CONFUCIANISM
AND
TOKUGAWA CULTURE

Edited by

PETER NOSCO

University of Hawai'i Press

Honolulu

© 1984 Princeton University Press
First published by Princeton University Press 1984
Published by University of Hawai'i Press 1997
All rights reserved
Printed in the United States of America

97 98 99 00 01 02   5 4 3 2 1

Library of Congress Cataloging-in-Publication Data

Confucianism and Tokugawa culture / edited by Peter Nosco.
p.   cm.
Includes bibliographical references and index.
ISBN 0–8248–1865–2 (alk. paper)
1. Neo-Confucianism—Japan—Congresses.   2.   Japan—
Intellectual life—1600–1868—Congresses.   3.   Japan—
Religion—1600–1868—Congresses.
I.   Nosco, Peter.
B5243.N4C66   1997
952'.025—dc20   96–27834
CIP

University of Hawai'i Press books are printed on
acid-free paper and meet the guidelines for permanence and
durability of the Council on Library Resources

CONFUCIANISM
AND
TOKUGAWA
CULTURE

FOR WM. THEODORE DE BARY

CONTENTS

ACKNOWLEDGMENTS
AND EXPLANATORY NOTES

The essays in this volume emerge from a symposium held in April 1981 at the De Andreis Gallery, St. John's University in the City of New York. The symposium was generously funded by the Division of Research Programs of the National Endowment for the Humanities, St. John's University, and the Japan Foundation.

The authors of the following essays benefited greatly from each others' suggestions, and still more from the comments of the discussants for the individual papers, Professors George Elison and Donald Shively. The symposium touched on a broad range of topics bound loosely by the theme of Neo-Confucianism and responses to it in Tokugawa (1600–1868) Japan. The task of integrating these topics and locating them within their broader East Asian context was left to Professor Wm. Theodore de Bary on the final day of the symposium. Professor de Bary brought his unique qualifications to bear on this set of issues, and we all benefited greatly from his success. Our indebtedness to him for this and for his contribution to the advancement of our own studies of the Japanese tradition is acknowledged, if only in part, by this volume's dedication.

Others have helped me a great deal: Rev. John Colman, C.M., introduced me to grantsmanship; Ms. Yuko Matsumura and Messrs. Kuang-mo Ho and Nien-chung Tu served as graduate assistants; Ms. Miwa Kai at Columbia and Mr. Kenji Niki at St. John's have assisted me greatly with reference materials; Dr. Chu Djang helped check Chinese entries in the Glossary; Ms. Sandra Esposito typed the manuscript; and Professors Joseph Kitagawa and Conrad Schirokauer were kind enough to read the entire text and to offer many helpful suggestions.

The following abbreviations are used in the notes:

JSZ—*Jiun Sonja zenshū*, 18 vols., ed. Hase Hōshū, 2nd ed. (Kyoto: Shibunkaku, 1974).

NRI—*Nihon rinri ihen*, 10 vols., comp. Inoue Tetsujirō and Kanie Yoshimaru (Ikuseikai, 1901–1903).

NST—*Nihon shisō taikei*, 67 vols., comp. Ienaga Saburō, Inoue

Mitsusada, Sagara Tōru, Nakamura Yoshihiko, Bitō Masahide, Maruyama Masao, and Yoshikawa Kōjirō (Iwanami Shoten, 1970–).

ZGR—*Zokuzoku gunsho ruijū*, 16 vols. (Kokusho Kankō Kai, 1906–1909).

Unless otherwise indicated, the place of publication of all Japanese works cited is Tokyo. Japanese, Chinese, and Korean names are reproduced in their native order with the surname first. A character glossary for foreign names and terms in the text begins on p. 269.

CONFUCIANISM
AND
TOKUGAWA
CULTURE

ONE

INTRODUCTION:
NEO-CONFUCIANISM AND
TOKUGAWA DISCOURSE

BY PETER NOSCO

Modern scholarship on the intellectual history of the Tokugawa period (1600–1868) can be said to have begun with the work of Maruyama Masao. In 1940 the then-young Maruyama published the first of three essays on Tokugawa political thought in the *Kokka gakkai zasshi* (Journal of the Association of National Scholarship). Tracing the ideological roots of Japan's modernity, Maruyama's work charted Tokugawa thought in an altogether new fashion. In 1952 the University of Tokyo Press published the essays as a single volume, and the significance of the work continued to grow, as attested to by Albert Craig's declaration in 1965 that, "All who write on Tokugawa thought must at some point ask themselves how their work relates to Maruyama Masao's . . . *Nihon seiji shisōshi kenkyū*."[1]

With the appearance of an English translation of Maruyama's work in 1974 (*Studies in the Intellectual History of Tokugawa Japan*),[2] Craig's statement may be truer than ever,[3] but the field has grown more complex, and Maruyama's name no longer stands quite so alone. The work of such scholars as Robert Bellah,[4] Wm. Theodore de Bary,[5]

[1] Marius Jansen, ed., *Changing Japanese Attitudes Toward Modernization* (Princeton: Princeton University Press, 1965), p. 155.

[2] Trans. Mikiso Hane (Princeton University Press, and Tokyo: University of Tokyo Press).

[3] More recently, Tetsuo Najita and Irwin Scheiner have written that Maruyama's work "remains the key reference point for all serious discussions of Tokugawa intellectual history." In Tetsuo Najita and Irwin Scheiner, eds., *Japanese Thought in the Tokugawa Period* (Chicago: University of Chicago Press, 1978), p. xi.

[4] *Tokugawa Religion* (Glencoe, Ill.: Free Press, 1957), and "Baigan and Sorai: Continuities and Discontinuities in Eighteenth-Century Japanese Thought," in Najita and Scheiner, *Japanese Thought*.

[5] With Ryusaku Tsunoda and Donald Keene, eds., *Sources of Japanese Tradition* (New York: Columbia University Press, 1958); with Irene Bloom, eds., *Principle and Practicality: Essays in Neo-Confucianism and Practical Learning* (Columbia, 1979); and *Neo-Confucian Orthodoxy and the Learning of the Mind-and-Heart* (Columbia, 1981).

David Earl,[6] George Elison,[7] Harry Harootunian,[8] Tetsuo Najita,[9] and (most recently) Richard Rubinger[10] in the West, and the researches of such scholars as Abe Yoshio,[11] Bitō Masahide,[12] Haga Noboru,[13] and Minamoto Ryōen[14] in Japan, as well as the analyses of those scholars represented in this volume,[15] have made Tokugawa thought more accessible and intelligible than ever before. One finds represented in their work and that of others a broad range of methodological and interpretive approaches that attests to the richness of this field.

The intellectual history of the Tokugawa period has been intimately identified from start to finish with the orthodox Neo-Confucian mode of thought, by which I mean the thought of the philosopher Chu Hsi (1130–1200) in China and of those later followers and interpreters in China, Korea, and Japan who regarded themselves as part of an elaborate and complex intellectual lineage which they traced directly to the master. Like the other papers in this volume, this introductory essay emerges from a conference on responses to Neo-Confucianism in Tokugawa Japan held at St. John's University and is concerned as much with the broad range of responses and reactions

[6] *Emperor and Nation in Japan: Political Thinkers of the Tokugawa Period* (Seattle: University of Washington Press, 1964).

[7] *Deus Destroyed, The Image of Christianity in Early Modern Japan* (Cambridge: Harvard University Press, 1973).

[8] *Toward Restoration: The Growth of Political Consciousness in Tokugawa Japan* (Berkeley and Los Angeles: University of California Press, 1970), and "Ideology as Conflict," in T. Najita and J. V. Koschmann, eds., *Conflict in Modern Japanese History* (Princeton: Princeton University Press, 1982).

[9] "Restoration in the Political Thought of Yamagata Daini (1725–1767)," *Journal of Asian Studies* 30 (1971): 17–29; "Political Economism in the Thought of Dazai Shundai (1680–1747)," *Journal of Asian Studies* 31 (1972): 821–839; "Intellectual Change in Early Eighteenth-Century Tokugawa Confucianism," *Journal of Asian Studies* 34 (1975): 931–944; with Irwin Scheiner, eds., *Japanese Thought*; and with J. Victor Koschman, eds., *Conflict in Modern Japanese History*.

[10] *Private Academies of Tokugawa Japan* (Princeton: Princeton University Press, 1982).

[11] *Nihon Shushigaku to Chōsen* (Tōkyō Daigaku Shuppankai, 1965), and *Jukyō no hensen to genkyo* (Kazankai, 1977).

[12] *Nihon hōken shisō-shi kenkyū* (Aoki Shoten, 1961); comp., *Ogyū Sorai*, Nihon no Meicho, no. 16 (Chūō Kōronsha, 1974); with Katō Shuichi, eds., *Arai Hakuseki*, NST, vol. 35 (Iwanami Shoten, 1975); and with Shimazaki Takao, eds., *Andō Shōeki, Satō Nobuhiro*, NST, vol. 45 (Iwanami Shoten, 1977).

[13] *Chihōshi no shisō* (Nihon Hōsō Shuppan Kyōkai, 1972); *Yonaoshi no shisō* (Yuzankaku, 1973); and *Bakumatsu kokugaku no kenkyū* (Kyōiku Shuppan Sentā, 1980).

[14] *Tokugawa gōri shisō no keifu* (Chūō Kōronsha, 1972); *Nihon kindaika to kinsei shisō* (Nihon Bunka Kaigi, 1976); *Edo no shisōkatachi* (Kenkyūsha, 1979); and *Kinsei shoki jitsugaku shisō no kenkyū* (Nihon Bunka Kaigi, 1976).

[15] See List of Contributors, pp. 267–268.

to Neo-Confucianism in the Tokugawa era, and what might arguably be regarded as responses to those very responses, as it is with Tokugawa Neo-Confucianism per se. This question of the relationship between Neo-Confucianism and Tokugawa discourse is by no means a simple one, and just as the work of recent decades has served to refine our understanding of Neo-Confucianism and Tokugawa thought, the essays in this volume challenge numerous commonly held assumptions on the subject, calling attention to responses to Neo-Confucianism in heretofore uncharted regions of the vast map of Tokugawa thought. They are, in this sense, part of an ongoing process of refinement, and it is hoped that they will serve to stimulate future advances in this inquiry.

Early Japanese chronicles state that Confucianism was introduced to Japan in A.D. 285 during the reign of Emperor Ōjin when Wani of Paekche brought copies from his native Korea of the *Analects* of Confucius (C., *Lun-yü*; J., *Rongo*) and the *Thousand Character Classic* (C., *Ch'ien-tzu wen*; J., *Senjimon*), a Confucian primer. Though the actual date of this event may have been a century or more later, it is equally likely that Confucian teachings were known by at least some of those immigrants from the continent who were reaching Japanese shores in increasing numbers at this time. The Confucianism to which the Japanese were first exposed already represented more than the humble, ethical teachings of Confucius and his followers. Over the centuries, those teachings had been overlaid and, to a certain extent, obscured by a complex set of correlative doctrines that combined to form an entire cosmology and were drawn from the Taoist and Yin-yang schools that had influenced ethico-religious practice in China.[16] However, for a variety of reasons Confucianism was eclipsed both in China and Japan by the doctrines of Buddhism which, particularly in Japan, were linked first to an aestheticism that enchanted courtly circles and later to a popular appeal that captured the faith of a broad audience.

Confucianism appears to have left its mark on Japanese society with its concern for hierarchical relationships and its emphasis on harmony within the home as the basis for harmony in the state, but equally plausible is the argument that in most instances Confucianism merely reinforced and justified social practices that had their antecedents in the pre-Confucian era. Prior to the Tokugawa, most Japanese were attracted more to the superstitious overlays of Confucian rites and practices than to the philosophical and ethical nucleus. Chinese

[16] Tsunoda et al., eds., *Sources of Japanese Tradition*, 1:54.

diviners were thus routinely consulted over such matters as building homes, selecting auspicious dates for travel or marriage and other similar activities, but Confucian advice on how to run the state or on how to regulate the affairs of man was largely ignored.

Aware of similar tendencies in China, and concerned over the relative strength of Buddhism, Chu Hsi transformed Confucianism and reinvigorated it as an intellectual discipline. He rejected the exegetical practices of his predecessors in the T'ang (618–907) dynasty and stressed the importance of studying the Way of the Sages as expressed in the Four Books: the *Analects*, the *Mencius* (C., *Meng-tzu*; J., *Mōshi*), the *Great Learning* (C., *Ta-hsüeh*; J., *Daigaku*), and the *Mean* (C., *Chung-yung*; J., *Chūyō*). In order to structure his thought, he developed a qualified monistic ontology that interpreted reality in terms of a singular natural principle (C., *li*; J., *ri*); and in order to guide the individual he counseled the methods of first the investigation of things (C., *ko wu*; J., *kakubutsu*), by which he meant the contemplation of one's physical environment with the aim of understanding the role of principle in it, and second the exercise of seriousness and reverence (C., *ching*; J., *kei*).

The joy of the Chu Hsi mode of thought was that it was both scholarly and spiritual: while it emphasized the quasi-scientific examination of the external world, it nonetheless provided for the development of the individual mind, recognizing the spiritual dimensions of such development. In this latter respect, Chu Hsi drew fruitfully from the teachings of Ch'an (J., Zen) Buddhism, but by transforming both the ends and the means, he made of it a genuinely Confucian doctrine. Regrettably, Chu Hsi's emphasis on seriousness at times lapsed, at the hands of his successors, into a humorless and dour tone far removed from those expectations that had inspired Neo-Confucianism in its earliest stages.

The Chu Hsi mode of thought was introduced to Japan in the early thirteenth century, perhaps as early as 1200, the year of Chu Hsi's death. For the most part, the philosophy was institutionally housed for nearly four centuries within Zen monasteries where it was regarded as a stimulating mental exercise that if properly directed, might point one toward the same truths as Zen. During these centuries, Zen enjoyed the patronage of the succession of military elites who ruled Japan, and since there were numerous similarities between the two modes of thought, Zen advocates were quick to assert that such Chu Hsi contemplative practices as "holding fast to seriousness and sitting quietly" (C., *ch'ih-ching ching-tso*; J., *jikei seiza*) were less developed stages of what they knew as "sitting in meditation" (C., *tso-ch'an*; J., *zazen*).

Chu Hsi's philosophy enjoyed a brief period of favor at the imperial court in the early fourteenth century during the reigns of Emperors Hanazono (r. 1308–1318) and Godaigo (r. 1318–1339), and emperors and shoguns alike summoned scholars to lecture on Confucian topics at intervals throughout the medieval period. Several thousand students, many of them Zen monks, attended the nonecclesiastical Ashikaga Academy (*Ashikaga gakkō*) where they studied a Neo-Confucian curriculum. Nonetheless, Neo-Confucianism did not achieve independent status during these centuries and remained in the shadow of its Buddhist patron.[17] However, since the Chu Hsi philosophy originally arose as a rational alternative to Buddhism, the possibility of a rupture between these two modes of thought always existed, and it was out of that rupture that the Chu Hsi philosophy came into its own in Japan. The rupture began with the introduction of texts representative of new developments within Neo-Confucianism which the Japanese obtained during their invasion of Korea in the 1590s, and it was more or less complete by the time the first Tokugawa shogun, Tokugawa Ieyasu (1542–1616), appointed the leading Chu Hsi advocate to his retinue in 1605.

The rapidity with which the major themes of medieval Japanese discourse are replaced by the new themes of Tokugawa discourse is impressive; yet one must acknowledge that the transformation is no less rapid or striking than the concurrent political transformation. During the space of little more than half a century, the Japanese polity was transformed through the efforts of three great empire builders—Oda Nobunaga (1534–1582), Toyotomi Hideyoshi (1536–1598), and Tokugawa Ieyasu—from a loose confederation of semiautonomous fiefdoms into the more centralized feudal system that distinguishes the Tokugawa as Japan's early-modern state. Where the predominant concerns of the medieval period had dealt with such Buddhist themes as human suffering in the world, and the quest for personal salvation or enlightenment, the discourse of the Tokugawa was concerned more with the achievement and maintenance of a stable and harmonious society, placing the responsibility for maintaining that delicate equilibrium at the heart of both man and the cosmos squarely

---

[17] On the Ashikaga Academy (*Ashikaga gakkō*), see Wajima Yoshio, *Chūsei no Jugaku*, Nihon Rekishi Sōsho, no. 11 (Yoshikawa Kōbunkan, 1965), pp. 226–261. Gidō (1324–1388), adviser to Ashikaga Yoshimitsu (shogun, 1368–1393), was typical of medieval authorities on Neo-Confucianism who felt that while Buddhism could include Confucianism, Confucianism could not include all that Buddhism had to offer. On Gidō and Yoshimitsu, see George Sansom, *A History of Japan, 1334–1615* (Stanford: Stanford University Press, 1961), pp. 161–166.

on the shoulders of man. Seventeenth-century discourse was characterized by the presence of a well-developed humanistic political discourse absent in the thought of the sixteenth century, and this discourse drew fruitfully from the assumptions and vocabulary of Neo-Confucianism for its descriptions of man and his society.

Our understanding of the nature of this transformation has changed as a result of recent research. Where it had once been assumed that the Neo-Confucianism present in early-seventeenth-century Japan was virtually identical to the original formulation of Chu Hsi, it is now understood that the pioneers of Neo-Confucian thought in Tokugawa Japan drew as much from Yi dynasty (1392–1909) Korean interpretations and Ming dynasty (1368–1644) Chinese interpretations of the Chu Hsi orthodoxy as they did from the original teachings of Chu Hsi; and where it had once been thought that Neo-Confucianism enjoyed a near-hegemonic role in the formulation of this new discourse, Herman Ooms makes apparent in the next essay in this volume that Neo-Confucianism was just one, though still a most important, ingredient in it.

Neo-Confucianism appears at the very start of the Tokugawa era as one of several modes of thought which are of use to the bakufu for its political purposes. While its long incubation during the medieval period did not result in the appearance of any Japanese Neo-Confucians of stature, the interval was sufficient for the thought to prepare for its larger role. Thanks to the official recognition that Neo-Confucianism would receive during the first Tokugawa century, however qualified that recognition may have been, Neo-Confucian thought would rapidly gain broader acceptance in Japanese society and culture, both politically and intellectually. This is hardly surprising in view of the fact that Confucianism had traditionally been directed toward precisely those issues which were now of immediate concern at all levels of Tokugawa society. Nonetheless, no single intellectual tradition would be privileged in Tokugawa Japan with exclusive government support, as had been and remained the case in China.

What is perhaps surprising is the extent to which Neo-Confucianism appears in tandem with Shinto and Buddhist elements in the new discourse. As Herman Ooms suggests in this volume, the Tokugawa bakufu was never at a loss for ideologues prepared to propagate affirmative teachings on man and society. Where Neo-Confucianism was prepared to provide arguments constructed from principles linking the terrestrial order to the cosmic, traditional Shinto, particularly its Yoshida denomination, was equipped to provide that element of mythification so useful in obfuscating the historical wellsprings of Tokugawa power.

In the Buddhist camp as well, one finds articulate spokesmen who, while not directly under the influence of Confucian thought, nonetheless addressed those same concerns of social order and ethical life toward which Neo-Confucianism had been directed. Such attempts on the part of leading Buddhists to assert that Buddhism might service the nation's interests were, of course, nothing new in the Japanese tradition, but the terms of the argument were different. Where Buddhism in past centuries had sought to expand its social and political role, in the Tokugawa it would seek to preserve its hard-won gains against new and more formidable challenges.

In his essay, Royall Tyler calls our attention to two figures who are significant in this regard, Suzuki Shōsan (1579–1655) and Kakugyō Tōbutsu (1541–1646). Shōsan maintained that Buddhism was the key to any enduring peace or stability under the banner of the Tokugawa, and he regarded Buddhism as containing within itself all that was necessary to provide for the individual. He imagined the shogun's role as that of the ultimate arbiter of Buddhism's doctrines and himself as nothing less than the shogun's loyal adviser. The legend surrounding Kakugyō Tōbutsu and Tokugawa Ieyasu is also instructive in this regard. According to the legend, the great deity of Mt. Fuji, Sengen Daibosatsu, heralded in 1583 the arrival of heaven's designated future ruler, none other than Tokugawa Ieyasu. Ieyasu is said to have made a pilgrimage to Mt. Fuji with his close Buddhist adviser Tenkai (1536–1643), and together they are said to have entered the Hitoana cave where they received the complete teachings of Sengen Daibosatsu, returning twice for further instruction in later years.

Of course, Neo-Confucianism was well equipped to contribute to the legitimizing function of the new discourse. Confucianism had traditionally served this function in China, but Japanese elites had long been accustomed to justifying their status more on the grounds of pedigree and precedent than merit or humanity. Yet once the validity of Neo-Confucian assumptions was acknowledged in the early Tokugawa, there arose the problem of reconciling Neo-Confucian norms with Japanese reality, as Kate Nakai indicates in her essay. For example, in a Confucian-inspired history of Japan, Hayashi Razan's (1583–1657) son, Hayashi Gahō (1618–1680), cast Tokugawa Ieyasu in the classic guise of the newly anointed recipient of the mandate of heaven, equipping him both morally and spiritually for the task of humane rulership. However, the obverse side of this issue—that heaven might withdraw its mandate from an inhumane regime—was of necessity skirted by all Tokugawa Confucian thinkers until the very last years of the Tokugawa.

Likewise, Chu Hsi's notion of the Way of the ruler, the Way of the minister, the Way of the parent, the Way of the child, and so on, divided the social system into constituent functions in such a way as to affirm the enduring stability and continuity of the status quo. This highly segmented way of interpreting society reappears in several guises in Tokugawa thought and may also be an indication of Neo-Confucianism's success in Tokugawa Japan. It was, after all, what Toyotomi Hideyoshi had attempted to do through legislation by disarming the peasants, removing samurai from villages, and "freezing" all individuals and their descendants into component, class-defined functions. Nonetheless, the economic realities of Tokugawa Japan propelled the (in Confucian eyes) despised merchant class into a position with considerable social leverage.

What is clear, however, is that Neo-Confucianism alone did not service these legitimizing functions for the Tokugawa bakufu, nor did it function with the degree of official orthodoxy that has heretofore been assumed of it. Whence, then, this concern with orthodoxy? Not surprisingly, the concern would appear to have originated among those who stood most directly to benefit from the official endorsement of their thought. For example, as Herman Ooms indicates, it was the descendants of Hayashi Razan who skillfully fabricated the impression of a monopolistic orthodoxy allegedly enjoyed by the premier Tokugawa Neo-Confucian, Hayashi Razan. Similarly, Suzuki Shōsan and those who spun the legend of Tōbutsu and Ieyasu understood the potential benefit that might devolve upon them through their endorsement of the status quo. It was not until the mid-seventeenth century that the issue of orthodoxy itself arose, and it may not have been until precisely this time that Neo-Confucianism began to enjoy a degree of acceptance that can be said even to approximate its status as orthodoxy in China. Yet, by this time, responses to Neo-Confucianism were already incipient, confirming the extraordinary degree of pluralism and intellectual diversity that characterized late-seventeenth-century thought in Japan. As Maruyama Masao observed in making something of a correction to his earlier thesis, "The diffusion of Neo-Confucianism as an ideology and the School of Ancient Learning's challenge to it developed almost contemporaneously. Moreover, if one asks not just about *scholarly* Confucianism but about the basic thought categories of Confucianism that constituted the *Aspektstruktur* of Tokugawa society, then one can argue that they tenaciously retained a currency until the very last instant of the Tokugawa regime."[18]

It is remarkable how quickly, deeply, and widely interest in Neo-Confucianism spread in Tokugawa Japan. The Japanese, like the Koreans some centuries earlier, appear to have taken Confucian thought seriously, almost passionately, and even if the degree of official interest in Neo-Confucianism may have been exaggerated, it would appear likely that the bakufu's interest in Confucian thought, and the attendant prestige which such interest bestowed, contributed to the currency of Confucian thought in Japan. Confucianism was, after all, able to provide answers to the differing questions of various shogunal governments from the start of the Tokugawa period until its end.

One can find the penetration of Confucian thought and vocabulary in any number of areas of intellectual pursuit in Tokugawa Japan. For example, the outburst during the years 1640 to 1720 of Japanese historical writings that sought to evaluate the Japanese past in light of Confucian historiographical principles is one indication of a new level of commitment to Confucianism in Japan, and Kate Nakai's analysis of historiography in the first half of the Tokugawa era reveals the extent to which Confucian thought adapts to Japanese concerns. Similarly, the new interest among seventeenth-century Shinto theologians in accommodating their doctrines to this new Confucian thought is at once a confirmation of the prestige that thought enjoyed in quondam intellectual circles and an example of Shinto's traditional sensitivity to major currents in the intellectual history of Japan. That such efforts in the Shinto camp were matched by leading seventeenth-century Neo-Confucians like Hayashi Razan and Yamazaki Ansai (1618–1682), who sought to fashion new Shinto theologies using a Neo-Confucian structure, attests to the mutually advantageous nature of such endeavors, and the eventual appearance of Confucian-Shinto popularists is further indication of Neo-Confucianism's penetration into the "ground bass" of Tokugawa thought.[19]

There is, however, perhaps no better indication of Confucianism's penetration into this substructure of Tokugawa culture than its appearance in the popular literature of the period. Tokugawa literature was, as Donald Keene indicates in his essay, prevailingly popular and thus mirrors elements in Tokugawa society and culture, however warped such mirrored images might be. Though generalizations are

[18] Maruyama, *Studies*, p. xxxv. Original emphasis retained.
[19] Following Shigeru Matsumoto's sense of Robert Bellah's term "ground bass" in Matsumoto's *Motoori Norinaga* (Cambridge: Harvard University Press, 1970), pp. 1–7.

difficult, Confucian philosophy tends to appear in Tokugawa literature as appealing more to the intellect than to the heart, and being more rational than emotional. In fact, Confucianism seems to emerge in Tokugawa literature as a highly charged metaphor for a complex set of identifications that would include Chineseness as opposed to Japaneseness, *giri*, or a preoccupation with moral behavior, as opposed to *ninjō*, or a resignation to the demands of the heart, craftiness as opposed to wit, and even stuffiness or aloofness as opposed to a more casual demeanor. China remained the central point of reference for the Japanese during all but the last years of the Tokugawa, and to the extent that in the popular mind to be Chinese meant to be Confucian, considerable literary license was possible in the interpretation of this metaphor.

The extent to which Confucian-related themes emerge in the popular culture of the Tokugawa may at first seem surprising to those familiar with the sheer complexity of Confucian thought, but of its popularity there can be little doubt. In a list of the accomplishments of an otherwise wayward son, Ihara Saikaku (1642–1693), the first truly popular writer in Japanese literature, cites a familiarity with Utsunomiya Ton'an's (1634–1710) lectures on the Confucian Way alongside such other accomplishments as familiarity with linked verse, flower arrangement, the tea ceremony, archery, and a mastery of a broad range of musical instruments.[20] Whether or not Utsunomiya Ton'an was a "popular" lecturer, one may surmise that familiarity with Confucian doctrine was as much an asset for Saikaku's townsman as wealth and liberal education were for Daniel Defoe's (1660–1731) "true-bred merchant."

There is probably a connection here with the spread of popular education in Tokugawa Japan, an education based on a curriculum which while not exactly Neo-Confucian was without doubt close. One of the major social issues confronting the Tokugawa regime of the seventeenth century was the problem of the "civilianization" of the *rōnin* (masterless samurai) classes in an age when their martial talents were no longer as necessary as they had been prior to the Tokugawa period. Virtually all Tokugawa men of letters were taught to read using a curriculum that included the Four Books and several lesser Confucian works. Of course, there was a need for teachers and tutors, and many current and former samurai found an educational niche for themselves in this new age of peace. In much the same way that Ihara Saikaku complained of the ease with which amateurs might

[20] Peter Nosco, trans., *Some Final Words of Advice* (Tokyo: Charles E. Tuttle, 1980), p. 41.

raise their shingle and proclaim themselves teachers and masters of versification, a Buddhist work called the *Gion monogatari* (Tale of Gion) speaks bitterly of those young men who, bored with being monks, might return to lay life by learning a bit about the Four Books and establishing themselves as independent scholars.[21] Of course, where there are teachers, there are also students, and this widespread interest in Confucian thought, as well as its identification with literacy, are further indices of the role Confucianism played in popular education and culture.

Related to this phenomenon of the penetration of Neo-Confucian assumptions and vocabulary into the popular culture of Tokugawa Japan is the appearance of a broad range of ideological responses in the Confucian, Buddhist, and nativist intellectual camps, a set of responses characterized by classicism and fundamentalism. Of these responses, that which took place within the Confucian arena is perhaps the best known. As Japanese scholars arrived at a more sophisticated understanding of the vitality and diversity that lay beneath the surface of Chinese and Korean Confucian circles, they naturally drew closer to teachings which were, if not orthodox, certainly representative of important strains within Chinese thought. In China the single most important Neo-Confucian alternative to the teachings of Chu Hsi were those of Wang Yang-ming (1472–1528), whose heterodox philosophy emphasized the unity between thought and action. In Japan, however, the most forceful challenge to orthodox Neo-Confucianism was mounted by the school of Ancient Learning (*kogaku*).

The school of Ancient Learning, which like the Wang Yang-ming school (J. *Yōmeigaku*) in Japan had prototypes within the intellectual history of China, based its teachings on the disarmingly simple proposition that if one wished to understand the truths of ancient Confucian teaching, then that cause could be better served by reading the ancient writings themselves than by studying the exegesis on those texts written by Chu Hsi or others. The major proponents of this school, Yamaga Sokō (1622–1685), Itō Jinsai (1627–1705), Jinsai's son Itō Tōgai (1670–1736), and Ogyū Sorai (1666–1728), succeeded first in establishing a highly systematic methodology for the study of ancient texts; second, in making Confucianism in Japan more recognizably "Japanese"; and finally in further enhancing the degree of philosophical variety available to intellectuals at that time.

For practical purposes, the school of Ancient Learning can be dated

---

[21] See *ibid.*, pp. 130–132; Royall Tyler's paper in this volume; and Rubinger, *Private Academies of Tokugawa Japan*, pp. 41–59.

from 1665, the date of Yamaga Sokō's publication of a work titled *Essential Teachings of the Sages (Seikyō yōroku)*. Though the leaders of Ancient Learning were drawn to it for differing reasons, Sokō's statement as to why he turned to the study of ancient texts spoke for many who later adopted this approach

> In the early 1660s, I learned that my misunderstandings were due to reading works by scholars from the Han, T'ang, Sung and Ming dynasties. I went directly to the works of the Duke of Chou and Confucius, and taking them as my model, I was able to straighten my own line of thought. From then on, I stopped using the writings of later ages, and by diligently studying works of the sages day and night, I finally clarified and understood the message of the sages. . . . Even if your speech and actions are disciplined and you learn a thousand and one quotations by heart, this clearly just takes you away from the main point and has nothing to do with the message of the sages.[22]

All Confucians had sought the "true message of the sages," but for Sokō and others in the Ancient Learning movement, that message was something that spoke for itself and did not require the exegetical overlay of later centuries in order to be comprehensible. Since Ancient Learning scholars insisted on dealing directly with texts two millennia removed from their own day, they developed techniques for handling such materials textually and linguistically and initiated the study of Chinese philology in Tokugawa Japan.

The Ancient Learning school's objections to Neo-Confucianism, however, were not limited to methodology. Itō Jinsai's remark that "one cannot hope to explain away everything in the world with the one word principle,"[23] and Yamaga Sokō's assertion that "anyone who eliminates human desire is not a human being at all,"[24] struck at the very heart of orthodox Neo-Confucian metaphysics. Related to these attacks on Neo-Confucian doctrine were the school's attempts to transform Japanese Confucianism into something more in tune with its new setting. Sokō was particularly moved by this concern. He was attracted to the original teachings of Confucius as an image of life in the idealized ancient Chou state, since he felt that those images provided an appropriate model for the application of Confucian doctrine in a paramilitary state, and in this regard he has been credited with being the early-modern formulator of the doctrine

[22] From his *Haisho Zanpitsu*, in *Yamaga Sokō bunshū* (Yūhōdō Bunko, 1926), p. 485.
[23] *Dōjimon*, NRI, 5:113.
[24] *Takkyō dōmon*, ZGR, 10:286.

of *bushidō*, or the Way of the Warrior. Similarly, Itō Jinsai's concept of benevolence (C., *jen*; J., *jin*), rooted as it was in terms of social goodness, reflected a deep-seated Japanese concern with the practical application of virtue in a social context, rather than an inclination to ponder virtue as an abstract concept.

No Ancient Learning scholar argued more forcefully and innovatively than Ogyū Sorai, the subject of Samuel Yamashita's essay in this volume. For Sorai, the assumption that one might through the workings of the human intellect arrive at an interpretation or explication of the original message of the sages was nothing less than arrogance and betrayed a serious lack of reverence for the classical texts. He regarded all later interpretations of the teachings of the early kings and Confucius as misreadings that had the lamentable result of obscuring the culture represented in those texts. He regarded the retrieval of these artifacts of classical Chinese civilization as essential to their reverencing, and he condemned those "who [spoke] on the authority of principle and their own minds." As Yamashita points out, Sorai also regarded human nature as lively, physical, and infinitely diverse, and in this regard his teachings may represent an acknowledgment of human individuality unprecedented within the Japanese Confucian tradition. Sorai's school not only attracted a sizable following during his lifetime, but actually continued to grow during the two decades following his death.[25]

A number of interesting comparisons can be drawn between developments in the Confucian arena during the first half of the Tokugawa period and corresponding developments in eighteenth-century Japanese nativism. In this regard, Kamo Mabuchi (1697–1769) and Motoori Norinaga (1730–1801), the two leading figures of eighteenth-century National Learning (*kokugaku*), provide the most fruitful comparison. Kamo Mabuchi's formative years overlapped with the period when the teachings of Ogyū Sorai were at their peak of acceptance and the early years of their decline. He had briefly studied Sorai's teachings under Watanabe Mōan (b. 1687) in Mabuchi's native Hamamatsu, and it appears that one of Mabuchi's closer friends during his earlier years in Edo was Hattori Nankaku (1683–1749), another of Sorai's students.

The connection between Mabuchi's thought and that of the Sorai school was, in fact, a strong one, but it was a connection based on Mabuchi's repeated rejection of several of the Sorai school's basic assumptions. Mabuchi's reaction against the teachings of Ogyū Sorai was evident as early as his involvement in the *Kokka hachiron* contro-

[25] See Maruyama, *Studies*, p. 136.

versy of the early 1740s in which Mabuchi had attacked Kada Arimaro's (1706–1751) notion that poetry was of negligible relevance to
the well-being of the state.[26] Kada Arimaro's position in the controversy represented a direct application of Ogyū Sorai's Chinese literary theory to verse from the native tradition, and it is worth noting
that at this time Sorai's teachings had just reached the tail end of their
period of broadest acceptance.

This rejection by Mabuchi of the Sorai school's teachings became
even more conspicuous during his last years. For example, while
Mabuchi shared Sorai's view that Chinese Confucianism was a man-
made Way—an assumption that lay at the heart of all Sorai's teachings—it was precisely this fact that Mabuchi most strongly objected
to in his vilification of the Confucian Way. He claimed that since
Confucianism was a man-made Way, it was a product of human cleverness and that such cleverness was incompatible with the "true"
dictates of the natural Way of Heaven and Earth. Furthermore, Mabuchi's assertion of the presence *in illo tempore* of Confucian virtues
such as benevolence, righteousness, and so on, was intended as a
rebuttal of claims to the contrary by Dazai Shundai (1680–1747), another of Sorai's students. Shundai had asserted that proof that the
Way did not exist in Japan prior to the introduction of Chinese learning "lay in the fact that there were no Japanese words for benevolence, righteousness, propriety, music, filial piety and so on."[27] Mabuchi's claim that those virtues existed "throughout the world like
the movement of the four seasons"[28] was a specific repudiation of
Shundai's position and was actually one of no fewer than thirty attacks on the Sorai school written during the years 1750 to 1790.[29]

A more subtle debt, however, was owed by Mabuchi to Neo-
Confucian teachings. In many ways his concept of the True Heart
(*magokoro*) resembled the Neo-Confucian notion of the original nature (C., *pen-jan chih hsing*; J., *honzen no sei*). Like Chu Hsi's original
nature, Kamo Mabuchi's True Heart represented the innate goodness
that man lost through a specific set of identifiable actions—succumb-
ing to desires and emotions in Chu Hsi's case, and adopting Chinese
ways in Mabuchi's. Moreover, the essential quest for both Chu Hsi
and Mabuchi was the attainment of human perfection in the present

[26] On the *Kokka hachiron* controversy, see Peter Nosco, "Nature, Invention, and
National Learning," *Harvard Journal of Asiatic Studies* 41, no. 1 (June 1981).

[27] From his *Bendōsho*, quoted in Saigusa Yasutaka, *Kamo Mabuchi*, Jinbutsu Sōsho,
no. 93 (Yoshikawa Kōbunkan, 1962), p. 288.

[28] *Koku-i kō*, in Yamamoto Yutaka, comp., *Kōhon Kamo Mabuchi zenshū: shisō hen*
(Kōbundō, 1942), 2:1095.

[29] Maruyama, *Studies*, pp. 136–137.

through recovery of that original goodness which each man enjoyed as his birthright. For Chu Hsi, this entailed the sage's return to the principle of heaven, while for Mabuchi it involved the unconscious observance of the Way of Heaven and Earth.

This structural affinity between Kamo Mabuchi's nativist ideology and Chu Hsi's Neo-Confucianism was almost certainly not deliberate on Mabuchi's part and merely indicates the extent to which many of the basic assumptions of Neo-Confucianism had penetrated the intellectual strata of Tokugawa Japan. Mabuchi remained unreserved in his criticism of Japanese Confucians throughout the last decade of his life and vehemently attacked their "ignorance about ancient Japan."[30] Nonetheless, as I have argued elsewhere, the reason why Mabuchi's position in the *Kokka hachiron* controversy more closely resembled that of his Confucian-inspired patron Tayasu Munetake (1715–1771) was due to their common faith in the traditional Confucian assumption that literature, in particular poetry, was of fundamental normative value in the governing of the state.[31]

Motoori Norinaga, the most significant of all Tokugawa nativists, likewise owed a great deal structurally to Confucian thought, in particular to the thought of Ogyū Sorai. Norinaga's ideological indebtedness to Sorai has been superlatively explicated by Maruyama Masao, and the arguments are well known. Like Sorai, Norinaga distrusted the human intellect as an instrument sufficient to glean the truths of revealed wisdom; where Sorai's attitude toward heaven was one of awe and reverence, Norinaga's attitude toward the divine presence in everyday life was no less wondrous; Norinaga agreed with Sorai's reducing the sage to mortal dimensions, and like Mabuchi it was precisely this human role in the creation of the Way of the Sages that made the Confucian Way so objectionable; and like Sorai's Confucian fundamentalism, Norinaga's nativist fundamentalism bound him to gleaning ancient truths from ancient texts, in this case the *Kojiki* (712), Japan's most ancient extant history. It can even be argued that Norinaga's highly deterministic view of human action—a view that

[30] A charge directed against Kaibara Ekken (1630–1714), a Chu Hsi follower, and "others like him," in *Tatsu no kimie Kamo no Mabuchi toikotae*, in *Kōhon Kamo Mabuchi zenshū: shisō hen*, 2:1013. Of all Japanese Neo-Confucians, the only one who seems to have won a degree of respect from Mabuchi was Arai Hakuseki, whom Mabuchi described as a man who "often made good points in his writings" (ibid., p. 1045). While Hakuseki was particularly well versed in Japanese history (see Kate Nakai's paper in this volume), Mabuchi's respect may also have derived in part from the fact that one of Hakuseki's students, Doi Motorari, was an early tutor of his patron Tayasu Munetake.

[31] "Nature, Invention, and National Learning," *Harvard Journal of Asiatic Studies* 41 (1981): 75–91.

interpreted every event and action as a direct manifestation of the will of a myriad of gods—resulted in an acknowledgment of human diversity that in substantial portion replicates Sorai's sophisticated view of human individuality. For Norinaga, the only authority for informing human action was that of ancient precedent. The Way of the Gods (*kami no michi*) was the way things were in the Divine Age; it could be learned through accounts of the Divine Age in works like the *Kojiki*; and since human reason was intrinsically incapable of comprehending the divine, personal shrewdness (*sakashira*) had no place in man's attempts to act in accord with the Way of the Gods. If one sincerely wished to behave in accordance with the Way of the Gods, then one's only recourse was to study the record of that Way and to place oneself at the discretion of the wishes of the gods.

In general, then, one can identify several respects in which nativist fundamentalism was indebted to Confucian fundamentalism.[32] First, Tokugawa nativists agreed with the Neo-Confucian assumption that at birth an individual's original inclinations were purely good and that the seeds of this goodness, though lost through a set of identifiable actions, were ultimately recoverable. Second, in the Ancient Learning school's approach, Tokugawa nativists saw a methodology suited to the examination of ancient texts from their own tradition. Third, the National Learning scholars were in fundamental agreement with the school of Ogyū Sorai, which believed that the sages, after all, were just men, but where Sorai and his followers found in this fact cause to celebrate, Tokugawa nativists regarded it as the central fallacy of Confucian teachings. Further, the nativists agreed with the Confucians generally that at some point in the past, life was preferable to what it was then—society was ordered, the state was well governed, men and their families enjoyed tranquility—and that the improvement of life in the present was contingent upon a sound understanding of life in the past.

Curiously, the classicism and fundamentalism that form such a conspicuous aspect of both Confucian and nativist thought in eighteenth-century Japan are also represented in Tokugawa Buddhism. Jiun Sonja (1718–1804), the subject of Paul Watt's chapter, had a degree of mastery of Sanskrit that was unprecedented among Japanese Buddhists, and his intention in acquiring this mastery was to draw closer to the original meaning of the most ancient Buddhist

---

[32] The question of whether Confucian fundamentalism preceded and *inspired* nativist fundamentalism is debatable. See my "Keichū (1640–1701): Forerunner of National Learning," *Asian Thought and Society* 5 (1980): 237–252.

scriptures with the aim of recovering *Butsu zaise no Bukkyō*, or "Buddhism as it was when the Buddha was alive." The recipient of a Neo-Confucian education, Jiun was familiar with the Ancient Learning school of Itō Jinsai and was acquainted with the teachings of Ogyū Sorai. His Buddhist response to Confucianism was in many ways reminiscent of the Buddhist-Shinto syncretism of nearly a thousand years earlier, when Buddhism likewise stood to gain politically, socially, and evangelically from such affiliations. The Buddhist-Confucian dialogue of Jiun and others in the Tokugawa was facilitated first by early Neo-Confucianism's indebtedness to certain Buddhist formulations in China, and second by Neo-Confucianism's long period of incubation in medieval Japanese Zen monasteries. As Paul Watt indicates, Jiun's mastery of Sanskrit and his profound concern with Buddhism's ability to meet the intellectual and ideological challenges of his day indicate both his commitment to this highly syncretic dialogue and his participation in the new fundamentalist discourse.

It is indeed significant that such disparate figures as Ogyū Sorai, Motoori Norinaga, and Jiun Sonja—paragons of rationalism in their respective traditions—all found limits on the ability of the human intellect to arrive at ultimate truths. Jiun, like his contemporary Motoori Norinaga, criticized Confucians for too great a reliance on this aspect of reason, and in this sense they can both be regarded as sharing the earlier sentiments of Ogyū Sorai. The conjunction of these various forms of fundamentalism, as well as the peculiar admixture of confidence in and distrust of rationalism present in their respective modes of thought, suggest that this phenomenon of fundamentalism in mid-Tokugawa thought deserves further study.

One controversial point in the evaluation of Neo-Confucianism and Tokugawa discourse has been the status of Neo-Confucian thought during the Tokugawa era's last century. Here again the Maruyama thesis has exerted great influence, although to an extent that may perhaps obscure certain important functions of Neo-Confucian thought during the Tokugawa era's last decades. It will be recalled that the school of Ogyū Sorai achieved the peak of its popularity during the two decades following Sorai's death. According to Maruyama, decline then set in, and the decline of the Sorai school "meant that Confucianism itself was relinquishing its leadership in the intellectual world" of Tokugawa Japan. Interpreting the Tokugawa environment as one that abhors a "vacuum," Maruyama sees the school of National Learning replacing Confucianism as the hegemonic movement in intellectual circles of that time.[33]

The question of "leadership" is a complex one, but it would certainly appear that Maruyama's assertion could lead one to underestimate the vitality, relevance, and persistence of Neo-Confucian topics and themes in the discourse of the late Tokugawa. One prominent feature of the Tokugawa period's last decades is the appearance of distinctive, often charismatic figures whose teachings were described as *yonaoshi*, or literally "rectification of the world." The term yonaoshi first appears during the 1780s, "becoming," as Herman Ooms has described elsewhere, "increasingly popular until the Meiji restoration as a word to indicate recurrent popular movements to redress the social and political wrongs of society."[34] Such movements appear to have arisen as a result of anxiety that the harmony and stability of the Tokugawa feudal order might be threatened or perhaps even in part lost. Consequently, one finds numerous figures in the late Tokugawa in pursuit of the renewal of that order, or at least the renewal of the contemporary perception of what that order might have represented.

Perhaps the best-known yonaoshi figure was Matsudaira Sadanobu (1758–1829), leader of the Kansei Reform movement of the closing years of the eighteenth century. In 1790, during his six-year tenure as head of the Council of Elders (*rōjū*), Matsudaira Sadanobu was the author and promulgator of a brief edict known as "The Kansei Prohibition of Heterodox Studies" (*Kansei igaku no kin*). The edict was addressed to Hayashi Kinpō (1733–1792), head of the Bakufu College, a position that had remained hereditary within the Hayashi family since the college's inception in the seventeenth century. It called upon Kinpō to reaffirm his school's commitment to more orthodox versions of Neo-Confucian teachings, and to repress heterodox teachings within the school. Several years later, a similar directive was promulgated to the heads of the domainal schools and colleges, though the effect of the edict outside the capital was less pronounced.

Some have taken the Prohibition of Heterodox Studies to be an affirmation of Neo-Confucianism's ever-increasing vigor and popularity in the Tokugawa era, while others have regarded it as the last gasp of an otherwise moribund tradition. The truth, as is usually the case, would appear to lie somewhere between these extremes. Ma-

[33] Maruyama, *Studies*, p. 143.

[34] *Charismatic Bureaucrat: A Political Biography of Matsudaira Sadanobu, 1758–1829* (Chicago: University of Chicago Press, 1975), p. 49. See also Anne Walthal, "Narratives of Peasant Uprisings in Japan," *Journal of Asian Studies* 42, no. 3 (May 1983).

tsudaira Sadanobu was in significant measure inspired by the attempts at reform of Tokugawa Yoshimune (1684–1751; shogun 1716–1745), whose Kyōhō Reform of the 1720s can be regarded as a major attempt to resurrect those values, policies, and attitudes that were identified with Tokugawa Ieyasu at the very start of the Tokugawa regime. Matsudaira Sadanobu, like Tokugawa Yoshimune before him, was confronted with serious fiscal and social dilemmas, and it is a common historical phenomenon for leaders faced with such problems to seek to resurrect the policies of the "founding fathers." In this sense, Matsudaira Sadanobu's policies might be designated, to modify a familial term, as restorationist "once removed."

There are two points here that are significant. The first is that by attempting to enhance the degree of ideological orthodoxy of the Bakufu College, and by identifying orthodoxy as something that had once been characteristic of the school at its start and that later somehow had been lost, Matsudaira Sadanobu was actually seeking to resurrect a misperception of the original status of Hayashi Razan and his immediate successors. This misperception was so beguiling that it had proved no less captivating to Yoshimune some seven decades earlier. Neo-Confucianism, as mentioned previously, was not the only or even necessarily the single most important factor in the complex discourse of the early Tokugawa. Thus Sadanobu's policies were based more upon his perception of the relationship between the bakufu and Neo-Confucianism in the early Tokugawa than on the actual reality of that relationship.

Second, by framing his attempts at reform in the context of the resurrection of past policies regarded as "tried and true," Matsudaira Sadanobu was evidencing a characteristic present in Confucian thought from the very beginning. Confucius, as is well known, insisted that he be regarded not as a reformer but rather as the faithful transmitter of teachings and traditions that might otherwise be lost. In this respect, Matsudaira Sadanobu was, almost certainly unconsciously, behaving in a manner consistent with the highest restorationist ideals of the Confucian tradition.

Despite these attempts at Confucian renewal, the Tokugawa bakufu in its last half-century began increasingly to exhibit those tendencies and problems that would eventually result in its final demise. Nonetheless, even in this time of decline, or perhaps one should say in particular during this period of decline, one can find examples of Neo-Confucian thought being used by intellectuals in order to resolve their own dilemmas, if not in the sense of affecting a reversal of social and political decline, at least in the sense of providing personal answers for how they as individuals might cope with such a situation. By these final decades of the Tokugawa era, numerous intellectuals of Confucian persuasion, but not necessarily figures directly involved in political movements, came to regard themselves, as Okada Takehiko points out in his chapter, as the direct heirs to an elaborate intellectual dialogue that had its origins in China in the late-Ming and Ch'ing (1644–1912) dynasties and of Yi-dynasty Korea.

These late-Tokugawa scholars exhibited a degree of eclecticism in their thought perhaps unmatched in the history of Tokugawa Confucianism from the time of Fujiwara Seika (1561–1617). As Okada indicates, these Neo-Confucians partook in significant measure from the teachings of not just Chu Hsi but also those of Wang Yang-ming, and there is perhaps no better indication of the continued vitality of Neo-Confucianism in Tokugawa Japan than the intensely personal commitment of these thinkers to its teachings for answers on matters relating to the mind, human nature, and the role of the individual in troubled times.

There has also been a tendency to imagine that with the advent of the Meiji restoration of 1868, somehow Confucianism ceases almost immediately to be a motivating factor for the individual in either personally or politically significant action. The role of the Wang Yang-ming school in stimulating activist behavior among its followers in the late Tokugawa and early Meiji (1868–1912) has been well documented, but in the same manner in which many scholars have underestimated the conservative motivations of the leaders of the Meiji restoration, intellectual historians have tended to de-emphasize the persistence of Confucian issues in the early-Meiji period.

Matsumoto Sannosuke's paper calls our attention to Nakae Chōmin (1847–1901), an intellectual whose standard characterization has been that of the classic Meiji liberal, or the "Japanese Rousseau" as he has often been called. Matsumoto demonstrates how Chōmin's concept of freedom and liberty was indebted to assumptions that can be traced ideologically through Itō Jinsai in the Ancient Learning school all the way back to Mencius (372–289 B.C.). Chōmin's notion that freedom required "cultivation" and "development" might seem odd to an intellectual historian familiar with the concept of freedom in the West, but these notions make perfect sense once they are regarded as structural resonances of those elements of personal cultivation and human development which are evidenced by Mencius as the first orthodox interpreter of Confucius' teaching. Freedom, in this context, thus becomes not something that is won and then retained, but rather something to which humans continually aspire and which requires nourishment no less than any other human virtue.

It is tempting, at this juncture, to step back and to attempt to locate some of the themes that have arisen in this discussion of Neo-Confucianism and Tokugawa discourse in the broader perspective of Neo-Confucianism in East Asian culture. In English no one has written more extensively or masterfully on these larger issues than Wm. Theodore de Bary.[35] In an essay first published in 1959, de Bary identified humanism, rationalism, historical-mindedness and ethnocentrism as characteristics of Neo-Confucian thought, and each of these in varying degrees and contexts is conspicuous in Tokugawa discourse and serves to distinguish Tokugawa thought from that of the medieval period.[36] Significantly, in Tokugawa discourse these themes are not limited to discussions within the Confucian arena alone, but also feature prominently in the myriad responses and reactions to Neo-Confucianism that reverberate throughout Tokugawa thought.

There are other features that likewise demand our attention. One cannot but be struck by the intellectually compelling quality of Chu Hsi's thought, since there is no other convincing explanation of the persistence of Neo-Confucian themes in a Tokugawa environment that valued knowledge of Chu Hsi's commentaries on the Four Books not as a possible stepping-stone to an official position, but precisely as an indication of intellectual mastery and achievement. Chu Hsi had been condemned in his own day as a heretic, and his many followers had been ordered not to attend his funeral, though they of course disobeyed and attended in large numbers. In China, as in Japan, Neo-Confucian thought appears first to have spread on its own intellectual and philosophic merits without the advantage of state sponsorship. Becoming established in local academies in the late-Sung and early-Yüan (1260–1368) periods, it was not until later that the thought became the curriculum of the official school system in China where it was incorporated, as is well known, into the examination system. It then appealed in succession to the Mongols of the Yüan, the Chinese of the Ming, and the Manchus of the Ch'ing, suggesting an element of breadth in Neo-Confucianism's appeal both to ruling elites and to educated members of the scholar-official class. One can also observe

[35] The following discussion is heavily indebted to remarks made by Professor de Bary in his role as discussant at the St. John's Conference.

[36] "Some Common Tendencies in Neo-Confucianism," in David S. Nivison and Arthur Wright, eds., *Confucianism in Action* (Stanford: Stanford University Press, 1959), pp. 25–49.

fruitful parallels between the highly competitive heterodox Confucian environment of the late-eighteenth and early-nineteenth centuries in Japan and the situation in late-Ming China, but the comparison requires qualification. In Japan the domainal schools enjoyed a degree of ideological independence that their Chinese counterparts would have envied, since in China the government pressured local academies to follow the teachings of Chu Hsi, understandably in light of the examination system's role in staffing China's complex bureaucracy. The only comparable instance of such pressure in the Tokugawa context—the Kansei Prohibition of Heterodox Studies—was of more symbolic than actual success.

While calling attention to this intellectually compelling quality of Neo-Confucianism, it must in the same breath be acknowledged, as Donald Keene indicates in his paper, that obedience to Confucian principles does not necessarily bring happiness or peace of mind. The peculiar moral and political dilemmas of leading activist figures in the last years of the Tokugawa and the early years of the Meiji suggest that taking one's role in the broader environment seriously—and, of course, all Neo-Confucians were in some sense devoted practitioners of seriousness—involved confronting the fundamental contradiction that arose at that time between the bakufu's professed ideals and the interests of the bakufu itself, between the shogun as "Barbarian-Subduing Generalissimo" (*sei-i tai shōgun*), as he was formally styled, and the shogun as caretaker of a government incapable, and daily more apparently so, of dealing with what the Japanese and their emperor perceived to be a foreign (that is, barbarian) menace. Adopting a Neo-Confucian perspective on the Meiji restoration of 1868, one might, albeit simplistically, regard this political watershed as an extraordinary exercise in the traditional Confucian theme of the rectification of names, that is, in the matching of reality and terminology.

The relationship between the secular rule of the shogun and the religious prestige of the reigning emperor—a relationship virtually irreconcilable in Chinese Confucian terms—had long lurked, like some dark secret, behind the fastidious veil of Tokugawa political thought. There had, of course, been tears in this veil. One is struck by the anecdote, cited in Kate Nakai's paper, of Tokugawa Mitsukuni (1628–1701), lord of Mito, who is said to have bowed toward Kyoto each New Year's morning declaiming to his closest vassals, "My lord is the emperor, the present shogun is the head of my family. One must take care not to misunderstand this situation." Takeuchi Shikibu (1712–1767) and Yamagata Daini (1725–1767), both followers of the teachings of Yamazaki Ansai (1618–1682), were outstanding eighteenth-century imperial loyalists;[37] and, of course, the intellectual horizon of the Tokugawa's last decades was crowded with spokesmen who, from a variety of Confucian and nativist perspectives, sought to rectify their world.

At the St. John's Conference, Wing-tsit Chan called the participants' attention to the possibility that the Japanese reaction to Confucianism was characteristic of those who inherit a mode of thought as opposed to those who generate that mode of thought. In other words, perhaps the Japanese attitude toward Neo-Confucianism in the Tokugawa period betrays the attitude of a purist whose enthusiasm through conversion is likely to exceed the enthusiasm of one who takes such matters for granted. In this sense, the Japanese reception of Neo-Confucian teachings in the Tokugawa is suggestive of deep-seated elements of both conservatism and conservationism in Japanese thought.

Nonetheless, it would be a mistake to conclude from this discussion either that the Japanese were merely passive recipients of an imported mode of thought or that Neo-Confucianism necessarily repeats developmental patterns when transplanted into non-Chinese East Asian settings. In the case of the former, Japanese history demonstrates time and again the failure of Chinese models in Japan, and to cite just one example relevant to this discussion, it remains a striking irony that the Japanese were never inclined to borrow the elaborate examination system so well established in China until the nineteenth century when the inspiration was arguably more Western than Chinese in the establishment of this meritocracy. In the case of the latter, it is likewise clear that to attempt to evaluate Neo-Confucianism's progress in East Asia as one that is bound by certain patterns and processes would undermine the intimate connection between ideology and society, a connection that by now requires no further defense. As this cursory examination of the topic of Neo-Confucianism and Tokugawa discourse has sought to demonstrate, the growth of Neo-Confucianism in Japan is suggestive of numerous parallels with its corresponding developments in China and Korea, but Neo-Confucianism's success in Japan was due at least as much to the refashioning of those doctrines by Japanese intellectuals as it was to the sheer flexibility of the Neo-Confucian system to accommodate itself to such transformation.

[37] See Herschel Webb, *The Japanese Imperial Institution in the Tokugawa Period* (New York: Columbia University Press, 1968), pp. 248–253.

By way of conclusion, then, we may observe the following points in assessing the nature of Neo-Confucianism's role in the evolving discourse of Japan's Tokugawa period: First, Neo-Confucianism is present at the very start of the Tokugawa as one of several modes of thought that vied for the attention of the new bakufu government; second, the teachings benefited from a measure of official recognition and rapidly penetrated the emergent popular culture; third, responses and reactions to Neo-Confucian teachings can be found throughout the vast landscape of Tokugawa thought, contributing to overall structural coherence as well as to pluralism and diversity; fourth, far from fading, the relevance of Neo-Confucian teachings is reaffirmed during the late Tokugawa, particularly in terms of the teachings' efficacy at assuaging personal moral and ethical uncertainty; and finally, the doctrine's success in affecting change to and response in Tokugawa discourse was due primarily to the intellectually compelling quality of Neo-Confucian thought which continues to find articulate spokesmen even today.

TWO

NEO-CONFUCIANISM AND THE FORMATION OF EARLY TOKUGAWA IDEOLOGY: CONTOURS OF A PROBLEM

BY HERMAN OOMS

For hundreds of years, scholars have identified Neo-Confucianism as the official ideology of the Tokugawa bakufu. Over time this speculative ascription of a legitimizing function to Neo-Confucianism has hardened into a solid historical fact. Today, the awareness is dim that the links established by such identification entail a considerable amount of interpretation. It is the intention of this paper to take a look at the nature of this linkage between Neo-Confucianism, the early bakufu, and ideology.*

There are good reasons why this particular view has acquired such authority. One can find both historical and theoretical explanations for its unquestioned acceptance. First of all, several converging interpretations of certain historical developments in the Tokugawa period seem naturally to compose this overall picture of bakufu ideology. The most striking are as follows.

Starting with Tokugawa Ieyasu (1542–1616; shogun, 1603–1605), rulers appear to have shown an interest in Neo-Confucian scholars and to have taken them into their service. Tokugawa Iemitsu (b. 1604, r. 1623–1651), the third shogun, even financed a school for Hayashi Razan (1583–1657) to propagate his teachings. Kumazawa Banzan (1619–1691) and Yamaga Sokō (1622–1685), punished by the bakufu for their "unorthodox" views, were living proof of the existence of an official ideological threshold. Tsunayoshi (b. 1646; shogun, 1680–1709) ardently lectured on Neo-Confucianism. Matsudaira Sadanobu (1758–1829; chief councillor, 1787–1793) in the 1790s revived the Hayashi school to secure a "Neo-Confucian orthodoxy"

* This paper is based on a larger study, in progress at the time of the conference, for which financial support was granted by the Japan Foundation, the Social Science Research Council, and the American Philosophical Society. Meanwhile the study has been completed and will be published by Princeton University Press, under the title: *Tokugawa Ideology: Early Constructs, 1570–1680.*

for the bakufu. And the Mito school, toward the end of the period, gave new relevance to Neo-Confucianism as a cure for the ills of the time.

All of this seems incontrovertible and overwhelming historical evidence for the existence of a Neo-Confucian bakufu orthodoxy. It is also possible, however, that these disparate data, all having somehow to do with the fortunes of public knowledge, were transformed into components of an ideology-picture precisely because their interpretation was governed by the unifying assumption that an official bakufu ideological apparatus was operating throughout the period.

Recent scholarship has reevaluated some of these events.[1] The bakufu never took an interest in the curriculum at the Hayashi school before 1790. Kumazawa Banzan and Yamaga Sokō were (only temporarily) the victims of personal politics, not of official policies. Matsudaira Sadanobu did not return to an earlier "orthodoxy." Nevertheless, the general thesis of a Tokugawa Neo-Confucian ideology has been largely unaffected by these piecemeal revisions.

A second reason for the tenacity of this thesis has its roots in a theoretical assumption about the functioning of political regimes. In this view, the Tokugawa case is simply a particular embodiment of a universal law that requires no further discussion: a law asserting that every regime needs an ideology as an indispensable accessory to power.

This modern view is not very novel, however, and has its own historiographical backing. In the *Tokugawa jikki* (The True Tokugawa Records) one reads:

Ieyasu had conquered the nation on horseback, but being an enlightened and wise man, realized early that the land could not be governed from a horse. He had always respected and believed in the Way of the Sages. He wisely decided that in order to govern

---

[1] On the Hayashi school's status, role, history, and number of students, and on Matsudaira Sadanobu's Ban of Heterodoxy, see my *Charismatic Bureaucrat: A Political Biography of Matsudaira Sadanobu, 1758–1829* (Chicago: University of Chicago Press, 1975), pp. 122–150; Robert L. Backus, "The Relationship of Confucianism to the Tokugawa Bakufu as Revealed in the Kansei Educational Reform," *Harvard Journal of Asiatic Studies* 34 (1974): 97–162, and his "The Kansei Prohibition of Heterodoxy and Its Effect on Education," ibid. 39 (1979): 55–106. Kumazawa Banzan was subjected to criticism by Razan and public harassment. He resigned from his post in 1657 but never stopped writing. Yamaga Sokō was victimized by the Great Councillor Sakai Tadakiyo and banished from Edo by Hoshina Masayuki in 1666, but eight years later he was allowed to return. For the last five years of his life, he could even lecture freely on his *Seikyō yōroku*, the cause for his punishment fifteen years earlier. See Wajima Yoshio, "Kanbun igaku no kin—sono Rinmon kōryū to no kankei," *Ōtemae joshidaigaku ronshū* 8 (1975): 139, 143–147.

the land and follow the path proper to man, he must pursue the path of learning. Therefore, from the beginning he encouraged learning.[2]

Tokugawa Ieyasu, enlightened about power's need for ideology, simply availed himself of a Neo-Confucianism just waiting in the wings to be put to use. Thus both history and theory, intertwined around an interpretive core, reinforce the standard ideology thesis.

The *Tokugawa jikki* was compiled in the first decades of the nineteenth century when the question of a bakufu-enforced orthodoxy had become a real issue. While, as will become clear, a considerable amount of retrospective fallacy informs the previous quotation, it is rather faithful to earlier portrayals of the beginnings of a Tokugawa ideology. In fact, this quotation and other similar ones are from Fujiwara Seika's biography by Hayashi Razan and Razan's biography by his two sons.

The classical story of how Neo-Confucianism came to be linked to the bakufu is found in Hayashi Razan's biography of his teacher Fujiwara Seika (1561–1619), written in 1620.[3] Here Razan tells how Ieyasu, only two weeks after his victory at Sekigahara on September 15, 1600, summoned the ex-monk Fujiwara Seika for an audience with him. Seika, who had broken with Buddhism and was deeply involved in Neo-Confucian studies, appeared in the garb of a Confucian literatus. He was invited to enter Ieyasu's service but declined the offer. Five years later, however, Razan himself (also an ex-monk) secured a post in Ieyasu's bureaucracy which he would hold for over fifty years.

This audience at the very opening of the Tokugawa period has come to symbolize the ascendance of Neo-Confucianism as the official doctrine of the Tokugawa regime. Razan has accordingly been portrayed by himself and others as the bakufu's official ideologue.[4]

These paradigmatic stories establish several points: (1) they build a

---

[2] Quoted in Masao Maruyama, *Studies in the Intellectual History of Tokugawa Japan* (Princeton: Princeton University Press, 1974), p. 15.

[3] An annotated version of the biography can be found in Abe Yoshio, ed., *Nihon no Shushigaku*, Shushigaku Taikei, vol. 13; (Meitoku Shuppansha, 1975), vol. 2, pp. 43–54. The reference is to pp. 46–47. Another edition is available in *Fujiwara Seika, Hayashi Razan*, NST, 28:188–198. See also Imanaka Kanshi, *Kinsei Nihon seiji shisō no seiritsu: Seikagaku to Razangaku* (Sōbunsha, 1972), pp. 34, 88–89, 95, 125–126.

[4] Nakae Tōju, for instance, criticized Razan for having sold out to the bakufu. He acknowledged Razan's reputation as a man of great learning, but accused him of merely posing as a Neo-Confucian scholar since he had accepted the highest Buddhist title of *hōin* from the bakufu in 1629. See his *Rinshi teihatsu juiben*, in *Nakae Tōju*, NST, 29:13–16.

linkage between the bakufu, Neo-Confucianism, and ideology; (2) this linkage is structured as an event involving specific actors—Ieyasu, Seika, Razan; (3) the event is characterized as a conscious decision by Ieyasu, portrayed as keenly aware of a power-ideology symbiosis; (4) it implies that a single and comprehensive body of thought, Neo-Confucianism, was "borrowed"; and (5) the shift from Buddhism to Neo-Confucianism is presented as a substitution of secular, rational thought for religious doctrine, and structured as a phenomenon of historical discontinuity.

One finds these five points uncritically woven into standard treatments of the subject. Yet each involves issues that raise serious questions, some general, others specific.

Broadly speaking, there is no denying that seventeenth-century Japan presents us with a well-developed political discourse that is absent in the previous century. It is also certain that within this epistemological field, a considerable Neo-Confucian vocabulary was deployed to talk and think about man and society. What is far from clear, however, is whether Neo-Confucianism monopolized this discourse, and whether its relationship to the Tokugawa power structure transformed it into an official orthodoxy. Are we indeed confronted with an official sponsorship of a discourse as an ideology, and if so, what do these terms mean? Moreover, when the first and second bakufu were established in the twelfth and fourteenth centuries, nothing even remotely analogous to the ideational construction of the seventeenth century occurred. Why did a political ideology develop (assuming that to be the case) precisely at that time, while in previous centuries political regimes seemed to have been able to get by with less fully articulated doctrines?

More specifically, the roles of the main actors have to be reevaluated as to their intentions. Can the establishment of an ideology be merely the result of a political mind making a deliberate decision and leaving its execution to an ideologue? Further, is this operation best described as the "borrowing" of a foreign doctrine?

Traditional accounts, one can conclude, assume an unproblematic, "natural" presence of an appropriate body of knowledge for administrative purposes—an "ideology"—from the very beginning of the period. For most historians, Tokugawa ideology is a primary given, a thing "*déjà en place*."[5] This body of thought, being of foreign ori-

---

[5] For the most recent examples, see Wm. Theodore de Bary and I. Bloom, eds., *Principle and Practicality: Essays in Neo-Confucianism and Practical Learning* (New York: Columbia University Press, 1979), pp. 14, 17, 137–138, 474, 476, 480–481. See also Maruyama, *Studies*, pp. 3–42. Japanese Marxist historians usually speak of "contradictions" between the social structure and the ideology, thereby assuming that an (inad-

gin, was "borrowed" by Tokugawa power (also already *in situ*) mainly through the mediation of Tokugawa Ieyasu and Hayashi Razan. This thought system clearly had a structure. Nevertheless, one is left with the impression that one is dealing with a commodity that was not the end product of a production process: as far as Japan was concerned, it was preconstructed in China, and all that was involved was not the building but the borrowing of a conceptual structure.

According to Maruyama Masao, the Japanese took over a monolithic block of Sung thought, structured in a continuative mode.[6] Professor Wm. Theodore de Bary stresses Neo-Confucianism's unfolding differentiation during the Ming dynasty. What was adopted was thus a diversified tradition which, however, had already realized its pluralistic potential in China.[7] Such characterizations of Neo-Confucianism have forced scholars like Maruyama and de Bary—their excellent contributions to the study of Tokugawa thought notwithstanding—into accepting the traditional picture that, for all practical purposes, early-Tokugawa political thought had a structure with little or no genesis of its own. They subscribe to the tale of a beginning. A historical beginning, however, in contrast to a genesis, is usually a rather simple matter, and is often more emblematic than real. A first step of inquiry consists thus of exposing the emblematic character of the links forged in the traditional account of the beginning of Neo-Confucianism in Japan, an account that has beguiled many historians.

Founders of dynasties are irresistible seducers. Later historians as well as their own contemporaries are too eager to ascribe major insights and decisions to them. An extreme example is David A. Dilworth, who refers to an "epochal decision by Tokugawa Ieyasu to shift the spiritual authority from Buddhism to the metaphysical and humanistic thought of Neo-Confucianism";[8] this decision, he also writes, was reflected by the conversions of Seika, Razan, and Yamazaki Ansai (1618–1682) to Neo-Confucianism. When did Ieyasu make this "epochal" ("monumental" or "about an epoch"?) decision so that it could be reflected in conversions by Seika—the year he left the monastery is unknown, but he married around 1598—and Razan (in 1597)? It could not have been the simple fact that in 1593 Ieyasu invited

---

equate) ideology was a given. One instance is Kinugasa Yasuki, *Kinsei Jugaku shisōshi no kenkyū* (Hōsei Daigaku, 1976).

[6] Maruyama, *Studies*, pp. 26–31.

[7] Wm. Theodore de Bary, ed., *The Unfolding of Neo-Confucianism* (New York: Columbia University Press, 1975); *Principle*, pp. 28–30, 156, 167, 174.

[8] de Bary, *Principle*, p. 476.

Seika to lecture on the *Chen-kuan cheng-yao* (The Essentials of Government of the Chen-kuan [627–649] Period), as Dilworth seems to suggest.[9] This treatise was not a Neo-Confucian work, and emperors and shoguns had heard lectures about it on many occasions in the past (for instance, in 1317, 1359, 1401, and 1503).[10] Further, what does it mean that in 1600 Seika declined an invitation by Ieyasu to join his service, withdrew gradually from the public realm and became a cultured recluse while Razan, hired in 1605, was forced two years later, in order to keep his post, to take tonsure again?[11]

All evidence indicates that Neo-Confucianism was never perceived by the early-Tokugawa shoguns as a tradition deserving specific support. Shinto and Buddhism, however, were. Every twenty years the bakufu allocated 30,000 *koku* for the ritual rebuilding of the Ise shrines.[12] Iemitsu also spent 500,000 *ryō* (one-seventh of the treasury left by his father, Hidetada, the second shogun) on the Nikkō mausoleum for Ieyasu.[13] Further, through daimyo levies, he gave 50,000 ryō and building material to Tenkai (1536?–1643), Razan's archrival in the bakufu, for the construction of Kan'eiji in Edo, a monastery housing thirty-six monks. This compares most unfavorably with the land grant and 200 ryō, given to Razan in 1630 to build a school for some twenty or thirty students—more a gesture of shogunal gratitude for twenty-five years of bakufu service than an expression of shogunal patronage of Neo-Confucianism. The bakufu did not even finance the school's Confucian temple, which was built a year later by the lord of Owari. In 1633 Iemitsu (on his way back from the Kan'eiji)

---

[9] Ibid., p. 477.

[10] Wajima Yoshio, *Chūsei no Jugaku* (Yoshikawa Kōbunkan, 1965), pp. 74, 99, 171, 184.

[11] Tetsuo Najita, in a short chapter on Tokugawa thought, also still finds space to grant Ieyasu the honor of identifying and discussing with Fujiwara Seika the crucial issues (power and loyalty) that were to dominate Japan for over two hundred years (*Japan* [Prentice-Hall, 1974], pp. 18–19). This is incorrect on two points. First, the discussion took place with Razan and not with Seika, who explictly declined involvement in such discussion. Second, a more plausible and immediate context for these discussions in 1612 was not the issue of general principles of governance, but rather the question of how to reconcile Ieyasu's obligation of loyalty to Hideyori with his decision to use power to get rid of him—an issue of "regicide" which Ieyasu had to confront before his Osaka campaigns. This explains Seika's refusal to respond. See Hori Isao, *Hayashi Razan*, Jinbutsu Sōsho, no. 118 (Yoshikawa Kōbunkan, 1964), pp. 159–164.

[12] Sakurai Katsunoshin, *Ise jingū* (Gakuseisha, 1969), p. 199.

[13] Conrad Totman, *Politics in the Tokugawa Bakufu, 1600–1843* (Cambridge: Harvard University Press, 1967), pp. 77, 82.

paid the school a quick visit. Ietsuna (b. 1641; shogun, 1651–1680) never set foot in the school.[14]

This absence of attention—let alone support—for Neo-Confucianism as a distinct tradition, characteristic of Iemitsu and Ietsuna, also typified Ieyasu's attitude. How else can one explain 112 recorded instances of Ieyasu's attendance at official expositions of Buddhist doctrine; his initiation into Tendai teachings; the absence in his bureaucracy of a *Jusha* (Confucian teacher) post—Razan was one of thirteen *ohanashishū*, or moral tale-tellers; his refusal in 1614 to grant Razan's request for support to open a school to be headed by Seika; and his patronizing the printing of numerous works on Buddhism, but of only two traditional Confucian works and not a single Neo-Confucian one?[15]

If Ieyasu and the next three shoguns, which brings us to 1680, gave no distinctive institutional support to Neo-Confucianism, what does one make then of Razan's position? Nakae Tōju (1608–1648) was right when he wrote that Razan's career was not that of a Confucian scholar.[16] It seems, however, that his career represents a continuous but only partially successful attempt to establish himself as one.

The following are some clues as to Razan's position as ohanashishū. During the Ieyasu and Hidetada years, Razan was a frustrated "*fonctionnaire*," an ambitious clerk-librarian whose talents were rarely called upon for lecturing, and whose future either as a scholar or bureaucrat was dim. In 1611 he complained to Seika that he felt like a fraud since he was not allowed to teach what Seika had prepared him for.[17] Although his position improved under Iemitsu, it still was not tailored to the advisory role a Confucian scholar should play. In 1650, for example, the lord of Mito commissioned a treatise on tobacco smoking by Razan, but when he started his monumental work on the history of Japan seven years later, he sought neither the service nor advice of the Hayashi house.[18] When Hoshina Masayuki (1611–1672), Iemitsu's brother, after reading the *Hsiao-hsüeh* (Elementary

---

[14] Hori, *Razan*, pp. 275–282.

[15] Kōmoto Takeshi, "Nihon kinsei shoki ni okeru seiji to shisō—Tokugawa Ieyasu no seiji to Bukkyō," *Shichō* 42 (1948): 51, 53 n. 1; Hori, *Razan*, pp. 223, 252, 255–256.

[16] See n. 4 of this essay.

[17] *Razan sensei bunshū*, originally published in 1662 (Heiankō Kogakkai, 1918), 2:27. The relevant passage is quoted in Minamoto Ryōen, "Fujiwara Seika to Hayashi Razan," *Bungei kenkyū* (Tōhoku Daigaku) 87 (1978): 4.

[18] Hori, *Razan*, p. 345. In 1664 Tokugawa Mitsukuni showed some interest in the historical views of the Hayashi house, but from 1672 on he stopped hiring Hayashi school graduates for his project.

Learning) four years earlier, ordered the composition of a Neo-Confucian compendium for the young shogunal heir (the future Ietsuna),
he called upon a doctor but not upon Razan.[19] According to Wajima
Yoshio, Razan's first assignment as a Neo-Confucian scholar for the
bakufu came only in 1656, one year before his death, when he lectured on the *Ta-hsüeh* (Great Learning) to the fifteen-year-old Ietsuna.[20]

From early on, however, Razan endeavored to increase the official
character of his position. His request in 1614 for funds to build a
school and his final success in 1630 are steps in that direction. In the
1650s and 1660s, however, the Hayashi house had to deal with serious competitors. In these decades, powerful daimyo closely related
to the Tokugawa, such as Hoshina Masayuki, regent (*hosa*) to the
young Ietsuna, Tokugawa Mitsukuni (1628–1700) from Mito, and
Ikeda Mitsumasa (1609–1682) from Okayama, through their interest
in ideology, made ideology a commodity. The Hayashi thus sought
to further their competitive advantage in an open but threatening
market. Sokō and Banzan were famous and held stipends equal to
Razan's (Sokō) or triple the amount (Banzan's 3,000 koku). In 1651
Iemitsu, shortly before he died, even thought of bringing both into
the bakufu. Razan's virulent attack on Christianity in 1651–1652, in
which he branded Banzan's teachings as a crypto version of Christian
doctrine, and his castigation of scholars producing military works
(Sokō) are better understood as political moves against strong competitors (rather than as proof that Razan was blinded by his own
fanatical rhetoric, as George Elison suggests).[21]

In 1658 Yamazaki Ansai appeared in Edo, becoming Hoshina Masayuki's mentor in 1665. Rumors spread that Hoshina would ask
Ansai to open his own school in Edo.[22] Hoshina was a fervent ideologue but had no use for the Hayashi school. As we shall soon see,
it was within this competitive context at the center of bakufu power
that the Hayashi brothers, in their biography of their father, Razan,
made a monopolistic claim on orthodoxy.

Ultimately, it was the Hayashi family that was responsible for creating the emblematic links between Ieyasu, the bakufu, Seika, Neo-
Confucianism, and Razan. The Hayashi helped establish the fiction

[19] Wajima, "Kanbun igaku," p. 139.

[20] Wajima Yoshio, "Hoshina seiken to Rinke no gakumon," *Ōtemae joshidaigaku
ronshū* 9 (1975): 87.

[21] Hori, *Razan*, pp. 397–399; Wajima, "Kanbun igaku," pp. 143–147. For Elison's
interpretation, see his *Deus Destroyed* (Cambridge: Harvard University Press, 1973),
p. 235.

[22] Wajima, "Hoshina seiken," pp. 85–86, 92.

of a Neo-Confucian bakufu-supported orthodoxy, which not only informed the text of Matsudaira Sadanobu's Ban on Heterodoxy in 1790, but still governs much of today's scholarship. They, and not the bakufu leadership, were eager to have Neo-Confucianism clearly marked as a separate tradition under their own aegis.

Razan's publication of Seika's collected works in 1620 gives the impression that he was Seika's spiritual heir. Yet Razan and Seika had become estranged not long after they met,[23] and Seika designated not Razan but Matsunaga Shōsan as his successor.[24]

Razan's own collected writings were published in 1662 by his two sons. In the two biographies appended to this edition,[25] his sons do not merely chronicle Razan's career, but construct a life history that established the ideological importance of the Hayashi family. They fabricate for Tokugawa Neo-Confucianism a beginning that bestowed unassailable authority upon the Hayashi house. For instance, they dramatize public lectures Razan gave in Kyoto in 1600 and 1603. In the first one, Razan lectured on Neo-Confucian texts, an event which "in the same year that the Great Divine Lord Tōshō [Ieyasu] established his military authority over the country, established in our country the authority of *dōgaku* [Teachings of the Way, Neo-Confucianism]."[26] This version establishes an even more direct link between Razan, Neo-Confucianism, and the bakufu than the more well known story of Seika's audience with Ieyasu.

It was thus in the 1650s and 1660s that orthodoxy became important: it was an issue, however, created not by the bakufu but by the Hayashi scholars who saw their position threatened. Their aim and motivation was not simply to promote correct learning, but to secure the power to produce official knowledge.

The previous analysis shows that the early bakufu under the first four shoguns did not "respond" to Neo-Confucianism: there existed neither privileged institutional support for it, nor any directives from above for the imposition of a well-formulated ideology. This, however, does not preclude the existence of more limited legitimation efforts by the new rulers to justify their newly acquired position of domination, nor does it disprove the existence of an ideology, along lines spelled out by Gramsci, as an epistemological construct produced by the private initiative of auxiliary groups to the political

[23] Minamoto, "Seika to Razan," p. 4.

[24] Hori, *Razan*, p. 100.

[25] *Razan sensei shishū*, originally published in 1662 (Heiankō Kogakkai, 1921), vol. 2: Furoku (Appendix), pp. 1–55.

[26] Ibid., pp. 3, 4, 36.

governing elite. Such a construct enables the ruling class to reduce its reliance on coercive power and instead to exercise a hegemonic rule which entails not only political domination but also moral and cultural leadership facilitating that domination.[27] The investigation of these two aspects of an early-Tokugawa ideology requires some clarification of theoretical assumptions.

First, it seems clear that one will not find further answers to the question of an overall ideology by focusing on the actions, aims, and motivations of alleged main actors (the shogun and the Hayashi scholars). The shoguns were uninterested in pushing an overall ideology, while the Hayashi were drawn to it belatedly as a weapon in their struggle to secure a place for themselves within the bakufu.

Further, the appearance of a body of political thought by the mid-seventeenth century remains to be explained as a problem in itself.[28] In the past, the presence of this body of thought has too easily been taken for granted. Assuming the content of Tokugawa political discourse to have been settled, scholars hurried into an analysis of the structure and function of this "ideology." They could do this because they assumed that "borrowing" answered the whole question of its establishment.

One can approach this problem through two kinds of inquiry. One consists of identifying the mechanism or logic by which such a thought construct was put together, that is, the "how" of its genesis. In general, the invocation of existing ideologies does not occur *in toto* but rather is a partial and piecemeal matter.[29] It seems justified, therefore, to assume that ideologies never take shape all at once. Their establishment is not an event but a process. The other inquiry consists of

[27] Antonio Gramsci, *Selections from the Prison Notebooks*, ed. and trans. Quintin Hoare and G. N. Smith (New York: International Publishers, 1971), pp. 57–59, 258, 261–262.

[28] In his day, Nietzsche argued that the problem with the "Science of Morals" was that the problem of morality itself was lacking. This is perhaps applicable to the question of the study of bakufu ideology-formation: "The suspicion was lacking that there was anything problematic here. What philosophers . . . sought to furnish was . . . only a scholarly form of *faith* in the prevailing morality, a new way of *expressing* it, and thus itself a fact within a certain morality, indeed even in the last resort a kind of denial that this morality *ought* to be conceived as a problem" (*Beyond Good and Evil*, trans. R. J. Hollingdale [Penguin Books, 1973], p. 91). Original emphasis retained.

[29] On the problem of ideology as a never-ending process of regularization and situational adjustment in a climate of indeterminacy, see Sally F. Moore, "Epilogue: Uncertainties in Situations; Indeterminacies in Culture," in S. F. Moore and Myerhoff, eds., *Symbol and Politics in Communal Ideology* (Ithaca: Cornell University Press, 1976), pp. 210–239. Moore suggests (p. 236) that ideologies we speak of as whole are only invoked piecemeal.

the search for plausible reasons why such ideological construction took place at that particular time in Japanese history.

In a general way, it is thus helpful to maintain a constructivist perspective on ideologies. Conceiving of them as thought constructs, one looks then for indications of a construction, of a conceptual engineering through an oriented activation according to a certain logic, of the symbolizing power of ideas from possibly more than one tradition. This logic is informed by the requirements of political practice, by schemes that aim at the efficacy of symbols in the world. It is thus not determined or constricted by the mechanism of borrowing. Rather, what ideas are selected and how they are appropriated is dictated by this logic. Whether one faces borrowed concepts or novel ones, the problem is the same—a politically guided putting-in-place of symbolizations.

Further, the existence or emergence of a comprehensive, effective discourse in society cannot be understood as the result of the purposeful planning of one or two individuals. It is therefore more useful to formulate explanations of this formation in terms of an overall strategy at the transindividual and transbiographical level rather than in terms of individual intentions. Interests are also at stake in its formation; interests that are not necessarily those of the whole society, but rather the sectional interests of certain classes or groups which are being served by such constructs in a variety of ways, not the least of which is that they help create those very groups that are their creators by giving these groups a clearer identity (at the expense of other groups). And, as described earlier, sectarian interests can also play a role in producing social knowledge, vying with each other for official recognition from which they would benefit.[30]

These considerations force one to cast one's nets more widely. While remaining within the perimeter of the bakufu proper, as is our task

[30] In formulating the problematik spelled out in these two paragraphs, I have relied on a variety of authors: Lucien Goldmann for the constructivist and transindividual view (*Essays on Method in the Sociology of Literature* [St. Louis: Telos Press, 1980], pp. 19, 44, 60–61); Pierre Bourdieu for conceiving of the problem in terms of a certain logic and schemes that are informed by praxis (*Outline of a Theory of Practice* [Cambridge: At the University Press, 1977], pp. 15, 16, 27, 109–110); J. C. Merquior for the conflict between sectional interests and those of the whole society (*The Veil and the Mask: Essays on Culture and Ideology* [London: Routledge and Kegan Paul, 1979], pp. 3–4); Michel Foucault for the idea of conceptualizing strategies (*The Archeology of Knowledge* [New York: Pantheon, 1972], pp. 64–70; *Power/Knowledge: Selected Interviews and other Writings, 1972–1977* [New York: Pantheon, 1980], pp. 61, 77, 114, 202–208. See also Bourdieu, *Outline*, pp. 6, 9). On the problem of positing acting subjects behind these strategies, see Foucault, *Power*, pp. 202–204, and Bourdieu, *Outline*, pp. 73–76.

for this paper, one has to trace the genesis of the early-Tokugawa discourse on society. This entails establishing a reference point outside Neo-Confucianism and scanning the broader epistemological horizon. Only then can one properly evaluate Neo-Confucian contributions to the formation of this discourse. This also means going back in time to the end of the Warring States period (1482–1558) to take into account the questions to which the earliest formulations of this discourse were answers.

In the decades straddling the year 1600, a fragmented society in constant flux was stabilized through sheer military force and was transformed into a new society that found validation for—and acceptance of—a new kind of authority. Within this transformation, what was the relationship between power and authority? What went into the construction of this authority? What were the mechanisms of symbolic signification that effected this creation? In the answers to these questions, one can detect the first stirrings of a discourse that took some one hundred years, that is, from around 1570 until the mid-seventeenth century, to mature.

In sixteenth-century Japan, the situation in terms of power and authority was experimental and open-ended. All central authority—imperial, shogunal, and even that of the provincial governors—was collapsing. At the local level, however, we find a newly emerging group of independent and contentious warlords, the daimyo. But even their power was tenuous. Victory one day was never a full assurance against defeat the next, and peace never more than a lull between campaigns. In the words of one daimyo in the 1550s: "Warriors may be called dogs or beasts; but no matter what, victory is their business," and "no matter how powerful you are, there is always someone more powerful than you."[31] One hundred years later, as we shall see, these self-confessed subhumans will pose as exemplars for mankind (and be recognized as such), their virtuous status firmly secured, dispensing benevolence at the tip of the sword. The self-presentation of the warriors, in these one hundred years, underwent a turnabout.

In the sixteenth century also, one does not come across extended discussions of the nature of society. One notable exception is the Tako House Code of circa 1544.[32] According to Tako Tokitaka (1467–1562), the central quality his age needed was *san'yō*, calculation. One

---

[31] The first quotation is from *Asakura Sōteki waki* written around 1552; see Nihon Kyōiku Bunko, *Kunkai* (Dōbunkan, 1910), 2:127. The second is from *Tako kakun*, written around 1544; see Kakei Yasuhiko, *Chūsei buke kakun no kenkyū, Shiryō-hen* (Kazama, 1967), pp. 305–307.

[32] The Tako House Code can be found in Kakei, *Chūsei*.

has to be able to calculate things, resources, and talent, for otherwise government is impossible.[33] Practical knowledge is necessary for the functional arrangement of society, which is compared to a house where the lord is the roof, his immediate relatives the beams, the elders the pillars, servants the gate, peasants the tatami floor, and so on.[34] The metaphor for society is the construction of a dwelling, not the still hierarchy of nature. Even religion rests on calculation because rebirth is nothing without it, since one's mind will unredeemably wander astray if one follows one's desires to live without knowing the limits of life.[35] In this text, society is discussed in functional terms, and even religion is subjected to such rational discourse. Again, one hundred years later one is confronted with a total reversal when religious and spiritual concepts are mobilized in a discourse on society. The Tako document identified a crucial social and political problem and talked about it in straightforward constructivist terms. Tokugawa society knew the same problem, but its texts formulated a discourse that was oblique and elaborate, as well as structural.

Undomesticated power was the crucial issue that kept sixteenth-century Japan in constant flux. It is as if power had no need for another name to obfuscate its true nature; no need to refer to "sources" other than itself: emperor, shogun, and provincial governors were useless as guarantors to daimyo, who were busy breaking down local resistance to their armies, and who survived by their own strategic cunning in battles against each other.

Yet, even while in the first half of the century sheer force could get by without apologetical justifications, voices were raised that proceeded to envelop it in new terms, out of which ultimately a new discourse was spun, a conceptual cocoon in whose dark center power could hide from view. This process started in earnest with Oda Nobunaga (1534–1582) in the 1570s. It is as if, alongside an unprecedented accumulation of power, Nobunaga had also to increase his symbolic stock in order to signify that power as something else.[36]

A first step in this direction, which other daimyo took as well, consisted of vague references to something beyond power called *kōgi*.[37]

---

[33] Kakei, *Chūsei, Kenkyū-hen*, pp. 262–266, 279–280.

[34] Ibid., *Kenkyū-hen*, pp. 283–286; *Shiryō-hen*, pp. 291–295.

[35] Ibid., *Shiryō-hen*, pp. 249, 257.

[36] Bourdieu has developed the metaphors of "symbolic stock" and "symbolic capital" (*Outline*, pp. 39, 41, 48, 171, 195).

[37] On kōgi, see Fukaya Katsumi, "Kōgi to mibunsei," in *Kinsei*, Taikei Nihon Kokkashi (Tōkyō Daigaku, 1975), 3:153; Asao Naohiro, "Bakuhansei to tennō," ibid., p. 209, n. 2. Recently, after this paper was drafted, two works were published in English where the complex developments, summarized in the next three paragraphs, are dealt with in detail. On kōgi in general, see Asao Naohiro, "Shogun and Tennō," in John

Kōgi meant "public affairs and ceremonies" and referred to the imperial and shogunal courts. In speaking of kōgi in the context of their own private regimes, these daimyo created for themselves a semblance of legitimacy by alluding to these two traditional sources of authority.

Nobunaga also referred to *tenka*, the realm.[38] Here the explicit appeal was to the whole that was intended to make partiality acceptable. Nobunaga's implicit argument was that his particular interests were not what they appeared to be, but rather were conditioned and hence transformed by a holistic focus. The symbolic capital that he was adding to his expanding warlord powers transformed his campaigns into a public, official program labeled the unification or military pacification of the whole realm. The tactic of "officializing" his position, however, was only the beginning of his legitimizing strategy.[39]

For this strategy to be successful, the center, Kyoto had to be controlled. After his conquest of the capital, however, it became clear to Nobunaga that the imperial and shogunal institutions did not provide the appropriate idiom to speak of his powers. Symbols signifying sharing or delegation would not do. Yet even autonomous power needs a base and a name as disguise. What Nobunaga had in mind became literally monumentally clear when he built Azuchi castle outside Kyoto, which became the ritual setting, an architectural *mise-en-scène*, for inaugurating a cult to himself shortly before his violent death in 1582.[40] The idiom which he then revealed to have made his own was religious (and, if anything, Shinto). He made himself the referent for his own power not as a supreme general but as a divine

---

Whitney Hall et al., eds., *Japan before Tokugawa: Political Control and Economic Growth, 1500–1650* (Princeton: Princeton University Press, 1981), pp. 248–270; Sasaki Junnosuke, "The Changing Rationale of Daimyo Control in the Emergence of the Bakuhan State," ibid., pp. 271–294. On *tenka* and Nobunaga's politics in Kyoto, see Fujiki Hisashi, "The Political Posture of Oda Nobunaga," ibid., pp. 149–193. On Azuchi castle, see George Elison, "The Cross and the Sword: Patterns of Momoyama History," in George Elison and B. L. Smith, eds., *Warlords, Artists and Commoners: Japan in the Sixteenth Century* (Honolulu: University Press of Hawaii, 1981), pp. 62–65; Carolyn Wheelright, "A Visualization of Eitoku's Lost Paintings at Azuchi Castle," in *Warlords*, pp. 87–111. On Nobunaga and Hideyoshi, see George Elison, "The Cross," pp. 53–85, "Hideyoshi, the Bountiful Minister," in *Warlords*, pp. 222–244. See also my *Tokugawa Ideology* (forthcoming, Princeton University Press).

[38] Okuno Takahiro, *Oda Nobunaga monjo no kenkyū* (Yoshikawa Kōbunkan, 1969–1970), 1:169, 389, 549; and 2:124, 125, 389, 417, 531–533.

[39] On "officialization" as a legitimizing tactic, see Bourdieu, *Outline*, pp. 21–22, 40.

[40] See Naitō Akira, "Azuchi-jō no kenkyū," *Kokka* 83, nos. 987, 988 (1975); Michael Cooper, ed., *They Came to Japan* (Berkeley: University of California Press, 1965), pp. 101–102; Okuno Takahiro, "Oda seiken no kihonrosen," *Kokushigaku* 100 (1976): 50.

ruler.[41] Generator and recipient at the same time of his own legitimacy, he erased all mediating references. Nobunaga achieved this by the idiomatic transposition of political discourse into an unmediated absolute mode.

This way of speaking of power as sacred authority was continued by subsequent supreme power holders. Toyotomi Hideyoshi (1537–1598), who was of peasant origin, endorsed and encouraged stories about his divine predestination and miraculous birth, even in his diplomatic correspondence with the Portuguese viceroy of the Indies in Goa and the Spanish governor-general of the Philippines.[42] He also explicitly relied on Yoshida Shinto teachings to formulate his views and made arrangements for a cult after his death.[43] Tokugawa Ieyasu

[41] Most Japanese historians accept the small evidence available about Nobunaga's self-deification and make good sense of it in the immediate political context. George Elison rejects that evidence and the notion of Nobunaga's cult to himself ("The Cross," pp. 74–75, 301–302 no. 62, 63). His meticulous analysis, while praiseworthy (and allowing for the pleasure of destroying another Deus), is not convincing. First, Elison has a tendency to play down political arguments in favor of psychological ones, even when explaining the behavior of historical actors that have proven themselves to be adroit and shrewd politicians. Such is the case with Hayashi Razan (see n. 21 of this essay), and even with Nobunaga (a "solipsist"; see "The Cross," p. 74, and "Hideyoshi," p. 231) and Hideyoshi ("insecure," "a social climber," and given to "theatricality"; "Hideyoshi," pp. 225, 241). In the present context, he accuses Father Luis Frois, who reported on the cult in some detail, of being swayed by "a sense of tragedy" ("The Cross," p. 75). Second, Elison often credits the Jesuit missionaries with reliable reporting (pp. 59, 227, 228) and even praises Frois for his "superb portrait" of Nobunaga (p. 66). Why then the appeal to a distorting (and fabricating) sense of tragedy on this particular point? Third, he does not explain why Frois, who earlier praised Nobunaga, a supporter of the Church, should suddenly paint him as an abomination. An obvious explanation is that Nobunaga had indeed turned into one—in the eyes of the missionary. And what could have been more shocking than that this supporter of the Church committed the ultimate sacrilege of taking on godly prerogatives? Fourth, if such were the case, then Frois's report has to be accepted as a description by Frois of Nobunaga's arrogation of divine powers, and not rejected (as if this were Nobunaga's text) because "Nobunaga's notion of divinity could not have been the biblical conception reflected by the missionary" (p. 75). Last, Nobunaga's cult makes political sense as one move in a long career of skillful and unprecedented political maneuvers by someone who had become sensitive to ideological issues during his campaigns against his religious adversaries, a point made by Japanese historians and again downplayed by Elison (pp. 70–73).

[42] Murakami Naojirō, ed., *Ikoku ōfuku shokanshū—zōtei ikoku nikkisho* (Yūshōdō, 1966), pp. 26–29, 51, 59, 78–79; Adriana Boscaro, ed., *101 Letters of Hideyoshi* (Tokyo: Sophia University, 1975), p. 37 n. 26.

[43] Ours is the land of the *kami*, and kami is mind (*kokoro*), and the one mind is all-encompassing. No phenomena exist outside it. Without kami, there would be no spirits or no Way. They transcend good times of growth and bad times of decline; they are yin and yang at the same time and cannot be measured. They are thus the root and source of all phenomena. They are in India under the name of

41

made provisions in his last will for a shrine in Nikkō where Iemitsu, his grandson, developed a regular cult to the *shinkun*, or Divine Lord, into which even the imperial court was drawn. It is worth adding that in Edo this cult was centered in the newly built Kan'eiji, which explains its importance to Iemitsu as compared to the Hayashi school's.

Nobunaga and Hideyoshi were self-made men. Through their cunning strategies they came to control enormous military power. However, strategic action (both in the military sense, and as competitive action calculated to foster personal interests and thus devoid of any persuasive dimension to convince others of the legitimate character of a taken course) is always motivated by self-serving intentions and can never lay claim to truthfulness.[44] Without redeeming truthfulness, however, the results of such action will not be accepted by others beyond the immediate threat of power. In order to be accepted, these rulers had to resort to a different mode of action that could validate such a claim. Only then could they become legitimate rulers and their position be seen as based on something other than coercive force. They had to resort to persuasion through symbolic manipulations. The medium for this transubstantiation of power into authority was ideology.

Ideology, however, does not offer an objective representation of social and political reality although it inevitably claims truthfulness for its formulations. The ideological experiments of these men, therefore, were not attempts at representing truly the awesome reality of their coercive power; they were efforts at signifying that reality in a new way. These warlords wanted to obfuscate the history they themselves had made. They sought to distort their role as strategists and to justify themselves as other than successful warlords. Victory was not their sole business as it had been, by their own admission, for the daimyo of half a century earlier, but acceptance of their victories was, and therefore their intentions had to be put beyond questioning—or at least they had to be bracketed. They had to create a false consciousness of their position, for they did not want their power

---

Buddhism; they are in China under the name of Confucianism; they are in Japan where they go under the name Shinto. To know Shinto is to know Buddhism and Confucianism. (Murakami, *Ikoku*, pp. 26–28, 78–79)

Hideyoshi's divine title was Toyokuni daimyōjin, written with the characters alluding to his name (*Toyo*tomi) and the country (*kuni*), also an abbreviation of a name for Japan in the *Kojiki*: "*Toyo*ashihara no nakatsu *kuni*" (Central Land of the Plentiful Reed Plains).

[44] The conceptual framework of legitimacy having to redeem the validity claims of truthfulness and correctness (discussed later) is borrowed from Jürgen Habermas, *Communication and the Evolution of Society* (Beacon Press, 1979), pp. 2, 3, 38, 66, 118, 209. Also for Habermas, strategic action and communicative action are technical terms.

to be recognized as such. Their aim, then, was to "defamiliarize" society from the reality of their power through its false recognition as something else.[45] One has the impression that they were afraid that naked power might be powerless. Indeed, a negative response to pure power could only be its direct challenge, while if power were surrounded by obfuscating significations, its rejection would also entail conceptual reformulations at the level of argumentation.

One can thus say that the symbolic manipulations of these men were a continuation of warfare, but by other means. This new effort at persuasion also involved strategies, but signifying strategies which, if successful, would obliterate their own traces including the military strategies of which they were a continuation.[46]

By mythologizing themselves, they dissolved the historical, contingent dimension of their persons and inserted them into a Shinto scheme of the sacred. In this way, they reduced greatly, if not totally, questions concerning their real character and intentions. Or, at least, to circumvent the subtle question of belief, one can say that this fiction went publicly uncontested; that they achieved complicity with a society that agreed to live by this fiction.[47]

Iemitsu, however, found himself in a different position. He was successor to a legacy of achievements not of his own making. He inherited his predecessors' formidable military power—he paraded an army of over three hundred thousand through Kyoto—and also an authority structure which he further consolidated and perfected. Iemitsu faced two problems. First, he had to find acceptance for his received position at the top. His personal motives were thus less of a problem. Certainly, his truthfulness had to be established, but the dissonance that had to be orchestrated away was lesser for him than for his predecessors. They were victorious generals, while he was

[45] On ideology as signification rather than representation, see Roland Barthes, *Mythologies* (New York: Hill and Wang, 1972), pp. 109–139. Barthes' position is that myths do not hide but distort and inflect, their very principle being to transform history into nature. The idea that ideology produces a false recognition (*une méconnaissance*) is Bourdieu's (see *Outline*, pp. 5, 50, 97, 133, 164, 232). Fredric Jameson discusses the notion of "defamiliarization" in his *The Prison-House of Language* (Princeton: Princeton University Press, 1972), pp. 52, 58.

[46] Foucault speaks of power as a continuation with other means (*Power*, p. 90). For the period of transition under discussion (1570s–1660s), it seems literally true that the construction of an ideology was a continuation of war with other means. The trace-effacing effect of ideological strategies is also central to Bourdieu's theory. See his *Outline*, pp. 22, 76, and Bourdieu and Jean-Claude Passeron, *Reproduction in Education, Society and Culture* (London: Sage Publications, 1977), pp. xi, 4–15.

[47] The concept of social complicity to explain the acceptance of ideas is very useful and comes from Bourdieu, *Outline*, pp. 6, 50, 133, 196.

heir to a peace that he had not forged on the battlefield. His second and larger problem was to justify a system of domination that only now, under his role in the 1630s and 1640s, had spread over the whole country and claimed to regulate the lives of all members of a highly and artificially stratified society.[48] His principal task was to persuade all that the system he presided over was not an arbitrary system of domination but a just social order. Rightness (correctness, appropriateness) was the claim he had to validate most.

Iemitsu accomplished the first task easily enough by casting himself as the successor to a founder whose sacred character validated his own position. The political order of domination, however, was not talked away by the sacred character of his grandfather. Not only the ruler, but the particular society that he presided over had to be signified in a way that discouraged questions about the historical, contingent, and hence contestable and reversible character of the whole power structure. The understanding of society had to be organized with formulas that left no place for opinions on power.

The level of justification required for this task was of a broader order than that which a mythologizing discourse could provide. Myths may have a constitutive power, but their efficacy is limited to establishing the legitimacy of rulers. They are unable to signify the legitimacy of a complex political order that already exists. But under Iemitsu, the general order of things, beyond the person of the ruler, had to be justified and clarified (illuminated, but precisely so as to leave the reality of power in the dark).

Justifications of this kind draw upon cosmologically grounded ethical philosophies that can provide rationalized world views in the form of dogmatizable knowledge.[49] In other words, narrative explanations through exemplars (the mythological mode of discourse) must make room, without necessarily disappearing themselves, for deductive explanations through philosophical arguments (a reasoned discourse) that establish ultimate grounds and unifying principles which explain the natural and human world as a whole. Such discourse, like

[48] The stratification started with Hideyoshi's famous Sword Hunt and Status Edicts, but only under Iemitsu's rule was bakufu control extended to the whole country. A shogunal delegation set foot iñ Kyushu, *tozama* territory, for the first time only in 1632. The same year, bakufu emissaries were also dispatched all over Japan. In 1635 Iemitsu revised the Regulations for Military Houses (*Buke shohatto*), widening their scope. He issued them as a set of laws without even requesting loyalty oaths from all the daimyo, as had been done on such occasions in the past. See Asao Naohiro, "Shōgun seiji no kenryoku kōzō," in *Kinsei* (Iwanami Kōza Nihon Rekishi, 1975), 106:10–14.

[49] The theoretical points in this paragraph and the preceding one were made by Habermas (*Communication*, pp. 103–104, 111, 161–162, 178, 179, 183–184).

the mythological one, also rests upon ultimate beginnings, but it transforms the originating actions of myth into "beginnings" of argumentation or fundamental principles beyond which one cannot go. Thus rulers and their order are accepted as long as political domination is made plausible as a legacy of an order of the world that was posited absolutely. In this way, the validity claim of correctness can be secured.

Traditional Shinto, needless to say, makes available mythologizing stratagems, whereas Neo-Confucianism provides the other kind of reasons most appropriate for this situation: arguments constructed from principles. But Yoshida Shinto had already worked many Neo-Confucian principles into its own constructs, mainly through establishing equations between Shinto mythological data (deities) and Neo-Confucian cosmological principles or ontological virtues.[50] This is probably why it is not surprising to find Razan dabbling in Shinto teachings throughout his career and even producing at one point a Shinto doctrine of his own.[51] It also may explain why Yamazaki Ansai turned to Shinto after an immersion in Neo-Confucian learning, drawing more and more equations (that strike one as totally arbitrary) between the two traditions.[52] Interestingly enough, Fujiwara Seika, who was also exposed to Yoshida teachings but whose interests, unlike Razan and Ansai's, moved away from the public realm, does not deal in any significant way with Shinto subjects. It is striking that: (1) Razan and Ansai, both servants of the bakufu and self-proclaimed Neo-Confucian scholars, were drawn to Shinto (which distinguishes them from Yoshikawa Koretaru, 1616–1694, and Watarai Nobuyoshi, 1615–1690, who "updated" Shinto with a Neo-Confucian vocabulary); and (2) within Yoshida Shinto enough Neo-Confucian concepts may already have been appropriated to provide the conceptual material for the task at hand. This suggests the intriguing hypothesis that the influx of Neo-Confucian learning in the early-Tokugawa period may not have been a necessary condition for the establishment of a bakufu ideology—possibly an extreme thesis,

[50] For an example of the large equation between the three traditions, see the quotation from a letter by Hideyoshi in n. 43. The most well known of these equations are between the three imperial regalia and Confucian virtues, or between Izanagi/Izanami and yin/yang. For examples, see n. 65 of this essay.

[51] The most well known formulation of Razan's particular Shinto doctrine is the *Shintō denju*, commissioned by Sakai Tadakatsu: see *Kinsei Shintōron, zenki kokugaku*, NST, 39:11–57. Other occasional notes on Shinto subjects can be found throughout Razan's collected writings. They span his career.

[52] For an example, see Ryūsaku Tsunoda et al., *Sources of Japanese Tradition* (New York: Columbia University Press, 1958), 1:358–360.

but one worth exploring. Without any doubt, however, Shinto concepts were appropriated in the construction of the discourse.

But let us set Razan and Ansai aside for the moment. They were both employed by bakufu rulers, but it can be argued that much of what they produced was not explicitly ordered by the bakufu. Many of Razan's writings pertain to his own private scholarship; and Ansai served Hoshina Masayuki, regent to the fourth shogun, for only seven years (from 1665 to 1672).[53] Moreover, Hoshina's extreme commitment to Neo-Confucianism was not shared by the bakufu leadership. Hoshina also became heir to Yoshida Shinto.[54] Strictly speaking, only one explicitly ideological document (produced anonymously and circulated in printed form during the Iemitsu years) seems to have been commissioned by the bakufu: the Tōshōgū goikun (Testament of the Deity Shining in the East, or simply "Ieyasu's Testament").[55] It is in this document that the needs of Iemitsu's reign were met through symbolic negotiations that signified the order of his regime as an embodiment of tendō, the Way of Heaven, a Confucian concept that had enjoyed common currency in Japan for quite some time.[56]

Briefly, the philosophy of tendō in Ieyasu's Testament posited the ruler not as an absolute master of his own house but as one who himself was loyal to tendō. Hence obedience to the ruler equaled

[53] Most of Razan's writings on Neo-Confucianism, except for the Shunkanshō and the Santokushō, which were written and published in the late 1620s (available in NST, 28:115–186), were personal study notes that were divulged only after his death, with the publication of his collected works in 1662. Ansai's teachings have been preserved mainly in the form of his personal study notes as well as lecture notes taken by his students. These, along with other writings of his school, were published in Nihon Koten Gakkai, ed., Yamazaki Ansai zenshū, 5 vols., 1936–1937. More recently, critical editions of some of his work have become available: for Shinto writings, see NST, 39:119–188; for Neo-Confucian writings by him and his main disciples, see Yamazaki Ansai gakuha, NST, vol. 31 (Iwanami, 1980), and Chōsen no Shushigaku, Nihon no Shushigaku (I), Shushigaku Taikei, vol. 12 (Meitoku Shuppansha, 1977).

[54] Hoshina Masayuki's early radical commitment to Neo-Confucian teachings was matched by his later fanatical enthusiasm for Shinto, and he did not get very far in giving the bakufu a Neo-Confucian tone. He legislated against junshi (loyal suicide by retainers upon the death of their lord) in 1663 as a barbaric practice, but its enforcement in 1668 was hardly less barbaric. In that year, retainers in the Utsunomiya domain committed junshi. The punishment: transfer of the heir to Yamagata with a loss of 20,000 koku, death penalty for two children of the dead retainers, and exile for other relatives. Hoshina's punishment of Yamaga Sokō was also revoked later by the bakufu (see n. 1 of this essay).

[55] The Tōshōgū goikun is to be found in Nihon kyōiku bunko: Kakunhen (Dōbunkan, 1910), pp. 252–342.

[56] Ishige Tadashi, "Sengoku-Azuchi-Momoyama jidai no rinri shisō: tendō shisō no tenkai," in Nihon Shisōshi Kenkyūkai, ed., Nihon ni okeru rinri shisō no tenkai (Yoshikawa Kōbunkan, 1965), pp. 141–168.

submission to heaven's mandate.[57] In this scheme, the warriors help to hold up Heaven's Way through the Way of the Warrior, an instrument not of evil but for killing evil.[58] Warrior rule is therefore inspired by two cardinal virtues: *jihi*, generous benevolence, a Buddhist virtue; and *shōjiki*, uprightness or straightforwardness, a Shinto term. Benevolence, the most fundamental of all virtues, paradoxically, is symbolized by the sword.[59] Thus it is established that military power, embodied in the warrior class, is indispensable for society. However, its character as an instrument of domination is made unrecognizable because benevolence is its principle. The practice of these virtues, central to a correct government, gives their practitioners a divine status.[60] The exercise of power by warriors becomes a dispensation of virtue by the virtuous.

It is worth noting that the Confucian term *jinsei*, benevolent government, is not to be found in the document. Moreover, *Ieyasu's Testament* is framed toward the beginning and the end by references to a divine exemplar for a *military* Minister of the Center: Sumiyoshi daimyōjin (Great Deity of Sumiyoshi).[61] One finds the identity of this god revealed in the *Warongo* (Japanese Analects), where he is spoken of as a divine shogun.[62] The *Warongo* is a contemporary syncretistic popular anthology of oracles and sayings, heavily indebted to Yoshida Shinto. The shogun's position continues to be grounded not in imperial authority but in divine paradigms.[63]

There is more, however, if one looks into some of Razan's writings and other anonymous works that started to circulate in printed form toward the end of Iemitsu's reign.[64] Here, through extended

---

[57] *Tōshōgū goikun*, pp. 285, 297, 329–330.

[58] Ibid., pp. 286, 294, 306.

[59] Ibid., pp. 256, 273, 309. This text also presents historical arguments of houses that collapsed, but these arguments are always validated by a spiritual tendō context.

[60] Ibid., p. 256.

[61] Ibid., pp. 256, 307–308.

[62] Katsube Mitake, *"Warongo" no kenkyū* (Shibundō, 1970), p. 9. The oracle by Sumiyoshi daimyōjin is the tenth in the first fascicle.

[63] Nowhere is there any mention of a delegation of authority from the emperor to the shogun. The emperor merely had special duties attached to his house (*kagyō*) which were mainly ritualistic (*Tōshōgū goikun*, p. 306).

[64] The most important of these works are the *Kanashōri*, the *Shingaku gorinsho* and the *Honsaroku* (all in NST, 28:238–302).

Shinto elements are routinely part of the discourse in these works that circulated first in manuscript form but by the 1650s in printed editions. The first two texts are almost identical and obviously related. The former seems to be the oldest (possibly composed before 1620) and the source for the latter. The *Honsaroku* argues in a vein similar to the *Tōshōgū goikun*, which was also published around the same time. The views presented in these works are very similar to those Razan reveals in his Shinto

variations on microcosmic-macrocosmic correspondences, through metaphoric manipulations à la Paracelsus, the cosmos, nature, society, and man's moral endeavors are marshaled into a grand and complex vision the sole orientation and impulse of which is political.[65] This discourse, infinitely expandable in all directions, refuses, however, to recognize man as a center of initiative other than for action confirming that general order. The rulers in this monistic scheme of things may be divine, but they have no monopoly on the sacred as Nobunaga or Hideyoshi had. All men, that is, all subjects, share in the same sacrality because they are part of an order that ought not to be upset lest one commit sacrilege: the *kami* or gods are spoken of as residing in the people, tendō's children.[66]

---

treatise. Tokugawa scholars and printers have attributed these works to various scholars (Seika and Banzan). Modern scholars have ascribed them to others. Imanaka Kanshi argues for a Razan authorship in his *Seikagaku* (pp. 38, 155–156, 187, 191). Hori rejects this hypothesis (*Razan*, p. 374). Ishige Tadashi has argued first for Fabian Fucan, and more recently for Bonshun (NST, 28:500). Obviously, correct authorship or scholastic genealogy (Shinto versus Neo-Confucian) was not important at the time. It should therefore be irrelevant for our approach to these texts. What is crucial about them is that they all contribute (with heterogeneous material) to the formation of a political discourse in the mid-seventeenth century.

[65] Some examples of this "mutual interlocking of everything with everything at every moment" (the expression is from Jean Soustelle, *La Pensée cosmologique des anciens Mexicains* [Paris: Hermann, 1940], p. 9) are the following. "Man's head is round because Heaven is round; the top cowlick on his head corresponds to the polestar; the eyes to the sun and moon; the five intestines and groups of five fingers and toes to the five elements" (*Santoku*, p. 175). The ethical world is based on the five constant virtues and the five relationships: to organize one's behavior according to them equals becoming one with tendō (*Kana*, p. 243). Nature's principles and the original principle of man's mind are the same (*Santoku*, p. 180). Heaven and man are thus one (*Kana*, p. 242). There are no principles besides mind (*Santoku*, p. 153), and no gods besides mind (*Shintō denju*, pp. 19, 57). Recapturing the prethought mind is a return to the [*Nihon shoki*'s] primeval chaos (*konton*) preceding creation (*Shintō denju*, pp. 25–26) or original *ki* (matter), which is none other than the deity Kunitokotachi (ibid., p. 33); the mind is the dwelling place of the gods (ibid., p. 12).

Since tendō is the order of all things, through obeying the gods one fulfills tendō (ibid.), whose mind is originally the same as man's (*Honsa*, p. 296). Rulers are caretakers of things that belong to tendō (ibid., p. 290): to observe tendō's rules in the public realm means to respect warrior laws (ibid., p. 289). Hierarchical stability is the principle of Heaven and Earth (*Razan bunshū*, 2:402), the will of heaven (*Santoku*, p. 129). *Kei*, reverence, is the mental attitude par excellence that maintains the hierarchy spelled out in the rites (ibid., p. 132); reverence means restraint, discretion, prudence, self-control (*tsutsushimu*: *Razan bunshū*, 2:204). Gods do not accept offerings unless they come from a pure heart (*Honsa*, p. 294). Amaterasu has to be believed: to follow the Way is *tenri*, the principle of heaven (ibid., p. 281).

[66] Ruling over the people is an act of divine veneration because "the people are the lords of the gods" (*tami wa kami no shu nari*) (*Shintō denju*, p. 14). (This is a literal translation. The character *shu*, lord, also stands for the Confucian ancestor tablet where,

By the mid-seventeenth century, the strategic cunning of the previous century was a far memory but also an ever-present fear—witness the Shimabara Rebellion of 1637. Political and personal power are thus absent from a discourse that talks not about an order to be achieved by divine protagonists, but an order that is, and that is as it ought to be—an order that had a very human and contingent history that is better forgotten. History is therefore dangerous and has to be obliterated or at least left in the background. Instead, a nature that is sacred takes the limelight. Everything is reduced to a synchronicity and immediacy that partakes of the mythical and eternal.

The process, sketched all too briefly here, consists thus of a gradual sacralization of the constituent elements of a new structure of domination as those elements become critically important. First the leaders, then the ruling class and the hierarchical structure of society itself, and finally the subjects are given cosmological and religious significance through a discourse that over a period of close to one hundred years comes to full maturation by appropriating elements from various traditions: Shinto, Buddhist and folk theologies and cosmologies, as well as Neo-Confucianism.[67] Nowhere does one find an exclusivistic concern to keep the texts within the confines of Neo-Confucianism. One is dealing rather with a process consisting of the appropriation of heterogeneous elements for the construction of a body of social knowledge, rather than with the borrowing of a ready-made philosophical system imposed as an official orthodoxy. The partitions between Neo-Confucianism and other traditions, especially Shinto, were highly porous as the careers and thought of both Razan and Ansai show. In this new discourse, "Neo-Confucianism" and "Shinto" were irrelevant as distinct doctrinal categories that by themselves would provide content and boundaries to the production of thought. Other categories discussed further in this essay played a far more important role in giving form and content to the Tokugawa discourse on society.

---

through prayer, the spirit of an ancestor can be called down and resides temporarily. The meaning of this sentence is thus: "the gods reside in the people.") To rule the country is an exercise of divine power; a lost tradition that goes back to Amaterasu (ibid., p. 19). People are all born as tendō's children; to alienate or harm them is an offense against tendō (*Tōshōgū goikun*, pp. 255, 293–294).

[67] The chronological sequence is a loose one. The first deification of a warrior-ruler certainly occurs with Oda Nobunaga. At the other end, the people are given a spiritual and religious definition, but only in a few rare passages, and only in later documents. Between these two extremes stands the full tendō philosophy. In Seika's work, one also finds references to tendō, but it is only with *Ieyasu's Testament* and the other anonymous works that the warrior class receives a privileged place. Furthermore, a very wide justification of the whole social order is worked out in cosmological terms.

If ever-expanding sacralization is the logic that characterizes the formation of this discourse, a number of questions still remain to be answered. These questions have to do with gauging the level of motivation and the degree of consciousness or calculated manipulation behind the formation of these symbolic constructs.

As already mentioned, *Ieyasu's Testament* appears to be the only explicitly ideological piece produced under direct Tokugawa sponsorship. Other writings that cosmologize the social order were written either anonymously or by someone like Razan, who, as mentioned earlier, was not an official ideologue for the bakufu, but rather an intellectual jack-of-all trades: Razan functioned as scribe, librarian, drafter of documents, ritualist, storyteller, and even as hawking companion. In other words, for most of his career he served less as the system's theologian than as its sacristan.[68] Sometimes, although rarely, he lectured, but he was in no way the only one to be invited by the bakufu to do so. He produced social commentaries, but just as often he composed them privately. Most importantly, he was not bound to one single tradition of learning. Yet, although there were no clear directives from above and no educational apparatus to diffuse an ideology,[69] scholars like Seika, Razan, and Ansai nevertheless mediated between the interests of the new ruling class and the beliefs or symbolizations called into being by these interests. The effect appears to be deception. These scholars seem to wear masks behind which they hide their real motives for presenting a fictitious picture of reality. Yet it is unclear where one would put the focal point of such a conscious conspiracy to deceive.

In retrospect, one can say that these men were spokesmen for the interests of the ruling class, so long as one keeps in mind that strictly speaking they were not appointed as such. No doubt, they formulated thoughts that became the dominant discourse of the time. In that sense, they produced an ideology, but this was not a doctrine imposed as an orthodoxy by the direct power of the "state."

However, insofar as their utterances were perceived as the solemn pronouncements of a public teaching, their semiofficial and quasi-public character served in and of itself a legitimizing function,[70] quite

[68] The theological construct of the Ieyasu cult at Nikkō was Tenkai's work, but Razan was in Nikkō on all eleven important shogunal visits (Hori, *Razan*, pp. 283, 290).

[69] In the first half-century (1630–1680) after the establishment of the Hayashi school, a total of only 310 students attended the school. By 1682 there were only seven domain schools in the more than two-hundred domains (Ooms, *Charismatic Bureaucrat*, pp. 127, 138).

[70] The legitimizing power, generated not through the content of a message but through

aside from the fact that this discourse set the terms and modality within which society ought to be discussed. It is interesting to recall that a scholar like Razan, certainly the most "official" of them all, maneuvered incessantly to increase the official character of his position and teaching in order to acquire a monopoly on the production of social knowledge (to his own benefit and the detriment of competitors). This indicates that such "official" character was far from a given and merely a desirable goal for Razan (neither he nor his successors attained the goal before Matsudaira Sadanobu's decree on heterodoxy, which was forced upon the Hayashi College under protest of its rector).[71]

Whatever masking functions this "ideology" may have performed, it also served as a veil,[72] in the sense that it expressed the genuine cognitive limitations inherent in the social perceptions of the ruling elite, perceptions which stemmed from their position in society. This new elite wanted to stay in power—hence their concern for order. But this desire for order, after a century of chaos, was shared by other segments of the population and was thus quite legitimate. The ruling class co-opted this social concern and made it exclusively their own. They may therefore have taken their statements about society, presented as truthful social knowledge, not as a knowledge distorted by (and masking) the calculation of particular interests, but indeed as veridical statements whose class bias escaped their consciousness. Social knowledge thus becomes an effective ideology precisely when it achieves such cognitive sublimation. However, both interpretations of ideology—the one as mask or conscious deception and the other as veil or naive self-delusion—refer back to the question of the acceptance of and belief in such an ideology.

How then was this ideology accepted, and in what marketplace did this effort at persuasion occur? Often these questions do not even arise because we simply assume that ideologies are produced for consumption by the ruled. Early-Tokugawa discourse, however, was intended mainly, if not exclusively, for internal consumption, that is to say, for the ruling or warrior class itself—an official consumption which further added to the symbolic capital and truth value of the discourse. Why mainly the ruling class? Because it was from this politically significant segment of society that a validation of the new

---

the perception by others of authority invested in the one who delivers it, is discussed by Bourdieu (*Outline*, pp. 170–171; *Reproduction*, pp. 20–22; "Le langage authorisé: note sur les conditions sociales de l'efficacité du discours rituel," *Actes de la Recherche en Sciences Sociales* 1, nos. 5/6 [1975]: 184–186).

[71] Ooms, *Charismatic Bureaucrat*, p. 134.

[72] For a discussion of ideology as veil or mask, see Merquior, *The Veil*, pp. 11–12.

order had to be secured. Legitimation becomes an issue only in a situation where various forces are competing for official power. These forces will therefore constitute the principal target of such efforts at persuasion. Three of the four teachers—Seika, Razan, Ansai, but not Suzuki Shōsan (1579–1655)—who were closely associated with the bakufu in the first half of the seventeenth century, as well as all of the anonymous works of the period, addressed themselves exclusively to the members of the new ruling elite.

Tokugawa discourse operated according to a clear strategy of inclusion and exclusion. This strategy, however, was not deployed toward existing traditions of thought in order to preserve the field for Neo-Confucianism alone. Its objective was the ruling class. Included were the warrior-rulers as the indirect patrons if not the producers of the discourse, as its consumers, and as its primary topic and inspiration. Other groups were excluded on all three accounts, since peasants or merchants were not those who produced, consumed, or inspired it. They were not even those upon whom it was directly "imposed." Nor was the discourse about them as peasants or merchants but as subjects, or, more precisely, as the nonrulers, that is, "the people." This discourse thus provided a clear identity to one class, the warriors, as the rulers or the virtuous—a much sharper identity than they had ever had in Japanese history. One is thus allowed to speak of this class as a transindividual agent as long as one keeps in mind that its relationship to any action one ascribes to it (such as constructing an ideology) is a dialectical one. This class did not exist as a real entity that simply produced a discourse about itself, for in this very production of knowledge, it also produced itself as a class.[73] All those outside this class suffered a negative identity as nonrulers, nonwarriors, that is, as the nonvirtuous.[74]

The early-Tokugawa discourse on society inhibited the consolidation of other groups or classes, since as a distinctive group, not to be talked about, talked to, or allowed to speak means not to exist as a group.[75] Although peasants and merchants as such were alien to this discourse, they were nevertheless affected by it. First, their unwor-

[73] Foucault discusses this dialectic in *Power*, pp. 202–204.

[74] The view of the people as the residing place of the kami or as tendō's children (see n. 66 of this study) was meant not to enhance the self-worthiness of the people, but to give warrior-administrators a sense of the limits of their power.

[75] This was the fate of the peasantry in general during the first half-century of the Tokugawa period. Moreover, certain groups were explicitly outlawed: Christians, Fujufuse followers, and what came to be known as the Kakure nenbutsu sect. The latter two sects were offspring of the powerful groups that had fought Nobunaga and Hideyoshi; the Christians were irredeemably compromised after the Shimabara Rebellion.

thiness of attention in the discourse sealed their social and political unworthiness. Second, this effect was further reinforced in that any systematic knowledge they could acquire through education was knowledge extraneous to themselves and their interests. Much later in the Tokugawa period, they would start to talk about themselves and be talked about. However, this occurred only when they became a problem—and this talk in itself was one way of being a problem— for the stability of the Tokugawa power arrangement and its symbolic constructs.

The issue of the acceptance (by the warrior class) of this ideology is more complicated. This is so because we instinctively equate acceptance with belief, especially when dealing with constructs which we today speak of as "symbolic" and therefore pertain to the category of belief/nonbelief or even make-believe, but belief in any case. These constructs, while varying considerably in detail and elaboration in different texts, were in wide circulation by the mid-seventeenth century. The basic premises and orientations of these texts were not contested or even taken as just one among many learned opinions about the world, but rather were regarded as the social truth to which there were no alternatives. This does not necessarily mean, however, that they were internalized as dogmatic points of belief or faith. It would be more precise to say that they were adopted in a complicitous understanding between the producers and consumers of these constructs (both belonging to the same social class, at least in the first half-century of the period)—an understanding that society could and should operate according to these fictitious truths, and that one must abide by this collective self-deception. In other words, in this case one can discuss consciousness and behavior without having to appeal to belief.[76]

The fourth scholar, Suzuki Shōsan, a Buddhist monk and ex-warrior, was specifically commissioned by the bakufu to straighten out through his sermons the minds of seditious peasants in one particular domain following the Shimabara Rebellion of 1637. It is worth noting, if only in passing, that in a time of crisis calling for ideological clarification, the bakufu sought the service of a Buddhist monk and not that of a Neo-Confucian scholar. These Shimabara peasants were the target of an indoctrination campaign because the rebellion was

---

[76] On the concept of self-deception, see Bourdieu (*Outline*, pp. 50, 196). The whole question of belief as an unworkable category, bound by historical developments in the West, has been analyzed by Rodney Needham, *Belief, Language and Experience* (Chicago: University of Chicago Press, 1972). Dan Sperber even argues that the dual concept of symbol/meaning is not universal either, but a culture-bound Western product (*Rethinking Symbolism* [Cambridge: At the University Press, 1974], pp. 49–50).

analogous to a situation fifty years earlier when large groups of peasants, in their resistance against warrior armies, had projected their interests in a world view that rejected the warriors. This was the only occasion, however, and a very limited one, during the first decade of the Tokugawa period, that the rulers were forced to incorporate some sector of the peasantry in their efforts at self-justification. By then, however, the peasantry at large was no longer a competitor for power. In fact, peasants had been eliminated as competitors by Nobunaga and Hideyoshi during the last decades of the sixteenth century.

In the sixteenth century, the organized peasants and commoners of several provinces had proven themselves the greatest obstacle to the expansion of Nobunaga and Hideyoshi's power. This resistance was reinforced by a world view that had no place for a warrior class.[77] These nonwarriors acknowledged authority to reside only in Buddha or the emperor and considered themselves their direct servants, denying any legitimacy to the intermediate power of the daimyo and samurai whom they saw as interlopers. Death in combat against Nobunaga, branded as "the enemy of the faith," was a guarantee of eternal salvation. It was precisely to undercut this world view that Nobunaga arrogated for himself divine status and cast himself in the role of protector of the emperor and guarantor of supernatural blessings (and not because he was a pathological megalomaniac, as one often reads).[78] The first ideological formulations of the period under study were thus put together as an ideological counter-strategy to the one of the peasants. By 1600, however, their power had been broken and their views outlawed.[79]

This leads to the question of whence came this sudden necessity for a comprehensive ideology, that is to say, an elaborate discourse

[77] Goldmann has drawn a distinction between world view and ideology (*Essays*, pp. 12, 22–24, 111–115; "Genetic Structuralism," in Elisabeth Burns and Tom Burns, eds., *The Sociology of Literature and Drama* [Penguin Books 1973], p. 114). In this paper I reverse Goldmann's definitions and use world view for a thought construct that, although inspired by class interests like ideology, lacks the totalizing comprehensiveness and applicability to other classes that are not its originators and which characterize the latter.

[78] On the world view of the Kaga *ikkō ikki* (the Ikkō sect's uprising in Kaga province), see Kuroda Toshio, *Nihon chūsei no kokka to shūkyō* (Iwanami, 1975), p. 338; Shingyō Kiichi, "Ikkō ikki no shisō kōzō ni tsuite no ichi shikiron," in *Nihon rekishi ronkyū* (Ninomiya Shoten, 1963), pp. 269, 276; Kasahara Kazuo, *Shinshū ni okeru itan no keifu* (Tōkyō Daigaku, 1962), pp. 110–111, 117–119, 174, 215, 219; Asao Naohiro, " 'Shōgun kenryoku' no sōshutsu," part 1, *Rekishi hyōron* 241 (1970): 74; part 2, ibid. 293 (1974): 26. For the psychological interpretation of Nobunaga's behavior, see George Sansom, *A History of Japan, 1334–1614* (Stanford: Stanford University Press, 1961), pp. 367–371; Cooper, *They Came to Japan*, p. 101.

[79] See n. 75 of this essay.

on the cohesion of the whole society presented as valid for all its members. It seems that one cannot simply assume that Tokugawa ideology succeeded in displacing a pre-Tokugawa ideology. One has the strong impression that during the period under review, one is witnessing not the displacement of one ideology by another, but the irruption for the first time in Japanese history of ideology *tout court*.

One can argue this thesis as follows. One starts by pointing out that the peasant world view just mentioned was only prevalent in a few provinces and was itself a response to a new form of warrior power that emerged in the sixteenth century, and is thus no candidate for the position of a society-wide ideology that supposedly was displaced by analogous Tokugawa constructs.

Three further considerations that may contribute to an explanation are the following. To begin, the social arrangements that were being destroyed by warrior power had never been the object of ideological significations. They consisted largely of a complicated patchwork of graded legal rights to the land, between workers on the land, landowners, property managers (often samurai), and commendees (temples and noble houses). This superimposition of rights had prevented, even at the very local level, any group of persons from building a clear, singular, exclusive relation to the land and had thus also hindered the development of organized local communities as genuinely bounded units. It is only when warrior bands started to cut into these legal relationships, and through force to build contiguous domains out of these legal estates, that: (*a*) the commoners, freed from the legal superstructure, started to organize themselves into self-contained, self-managing local communities; (*b*) these commoners now suddenly encountered a new, single enemy, the warriors; (*c*) a legitimacy conflict thus arose over control of the land between commoners and warriors; and (*d*) a more comprehensive social unit emerged victorious from this struggle, the contiguous domain that was a microcosmic society. This novel social creation that incorporated the new commoner social unit of the village demanded a clarification of the status different classes of people would hold within it. Further, this was the first time in Japanese history that commoners in such great numbers were involved in a struggle for power against their domination by another group clearly perceived by them as an undesirable class. Finally, the very transparent, arbitrary character of this domination called for justifications or rejections at the level of arguments about legitimacy.

One can thus conclude that a totally novel situation in Japanese history necessitated the production of an all-embracing new discourse on society, and indeed the situation was such that the production of an ideology became for the first time in Japanese history an integral part of the strategy for power. This new power, of national dimensions, had to produce a truth about the whole of society, not a new truth about a society that was already there, but a truth about a society that was being fashioned for the first time.

That truth, however, was of the nature of a lie (or, less radical, a half-truth) presented as a truth (or the whole truth). The complete truth about the new society included the fact that it was (also) an arbitrary system of domination by a few over all. That system had to be signified through schemes effecting a distorted (or incomplete) knowledge of itself.

What bakufu power thus presided over was the successful orchestration of a deliberate oversight of itself—the organization of social thought that drew attention away from its arbitrary domination. The symbolic objects of this ideology ought thus not be seen as motives or reasons for power but rather as its obfuscating significations, and their construction as a gigantic production of a cognitive simulacrum.[80] Again, this does not mean that the people who conducted their lives under this regimen of truth (both the rulers and the ruled) were gullible or naïve, or took the ramifications of power literally as emanations of virtue. Perhaps some did or at least pretended to do so. What is socially and historically significant, however, is not the extent to which all this was subjectively internalized and consciously believed, but the extent to which as well as the manner in which Japanese society at one point, to borrow a phrase from Marcel Mauss, started to pay itself in the false currency of its false dreams.[81]

The ultimate achievement of an ideology is to have the social order perceived as the world of the realized ought-to-be, as a self-evident world where one is no longer even aware of questions of legitimacy—a social perspective that is accepted in the same way that a currency or a language is, and where the question of its free acceptance or its forceful imposition does not even arise. From our more distant and more totalizing perspective, this is difficult to accept since we see the ideology as a transparent deception, whether veil or mask. The coherence of the bric-a-brac of ideological constructs, however, is not one that is informed by the rigor of logical rules that govern reason but by the requirements of praxis. Ideology brackets that kind of logic, but not political reality.[82] Through ideology, a group or

[80] Some of these formulations are borrowed from Bourdieu (*Outline*, pp. 6, 21) and from Jean Beaudrillard, *Oublier Foucault* (Paris: Ed. Galilée, 1977), pp. 55–56, 81.

[81] Quoted by Bourdieu, *Outline*, p. 195.

[82] This idea is discussed by Bourdieu (*Outline*, pp. 109, 115, 168, 230–231). Symbolic constructs, such as ideology, are informed by a particular associative logic, which

class or society aims for the naturalization of its own arbitrariness. By absolutizing its own relative character, it achieves a sort of genesis amnesia and turns economic and political contingent formations into a destiny. Both Shinto and Neo-Confucianism made available a language that could perform this task. By establishing this peculiar regimen of truth, ideology thus effected recognition of a historically mediated reality as an immediate reality, in order to halt possible further mediations and transformations.[83]

Later developments in the Tokugawa period seem to bear out the validity of these interpretations. At the end of the eighteenth century, under pressure of social crises, the bakufu had to resort to new but weaker justifications when it argued that its authority was an imperially delegated authority, in other words, a mediated authority.[84] The bakufu thereby implicitly admitted that its authority could be revoked and in this way opened the road to the argument for a restoration of the emperor. Around the same time, the peasants started to argue that they and not the warriors were repositories of virtue, thus legitimizing their protest and extolling their martyred heroes as gods.[85] Then also Andō Shōeki (1703–1762?), an articulate and critical thinker, exposed all ideologies (Neo-Confucianism in particular) as ploys to rob the peasants, and accused Hayashi Razan of having contributed to this deception.[86]

Until this happened, however, the new perception of reality contributed its own symbolic strength to the reproduction of the system of domination by freezing the aspirations of the people within the boundaries set by the new "common sense." It is within the new limits, seen as naturally given, that people conducted and planned or accepted their lives: poor samurai and poor peasants accepting their low economic position, and wealthier merchants and peasants resign-

---

is governed, as Rodney Needham argues, by proportional analogies (*Reconnaissances* [Toronto: University of Toronto Press, 1980] chap. 2).

[83] On "genesis amnesia," see Bourdieu (*Outline*, p. 79; *Reproduction*, p. 9); on naturalization, Bourdieu (*Outline*, p. 164; "Genèse et structure du champs religieux," *Revue Française de Sociologie* 12 [1971]: 300, 310, 315); on the concept of a regimen of truth, Foucault (*Power*, p. 131).

[84] The delegation theory of shogunal power was formulated by a bakufu official for the first time in the writings of Matsudaira Sadanobu around the year 1800 (Asao Naohiro, "Bakuhansei," p. 191).

[85] For the language and justifications used by the peasants in the 1780s, see Anne Walthall, "The Ethics of Protest by Commoners in Late Eighteenth Century Japan" (Ph.D. diss. University of Chicago, 1979).

[86] Andō Shōeki held that all thought systems were schemes to "rob the world," and all scholars (and he points out Razan) were engaged in "robbing the common people" (Maruyama, *Studies*, pp. 253–256).

ing themselves to their low social status. The bulk of the population learned in their practice how to make a virtue (in all the meanings of the word) out of necessity, and in their thinking to filter reason out of necessity, generating an ethic that supported them within their limited life-possibilities.[87]

To take on the problem of ideology from a variety of angles means to get ensnarled in a web of methodological issues, theoretical assumptions, interpretive language traps, and one's own political views. Admittedly, such problems underlie any interpretive endeavor, whether one is conscious of them or not, but they seem to pullulate when ideology is the subject. Throughout this paper, one focus was kept on the complexity of these inescapable issues. This confrontation was necessary in order to develop an interpretive language tailored to the task at hand.

Past studies of Neo-Confucianism, working within different frameworks, have generated their own appropriate analytical and descriptive terminology. This is the case, for instance, with the modernization perspective, which tends to emphasize Neo-Confucian contributions to the rationalization of Japanese thought. The history of Neo-Confucianism has also been organized as a gradual unfolding of a polarized thought system.[88] These approaches, however, while

---

[87] For further theoretical elaborations on some of these statements, see Bourdieu, *Outline*, pp. 77, 87, 164, 166–167, and "Genèse," pp. 310–311.

[88] For Maruyama, the seventeenth century was still caught in the metaphysical and religious thinking of the "dark ages": significant "progress" was made only in the early eighteenth century with Ogyū Sorai (1666–1728). Almost all other scholars routinely praise Neo-Confucianism's contributions to advance the process of rationalization and secularization.

Professor de Bary has sometimes characterized the history of Neo-Confucianism as an unfolding of a polarized thought system. This unifying interpretation explains what ties together all variants, sometimes referred to as the result of an inner logic (*Principle*, pp. 28–30, 156, 167, 174; however, see also p. 32 for qualifications to this kind of view). He also corrects the interpretation of a linear secularizing growth by pointing out that it was accompanied by the rise of new religious attitudes (pp. 4–5). This very valuable correction brings to the fore the neglected spiritual side of Neo-Confucianism, but it also seems to relegate Neo-Confucianism's spiritual value to the private domain of individual religious quests, suggesting perhaps that a religious dimension was absent from the bakufu's "ideology." The social significance of Neo-Confucianism, it is occasionally suggested, lies in its role as an early driving force in the process of modernization (pp. 2–4, 154).

Professor de Bary plays the modernization theme pianissimo and presents it as an aside. With David A. Dilworth, however, modernization becomes the framework and reveals its glaring ahistorical character. Unblinkingly, he asserts (in a prose where centuries act, and human actors set variables in motion) that "the first half of the seventeenth century in Japan launched a full-scale 'modernization process' in its own

bringing out interesting and important aspects of Neo-Confucianism, are unable to generate questions enabling an examination of the relationship between a political system and certain ideas at a particular historical juncture. Thus they cannot shed light on problems of ideology.

This study leads then to the following concluding remarks. It is clear that during the period under review no single tradition was privileged with exclusive bakufu support that would have turned its teachings into an enforceable orthodoxy, as was the case in Ming China.[89] An elaborate discourse on society developed, however, during those decades; one that benefited the bakufu in very tangible ways. At the very least, it is certain that if this discourse had run counter to bakufu interests, it would have been suppressed. In this sense, a negative standard of orthodoxy was operating: the bakufu outlawed the teachings and activities of a few groups that had to go underground, or turn *kakure* (the kakure Christians, the kakure *nenbutsu* groups, and the *Fujufuse* Nichiren Buddhists, the last two having their origins in the peasant resistance of the sixteenth century).

This had an important consequence. The new discourse that was allowed to develop of its own filled the whole epistemological space available under the bakufu regime by referring to the system of domination only in oblique terms, leaving no room for calling that political reality by its proper name. In this way, a buffer zone of authoritative (and authority) symbols and significations was erected around power, reducing to an absolute minimum, if not totally eliminating, any ground for directly challenging that power. This power, while thus indirectly responsible for the space where this construction took place, since it was not named, posed as if it did not exist.

One can conjecture even further that without such symbolizing buffer, power could not have operated. In broad daylight it would have been recognized for what it was and run the risk of rejection and direct challenge. The network of significations served power.[90]

---

right" (ibid., p. 471). The quotatation marks and the "in his own right," meant to soften surprise in the reader's mind, are dropped later for the adjective "geniune" when he writes of Ieyasu's "setting in motion new social and intellectual variables characterizable as a genuine modernization process"; of the Japanese people undergoing a process of "spiritual modernization by internalizing the Confucian value system" (p. 476); and indeed of "Neo-Confucianism as the intellectual motive force of the Edo modernization process" (p. 478). Has China, the birthplace of Neo-Confucianism, been modernizing since the eleventh century?

[89] See de Bary (*Principle*, pp. 15–22) for a contrast between Mandarin and bakufu orthodoxies.

[90] This view is the opposite of Clifford Geertz' latest thesis on power and ritual in

In order to be challenged, power had first to be identified and given its real name, an effort that by itself would alert the bakufu. That is why Andō Shōeki's writings, which did precisely that, had to stay underground during the Tokugawa period.

What seems remarkable is that contributions to this obfuscating operation of a fictionalizing discourse flowed forth with such abundance from a variety of traditions and directions. Neo-Conficianism proved to be a great supplier of appropriate concepts for this purpose, but so were Shinto, folklore, and even folk religions like the Fuji kō, as Royall Tyler indicates in his paper. Teachers, scholars, and religious leaders—all were eager to draw the bakufu's attention, obtain its blessings, and increase their own importance. The Hayashi scholars wanted the bakufu to make their own house the keeper of Neo-Confucian orthodoxy. Tenkai won his battle against other monks to secure the Nikkō cult for the Tendai sect.[91] Suzuki Shōsan's dream of his life was to see the bakufu declare his brand of Buddhism, over and against Neo-Confucianism and other Buddhist orders, as the only teaching in the realm appropriate to the times.[92] The founder of the Fuji kō, as Tyler shows, claimed a special relationship with Ieyasu and credited his own teachings with Ieyasu's success in bringing peace to the realm.

During the rest of the Tokugawa period, this stampede at the doorsteps of the bakufu continued. Over and over again, new men sought to prove how the bakufu would be better served by their own formulas, thus providing the system of domination with ever-new screens from behind which to operate. For bakufu power it did not matter much how the screen was embroidered, as long as it was not transparent.

Tsunayoshi made his own contribution by bringing Neo-Confucianism into the limelight. Arai Hakuseki (1657–1725), as Kate Wildman Nakai spells out in a forthcoming book,[93] for a brief period succeeded in surrounding the shogun with a monarchial aura. During

---

Bali, that is, "power served pomp, not pomp power." See his *Negara: The Theatre State in Nineteenth Century Bali* (Princeton: Princeton University Press, 1980), p. 13.

[91] Tenkai's rivals were Bonshun and Sūden. For the details of this struggle, see Tamamuro Fumio, "Sūden to Tenkai," in Wakabayashi Tarō, ed., *Nihon shūkyōshi no nazo* (Kōsei, 1976), 2:53–63; Miyata Noboru, "Tōshō daigongen," ibid., pp. 65–74. For a partial treatment in English, see A. L. Sadler, *The Maker of Modern Japan: The Life of Tokugawa Ieyasu*, originally published in 1937 (Rutland: Charles E. Tuttle, 1978), pp. 324–331.

[92] Suzuki Tesshin, ed., *Suzuki Shōsan Dōnin zenshū* (Sankibō Busshorin, 1962), pp. 209, 257, 268, 272–275, 328.

[93] *Shogunal Politics: Arai Hakuseki and the Premises of Tokugawa Rule* (Cambridge, Mass., and London: Council on East Asian Studies, Harvard University, 1988).

the Kansei Reforms of the end of the eighteenth century, Matsudaira Sadonobu (the first bakufu leader to have explicitly legislated a policy in the realm of ideology) created an opportunity for Ansai followers to put their stamp on the bakufu's training program for its officials. Sadanobu, however, had a number of applicants, selling their ideological wares and longing for a bakufu patent. A follower of Motoori Norinaga (1730–1801) recommended his master's teachings to Sadanobu.[94] The Fuji kō, by now a millenarian and quite popular movement, seems to have made a similar attempt (see Tyler's paper).

Only a few years later, the *Tokugawa jikki* were compiled. The work reiterated that "Ieyasu had conquered the nation on horseback, but . . . wisely decided that, in order to govern the land . . . he must pursue the path of learning." In retrospect, this mythological Ieyasu proved to be right: from beginning to end, the bakufu was never at a loss for volunteers, ready to purvey teachings speaking eloquently about man and society (but keeping silent about power) in a way most inoffensive to its own interests. They all went about propagating their doctrines with great zeal, whether the bakufu acknowledged their existence or not.

[94] Shigeru Matsumoto, *Motoori Norinaga: 1730–1801* (Cambridge: Harvard University Press, 1970), p. 128.

THREE

TOKUGAWA CONFUCIAN HISTORIOGRAPHY: THE HAYASHI, EARLY MITO SCHOOL AND ARAI HAKUSEKI

BY KATE WILDMAN NAKAI

In the years between 1640 and 1720, there appeared in Tokugawa Japan a number of significant historical works. These include *Honchō tsugan*, compiled between 1644 and 1670 by Hayashi Razan (1583–1657) and his son Gahō (1618–1680); *Ōdai ichiran*, written by Gahō in 1652; Yamaga Sokō's (1622–1685) *Buke jiki* (1673); Arai Hakuseki's (1657–1725) *Tokushi yoron* (1712) and *Koshitsū* (1715); and the *Dai Nihonshi*, the compilation of which was inaugurated in 1657 by Tokugawa Mitsukuni (1628–1700), daimyo of Mito, and brought to a preliminary stage of completion with the presentation of a copy to the bakufu in 1720.

These Tokugawa histories were inspired or strongly influenced by the tradition of Chinese historiography that reached a new peak during the Sung dynasty in the works of Confucian statesmen and scholars like Ssu-ma Kuang (1019–1086) and Chu Hsi (1130–1200). For instance, the title of Hayashi Gahō's *Honchō tsugan* (The Comprehensive Mirror of This Court) refers explicitly to the *Tzu-chih t'ung-chien* (J., *Shiji tsugan*; The Comprehensive Mirror for Aid in Government), Ssu-ma Kuang's effort to provide an inclusive survey of Chinese history between 403 B.C. and A.D. 959. The title of Arai Hakuseki's *Tokushi yoron* (Additional Discussions [Stimulated by] the Explication of History) contains a similar allusion. *Tokushi yoron* was based on a series of lectures on Japanese history presented to the sixth Tokugawa shogun, Ienobu, in the spring of 1712. These lectures emerged, in turn, out of Hakuseki's long-standing assignment to lecture before Ienobu on Chu Hsi's redaction of Ssu-ma Kuang's account, the *T'ung-chien kang-mu* (Outline and Commentary on the Comprehensive Mirror).

Behind such allusions to Chinese historical works lay deeper parallels. The Hayashi, Hakuseki, and the historians employed by Mitsukuni alike addressed themselves in their own studies to the types of questions that had occupied generations of Chinese Confucian historians and brought to bear on the material available to them the principles of judgment elaborated and refined by figures such as Ssu-ma Kuang and Chu Hsi: had rulers and their subordinates acted in a manner appropriate to their given sociopolitical circumstances; what constituted the legitimacy, or lack of it, of a particular regime; and how had authority been transferred from one regime to another?

In that these Tokugawa historians sought to apply principles basic to Chinese Confucian historiography to the substance of Japanese history, their efforts afford an excellent opportunity to gauge the interaction between Chinese Confucian concepts and Japanese sociopolitical reality. Their works point up various problems inherent in that interaction; concepts formulated and refined in the Chinese environment were not necessarily readily applicable to the Japanese historical setting. Transplantation into a new environment governed by different dynamics heightened tensions already present in the original Chinese tradition. While particularly clear-cut in the area of historiography, these problems are relevant to the entirety of the Tokugawa experience with Confucianism. The modern observer may take advantage of the sharp contours they project in this area to enter into the larger questions of how Confucianism was incorporated into Tokugawa life as well as the factors behind its reshaping at the hands of Tokugawa thinkers.

In this essay I propose to explore two or three facets of these larger questions through a comparison of some features of the historiography of Hayashi Razan and Gahō, the early Mito school, and Arai Hakuseki. The discussion will focus in particular on the implications of their respective approaches to one of the knottiest problems raised by the application of the criteria of Chinese Confucian historiography to the substance of Japanese history: evaluation of the relationship between the emperor and shogun. This was an issue which threw into sharp relief the discrepancy between Japanese historical reality and the premises of Chinese historiography regarding such matters as the basis of political legitimacy and the transfer of authority.

As the Hayashi, the Mito historians, and Hakuseki were associated with the Tokugawa and as all drew more or less from the Chu Hsi line of Neo-Confucianism, to center the comparison on these three groups serves to limit variables. Yet despite such points in common, each stood in a different relationship to the contemporary political order and adopted a different approach to dealing with the world around him. The ways in which the three groups sought to ultilize Confucian historiographical principles and the conclusions they thereby reached about the course of Japanese history reflect these differences, testifying to the significance of such situtational factors to the process of adapting Confucianism to the concerns of Tokugawa Japanese.

Before proceeding to a more specific discussion of these points it will be useful to review briefly the characteristics of Chinese Confucian historiography most pertinent to the issues to be considered. As is often noted, Chinese historiography was deeply didactic in nature. History was regarded as offering a "mirror" for the present. Through the study of history one could perceive and take to heart the basic patterns of social and political conduct, good and bad, applicable to all ages. However, the mirror of history had two distinct, not fully congruent, sides to it. One projected an image of history as a means of remonstrance. To write history was to delineate the way to rectify current evils. Confucius was held to have acted on just such a concept of the function of history in editing the records of his native state of Lu. The transformation of those records into the *Ch'un ch'iu* (Spring and Autumn) was in turn regarded as the achievement that more than anything else qualified Confucius to be ranked as a sage with Yao, Shun, Yü, T'ang, Wen, Wu, and the duke of Chou. Mencius provides the *locus classicus* for both this view of Confucius and the function of history: "Again the world fell into decay and principles faded away. Perverse speakings and oppressive deeds waxed rife again. There were instances of ministers who murdered their sovereigns, and of sons who murdered their fathers. Confucius was afraid and made the *Spring and Autumn*. What the *Spring and Autumn* contains are matters proper to the sovereign. On this account Confucius said, 'Yes! It is through the *Spring and Autumn* that men will understand me and it is because of the *Spring and Autumn* that men will condemn me.' "[1]

The Sung revival of Confucianism brought a renewed affirmation of the remonstrative function of history. Ssu-ma Kuang, confronting the volume of dynastic histories and official and private records that had accumulated over the centuries, sought to follow the path set forth by Confucius by extracting the essential points from that mass of materials and thereby make the lessons of history available to those concerned with government from the emperor on down.

In the *Tzu-chih t'ung-chien*, Ssu-ma Kuang began his consideration of Chinese history at the point where the *Ch'un ch'iu* left off. More precisely, he began where the *Tso chuan*, the major commentary on the *Ch'un ch'iu*, ended. The *Ch'un ch'iu* ends with the untimely appearance and capture of a fabulous unicornlike *lin* in 481 B.C., two years before the death of Confucius. However, the *Tso chuan* carried

---

[1] *Mencius*, 3:B9. Adapted from James Legge, *The Chinese Classics*, 2:281–282.

its elucidation of the events recorded in the *Ch'un ch'iu* down to the destruction in 453 B.C. of Chih Po, minister of the state of Chin, by the heads of three other leading Chin families, the Han, Wei, and Chao. This incident was taken to herald the dismemberment of Chin in 403 B.C. at the hands of the same three families. Ssu-ma Kuang began his narrative by discussing the Chou king's admission of these three families to the ranks of the feudal lords, thereby tacitly sanctioning their act of usurpation. This abrogation by the ruler of the hierarchical moral order on which his own authority rested made inevitable, Ssu-ma Kuang declares, the final destruction of the Chou ruling house and the descent into social and political chaos.[2] Beginning with this perspective, in the *Tzu-chih t'ung-chien* Ssu-ma Kuang surveyed the events which brought about the oscillating cycle of order and disorder, the rise and fall of successive dynasties from 403 B.C. to A.D. 959, the year before the founding of his own dynasty, the Sung.

The Southern Sung scholar Chu Hsi affirmed even more strongly the remonstrative value of history. The *T'ung-chien kang-mu*, the redaction of Ssu-ma Kuang's work initiated by Chu Hsi, was intended to make the lessons of the *Tzu-chih t'ung-chien* yet more explicit. In the *T'ung-chien kang-mu*, Chu Hsi divided the material covered into "major events" (*kang*) and "background information" (*mu*), seeking both to emphasize the import of certain events in the manner of Confucius in the *Ch'un ch'iu* and to provide an elaboration of that import similar to that offered by the traditions of commentary on the *Ch'un ch'iu*, such as the *Tso chuan*.

While the ideal of using history to criticize the present was thus deeply embedded in the Chinese historiographical tradition, other Confucian assumptions acted to hedge the expression of such criticism. Among these was the Confucian opinion that the subject, although he might properly remonstrate with his ruler, should not display the ruler's faults before the ages. This opinion led to the conclusion that the historian should leave definitive judgment of the events of his own time and dynasty to future ages and confine himself to appraisal of the past, a principle observed by Ssu-ma Kuang and Chu Hsi, as well as by the dynastic histories. Moreover, it was held, even in his appraisal of the past, the historian should be judicious in his presentation of events which paralleled controversial matters of his own time.

These checks on the remonstrative function of history dovetailed

---

[2] Rai Tsutomu, "Kaisetsu," in *Shiji tsugan sen* (Heibonsha, 1970), pp. 496–498. Ssu-ma Kuang, *Tzu-chih t'ung-chien* (Peking, 1957), 1:2–6.

with the other didactic purpose projected by the mirror of history: legitimation of those currently in power. History, in recording the reasons for the fall of the previous regime, offered an explanation for the existence of the present one. If the *Ch'un ch'iu* served as a model for remonstrative history, the *Shang shu* (Book of History), the other major historical classic supposedly edited by Confucius, provided a precedent for using history as a means of legitimation. Concurrent with the premise that definitive judgment of the present should be left to future generations, the corollary developed that it was the responsibility of the current dynasty to make such judgment of the past. Eventually, compilation of the history of the previous dynasty came itself to be seen as an act establishing the legitimacy of the present dynasty.

The tendency of Confucian historiography not to discriminate fully between normative and descriptive modes of analysis increased the ambiguity of the relationship between these two sides, remonstrative and legitimizing, of the mirror of history. Differentiation between "name" (C., *ming*; J., *mei*) and "substance" (C., *shih*; J., *jitsu*) was fundamental to the Confucian world view; however, the mirror of history was assumed to reflect both normative ideal and objective reality. The traditional evaluation of Confucius' achievment in writing the *Ch'un ch'iu* epitomized this assumption. Confucius was held to have simply described things as they were; his successors also believed that through his selection of what to record and what to leave out, and by his choice of terms to refer to those involved in the events recorded, Confucius had clarified the ways in which the figures appearing in the *Ch'un ch'iu* had succeeded or failed in fulfilling the moral norms specific to their status and situation. "Confucius simply described things as they were," claimed Chu Hsi, "and right and wrong became apparent of themselves."[3]

The norms built into the Chinese Confucian mirror of history included a number of premises about the nature of political authority and the mode whereby it might be transferred from one regime to another. Chinese historians assumed, for instance, that China should be unified under the rule of one figure who combined in his person military and civil, sacerdotal and temporal authority. This comprehensive authority could not be divided properly among different claimants to the title of ruler. Such would be an abrogation of the "name" of ruler. However, Chinese political thinkers agreed, it conformed to the universal order of things for this comprehensive au-

---

[3] *Chu Tzu yü-lei*, chuan 83, quoted in Bitō Masahide, "Arai Hakuseki no rekishi shisō," in *Arai Hakuseki*, NST, 35:556.

thority to be transferred from one lineage to another in accordance with heaven's loss of confidence in the former and selection of the latter as its agent in governing "all under heaven."

The actual patterns of Chinese history by and large substantiated conviction in the validity of these norms. Even if the founders of later dynasties were not paragons of virtue comparable to the mythic sages of antiquity extolled by Confucian tradition, the succession of dynasties gave credence to the idea that heaven granted its mandate to "the one man" worthy of being entrusted with the government of all under heaven and withdrew it from a lineage which had failed to preserve that trust.

The general plausibility of the norms built into the Chinese mirror of history meant that the tension between the remonstrative and legitimizing sides of Confucian historiography, the contradiction inherent in its simultaneous affirmation of normative and descriptive analysis, became most apparent in the historian's treatment of periods which did not fit the assumed normative pattern. A classic instance was the Three Kingdoms period following the fall of the Han, when China was divided into three spheres of influence, that of Wei in the north, Shu in the southwest, and Wu in the southeast. Disagreement about how to deal with the aberrations of this period was one of the reasons that led Chu Hsi to embark on a revision of Ssu-ma Kuang's *T'ung-chien*

The chronological annals' (C., *pien-nien*; J., *hennen*) transdynastic format adopted by Ssu-ma Kuang and continued by Chu Hsi dealt with events under the reigns and era-names of successive rulers. It thus posed particular problems in handling an era like the Three Kingdoms when there was no single ruler of a unified China. Ssu-ma Kuang's solution was to use the reigns and era-names of one of the three to provide a chronological framework applicable to all three. He chose Wei, which occupied the heartland of the traditional Chinese empire and was in the strongest military position of the three. Ssu-ma Kuang thus ended the Han annals with the reign of Han Hsien-ti and began the Wei with Ts'ao P'i's accesion as king of Wei upon the death of his father, Ts'ao Ts'ao, and his securing of the abdication of Hsien-ti in his favor.

Ssu-ma Kuang explicitly denied the Shu ruler's claim to be the legitimate heir of the Han on the grounds that his purported descent from an offshoot of the Han imperial line could not be substantiated.[4] At the same time, in establishing a chronological line of succession from Han to Wei to the next dynasty of Chin, he strove to make

---

[4] Ssu-ma Kuang, *Tzu-chih t'ung-chien*, 1:2188.

clear that he was not thereby recognizing Wei as more "legitimate" than its rivals. He took the self-deprecating stance that he was not setting up standards of praise and blame in the manner of Confucius in the *Ch'un ch'iu*.[5] However, the prevalence of the practice of using titles and era-names to indicate or disavow the legitimacy of a particular dynasty made it almost impossible for Ssu-ma Kuang to sustain the distinction between "legitimacy" and "chronological point of reference." He could not describe objective reality without also passing normative judgment. Consequently, in using Wei reigns and era-names as the chronological framework for the Three Kingdoms period, Ssu-ma Kuang, in effect, presented Wei as the legitimate dynasty and Shu and Wu as regional powers.

Chu Hsi took exception to Ssu-ma Kuang's handling of the Three Kingdoms question. Ts'ao P'i, he held, having forced the abdication of Han Hsien-ti, should not be regarded as the founder of a new dynasty. Chu Hsi chose instead to treat Shu Han as a continuation of the legitimate Han dynasty and used the Shu Han reigns and era-names, instead of those of the Wei, as the chronological framework for the events of this period.[6]

Various factors may be seen at work in these two resolutions of what was unquestionably a problematic period to handle according to the principles of Confucian political thought and historiography. On the one hand, as Morohashi Tetsuji points out, there was a difference in temperament and approach to the world. Ssu-ma Kuang's tacit recognition of Wei as legitimate accorded with his generally "realistic" outlook, while Chu Hsi's denial of Wei's legitimacy was consistent with his more uncompromising emphasis on clarifying the moral issue at stake. On the other hand, ideological considerations pertinent to the immediate circumstances confronted by each also likely played a part. The founder of the Sung had come to power in a manner which had many parallels with the Wei usurpation of imperial authority from the Han. The editors of the *Ssu-k'u t'i-yao* (Summaries of the Four Treasures, 1782), Morohashi notes, held that these parallels were responsible for Ssu-ma Kuang's favoring of Wei. The situation of the Southern Sung, by contrast, was in many ways comparable to that of Shu Han, leading Chu Hsi to take the side of Shu.[7] One may add that the "temperamental" and "situational" factors behind the position of each were not necessarily unconnected.

[5] Ibid., pp. 2185–2188.

[6] Morohashi Tetsuji, "Shina no jingi oyobi shōtōron," in *Morohashi Tetsuji chosakushū* (Taishūkan Shoten, 1977), 3:332–337. Katō Shigeshi, "*Dai Nihonshi* to Shina shigaku," in *Honpō shigakushi ronsō* (Fuzanbō, 1939), 2:901–904.

[7] Morohashi, "Shina," pp. 336–337.

Stress on the importance of rectitude over that of substantive authority, while undoubtedly traceable to individual differences in outlook, also accorded with the geopolitical circumstances noted by the editors of the *Ssu-k'u t'i-yao*.

The problems Ssu-ma Kuang and Chu Hsi grappled with in their discussion of the Three Kingdoms period were of immediate relevance to Tokugawa historians like the Hayashi, the early Mito school, and Arai Hakuseki. In the Chinese context, an era like that of the Three Kingdoms could be dealt with as a temporary aberration. However, Tokugawa historians seeking to evaluate the course of Japanese history confronted a much more persistent gap between Confucian norm and substantive reality. In effect, they had to cope with a succession of Three Kingdoms dating back to the seventh and eighth centuries.

At that time, ideologues associated with the Yamato court had sought to graft the Chinese idea of an all-powerful monarch whose authority was symbolized by such prerogatives as promulgation of the calendar and designation of era-names onto the existing Japanese concept of legitimation by divine descent. In the following centuries, the imperial line lost to others the active temporal powers over the nation that, according to Chinese assumptions, formed the core of monarchal authority. However, it retained a preeminent claim to the symbols of Chinese-style monarchy, such as the prerogative to proclaim era-names and to grant appointments in the imperial system of ranks and offices. Those who succeeded to the substance of the temporal authority of the imperial line, first court nobles intimately associated with it and then a succession of military figures culminating in the Tokugawa shogun, found upholding the idea of a permanent mandate vested in the imperial line and claiming to rule under the aegis of imperial sanction preferable to overthrowing the descendant of the Sun Goddess and ruling in the name of a direct mandate of their own.

The Tokugawa conformity to this established pattern meant that their stance toward the court entailed fundamental ambiguities. As overlords of the entire nation, the Tokugawa issued a code of governance for the court, limiting the scope of its initiative and autonomy in much the same way as they held the daimyo in check through the *Buke shohatto* (Laws Governing the Military Households). They also provided the court with economic support through endowments of land comparable to those granted their vassals. At the same time, however, the Tokugawa, utilizing the titles, ranks, and offices awarded by the emperor as one of the cornerstones of their own legitimacy and as a major mechanism for rewarding their vassals and ordering their status, officially presented themselves as deferring to the supreme authority of the imperial line.

To trace the transfer of authority and establish the locus of legitimacy in such a historical context was a highly problematic task. Just as objections could be made to setting up either Wei or Shu Han as the legitimate successor of the Han dynasty, from the Confucian perspective it was difficult to identify either the shogun or emperor unequivocally as the legitimate ruler. In the original Confucian conception, the authority of the ruler as "the one man," although terrestrially all-encompassing, was conditional. Decline in the scope of his actual power, as had occurred with the Japanese emperor, was taken to indicate that heaven found him lacking. On the other hand, to rule, as did the shogun, in the shadow of another without the full symbolic attributes of "the one man" governing "all under heaven" associated with a definitive "change of mandate" (C., ko-ming; J., kakumei), smacked of usurpation.

As the Tokugawa historians considered here struggled to resolve such problems, they, like Ssu-ma Kuang and Chu Hsi before them, read the mirror of history in divergent ways. The different images each perceived likewise reflect situational factors comparable to those influencing the positions taken by their Sung mentors. It is appropriate at this point to consider what some of those situational factors were.

As scholars in the service of the bakufu, the Hayashi ranked at the head of Tokugawa Confucians. They owed this preeminent position in considerable measure to their recognition that it depended on performing according to the expectations of their lord and to their readiness to work within their allotted place in the Tokugawa sociopolitical order. For example, they accepted the necessity to shave their heads and to conform to a monklike style of dress and nomenclature despite their personal commitment to distinguishing the Way of the Sages from the Buddhist teachings to which in Japan it had previously been joined. The Hayashi rationalized this judicious attitude toward authority by distinguishing between their private views and their public role. Privately, they would uphold the Way; publicly, they would fulfill their duties as bakufu Confucians and within that capacity advance the Way as far as possible.

The Hayashi approach to history was consistent with this general attitude. Both Razan and Gahō expressed a commitment to the concept of history as an instrument of remonstrance. However, having been closely involved in various projects to bolster the authority of the bakufu from diplomatic correspondence to the formulation of the code defining daimyo obligations, they quite naturally tended to put greater emphasis on the significance of history as an instrument of legitimation. More importantly, they were keenly aware that, irrespective of the question of remonstrance versus legitimation, the bakufu leadership was far less committed than they to the act of writing history as such. In the diary that he kept while compiling *Honchō tsugan*, Gahō recorded his frustration over the tendency of influential figures within the bakufu to regard his project as a decorative undertaking of secondary importance that took too long and cost too much to complete.[8] Similarly, he complained about the time and energy consumed in resolving a dispute among the bakufu leadership over whether the names of the *rōjū* (Council of Elders) should appear in the preface. "The military vassals of today know nothing of literature. But they all have their own opinions, and the ideas of each are at odds with those of his colleagues. It is as if they do not understand a single word of these 300 volumes."[9]

At the same time, Gahō recognized that this situation required him to tread cautiously if the project was to be seen safely through to completion. In 1664, shortly after the work of compilation had been resumed in earnest after a hiatus of over a decade, Gahō recorded his conviction that if he were to express his own views too forcefully on controversial issues, challenging the assumptions of "powerful ministers," the whole endeavor might well be aborted.[10] Similarly, in the entry describing his anger over the matter of the preface, he noted that he nonetheless bowed to the "opinions" of the "military vassals" and revised his draft of the preface in accordance with the wishes of the powerful Hoshina Masayuki (1611–1672).

These considerations played an important part in the format adopted by Gahō. He took Ssu-ma Kuang's *T'ung-chien* as his model and went to some lengths to secure permission to change the title of his history from *Honchō hennen roku*, the title used by Razan, to that of *Honchō tsugan*.[11] Yet, as he himself admitted, there were important ways in which he diverged from the *T'ung-chien* model. For one, *Honchō tsugan* did not incorporate those sections in which the compiler voiced his own judgment of the import of the events recorded. Gahō wrote that he was "not without regrets" about the decision to leave out these sections, known as the *giron* or *ronsan*, but since the shogun had not instructed him to engage in such evaluation of events,

---

[8] Bitō Masahide, *Genroku jidai* (Shōgakkan, 1975), p. 188.

[9] Tsuboi Kumazō, "*Kokushikan nichiroku o yomu*," *Shigaku zasshi* 29, no. 4 (1918): 325; *Kokushikan nichiroku*, vols. 16–17 of *Honchō tsugan* (Kokusho Kankōkai, 1919), 2:920–921.

[10] Tsuboi, "*Kokushikan nichiroku o yomu*," p. 324; *Kokushikan nichiroku*, 1:41

[11] Hanami Kazumi, "*Honchō tsugan kō*," in *Honpō shigakushi ronsō*, 2:801–802.

it would not have been proper to include them. Moreover, there were various incidents in Japanese history that raised complex questions of right and wrong. In dealing with such incidents "in a book intended for the shogun's eyes it is incumbent upon one to be circumspect." For example, he noted, Razan had held the personal view that Shōtoku Taishi's failure to chastise Soga no Umako for the assassination of Emperor Sushun was tantamount to complicity in that act. However, "in a book intended for the shogun's eyes one cannot freely express such personal views" about a figure of authority revered as a paragon of virtue.[12]

The same reasoning led him to reject the suggestion of another Confucian scholar that he should follow the format of Chu Hsi's *T'ung-chien kang-mu*, geared to the passing of measured judgment, rather than that of Ssu-ma Kuang. "In the history of this country there are things about which it is difficult to express a formal judgment (*kōgen*), things the right and wrong of which are yet to be decided, things which call for discretion (*kitan*) in how they are presented." Moreover, he added, "At present no one is familiar with the principles of the *Ch'un ch'iu kang-mu* style; were I to pass formal judgment, who would appreciate my perception?"[13]

Gahō reconciled his effort to avoid controversy with the traditional Confucian view of the responsibility of the historian by noting that his labors might pave the way for someone in the future to play Chu Hsi to his version of Ssu-ma Kuang, and that once the compilation of the body of *Honchō tsugan* was complete he might undertake such an endeavor himself.[14] However, Gahō's ready acceptance of the need for circumspection points up the paradox that while the Hayashi connection to the bakufu motivated them to use Confucian historiographical principles as a means of enhancing the legitimacy of the bakufu, their assessment of the perspective of those they served induced them to approach cautiously the conflict between Confucian norms and Japanese reality.

If the Hayashi approach to the writing of history reflects one dimension of the interaction between Confucianism and the Tokugawa environment, the approach of the compilers of the *Dai Nihonshi* reflects another. The *Dai Nihonshi* was an even more ambitious undertaking than *Honchō tsugan*. By the time of Mitsukuni's death in 1700, the Mito domain had taken on almost 130 scholars to work on the project; the office in charge of the compilation of the *Dai Nihonshi*

---

[12] Tsuboi, "*Kokushikan nichiroku o yomu*," p. 324; *Kokushikan nichiroku*, 1:41.
[13] Hanami, "*Honchō tsugan kō*," pp. 802–803; *Kokushikan nichiroku*, 1:18.
[14] Ibid.

maintained a normal staff of thirty to forty people, and it was said that the cost of the project constituted a third of the domain's operating expenses.[15]

Underlying this immense undertaking was a convergence of psychological factors specific to Mitsukuni as sponsor and overseer of the project and sociopolitical factors more broadly applicable to the Mito domain as a whole. Mitsukuni's commitment to manifesting the Way through history had its source at least partially in the complexities of his family background. Born in 1628, Mitsukuni was the third son of the first daimyo of Mito, preceded in order of birth by a full brother born six years earlier and a half-brother born three years earlier. Evidently, out of deference to the mother of the half-brother, Mitsukuni's father did not acknowledge the birth of either Mitsukuni or his elder full brother, Yorishige. Indeed, it is said that he ordered both of them disposed of at birth, and whether or not that order was intended to be taken literally, Yorishige was raised by foster parents in Kyoto until the age of eleven, and Mitsukuni was raised by a Mito vassal until the age of six. However, the half-brother born between Yorishige and Mitsukuni died young; in 1632 their father brought Yorishige back from Kyoto, and the following year Mitsukuni was designated heir to the 280,000 *koku* Mito domain (1 *koku* = approximately 5 bushels of rice). Yorishige later became daimyo of the 120,000 koku domain of Takamatsu in Sanuki, but the psychological and moral implications of the circumstances involved in his selection as heir evidently weighed heavily on Mitsukuni.[16]

As an adolescent, Mitsukuni gave expression to this sense of psychological burden through rebellious and delinquent behavior. However, at the age of eighteen he read the biography of Po Yi and his younger brother Shu Ch'i in the *Shih chi* (Records of the Grand Historian) and therein found a way to resolve his personal dilemma. As described in the *Shih chi*, the father of Po Yi and Shu Ch'i chose the latter as his heir; upon the father's death Shu Ch'i sought to yield the succession to his elder brother, but Po Yi refused on grounds that such would be contrary to their father's will, and he fled into the wilderness. Faced with his brother's self-abnegation, Shu Ch'i left behind his official position and joined Po Yi in the wilderness.

According to various accounts of Mitsukuni's life, upon reading the story of Po Yi and Shu Ch'i he determined to emulate their renunciation of selfish interests and to pass the succession of the Mito domain to the son of Yorishige. Upon his succession as second dai-

[15] Bitō, *Genroku jidai*, p. 198.
[16] Noguchi Takehiko, *Tokugawa Mitsukuni* (Aṣahi Shinbunsha, 1976), pp. 63–78.

myo of the Mito domain in 1661, Mitsukuni did indeed designate a son of Yorishige as his heir, and he continued throughout his life to find a meaningful self-image in the ideal of self-abnegation. Upon his retirement in favor of Yorishige's son in 1690, Mitsukuni took up residence in a country villa which he named Seizansō, "Villa of the Western Mountains," a reference to the site of Po Yi and Shu Ch'i's retreat. He also used the *gō* (literary pseudonym) Bairi, a reference to the burial site of Wu T'ai Po, another exemplar of the ideal of self-abnegation.[17] Mitsukuni's commitment to this ideal did not mean, however, the adoption of a passive attitude toward the world. To the contrary, it was also expressed in expecting of others what he expected of himself. It may be noted, for instance, that he later urged Tsunayoshi—whose succession as the fifth shogun following the death of his brother, Ietsuna, was due in part to the fact that another brother, Tsunashige, born between Ietsuna and Tsunayoshi, had died a few years earlier—to follow Mitsukuni's example and designate Tsunashige's son as his heir.[18]

The psychological complexities of Mitsukuni's outlook were reinforced by what may be termed the complexities of the place of Mito in the Tokugawa political order. Together with the domains of Owari and Kii, Mito ranked at the head of the Tokugawa collateral houses. The three were alike established for sons of Ieyasu. However, Mito was set apart from the other two in several important ways. The honorary court rank and office of the daimyo of Mito was by custom one step below that of the daimyo of Owari and Kii. In comparison to the rank of *junii gondainagon* (Major Councillor, Junior Second Rank), attainable by the latter, the daimyo of Mito received no higher than the rank of *jusan'i gonchūnagon* (Middle Councillor, Junior Third Rank). Similarly, Mito, with an assessed yield of 280,000 koku, was considerably smaller in size than Owari (630,000 koku in 1635) and Kii (550,000 koku). In that it was customary for the daimyo of Mito to remain permanently in Edo, the domain also had somewhat less autonomy than the other two. Noguchi Takehiko argues that these differences in the treatment of Mito compared to Owari or Kii led to a classic instance of an effort to compensate for feelings of inferiority. On the one hand, the Mito daimyo and his retainers were animated by a sense of being unfairly discriminated against and a determination to prove Mito's superior worth. On the other hand,

[17] Ichimura Kisaburō, "*Dai Nihonshi* no tokushoku ni tsuite," in *Honpō shigakushi ronsō*, 2:912.

[18] Mikami Sanji, *Edo jidaishi* (Fuzanbō, 1943), 1:667–669.

the idea gradually took shape that Mito had a special mission to advise the shogun and defend the Tokugawa house.[19]

The particular features of Mitsukuni's family background which helped shape his psychology were unique to him. The sense of mission that resulted from the peculiarities of Mito's position within the Tokugawa political order was, however, of broader relevance. Insofar as Mitsukuni's own attitude and concerns contributed to the formation of that sense of mission, his identification with the Confucian image of moral uprightness and self-abnegation, epitomized in the stories of Po Yi and Shu Ch'i and Wu T'ai Po, took on a larger political significance. Put broadly, a key aspect of Mito's mission came to be conceived of as awakening in the bakufu leadership a comparable commitment to self-rectification.

In the first half of the Tokugawa period, this dimension of the Mito sense of mission received its most concrete expression in the compilation of the *Dai Nihonshi*. Bitō Masahide points out that the timing of the various stages of the compilation suggests a sense of rivalry with the bakufu. The confrontation with the story of Po Yi and Shu Ch'i at the age of eighteen, which offered Mitsukuni a way to resolve his personal moral and psychological predicament, has traditionally been held to have brought him to realize the power of history as an instrument of moral guidance, and the preface to the *Dai Nihonshi* describes this confrontation as inspiring in Mitsukuni the determination to compile a history of Japan. However, it was not until twelve years later, immediately after the Meireki fire of 1657, that Mitsukuni set in motion specific plans for a comprehensive national history by establishing a compilation office in the Komagome Mito residence. The timing of this action would seem not unconnected with the loss in the recent fire of the copy of *Honchō hennen roku* presented to the bakufu by Hayashi Razan.[20]

The Mito project took more definite shape in 1672, two years after the completion of *Honchō tsugan*, with the shift of the compilation office from the Komagome residence to the Koishikawa one and the naming of it as the Shōkōkan. The name came from Tu Yu's preface to the *Tso chuan* in which he referred to "illuminating the past (so as to enable) pondering the course of the future" (*shōō kōrai*).[21] Presumably, it was around the same time that Mitsukuni also decided to adopt the *kiden* (chronological annals plus biographies) style characteristic of the Chinese dynastic histories instead of the simpler *hennen*

[19] Noguchi, *Tokugawa Mitsukini*, pp. 39–50.
[20] The fire had occurred the previous month; Bitō, *Genroku jidai*, p. 197.
[21] Ichimura, "*Dai Nihonshi* no tokushoku ni tsuite," p. 912.

(chronological annals) style used by the Hayashi. In the kiden format
the actions of an individual could be considered from two perspectives, once within the annals section and once within a biography
devoted to that individual, making it possible to point up the various
implications of those actions. If the original decision to establish a
compilation office reflected perhaps an intent to continue the interrupted bakufu project, adoption of the kiden form indicated a readiness to pass the "formal judgment" on the actors of the past eschewed by the Hayashi.[22] Mitsukuni was in essence taking the stance
of Confucius in writing the Ch'un ch'iu. To pass such formal judgment was properly the responsibility of the sovereign. But with neither the court nor the bakufu assuming this responsibility, Mito would
act on their behalf and hold up the unequivocating mirror essential
to the task of rectifying both self and society.

The intent to draw explicit attention to the moral lessons of history
was further manifested in the decision to incorporate into the Dai
Nihonshi sections for the voicing of the compilers' judgment of the
import of the events recorded. The official order to add these sections
(ronsan) to the body of the text was issued in 1716 by Mitsukuni's
heir, Tsunaeda, sixteen years after Mitsukuni's death. When, in the
early 1800s, Fujita Yūkoku called for the removal of the ronsan from
the main text, he offered as a reason the fact that the writing of the
ronsan had not been overseen personally by Mitsukuni. Underlying
Yūkoku's demand, and its eventual acceptance by the domain, was
an important shift in ideological perspective within the Mito school
of Confucian scholarship. The leaders of the later Mito school no
longer found acceptable the conclusions drawn from the mirror of
history by the author of the ronsan, Asaka Tanpaku, and to bolster
their case they argued that the ronsan did not reflect truly the views
of Mitsukuni.[23] However, Tanpaku was a protégé of Mitsukuni and
a key figure in the process of compilation of the Dai Nihonshi from
the time of his entry into the Shōkōkan in 1683 until the presentation
of a copy of the text, including the ronsan, to the bakufu in 1720.
He played an important part in formulating the distinctive position
of the Dai Nihonshi on various knotty historiographical questions. It
thus seems fair to take the ronsan, both in content and as the expression of an intent to pass didactic judgment on the actors in Japanese
history, as representative of the perspective of the early Mito school,
including that of Mitsukuni.[24]

[22] Bitō, Genroku jidai, p. 198.

[23] Ogura Yoshihiko, "Kaidai," in Kinsei shiron shū, NST, 48:549–550, 557–560.

[24] Bitō Masahide, "Rekishi shisō ni okeru Nihon to Chūgoku," in Nihon bunka to
Chūgoku (Taishūkan Shoten, 1968), p. 192.

Reflecting the dual nuances of the Mito sense of mission, the implications of that didactic intent were twofold: first, like the Hayashi, the Mito scholars looked to history to legitimate the Tokugawa order which they believed Mito was charged to defend; and second, they regarded the writing of the *Dai Nihonshi* as a prime means of carrying out the remonstrative function vis-à-vis the bakufu leadership and the shogun, which they regarded as Mito's special responsibility. This evaluation of the significance of the act of writing history implied a commitment to Confucian norms as such that added to the inherent tension between those norms and Japanese historical reality. At the very least, the Mito scholars had to confront that conflict more explicitly than did the Hayashi.

In addition to the views of the Hayashi and Mito scholars, the works of Arai Hakuseki offer yet a third perspective on the writing of Japanese history in a Confucian mode.[25] Like the Hayashi, Hakuseki served the bakufu in an advisory capacity, but his relationship to the bakufu differed notably from theirs. The Hayashi came to occupy a niche within the Tokugawa sociopolitical order as hereditary Confucians attached to the bakufu; as such they participated, as noted previously, in the creation of the ideological foundations of the bakufu as it took shape during the reigns of the first three shoguns, and like their social superiors, the major *fudai* (hereditary vassal) daimyo, they could be considered part of the bakufu establishment consisting of the shogun and his leading vassals.

Hakuseki, by contrast, came from outside that establishment in two senses. Personally he was of obscure origins, and although as tutor to Tokugawa Ienobu, the man who ultimately succeeded Tsunayoshi as the sixth shogun, he managed to exercise substantial unofficial influence on bakufu policy, his formal position within the *kakaku* (house status) structure, governing access to bakufu office, remained ambiguous to the end. Ienobu, the shogun Hakuseki served, was also in a sense an outsider. Like Tsunayoshi before him, Ienobu came to the post of shogun from a collateral line because his predecessor failed to produce an heir. In both cases, the entry into the fudai-centered bakufu establishment of an outside group associated with the new shogun created a considerable amount of friction between those whose interests were identified with the bakufu as an institution and those whose primary ties were to the shogun as an individual. During the reign of Tsunayoshi, this conflict both led to

[25] The interpretation of Hakuseki and his historical writings sketched in this essay is developed more fully in my *Shogunal Politics: Arai Hakuseki and the Premises of Tokugawa Rule* (Cambridge, Mass., and London: Council on East Asian Studies, Harvard University, 1988).

and was, in turn, exacerbated by the efforts of the shogun to develop a more autocratic style of government in which a group of personal attendants acted as a buffer between him and the bakufu leadership. The use of personal attendants in this fashion continued under Ienobu, and Hakuseki, seeking to reduce the power of the fudai establishment on the one hand and to enhance the monarchal authority of the shogun on the other, endeavored to fashion an ideology supportive of this trend toward shogunal autocracy. To this end, among other things, he had the shogun adopt the title of king of Japan (Nihon *kokuō*) in relations with Korea, and he imported a more monarchal style of court dress and architecture from Kyoto. In so doing, he, in effect, attempted to dismantle the ideological structure created by the Hayashi and to erect a new structure in its place.

Hakuseki's concept of monarchy had its source in the traditional Chinese Confucian view of the king as a ruler with both temporal and sacerdotal powers backed by the authority of heaven's sanction. Thus it was only natural that he should employ the Chinese historiographical principles so closely linked to this view of kingship as a means of justifying his innovations. At the same time, this polemical aim gave his historical enterprise a different orientation from that of the works of the Hayashi and the Mito scholars. Hakuseki's purpose was not to compile an official, comprehensive survey of the historical records of the past in the manner of *Honchō tsugan* or the *Dai Nihonshi*. His was rather a private, explicitly interpretative history. The compilers of *Honchō tsugan* and the *Dai Nihonshi* sought to make them look like their Chinese models in both format and language; as Hayashi Gahō put it, "to make them comprehensible to a Chinese."[26] Hakuseki, by contrast, wrote in Japanese and the format he devised to express his arguments had no Chinese antecedent. But while compared to the others he was less concerned with the forms of Chinese historiography, in terms of the conflict between the norms of Confucian historical analysis and Japanese reality, he was by far the most favorably disposed to Confucian norms.

The divergent perspectives of the three on this question are revealed most clearly in how they dealt with the relationship between the emperor and the shogun. As noted previously, Chinese Confucian political theory assumed that civil and military, temporal and sacerdotal authority should be united in a single ruler, and that while it was improper for such unified authority to be divided among different claimants to the throne, it could be transferred from one dynasty to another. From the Confucian perspective, consequently, the

---

[26] Hanami, "*Honchō tsugan kō*," p. 800.

nominal division of authority between shogun and emperor raised questions about the legitimacy of each. The Hayashi, Mito scholars, and Hakuseki each took a different approach in dealing with this anomaly. None, it should be emphasized, had any intent of challenging or undermining the legitimacy of the bakufu. To the contrary, all in some manner used the concept of transfer of the mandate from one lineage to another (*ekisei kakumei*) to justify bakufu rule.

For example, Hayashi Gahō ends *Ōdai ichiran*, a shorter, more anecdotal, somewhat less judicious review of the same period covered in *Honchō tsugan*, by presenting Ieyasu in the classic guise of the newly anointed recipient of the mandate. He declares that with the battle of Sekigahara in 1600, "Evildoers and bandits were vanquished, and the entire realm submitted to Lord Ieyasu, praising the establishment of peace and extolling his martial virtue. That this glorious era that he founded may continue for ten thousands upon ten thousands of generations, coeval with heaven and earth!"[27] Hakuseki begins *Tokushi yoron* with the proposition that "in our country the government of the realm after nine epochal changes fell to *buke* (military house) rule; in the age of buke rule there were five further epochal changes leading to the rule of the present house." He ends by speaking of "Lord Ieyasu bringing the realm to submit through the agency of his martial virtue."[28] Since the *Dai Nihonshi* concludes in the early fifteenth century with the end of the period of division between the northern and southern courts, it does not refer directly to the achievements of Ieyasu. However, as discussed more fully later in this essay, the termination of the *Dai Nihonshi* at this point suggests that the legitimate imperial dynasty had come to an end. The *Dai Nihonshi* also alludes to Ieyasu as the eventual recipient of heaven's mandate by pointing to the retribution ultimately meted out to the Ashikaga, the immediate victors in the wars of the period of division, and the ultimate recognition of the merit of the apparent loser, Nitta Yoshisada, the putative ancestor of the Tokugawa.[29]

While thus making use of the concept of ekisei kakumei to justify Tokugawa rule, the Hayashi family, the Mito scholars, and Hakuseki differed substantially in how they sought to resolve the implications of this stand with the anomalous actuality of Tokugawa relations with the court. We may compare their respective approaches to this

---

[27] *Ōdai ichiran* (Kyoto: Ōmori Yasuemon, 1664), 7:60b–61a.

[28] *Tokushi yoron*, in NST, 35:184, 428.

[29] Bitō, *Genroku jidai*, pp. 209–212, "Rekishi shisō ni okeru Nihon to Chūgoku," p. 196. *Dai Nihonshi sansō*, in NST, 48:164–165, 173. See H. Paul Varley, *Imperial Restoration in Medieval Japan* (New York: Columbia University Press, 1971), for an analysis of the period of divided courts and a summary of Japanese historiography on it.

issue by examining how each dealt with the events that more than any other raised questions about the legitimacy of the imperial line and the relations of the bakufu to the court: the division between the northern and southern lines following Godaigo's forced abdication in 1331, the ultimate disappearance of the southern line, and the continuation of the imperial succession by the descendants of the northern emperor set up as a puppet by Ashikaga Takauji in 1336. It was a situation which although not directly analogous to that of the Three Kingdoms, involved quite comparable elements. However, it was further complicated by other factors. The Tokugawa shoguns received their appointment as such from an emperor descended from the northern line, a fact which, insofar as the emperor was affirmed as an agent for legitimizing Tokugawa rule, operated as an impetus for establishing the legitimacy of the northern line over the southern. On the other hand, as noted previously, the Tokugawa explicitly sought to utilize the reputation of the Ashikaga as traitors to the southern court and a claim of descent from the loyalist Nitta to justify their own succession to the post of shogun.

Confronting this innately contradictory mélange, the Hayashi, reluctant to break out of the framework of pragmatic inconsistency that marked the bakufu's definition of its relations with the imperial line, in effect chose to sustain that framework at the expense of a cohesive evaluation of the developments of the period of divided courts according to the premises of Confucian political historiography. The Mito scholars sought to achieve a delicate balance among the contradictory elements, that is, a reconciliation, if not a definitive resolution, of Confucian assumptions with the idea that ultimate sovereign authority was permanently vested in the imperial line. Hakuseki applied the premises of Confucian historical analysis to the events of the period in such a way as to create a convincing foundation for his position that the shogun should rule as a national monarch, as heir to the mandate in the Chinese mode.

In one sense, Hayashi Gahō treated the period of divided courts as marking a transition from court to buke rule. He describes Godaigo in the terms standardly used for one whose actions bring about the loss of the dynasty's mandate: Godaigo was shortsighted in his governmental decisions, arbitrary in meting out punishments and rewards, receptive to the suggestions of a scheming consort but resistant to the remonstrances and advice of loyal associates. Consequently, the "realm viewed buke rule as preferable."[30] In line with his ultimate presentation of Ieyasu as recipient of the mandate, Gahō also depicts

---

[30] *Ōdai ichiran*, 6:10a–b.

Takauji as acting as a candidate, albeit an unworthy one, for receipt of the mandate lost by Godaigo. Thus, for instance, he notes that with Takauji's issuing of the *Kenmu shikimoku* legal code in 1336 "the realm returned to buke rule."[31] At the same time, however, Gahō hedged this portrayal of a transferal of the mandate from the court to the buke by continuing to use the framework of imperial annals for the discussion of events in the period after Godaigo. In so doing he had to confront from a different perspective the question of Godaigo's place in the history of the imperial house.

Gahō records in his diary that in 1664 Mitsukuni asked him how he intended to handle this question. Gahō responded that it was necessary to weigh various factors carefully before reaching a conclusive decision. "Kōgen and Kōmyō represented the senior line and Godaigo the junior. However, the succession of Kōgen and Kōmyō was due to the wish of traitorous vassals. . . . Ssu-ma Kuang established Wei as the legitimate line. Most scholars criticize his argument as improper. However, if in this work I simply present the ancestors of the present emperor as usurpers and declare the southern court the legitimate ruler, once the book appears, how is the court likely to regard it?"[32] Gahō recognized that according to the criteria of most Confucian scholars, including Chu Hsi, whatever the faults of Godaigo himself, in that he had been deposed by a traitorous vassal, his line should be regarded as the legitimate one and the northern line as a puppet. However, to make such a judgment explicit would contradict the bakufu's stance of loyalty to the current line of emperors. Faced with these options, Gahō chose to give priority to the presentation of the legitimacy of the northern line and used the northern era-names and reign titles as the chronological framework for the period in question.

In *Ōdai ichiran*, written in 1652, Gahō ended Godaigo's reign as a legitimate emperor with his forced abdication in 1331. The events of Kenmu, Godaigo's flight to Yoshino, and his death there were handled under the chronological framework of the northern emperors Kōgen and Kōmyō. Some years later in *Honchō tsugan*, Gahō adopted a more complicated formula designed to show the transformation of the southern line from legitimate ruler to regional power as occurring at the death of Godaigo in 1339. From 1331 to 1333 in the title of the annals, Godaigo and Kōgen were listed jointly with Godaigo given first place and Kōgen second. From 1333 to 1336 Godaigo was listed as the sole ruler, and from 1336 to 1339 he was again given first place

---

[31] Ibid., 6:13b.
[32] *Kokushikan nichiroku*, 1:41.

in a joint listing with the northern emperor Kōmyō. However, with Godaigo's death and the accession of his son, Gomurakami, this order was reversed, with Kōmyō listed first and Gomurakami listed second, and from 1392 only the reign and era-names of the northern line appeared in the title of the annals.

In his conversation with Mitsukuni, Gahō indicated that he saw Ssu-ma Kuang's handling of the Wei-Shu issue as offering a justification for overlooking the problematic origins of the northern line. In fact, however, there was a significant difference in the approach of Gahō and Ssu-ma Kuang to these two comparable eras. Ssu-ma Kuang struggled with the normative dimensions of the historiographical use of era and reign titles in an effort to make Wei a chronological point of reference without thereby recognizing its legitimacy. Gahō, by contrast, eschewing explicit discussion of the grounds for establishing the northern line as legitimate, relied on the normative qualities of the use of reign titles to obviate such specification.

Similarly, he left ambiguous the meaning of that "legitimacy" in light of the relations between the buke and the imperial court thereafter. Ōdai ichiran ends with the reign of Ōgimachi (1557–1586). The termination of the imperial annals at that point, combined with Gahō's acclamation of Ieyasu's victory at Sekigahara and the founding of an era of peaceful rule, suggested that these events should be regarded as marking the start of a new dynasty. In Honchō tsugan, which goes up through the reign of Goyōzei (1586–1611), this issue is more blurred. If the definitive establishment of Tokugawa rule was to be regarded as dating from the elimination of the Toyotomi in 1615, the suggestion of the founding of a new dynasty could be considered sustained. On the other hand, the extension of the imperial annals to 1611 allowed for the incorporation in them of the imperial award of the title of sei-i tai shōgun (Barbarian Subduing Generalissimo) to Ieyasu in 1603 and to Hidetada in 1605, and implied that the reigns of subsequent shoguns should also be viewed within the larger context of the reigns of the emperors who followed Goyōzei.

Gahō appended to Honchō tsugan an analysis of the history of the imperial line according to the events occurring within each calendrical cycle of sixty years, which came as close as anything to the "giron" that he said he might attempt to add once the main project was completed. The summation of the relationship between the Tokugawa and the imperial line that he provides at the end of this analysis may be taken to indicate the normative image of that relationship that he wished his mirror to project. He writes:

Hideyoshi died and his heir was young and ineffectual. The populace all turned in voluntary submission to our great divine lord (*daishinkun*). In 1600 came the victory at Sekigahara. A great wind blew the clouds high into the firmament. The work of founding was complete, the task of maintenance was accomplished. Enlightened rule continued generation after generation; peace prevailed throughout the realm. Not since the time of Yoritomo had the world known such prosperity. . . . [Since that time] the court has relied on the buke with increasing respect, the buke have looked up to the court with ever more fervor. May their lineages continue together for a hundred thousand cycles, eternally governing the multitudinous populace.[33]

The juxtaposition of the portrait of the Tokugawa as heirs to the mandate with the harmonious picture of the court relying on the buke and the buke looking up to the court testifies to Gahō's desire both to utilize the principles of Confucian historiography to uphold the authority of the Tokugawa and to stay within the existing pragmatic framework of bakufu legitimacy. It also shows that for all its outwardly Chinese format and its incorporation of Chinese Confucian elements, Hayashi historiography was fundamentally eclectic. In his record of his conversation with Mitsukuni in 1664, Gahō describes himself as telling Mitsukuni that although he felt that for the moment he could do no more than record the facts meticulously without passing judgment, one who, like Mitsukuni, was knowledgeable about such matters, would "be able to recognize the points on which I wish to remonstrate."[34] In fact, however, the direction of Gahō's remonstrance, other than that the status quo should be preserved, remained ambiguous.

Gahō concluded his description of his 1664 conversation with Mitsukuni by noting that the latter "smiled approvingly."[35] The smile may be taken as an expression of appreciation for the problems adumbrated by Gahō and, to a certain extent, of agreement with his proposed approach to dealing with them. The ultimate resolution of the northern-southern court issue reached by the Mito scholars had, in fact, a number of features in common with Gahō's judicious affirmation of the legitimacy of the northern line. To reach that eventual solution, however, the Mito scholars took a quite different route from that followed by the Hayashi, and the explicit rationalization which

[33] *Honchō tsugan, furoku*, 2:751.
[34] *Kokushikan nichiroku*, 1:41–42.
[35] Ibid.

they offered for their decision distinguished it from the ambiguous effort of the Hayashi to sustain the legitimacy of the northern line.

Like the Hayashi, the Mito scholars held that Godaigo did not behave in the manner incumbent upon a ruler; they further specified that his lack of rectitude was responsible for the ultimate failure of the southern line to perpetuate itself. The ronsan to the *Dai Nihonshi* pointed to the arbitrary and inconsistent behavior of the restoration government toward the *bushi* (military) class as creating disorder and unrest throughout the realm and concluded that while Takauji's treasonous action in taking advantage of this unrest was "beyond calculation, it was also the consequence of the court itself breaching the bonds of morality."[36] The last emperor of Godaigo's line, Gokameyama (r. 1383–1392), weighed down by the "legacy of the faults" of Godaigo and his son, Gomurakami, yielded the regalia to the northern court in 1392 "because he knew that heaven had already withdrawn its mandate."[37]

However, applying the same principles to the issue that Chu Hsi adduced in his criticism of Ssu-ma Kuang's handling of the Wei-Shu question, the Mito scholars also held that the southern line had to be recognized as legitimate. Taking upon themselves the duty to elucidate the moral lessons of Japanese history, they made clarification of this point one of the central aims (*toppitsu*) of the *Dai Nihonshi*. In acccordance with this purpose, the *Dai Nihonshi* was originally intended to terminate with the rejoining of the courts in 1392, indicating that with the end of the southern line, the legitimate dynasty had likewise ended. The five northern emperors from Kōgen (r. 1331–1333) to Goen'yū (r. 1371–1382) who had occupied the throne in Kyoto were excluded from the imperial annals section and discussed in the general biographies section as pretenders, and the Ashikaga and those associated with them were identified as "traitors" (*zoku*).[38] These arrangements pointed up one of the morals that the compilers of the *Dai Nihonshi* wished to draw: it was incumbent upon ruler and subject alike to conform to the norms of rectitude inherent in the status of each. The failure of Godaigo to do so brought about the end of his dynasty; the failure of the Ashikaga to do so left them blackened with the name of "traitor" and a legacy of social and political chaos. The same arrangements also, as noted previously, established a base for presentation of the Tokugawa, as descendants of the loyalist Nitta, as heirs to the mandate forfeited by Godaigo. The

[36] *Dai Nihonshi sansō*, in NST, 48:177–178.

[37] Ibid., pp. 66–69, 164–165.

[38] Matsumoto Sannosuke, "Kinsei ni okeru rekishi jojutsu to sono shisō," in NST, 48:580–581; Ogura, pp. 552–553.

Nitta loyalty and self-abnegation in the face of the ruler's lack of rectitude illustrated precisely the qualities classically held to be exhibited by those selected by heaven to receive its mandate.

Had this original plan been followed through, the Dai Nihonshi would have been an authentic Confucian history in the Chinese mode. However, various considerations impelled a modification of this early arrangement. One was acknowledgment of the point raised by Gahō: the emperors of the Tokugawa period were descendants of the northern line. Describing his reaction to the original plan to put the five northern emperors in the biography section as pretenders, Asaka Tanpaku wrote: "If the situation were one of dynastic change as in China, and one were compiling the history of the preceding dynasty, such a format might be acceptable. But here the imperial house has continued as one lineage, and while there were the so-called northern and southern lines, both were alike the descendants of the heavenly founder. Moreover, the so-called 'five rulers' (goshu) of the northern court are in fact the direct ancestors of the present emperor. How could they properly be relegated to the biographies section?"[39]

In accordance with this conclusion, the Dai Nihonshi eventually was extended beyond the reign of Gokameyama to include the reign of the contemporary northern emperor Gokomatsu (r. 1382–1413), pointing to the ongoing legitimacy of the northern line. In addition, the five northern emperors from Kōgen to Goen'yū were taken out of the general biographies section and allotted a kind of semilegitimacy through the appending of an account of the events concerning them to the annals of the reign of Gokomatsu.[40]

However, more lay behind this rearrangement than simply pragmatic recognition of the necessity to affirm the legitimacy of the emperor who granted the Tokugawa shogun his titles of authority. At work as well was the aim to focus the shogun's efforts at self-rectification—the stimulation of which was one of the main purposes of the Dai Nihonshi—in a particular direction. That aim was fueled, in turn, by the complexities described previously of Mito's attitude toward the bakufu. In effect, the Mito scholars, by upholding the ultimate sovereign authority of the emperor, sought to impress upon the shogun the need for restraint in the exercise of his authority. On the one hand, through the delineation of the supreme position of the emperor, the Mito scholars established a specific context for their call upon the shogun to strive for self-abnegation. One may assume that this call for the shogun to take a more self-abnegating stance in con-

[39] Cited in Matsumoto, "Kinsei," in NST, 48:580.
[40] Matsumoto, "Kinsei," in NST, 48:580–581; Ogura, "Kaidai," pp. 552–553.

formity with his position of subordination to the emperor was motivated at least in part by Mitsukuni's negative reaction to the course of eccentric autocracy followed by Tsunayoshi, during whose reign the *Dai Nihonshi* took definitive shape. At the same time, the superior authority of the emperor could be used as a point of reference for establishing Mito's autonomy vis-à-vis the bakufu. An anecdote in a near contemporary collection of Mitsukuni's sayings and deeds offers an insight into these various considerations. Mitsukuni is described as putting on the court dress appropriate to his *kan'i* (honorary court rank and office) every New Year's morning and bowing toward Kyoto and as having told his close vassals, "My lord (*shukun*) is the emperor. The present shogun is the head of my family (*soshitsu*). One must take care not to misunderstand this situation."[41]

The revision of the original structure of the *Dai Nihonshi*, undertaken for the reasons described, inevitably introduced a contradictory element into the neat consistency of the original, thereby also creating the danger that the clarity of the moral lesson that the compilers wished to set forth would be obscured. To prevent that from happening, the compilers had to find a means of reconciling the contradictory elements that would preserve the desired didactic message. One of the instruments through which the Mito scholars sought to achieve this end was a new emphasis on the significance of the regalia as the indicator of imperial legitimacy. The yielding of the regalia to the northern line in 1392 by Gokameyama, who as the legitimate ruler had held them up to then, indicated that henceforth it was the northern line that should be regarded as legitimate.

By and large the early Mito scholars sought to keep this emphasis on possession of the regalia as evidence of legitimacy from leading to the conclusion that possession of the regalia was sufficient in itself to confer legitimacy. In the ronsan on Gokomatsu, Asaka Tanpaku declared, "The weight of the regalia depends on winning the hearts of the people. If the people cleave to the ruler the regalia carry weight; if their hearts are distant from him, then the regalia do not carry weight." Nevertheless, he also imputed to the regalia a kind of magical power that ensured they would automatically go to the appropriate recipient. He concluded that same section by remarking, "The regalia as spiritual entities (*reibutsu*), of themselves have that to which they cleave."[42] In effect, possession of the regalia took the place of the criteria adduced by Ssu-ma Kuang and Chu Hsi, such as the extent of the putative ruler's authority or manner of succession to

[41] Miki Hanzaemon, ed., *Tōgen iji*, ZGR, 3:329.
[42] *Dai Nihonshi sansō*, in NST, 48:69.

the throne, as the central evidence of heaven's will. As Matsumoto Sannosuke points out, the ultimate consequence of such restructuring of the concept of heaven's will was to remove the imperial line as a whole from the purview of mandate thought even while using the latter as a criterion for judging the conduct of individual emperors.[43]

The affirmation of the eternal sovereignty of the imperial line also impelled an effort to define more precisely the role of the shogun, to establish a "name" against which he could measure the "substance" of his actions. This the Mito scholars sought to do through the creation of a new historiographical category, the shogun *den*, in nature somewhere between the annals established for the ruler and the biographies set aside for subjects, wherein events pertaining to the shoguns and their vassals were covered. The proposer of this innovation, Miyake Kanran, pointed out that the reality of the shogun's role could not be accommodated readily within the standard categories of Chinese historiography. In China feudal lords or princes had been enfeoffed by the emperor as during the Chou and Han, buffer states had been established on the frontier as during the Ch'in and T'ang, and the land had been partitioned during periods in which there was no established ruler such as the Five Dynasties. However, none of these categories fit the situation of the shogun. The shogun occupied a position between the emperor on the one hand and the nobility and populace on the other. While he was appointed by the emperor and ranked as a subject, the shogun in fact "[held] the powers of financial administration over the lands of the realm; the prerogatives to appoint governors and government officials, to mount punitive expeditions, to cause to live or to die, to eradicate or create, all devolve[d] upon him. From the Chou and Han to the Sung and Yüan, among the records of [Chinese] rulers and subjects, there has been no comparable situation."[44] As Asaka Tanpaku described the arrangement, "While in name it belongs to the category of biography (*retsuden*) [indicating that the shogun was not the ruler], in substance it is like the main annals (*hongi*) [where events concerning the ruler were covered]."[45]

This Mito innovation involved a certain ambiguity. On the one hand, the creation of an official category for the shogun reflecting his actual powers could be taken as evidence of an intent to uphold those powers. On the other hand, such was the normative weight of the established names of "ruler" and "subject" and of the assumption

[43] Matsumoto, "Kinsei," in NST, 48:591.

[44] Ibid., p. 581; Miyake Kanran, "Shōgunden shigi," in *Kanranshū*, ZGR, 13:432.

[45] Matsumoto, "Kinsei," in NST, 48:582; Asaka Tanpaku, "Chōshū kiden girei no ato ni shosu," in *Tanpaku Sai bunshū*, ZGR, 13:305.

that reality should conform to name that, depending on the point of view of the reader, the remarks of Kanran and Tanpaku concerning the nature of the shogun den could be interpreted as a criticism as well as an affirmation of the "reality" of shogunal rule. One may say that this ambiguity, rather than inadvertent, was itself true to the complexities of the Mito attitude toward the bakufu.

In many ways Hakuseki took a view of the events of the period of divided courts comparable to that of the early version of the *Dai Nihonshi*. Applying uncompromisingly the criteria of Chinese Confucian historiography, he held that Godaigo was both the legitimate ruler and responsible for the loss of the mandate, and that, as a consequence, the legitimate imperial line came to an end with the southern court. He writes of the Kenmu restoration: "Both samurai and the populace knew that government under the emperor was far inferior to what there had been during the period of buke rule. Thus everyone, no matter who, throughout the realm longed to take as ruler whoever could revive the age of buke rule. Thus since this person [Takauji] fortunately became an enemy of the court, although they disliked that name, they longed for what in fact was involved."[46] Since Godaigo "had occupied the awesome position of emperor and took with him the regalia, . . . those court nobles who knew the meaning of loyalty and rectitude largely went to the southern court. . . . The same was true among the buke." However, Godaigo's lack of kingly qualities made it impossible to establish the southern court on a firm basis: "That nevertheless [the southern line] was ultimately unable to carry forward its succession was entirely due to the circumstances that heaven did not join with it because of the lack of virtue of its founder."[47]

Similarly, Hakuseki took the northern court to be no more than a puppet of the Ashikaga. "The northern court was nothing more than something established by Lord Ashikaga for his own purposes; it could not be considered the legitimate imperial line, and the people of the day spoke of it as the pretender or the court of the pretender."[48] However, unlike the Mito scholars, Hakuseki did not temper this "Chinese" interpretation of Japanese history. To the contrary, in line with his aim to justify the assumption by the shogun of a more monarchal role, he continued to adhere to the assumptions of Chinese Confucian historiography in his interpretation of the post-1392 period. This is shown by his approach to the elements utilized

[46] *Tokushi yoron*, in NST, 35:356.
[47] Ibid., pp. 275–276.
[48] Ibid.

by the Hayashi and the Mito scholars for establishing the ultimate legitimacy of the northern line, the transferal of the regalia, and the chronological framework of the post-1392 period.

Hakuseki agreed that the regalia were symbols of legitimacy, but he imputed no spiritual powers to them. Transfer of the regalia to the pretender's court by the line that failed to gain heaven's support because of its founder's lack of virtue could hardly transform the Ashikaga puppet into a legitimate emperor. Consequently, Hakuseki laid no particular emphasis on the transfer and simply dealt with the arrangements for the return as one of the events of the shogunal reign of Yoshimitsu, appending the brief parenthetical note, "After fifty-six years south and north were reunited."[49]

As noted earlier in this essay, Hakuseki divided Japanese history into nine epochs of rule by the court and five epochs of rule by the buke, culminating in rule by the Tokugawa. As he presented it, these ages overlapped; the age of court rule terminated with Godaigo, while the age of the buke began with Yoritomo. However, from the time of Takauji, "the court existed only as an empty vessel propped up by others, and the realm was completely under buke rule."[50] In line with this proposition, in the first section of *Tokushi yoron*, treating the age of the court, Hakuseki related events to the reigns of the emperors, and at the beginning of each reign he identified the emperor in question in terms of parentage, the date of his designation as crown prince, and the date of his accession. In the second section he broke away from this format and examined the actions of the buke rulers from Yoritomo to Takauji as they expanded the military authority abandoned to them by the increasingly decadent emperors. In the third section he related events to the reigns of the buke leaders who attempted to govern the realm from the time of Takauji on. In this section he referred to the emperors only in passing. Thus, for instance, while in *Ōdai ichiran* and *Honchō tsugan* Hayashi Gahō treated the events of the last reigns of the Ashikaga shogun and the rule of Oda Nobunaga and Toyotomi Hideyoshi within the context of the reign of Emperor Ōgimachi (r. 1557–1586), Hakuseki barely touched upon the accession of Ōgimachi in the course of discussing the events of the era of shogunal rule of Ashikaga Yoshiteru (r. 1546–1565). In his summation of the course of "the realm under Hideyoshi," he did not even allude to Ōgimachi's abdication or the accession of his successor.

This chronological format led to the presentation of Ieyasu as heir

---

[49] Ibid., p. 264.
[50] Ibid., p. 186.

to the heavenly mandate to rule the realm. However, unlike the Ha-yashi, Hakuseki did not intend his presentation of Ieyasu as heir to the mandate to constitute an affirmation of Tokugawa rule as it was. Rather, he sought to make that presentation the basis for a justification of the transformation of the shogun into a king. To that end he upheld unsparingly the premise advanced by generations of Chinese Confucian historians like Ssu-ma Kuang that the ruler should combine in his person civil and military, temporal and sacerdotal authority, and that failure to preserve this unified authority was an invitation to political disorder and social chaos. Evaluating emperor and buke alike according to this premise, Hakuseki depicted both as lacking: the emperor, on the one hand, for sanctioning usurpation of his powers just as the Chou king had done by admitting the heads of the houses of Han, Wei, and Chao to the ranks of the feudal lords; and, on the other hand, the succession of buke leaders for continuing to seek to rule in the shadow of an emperor who had lost the support of heaven. As noted previously, reflecting the weight of this Chinese Confucian premise of the norm of unified rule, the effort of the Mito scholars to define a new role for the shogun between that of ruler and subject involved a certain ambiguity. The image of the history of buke rule projected by Hakuseki's historical mirror was far less equivocal. Clearly with the intent of justifying a break with the buke tradition of "utilizing awe for the imperial house to control the realm," Hakuseki defined the succession of buke rulers from Yoritomo to Hideyoshi as *pa* (hegemons; J., *ha*) of one sort or another who sought to "raise up the emperor (*tenshi o hasamite*) and issue edicts in his name."[51]

The historical endeavors of the Mito scholars and Hakuseki may be read in a sense as responses to the unresolved contradictions of the Hayashi effort to join Chinese Confucian historiographical principles to Japanese historical reality. Tokugawa historiography of the late-eighteenth and nineteenth centuries reflected, in turn, the working out of the dialectical tensions present in the manner in which the Mito scholars and Hakuseki sought to reconcile Chinese Confucian norms and Japanese reality.

Historians of the late-Tokugawa period such as Fujita Yūkoku or Rai San'yō found untenable the ambiguity of Miyake Kanran and Asaka Tanpaku's affirmation of the name of shogun as something between ruler and subject. In place of this modification of Confucian historiographical and social categories, they advanced another: for the shogun, the effective ruler, to revere as sacrosanct the kingly au-

---

[51] Ibid., pp. 277, 428.

thority inherent in the "name" of emperor had a social value of its own. The respect for a fixed hierarchical order thus demonstrated by the shogun would set in motion a chain reaction of respect for superiors throughout society. Holding to such a position, late-Tokugawa historians took exception to Hakuseki's effort to bring about a fusion of the name and reality of kingly authority in the person of the shogun. Hakuseki's readiness to grant the shogun the name as well as the substantive authority of a king they saw as lending comfort to traitors.[52] However, even if they rejected the form of the union of name and substance proposed by Hakuseki, their own implicit affirmation of a separation of the two necessarily was undermined by the weight of the idea that properly name and substance should be united. The ongoing strength of that assumption, so basic to Confucian thought and nurtured in the Tokugawa environment by Hakuseki and, to a somewhat lesser extent, by the early Mito thinkers, thus combined with the renewed affirmation of the imperial line's eternal possession of the name of king to encourage the idea of an alternative fusion of name and substance: in the person of the emperor rather than shogun. Historical interpretations which took shape in a context firmly supportive of Tokugawa rule contributed in the end to the erosion of the position of the shogun and to the idea that he should return his authority to the emperor.

[52] For these late Tokugawa developments see Bitō, "Rekishi shisō ni okeru Nihon to Chūgoku," pp. 200–203, and "Sonnō jōi shisō," in *Iwanami kōza Nihon rekishi* (Iwanami Shoten, 1977), 13:77–85.

FOUR

THE TOKUGAWA PEACE AND POPULAR RELIGION: SUZUKI SHŌSAN, KAKUGYŌ TŌBUTSU, AND JIKIGYŌ MIROKU

BY ROYALL TYLER

In his "Author's Introduction" to *Studies in the Intellectual History of Tokugawa Japan*, Maruyama Masao observed: "It was not really until the late seventeenth century that the Confucian classics and the authoritative commentaries on them came to be printed and circulated, and the doctrines of Confucianism *as an ideology* came to penetrate society in general."[1] With this statement Maruyama partially corrected the assumption "that what I called the 'Neo-Confucian' mode of thought had achieved a general social ascendancy in the early Tokugawa period, and that the universality of its acceptance began to crumble subsequently in the late seventeenth and early eighteenth centuries."[2] This paper will not dispute Maruyama's self-correction, since the men it discusses were not properly speaking "Confucian" at all, and since they certainly were not spokesmen for Confucianism "as an ideology." It will, however, suggest first that the compelling quality of the Confucian mode of thought in the early seventeenth century and its widespread appeal are linked to a broad concern with precisely those issues toward which Confucian discourse had traditionally been directed; and second that interest in the general Confucian mode of thought did not spread only from the top downward, but was also shared from the outset by many at the lower levels of society.

The essential character of what I call here a "Confucian mode of thought" is an absorbing religious or philosophical concern with achieving, and more particularly, with maintaining a stable and harmonious society. It goes without saying that Confucianism has an

[1] Masao Maruyama, *Studies in the Intellectual History of Tokugawa Japan*, tr. Mikiso Hane (Princeton: Princeton University Press, and Tokyo: University of Tokyo Press, 1974), p. xxxiv. Original emphasis retained.

[2] Ibid.

essential ethical dimension and that it has much to say about self-cultivation, but this discussion does not directly address those aspects of the matter. Such a concern with social questions was not characteristic of what is commonly called *chūsei*, the "medieval" period (1185-1600) of Japanese history. The outstanding concerns of chūsei have to do with suffering, the passions, the enlightenment, and they thus belong to the province of Buddhism. Buddhism, however, was no longer at the forefront during the Tokugawa, despite the efforts of articulate spokesmen. In addition to Jiun Sonja, the topic of Paul Watt's paper in this volume, two seventeenth-century figures are valuable for an understanding of Buddhism's role during the early Tokugawa and for an understanding of popular religion at that time. The first of these is Suzuki Shōsan (1579-1655), an unorthodox Zen teacher; and the second is Kakugyō Tōbutsu (1541-1646), the ultimate founder of the Edo-period and modern cult of Mt. Fuji. The concern with a stable and harmonious society eventually gave rise to anxiety that the harmony and stability of the Tokugawa order was threatened or had been lost. This anxiety produced successive redefinitions of the efficacious essence of Confucianism itself, and (on a nonintellectual level) a thirst for the *renewal* of that order—or at least of what that order was felt to have been. The career of my third figure, and the cult inspired by his example, exemplify this trend in Tokugawa thought among the townsmen of Edo. This figure is Jikigyō Miroku (1671-1733), who turned the Fuji cult into a powerful popular movement.

Suzuki Shōsan

Fujiwara Seika (1561-1619), the founding Confucian of the Tokugawa period, once wrote, "Buddhist writings are not the urgent concern of our time."[3] Seika himself had been a Zen monk. So had Hayashi Razan (1583–1657) and Yamazaki Ansai (1618–1682), both illustrious upholders of Neo-Confucian philosophy. Another former Buddhist monk was Asayama Soshin (1589-1664), a Confucian scholar known to have expounded the *Mean* to Emperor Gokōmyō and author of a popular Confucian *kanazōshi* (storybook) entitled *Kiyomizu monogatari* (Tale of Kiyomizu). *Gion monogatari* (Tale of Gion), a Buddhist rejoinder to this work, contains a diatribe against young men who, bored with being monks, return to lay life, learn a bit

---

[3] From "Letter to Hayashi Saburō," quoted in Itō Kokan, *Nihon Zen no shōtō Gudē* (Shunjūsha, 1969), p. 61.

about the Four Books, and set themselves up as scholars.[4] Such a charge suggests that men like Soshin himself were not rare. Suzuki Shōsan, an ardent Buddhist whose life and sympathies were devoted to the bakufu, might well have been alarmed.

Shōsan was born in Mikawa, the base province of Ieyasu himself, in 1579, and he fought as a *hatamoto* both at Sekigahara and at Osaka. Shōsan had turned toward Buddhism at an early age, having been preoccupied by the problem of death. As a warrior he had in time of peace sought out many Zen masters, and in battle he pitted himself against death itself, sometimes attacking alone against hopeless odds. In old age he recalled that he had once felt ready for anything, having even considered taking a casual tour of the Hitoana. This cave near the base of Mt. Fuji was reputed to have been the entrance to hell, and thus a place whence none who entered returned alive.[5] As a matter of fact, throughout all but the last decade of Shōsan's life, the Hitoana was Kakugyō Tōbutsu's only residence.

It was either in 1621 or 1623 that Shōsan at last became a monk and gave himself fully to practice and teaching.[6] His works include the moral tracts of *Mōanjō* and *Banmin tokuyō*; the anti-Christian tract *Ha Kirishitan*; two *kanazōshi* titled *Nenbutsu sōshi* and *Ninin bikuni*; and a collection of didactic tales entitled *Inga monogatari*. In his last years, his sayings were compiled by a disciple named Echū (b. 1628) and published under the title *Roankyō*. Echū also published a further collection of sayings, letters, and so on, as *Hogo shū*.[7]

Shōsan's personal study was death and dying. Indeed, he often urged people to "rehearse death" (*shi o narau*), and he sometimes said that his teaching was "Buddhism for cowards," that is, Buddhism

---

[4] *Gion monogatari*, in *Tenri toshokan-zō kinsei bungaku mikanbon sōsho* (Kyoto: Yōto-kusha, 1949), p. 61. The text of *Kiyomizu monogatari* is included in the same volume. *Kiyomizu monogatari* was published in 1638. *Gion monogatari* is undated, but it likely appeared shortly afterward.

[5] *Roankyō*, 1:63, in *Suzuki Shōsan Dōnin zenshū*, ed. Suzuki Tesshin (Sankibō Busshorin, 1962), p. 157; and *Selected Writings of Suzuki Shōsan*, tr. Royall Tyler (Ithaca: Cornell University China-Japan Program, 1977), p. 99. The passage in my published translation speaks of the "lava caves on Mt. Fuji." Until I studied the Fuji cult, I had no clear idea what the Hitoana was.

[6] *Kansei chōshū fu* and *Suzuki-shi keifu* (in *Suzuki Shōsan Dōnin zenshū*) both give 1623. However, *Sekihei Dōnin gyōgyō ki* (in *Zenshū*) gives the date 1621, and describes Shōsan's activities as a monk between 1621 and 1623.

[7] All of Suzuki Shōsan's works except *Inga monogatari* are included in *Suzuki Shōsan Dōnin zenshū*, together with various biographical materials. *Selected Writings of Suzuki Shōsan* contains translations of *Mōanjō*, *Banmin tokuyō*, *Ninin bikuni*, most of *Roankyō*, and *Kaijō monogatari*, a tale by Echū. A translation of *Ha Kirishitan* is given by George Elison in *Deus Destroyed* (Cambridge: Harvard University Press, 1973).

for those who are afraid of death.[8] At the same time, he held that a man ignorantly afraid of death is hopelessly closed.[9] Shōsan once said, "No matter how long I live, I have nothing to talk about except death."[10] In this respect, his goal was to die fully conscious and unmoved.

Shōsan is known as the founder (although he had no successors) of Niō Zen; and as a Zen master who taught the nenbutsu. In either practice, his style was vigorous indeed. When he taught, he sometimes struck the pose of a Niō (Guardian King) and told his listeners to catch that martial spirit. He also urged practitioners to receive that same spirit by contemplating an image of a Niō, or of Fudō, and he reminded them that the beginner (Shōsan considered almost everyone a beginner, not necessarily exluding himself), open as he is to the assault of the passions, can gain nothing from the mood of a tranquil Buddha.[11] With respect to *zazen*, accordingly, he taught not calm sitting, or a sitting that aspires to calmness, but meditation done with clenched fists, gritted teeth, and eyes set in a fierce glare.

Shōsan's nenbutsu was much the same, for he often taught that the invocation should be recited with the attitude just described. Shōsan distinguished various manners in which the nenbutsu could be recited, but judging from his words, the most congenial styles for him were the "nenbutsu of severing" and the "nenbutsu of the brink of death." In the former, "you take the nenbutsu as a sword, . . . and sever and clear away all thoughts both of good and of evil"; in the latter, "you decide that this very moment is your last, and with 'Namu Amida Butsu' . . . work at dying."[12]

This was the way in which Shōsan himself practiced. He believed that few if any masters of the past had *truly* practiced; whereas for himself he was certain that he at least had done his best.[13] This rather striking claim suggests that Shōsan placed a hitherto unusual value upon effort. For Shōsan, effort seems to have been less a Buddhist than a concretely social issue. His idea of effort had less to do with *shugyō* (religious practice), and more to do with a secularized notion of hard work.

On the whole, Shōsan, adamant Buddhist though he was, took Buddhism quite for granted. That is, Buddhism (*Buppō*) was for him

[8] *Roankyō*, 1:72; *Zenshū*, p. 161; *Selected Writings*, p. 104.
[9] *Roankyō*, 1:75; *Zenshū*, p. 162; *Selected Writings*, p. 105.
[10] *Roankyō*, 3:129; *Zenshū*, p. 276; *Selected Writings*, p. 190.
[11] *Roankyō*, 3:36; *Zenshū*, p. 138; *Selected Writings*, p. 75.
[12] *Roankyō*, 3:36; *Zenshū*, p. 248; *Selected Writings*, p. 162.
[13] He left, however, a statement that after all he had "gotten nowhere." See *Roankyō*, 1:34; *Zenshū*, p. 148; *Selected Writings*, p. 90.

a sort of given. Although he claimed at times to champion Sōtō Zen,[14] he acknowledged no master, and thus avoided belonging to any lineage, Zen or otherwise. Likewise, he taught exclusively according to his own lights; and although he spoke often of the urgent need for the land to cleave to the True Dharma (*shōbō*), he did not define this True Dharma in terms which otherwise would appeal to any distinctively Buddhist thought. He claimed, for example, that Buddhism is indispensable to the development of true martial courage;[15] but this simple argument does not *require* acknowledgment of Buddhism at all. Perhaps if Buddhism had not been so entrenched in the Japan of Shōsan's time, with a thousand years of diffusion and acculturation, Shōsan might not have been able to champion "Buddhism" so easily, while having little or nothing to do with Buddhism in an institutional or even doctrinal sense.[16]

Certainly, Shōsan felt dissatisfaction with the Buddhist world of his time and urged reform. Similar sentiments had often been voiced by other monks, however, like Ikkyū (1394–1481), whose language and tone Shōsan adopted more than once.[17] Ikkyū, for all his unorthodox behavior, had eventually been offered, and had accepted, the post of abbot of Daitokuji. Thus he acknowledged unmistakably his position in Rinzai Zen and his debt to his own line. No matter what else Ikkyū may have done, or how little "Zen" (as distinguished from "Buddhism") may be found in those popular writings attributed to him,[18] the Buddhist character of his career is thus beyond question. Shōsan's insistence upon "Buddhism," on the other hand, was highly conservative, and perhaps fundamentally uncritical, as though he held to Buddhism first of all because that was what he had always known and hence preferred.

"You have Buddhism; I have none," Shōsan once said in irritation

---

[14] For example, *Roankyō*, 3:63; *Zenshū*, p. 256; *Selected Writings*, pp. 170–171.

[15] For example, *Roankyō*, 1:107; *Zenshū*, p. 171, *Selected Writings*, p. 115.

[16] His independence would also have been restricted if he had not been (as a monk) a former *hatamoto*, and if his temple (the Onshinji in Mikawa) had not been built for him by his own brother on land which that same brother held in fief. It is true, however, that in his own temple Shōsan carried out assiduously the normal functions of a temple priest.

[17] Shōsan's kanazōshi *Ninin bikuni* incorporates much material from *Gaikotsu* and from an older *Ninin bikuni*, both of which are attributed to Ikkyū. Some of Shōsan's diatribes against the incompetence of the monks of his own time strongly recall Ikkyū.

[18] *Gaikotsu* was translated by R. H. Blyth, "Ikkyū's Skeletons," *Eastern Buddhist* 4, no. 1 (Spring 1973):111–125. Two other works were translated by James Sanford, "Mandalas of the Heart: Two Prose Works by Ikkyū Sōjun," *Monumenta Nipponica* 25, no. 3 (Autumn 1980):273–298.

96

to a visitor.[19] This may sound like a Zen master's paradox, but in Shōsan's case there is a kind of literal truth to it. Shōsan's nenbutsu, for example, comes close to being nonreligious.[20] Of course, he did not teach devotion to Amida, but beyond this his attitude toward the practice was one of sheer practicality. He taught it simply because it was an invocation both convenient and universally known. To those whose profession or avocation required them to chant other things, he substituted these other sounds for the nenbutsu. Thus he told a Nō actor to concentrate on his *utai* (chanting), and a *kouta* singer to give her all to singing kouta.[21] In the same spirit he might urge a monk to recite long and vigorously any convenient liturgy or *darani*. Such an approach was not necessarily broad-minded. On the contrary, it meant that Shōsan insisted single-mindedly on a certain kind of *work*. From one plausible standpoint, digging a flower bed and digging a latrine or a grave are not, after all, the same thing. Shōsan, however, might have insisted that they *are* all the same thing because they all involve the same work.

There were only two persons whose achievement Shōsan acknowledged without qualification. One was the Buddha Shakyamuni, and the other was Tokugawa Ieyasu. Shakyamuni, of course, was a figure remote in time, and for that matter, in perfection. On the other hand, Ieyasu was for Shōsan a figure of the present. Shōsan's ambiguous character as a Buddhist may have had precisely to do with his relationship to the Tokugawa house and to the world which Ieyasu had brought into being. It was to the shogun that Shōsan gave the loyalty and devotion which Ikkyū had acccorded to his spiritual lineage, and to Zen as an institution. Ikkyū revived and rebuilt Daitokuji after the Onin War. What Shōsan aspired to revive and to rebuild was Buddhism itself; moreover, he aspired to do so *in the service* of the lord. He believed that Buddhism, not Confucianism, was the key to lasting peace and the stability of the Tokugawa order. By this he seems to have meant that whereas "Buddhism" can effect an essential transformation, thus creating what one might venture to call the "new Tokugawa man," "Confucianism" deals only with external injunctions. Nevertheless, Shōsan's discourse, and his written discourse especially, were replete with ethical terms and admonitions ordinarily identified with Confucianism.

The central concern of Shōsan's teaching was thus public in char-

---

[19] *Roankyō*, 3:116; *Zenshū*, p. 273; *Selected Writings*, p. 186.

[20] I have in mind, for example, the claim made by Transcendental Meditation to be a nonreligious practice.

[21] *Roankyō*, 2:82 and 3:50; *Zenshū*, pp. 215 and 253; *Selected Writings*, pp. 135–136 and 167.

acter. Now that peace had been achieved, Shōsan wished to see all people working in harmony, each in his place, so that this peace should last forever under the shogun's rule. In this respect, he was hardly different from the Confucians around him, for all his insistence that "Buddhism" could do it better. That is why Shōsan addressed his teaching to all four classes. He insisted that they work together, each in its own proper way. That, too, is why he refused to shave anyone's head and let him become a monk, for when warriors applied to Shōsan for the tonsure, he sent them back to their lords, saying, "For practice, nothing's better than service."[22] As for the other classes, the possibility of someone from them becoming a monk does not arise in Shōsan's surviving discourse.

Such was Shōsan's constant theme. He urged everyone to do the work allotted to him by birth, for the good of all. Thus the proper work of the warrior was to serve his lord; that of the farmer, to till his fields; that of the artisan, to follow his trade; and that of the merchant to amass profit—not for himself, however, but so as to make available to all the necessities of life and work. As each person went about his normal occupation, he might dedicate his efforts to "all beings," and so achieve selflessness and mastery over the passions. In particular, a farmer could say the nenbutsu "in time with each stroke of the hoe,"[23] while a samurai could give up all thought of self to guard and to serve his lord. To merchants Shōsan promised the same reward as to the others:

Say the nenbutsu all the while, and perceive that life is no more than a journey through the floating world. When you thus conduct your commerce without greed, having given up all clinging, the devas will protect you, the gods will be generous toward you, your profits will be enormous, and you will become a man of the greatest wealth. . . . You will at last find risen within you great faith, fierce and unshakable. Walking, standing, sitting, or lying you will be in meditation. Quite naturally enlightenment will mature in you until the subtle delight of nirvana is yours, until you are an unobstructed man of great freedom, and tread alone both yin and yang.[24]

In this passage, the promise of marvelous freedom ends up being subordinate to the admonition to get the job done. Moreover, it is not on the face of it a convincing promise at all.

---

[22] *Roankyō*, 3:13; *Zenshū*, p. 239; *Selected Writings*, p. 147.
[23] *Banmin tokuyō*; *Zenshū*, p. 69; *Selected Writings*, p. 68.
[24] *Banmin tokuyō*; *Zenshū*, p. 72; *Selected Writings*, p. 73.

In his concern for the stability of the social order, Shōsan left the individual no more room to move than any advocate of *taigi meibun* (a fixed role for each person in an immutable social order) ideals. For himself, when asked why he became a monk, he could only reply that it was his karma to do so.[25] He certainly never claimed the enlightenment which he promised to his readers, but he left the strong impression first that whatever this enlightenment or great freedom might be, the pursuit of it and its attainment were essentially a private matter, and second that this private aspiration should have no effect upon one's conduct except to bring one closer to a public ideal. Thus Shōsan's teaching establishes a clear distinction between public and private affairs, and despite all Shōsan's protests, it identifies what is left of any recognizably Buddhist endeavor with the private, less valuable side. Any irruption of this private aspect of the individual's existence into the realm of public morality, any externally detectable pursuit of enlightenment which might affect the individual's social performance, would thus instantly become "selfish." Here Shōsan came very close to the standard Confucian criticism of Buddhism.

Shōsan did actually accord to monks a social role, although to read him one wonders where the next generation of monks was to come from. He made them the spiritual counterpart of the physician: "The physician is an officer (*yakunin*) who cures the ailments of the flesh, while the disciple of the Buddha is an officer who cures the diseases of the mind."[26] His explanation of the monk's healing the "diseases of the mind" was very simple, for he said, "Alas, if the affairs of the whole land were governed in accordance with Buddhism, I believe the one word 'beast' would be enough to rule it." Lest anyone be tempted to indulge in beastly behavior (that is, to indulge his own desires at the expense of the collective good), it would be the function of priests constantly to remind their temple patrons (*danka*) never to be beasts. Priests would be held accountable for their temple patrons' conduct, just as the patrons would be held accountable for their priest's. The terrible nature of beastliness would be dinned into children's ears from infancy. "Once that was done," Shōsan said, "things wouldn't be like the way those Confucians teach humanity, morality, propriety, wisdom, etc., nowadays. People would be very simple. So every time a patron came to the temple, all the priest would need to say would be, 'Don't be a beast.' "[27] Thus Shōsan proposed to place the professional representatives of Buddhism at the service of law and

[25] *Roankyō*, 3:19; *Zenshū*, p. 244; *Selected Writings*, p. 158.
[26] *Banmin tokuyō*; *Zenshū*, p. 63; *Selected Writings*, p. 56.
[27] *Roankyō*, 1:172; *Zenshū*, pp. 188–189; *Selected Writings*, pp. 129–131.

order. Nor were monks or priests the only such "officers" he had in mind. Indeed, all people were "officers" entrusted with carrying out their designated social function. Thus he said that "to be a farmer is to be an officer entrusted by Heaven with the nourishment of the world."[28] In all this there is hardly more than a vestige of distinctly Buddhist thought.

Shōsan insisted repeatedly that Buppō (Buddhism, or the buddha's teaching) and *sehō* (the world's teaching) are one and the same. Thus Shōsan said: "Since ancient times there have been plenty of clerical and lay devotees, but they're all just learned Buddhists. Not one of them says to use the teaching of the world (sehō) in everything. No doubt there *are* people who say that, but so far I haven't heard of them. I think perhaps I'm the first."[29]

This statement recalls the medieval commonplace that "nirvana and the passions are the same"; but it is also different. For Shōsan there was no distinction between Buppō and the *ideals* of the Tokugawa bakufu. He took the social order, as envisioned and as made possible by the bakufu, to be a given: to be indeed "the dharma" (*hō*). His devotion was inspired by a gratitude and an awe before Ieyasu's achievement which was shared surely by most people in Shōsan's time; it was also inspired by his intense concern that this achievement should stand. Moreover, his devotion was especially lively because of his being an intimate Tokugawa vassal. Thus for Shōsan the Buddha had no interests apart from those of the shogun—the Buddha being far removed from this world in time and space, and the shogun very present. In this way, Shōsan served both loyally without seeing any ultimate difference between them. It is no wonder, then, that Shōsan was almost baffled to find that the shogun persisted in not proclaiming the True Dharma (shōbō).

It greatly troubled Shōsan that there was no bakufu-approved orthodoxy for Buddhism, as it appeared to him that there was in other fields. "Buddhism alone," he said, "has no standard, and no discerning supervision. We have people's own arbitrary versions of Buddhism, and the Buddha's teaching is dead."[30] "Alas," he exclaimed on another occasion, "if the ruler himself were to set Buddhism straight, the thing could be done effortlessly, with a single sentence. . . . [Indeed] I could set Buddhism straight right now, throughout the land, with just one sentence." When someone asked for the sentence, Shōsan replied: " 'Let all sects work toward Buddhahood.' With this

---

[28] *Banmin tokuyō*; *Zenshū*, p. 69; *Selected Writings*, pp. 67–68.

[29] *Roankyō*, 3:41; *Zenshū*, p. 251; *Selected Writings*, p. 166.

[30] *Roankyō*, 3:123; *Zenshū*, p. 275; *Selected Writings*, pp. 188–189.

one sentence I'd instantly turn Buddhism into the True Dharma."[31] Again, Shōsan sometimes imagined himself winning a debate before the assembled bakufu officials: a debate with the representatives of the various sects over the true meaning of Buddhism. "They can cut off my head," he said, "if someone better than I comes along."[32] Once the truth of Buddhism has thus been determined, "those who are wrong will be suitably instructed, and the True Dharma will be manifest on the spot."[33]

Thus Shōsan entrusted to the shogun, in his imagination at least, the authority to decide the right and true in Buddhism; and for his part, he was the shogun's loyal adviser. The shogun would surely recognize the right and true, for it would coincide with the best interests of his government and of his people. Indeed, he would recognize the True Dharma as the essence of his very own mind. Shōsan burned to put his message before the shogun, who by the time he died was Hidetada. He never actually did so, however.

To my mind, Suzuki Shōsan represents one possible dead end in the evolution of Buddhist thought. It is no doubt true that all is one, but there are still distinctions to be made. Beyond Shōsan, nothing distinctively Buddhist remains. It is no wonder that many of Shōsan's contemporaries had turned to another mode of thought which dealt more naturally with public affairs, and which served better to celebrate, by the aptness of its approach, the great achievements of the time.

Kakugyō Tōbutsu

For one of Shōsan's older contemporaries, Buddhism had already fallen away. This contemporary was no Confucian, either. Instead, he was a great ascetic, the kind of man whom in certain cases Shōsan praised but more often condemned.[34] Kakugyō Tōbutsu[35] (1541–1646) founded the modern cult of Mt. Fuji and thus became the originator

[31] *Roankyō*, 1:9; *Zenshū*, pp. 140–141; *Selected Writings*, pp. 79–80.

[32] *Roankyō*, 1:69; *Zenshū*, p. 159; *Selected Writings*, p. 102.

[33] *Roankyō*, 1:9; *Zenshū*, pp. 140–141; *Selected Writings*, pp. 79–80.

[34] In general, Shōsan thoroughly disapproved of ascetics and hermits, and attributed to them the basest of motives for living such a life. However, he had great praise for the legendary Zen eccentric P'u-hua (J., Fuke), and also spoke well of the famous Japanese Tendai eccentric Zōga Hijiri.

[35] There are several variants of this name. Formally written, the name is Kakugyō Tōbutsu Kū, in which the Kū is an honorific title unique to the Fuji cult. Moreover, Kakugyō may also be written with the character for "writing" (*kaku* in Japanese); while Tōbutsu may also be written Tōkakubutsu with the characters for "east" and "awakening."

of what might be called Japan's first "new religion." Although a product of the *shugendō* (mountain asceticism) tradition, Kakugyō was not a Buddhist, as the bakufu itself noticed when Kakugyō came at last to its attention. Instead, he was in direct communication with Sengen Daibosatsu,[36] the deity of Mt. Fuji. Like Shōsan, Kakugyō was urgently concerned with the issue of peace and social order, and his legend emphasizes an intimate (if fanciful) connection between himself and Ieyasu. According to this legend, it was Kakugyō who made Ieyasu's achievement possible.

Surviving materials on Kakugyō are regrettably unreliable. There is available only one basic account in two variants. Generally known as *Gotaigyō no maki*,[37] it bears as author the name of one of Kakugyō's disciples, and the date 1620. This claim is unlikely, however, and *Gotaigyō no maki* in its present form probably dates from no earlier than the mid-eighteenth century.[38] One might still hope that the bulk of the account is roughly authentic, at least insofar as it represents a view of Kakugyō which does date from about the mid-seventeenth century; furthermore, since the legend of Kakugyō and Ieyasu is at least a plausible invention for the period in which Shōsan lived, this legend is discussed here *as though* it were contemporary with Shōsan. It is, of course, possible that more precise information awaits discovery.[39]

Kakugyō was born in Nagasaki in 1541. *Gotaigyō no maki* makes

---

[36] This name is derived from Asama Daimyōjin, an early name for the deity. The characters for *Asama* soon came to be given their Chinese-style reading, *Sengen*; and from this sound evolved two homophonous names written with different characters. The second of these (see Glossary) was the one most often used in the Fuji cult. In legend the deity was also known as Konohanasakuya-hime (the official deity of the Asama Shrine in Fujinomiya), or as Kaguya-hime (the heroine, for example, of *Taketori monogatari*); but the Fuji cult did not use these two names.

[37] Under the title *Kakugyō Tōbutsu Kū ki*, this has been published in *Minshū shūkyō no shisō*, ed. Murakami Shigeo and Yasumaru Yoshio (Iwanami, 1971), NST, 69:452–481.

[38] Inobe Shigeo, "Fuji no shinkō," in *Sangaku shūkyō no seiritsu to tenkai*, ed. Wakamori Tarō, Sangaku Shūkyō Shi Kenkyū Sōsho, vol. 1 (Meicho Shuppan, 1975), pp. 134–135; and Itō Kenkichi, "*Kakugyō Tōbutsu Kū ki* to Kakugyō kankei monjo ni tsuite," in NST, 69:646–648.

[39] Itō Kenkichi stated that a good deal of holograph material by Kakugyō does survive. These documents are kept very close by the branch of the Fuji cult that owns them; indeed, Itō and a colleague were the first researchers to be allowed to see them. Itō found apparently authentic documents written by Kakugyō and dated 1580. He saw nothing in these papers which suggested the connection with Ieyasu. Nonetheless, the legend of Kakugyō and Ieyasu may still date from the first half of the seventeenth century. The only firm evidence for even a distant connection between Ieyasu and Kakugyō is a still extant document which bears Ieyasu's seal and which exempts the village of Hitoana from taxation.

the doubtful claim that he was a Fujiwara,[40] and thus the name Tōbutsu would refer both to his Fujiwara descent and to his embodiment of the divine nature of Mt. Fuji. In his late teens, Kakugyō
began to lead the life of an ascetic and moved northward. Eventually,
he undertook a retreat in a cave in the province of Mutsu where he
had a dream vision of En no Gyōja. En no Gyōja asked him why he
had undertaken so arduous an ascesis. Kakugyō answered: "At the
wish of my father and mother. The world is at present in ceaseless
warfare, so that the very Sovereign, above, is ever uneasy in his
mind; and so that the people, below, are suffering. I wish to bring
comfort to these, but it is beyond human power to do so. Therefore
I have undertaken this great practice."[41] En no Gyōja told Kakugyō
that he should go to Mt. Fuji which, he assured Kakugyō, is the
"pillar of the world." Kakugyō accordingly went to Mt. Fuji and
began to live in the Hitoana, the celebrated cavern on the west side
of the mountain.

Kakugyō moved into the Hitoana about 1560. Apparently, no ascetic had lived in it before. Kakugyō's choice was significant, since
by moving into the Hitoana he was able to ignore and bypass the
established shugendō cult of Fuji.

Fuji had, of course, been regarded with awe since early times. The
present Asama Jinja in Fujinomiya (near the base of the mountain, to
the southwest) was founded in the early ninth century;[42] more per-
tinently, a brief account of Fuji which dates from about 877 makes it
clear that there were in those days pilgrims who engaged in ascetic
practices upon the mountain's slopes.[43] The medieval shugendō of
Fuji was founded by one Matsudai Shōnin who, in the mid-twelfth
century, built a chapel to Dainichi upon the summit.[44] Matsudai's
succession developed into a *yamabushi* (mountain ascetic) community
affiliated with the Honzan-ha of shugendō (that is, with the Shōgoin
in Kyoto, and hence with Tendai), and based at Murayama (presently
the hamlet of Moto-Murayama) on the southwest side of the mountain. Shugendō activity out of Murayama flourished greatly, and in
late Kamakura and Muromachi times Fuji became an object of pop-

[40] *Gotaigyō no maki (Kakugyō Tōbutsu Kū ki)*, in NST, 69:453.

[41] Ibid.

[42] Endō Hideo, "Fuji shinkō no seiritsu to Murayama shugen," in *Fuji, Ontake to
Chūbu reizan*, ed. Suzuki Shōei, Sangaku Shūkyō Shi Kenkyū Sōsho, vol. 9 (Meicho
Shuppan, 1977), p. 30. The shrine, roughly as it exists today, was built by Sakanoue
no Tamuramaro, who is credited also with having patronized the original construction
of Kiyomizudera in Kyoto.

[43] *Fujisan ki*, by Miyako no Yoshika (d. 879), in *Gunsho ruijū*, part 6, p. 968.

[44] Endō, "Fuji shinkō," p. 31.

ular pilgrimage as well. Murayama's downfall began in 1560 when Imagawa Yoshimoto, with whose interests it had unfortunately become identified, lost the battle of Okegahazama to the forces of Oda Nobunaga. The Takeda house then seized control of the area and naturally showed Murayama little favor. The pilgrimage out of Murayama was still alive in 1608,[45] but Murayama lost most of its land in a legal judgment rendered in 1679, and the line of yamabushi at Murayama, having somehow managed to linger on, was at last declared extinct by the Shōgoin about 1930. The life of the vigorous Fuji cult had long since passed to Kakugyō's spiritual heirs.

Much that is essential in shugendō thought and practice comes from outside Buddhism, but the Buddhist coloring of shugendō is obvious. Kakugyō, however, not only ignored the shugendō community on Fuji, but also dropped almost all Buddhist language from his discourse. Thus he was neither a yamabushi nor a Buddhist. Like Shōsan, he championed a fully respectable ideal from an independent stance. The object of his devotion was the mountain-as-deity, which he called Sengen Daibosatsu, or Sengen Dainichi. *Dainichi* in this latter title refers more to the sun than to the Buddha Mahāvairocana, and is a mere vestige of the medieval, shugendō usage. For Kakugyō, Mt. Fuji was the one God.

Kakugyō had a close relationship with Sengen, who taught him many things. One of these was a powerful gift of healing which Kakugyō put to use in the year 1620. An epidemic was then abroad in Edo, and Kakugyō was persuaded to come down to Edo with two disciples in order to relieve the people's distress. He was so successful that his activities came to the attention of the bakufu. Puzzled by both the person and teaching of this unusual man, the bakufu detained Kakugyō and his two disciples on the suspicion that they were Christians. The three were interrogated by the highest bakufu authorities in these matters, and when the officials demanded to know what deity Kakugyō worshiped, Kakugyō replied: "We reverently serve our two parents and the five grains; and morning and night we worship Fuji Sengen Daibosatsu, the sun, and the moon. We have no other objects of worship."[46] At last the officials were satisfied, and Kakugyō returned to the Hitoana. All this happened just a year or two before Shōsan became a monk.

Neither Kakugyō's devotion to the sun, moon, and stars (*sankō*, or the Three Luminaries) nor his service to "our two parents" differed from his devotion to Sengen. Another of the gifts which Ka-

[45] Ibid., p. 52.
[46] *Gotaigyō no maki*, in NST, 69:480.

kugyō received from Sengen consisted of special words and invocations which Kakugyō wrote with new, coined ideographs. These remained in the cult, giving the key formulas of the cult a most curiously barbaric air.[47] The chief of these new characters form a pair read together as *moto no chichihaha*, or our original father and mother. Such primordial parents likewise were Sengen. Kakugyō apparently made no particular distinction between one's biological parents and *moto no chichihaha*. Indeed, he ordered his two disciples to return home, after his death, that each might serve there his ancestors and parents and leave them descendants.[48] One is reminded of Shōsan's sending warriors back to their lord with the reminder that service is Buddhist practice.

Kakugyō's reverence for the "five grains" is not much developed in *Gotaigyō no maki*, but it is worth noting. "The five grains" in practice means rice, that is, food. On one of his mystical diagrams of Mt. Fuji, Kakugyō wrote a series of characters in which each character has on the left the rice radical, and on the right the elements sun, man, moon, water, earth, wind, fire, and *on* (gratitude toward a benefactor).[49] This is a clear statement that rice, the essential food, is fundamental to man as well as the cosmos, and that the entire natural and moral (I refer to the *on*) order participates in the nature of rice, an idea on which Jikigyō Miroku later expanded. Thus Kakugyō had nothing to say about enlightenment or salvation. The object of his "great practice" (*taigyō*) was peace and ease for all the people in the world, just as they are, each in his place. It was Fuji, or Sengen, that was for Kakugyō and for Jikigyō after him the source of abundance for all.

Kakugyō's mission was to bring this peace and abundance into being by calling down through his mighty practice Sengen's blessing. His practice consisted particularly of a *tsumetachi-gyō*, or tiptoe practice. Kakugyō stood in the Hitoana upon a piece of wood some twelve centimeters square (four *sun* and five *bu*). During this time he neither moved nor slept. In principle, the practice was interrupted only three times by day and three times by night for a rigorous bout of *mizugori*, repeated immersion in cold water. The significance of the practice appears in *Gotaigyō no maki*, where after having revealed to him another mystical diagram of Fuji, Sengen is said to have spoken to Kakugyō as follows: "The diagram which I have given you is the pillar of the world. Your great practice too is the pillar of the world.

[47] The principal of these is KŌ-KŪ-TAI-SOKU-MYŌ-Ō-SOKU-TAI-JIP-PŌ-KŌ-KŪ-SHIN-NA-GETSU-DAI-GA-NICHI. NST, 69:482–483.

[48] *Gotaigyō no maki*, in NST, 69:480.

[49] NST, 69:482.

Thus your practice of standing upon the square of wood is to be the pillar of the world."[50] In becoming identical with the mountain (Sengen), Kakugyō was bringing heaven and earth into attunement, thus making possible the birth of a stable order.

Ieyasu was essential for the success of this endeavor. It was he who, by Sengen's grace (according to the legend), actually carried out the work of establishing the peace. Indeed, Kakugyō's taigyō may be intentionally homophonous with taigyō, the "great work" of a dynastic founder.[51]

According to Gotaigyō no maki, Kakugyō's parents deeply lamented the chaotic state of the world in their time, and grieved that it was beyond their power to quell the disorder. They therefore prayed that heaven grant them a son who might achieve what they could not. That is why Kakugyō declared to En no Gyōja (in his vision) that he was practicing at the wish of his parents. At last, in the seventh month of 1583, Kakugyō was told by Sengen to expect the arrival of him whom heaven had designated to be "the military ruler (bushō) over generations to come."[52] Of course, it was Ieyasu who came. He entered the Hitoana accompanied only by the celebrated Tendai prelate Tenkai (1536–1643).[53] There Kakugyō gave him, at Sengen's behest, all the teachings which he himself had received from Sengen. Ieyasu returned in 1588 when he was on his way to take over the eight provinces of the Kantō,[54] and again in 1606 when he retired to Sunpu. On all these occasions he expressed the deepest gratitude to Kakugyō and to Sengen for his every success. Likewise, on each of these three occasions Kakugyō gave him instruction.

Kakugyō's instruction, as recorded, took the form of sermons. The first of the three sermons is the major one and offers the following thoughts:

(a) Mt. Fuji is the "pillar of the land," and the "root origin (kongen) from which the ten thousand things are born."

(b) Hence it is thanks to the divine might of the deity of Fuji that the "Offspring of the Divine Grandchild [the emperor] . . . rules from generation to generation."

[50] Gotaigyō no maki, in NST, 69:458.

[51] The tradition of the Fuji cult reads the characters of "great practice" as taigyō rather than as daigyō.

[52] Gotaigyō no maki, in NST, 69:473.

[53] This claim is, among other things, anachronistic. It was in 1589 that Ieyasu formed his close bond with Tenkai.

[54] 1588 is the date given by the text, but 1587 is the year when Ieyasu took charge of the Kantō. The date below (1606) is not given in the text, but can be inferred.

(c) Kakugyō has accomplished a most difficult practice "as the first condition for [Ieyasu's] rule."

(d) Ieyasu is winning the land not for himself, but for the sake of all the people.

(e) Heaven provides man with all he needs.

(f) Nonetheless, modesty and frugality are essential. "Outside of rice, salt, and water, all else is foolish pride." Again, "One who does not know this is not in accord with the mind of heaven."

(g) One who is thus attuned to the mind of heaven will flourish prosperously, and likewise his descendants for many generations. One who does not will be destroyed.

(h) When the shogun thus "devotedly practices humanity, righteousness, propriety, wisdom, filial piety, purity, loyalty, and good faith, . . . then all from the shogun on down will cease doing evil, and with upright hearts will enjoy prosperity."

(i) In this situation, the people shall live out their lives in security, and each person shall honorably "preserve his inherited station" (mi no hodo o mamori).

(j) As shogun, Ieyasu will be the "fountainhead of all things" (moromoro no minamoto), and likewise the "source of kami and Buddhas" (sho shinbutsu no moto). Thus his teaching will make him the "origin of the world's teaching" (sehō no kongen).

(k) When the shogun is the "source of kami and Buddhas," evil is crushed, and virtue rewarded; provincial governors and government officials are loyal to their lord; and the people observe the five relationships. Under these circumstances, the shogun fulfills the function (yaku) of, for example, Shakyamuni (Shakabutsu) himself.[55]

Shōsan might well have disagreed vigorously with some aspects of Kakugyō's speech, but in his rebuttal he would have said much the same thing. In the first place, he would have left out all mention of Mt. Fuji. Nonetheless, it is interesting that Kakugyō's affirmation of Fuji as the central pillar of the world coincides here with an affirmation of the centrality of Ieyasu's role. I am not aware of any such concrete valuation of a mountain, no matter how impressive, in shugendō thought. In shugendō, whatever mountain is the locus of practice may be felt to have the nature of a world axis, but one mountain's character as a world axis does not exclude another's; the thought is not connected with any idea of a concrete, exclusive, and temporal order. In this respect, the thought which is here represented as having

---

[55] The text of this sermon is in Gotaigyō no maki, in NST, 69:473–475.

been Kakugyō's resembles Shōsan's own attitude toward the shogunal role.

In the second place, Shōsan would have refused to recognize Kakugyō's claim to be at the source of Ieyasu's accomplishment. Conversely, he would have reminded the shogun (if the shogun had been listening) that unless he recognized and proclaimed the True Dharma, as urged by Shōsan, the future of the Tokugawa peace would indeed be in doubt. In other words, Shōsan might have claimed for himself the role played here by Kakugyō. Moreover, the content of the True Dharma was quite compatible with what Kakugyō proposed.

Shōsan would surely have agreed with this affirmation of the value of selfless labor for the common good, both on the part of the shogun and the people. Shōsan, like Kakugyō, held such selfless devotion to be essential, and he developed at much greater length the importance of each person's following his own calling and fulfilling, for the good of all, the social role which had fallen to his lot. Nonetheless, Shōsan did not emphasize, as Kakugyō did, the prosperity that the good man would achieve both for himself and his descendants, and he mentioned wealth only in connection with merchants. He promised instead the spiritual riches of "great freedom."

The most striking parallel between Shōsan and Kakugyō lies in Kakugyō's statement that the shogun should be the "fountainhead of all things" and the "source of the kami and Buddhas." The word *minamoto* (fountainhead) is precisely the one Shōsan used in the passage quoted previously in this essay:

> For swords there is the Hon'ami line, men who can tell forged inscriptions from genuine ones, and determine the value accordingly. Calligraphy too has a standard authority (minamoto), so that one knows whether or not an item is the real thing. All the arts are the same. That's why they last. The thing is that government (bakufu) decrees concerning them are correct. Buddhism alone has no standard authority, and no discerning supervision. All we have are people's arbitrary versions of Buddhism, and the Buddha's teaching is dead. This pains my whole being. It's because the government consistently singles Buddhism out for neglect, and lets people be as they please.

Here Shōsan was decrying not only an indifference on the part of the bakufu toward Buddhism itself, but a failure to act decisively to achieve its own ideals. Therefore, Shōsan continued on:

> My chest is bursting with the desire to put a proposal on this matter before the authorities, but it's turned out that Heaven

hasn't allowed me to do so. When our present Lord (Ietsuna, 1641–1680) turns fifteen, perhaps he'll take the proper measures. When he's twenty, a direct appeal may perhaps move him.[56]

Shōsan did indeed believe that the shogun should act as a Shakabutsu. With respect to the birth of this same shogun, Ietsuna, Shōsan once told the following story:

> I was at Sogi-no-yu in Mino when there came the announcement that the shogun had an heir. "Aha, this is very auspicious," I boldly remarked. "Right off, the boy has a tiger, rabbit, dragon, and snake in sequence. What sort of sage has just come into the world? This Great Shogun has certainly brought ample virtue with him!" Surprised, the people around me asked me what I meant. I said "Well, His Lordship (Hidetada) has not been well in recent years, so that everyone has been troubled, from the hereditary vassals, to the daimyo of each province, and on down to the humblest folk. In the remotest areas people have been as though waiting for something, and anxious. Then, "Hooray! An heir is born!" came the news, and the whole land was at peace. Suddenly men's minds were still. Doesn't this mean he brought peace to the land with his birthcry? Can you imagine the power to bring peace to the realm at the very moment of your birth? In what era will you find a lord like that? His reign is bound to be one of great peace.

Shōsan then noted that his statement had come to the ears of the shogun himself, who had been "extremely pleased." Shōsan concluded: "Nevertheless, I cling to my own life. I'd like to see this Lord raise up Buddhism before I die."[57] Shōsan was close enough to the bakufu to know that things had not gone quite the way Kakugyō had promised to Ieyasu. His faith was lively, however, and he did remain hopeful.

Jikigyō Miroku

Jikigyō Miroku was no one even to dream of addressing the shogun. Born in the province of Ise in 1671, he went at age twelve or thirteen to seek his fortune in Edo, where he lived through the Genroku period (1688–1704) as a small townsman. He was an oil seller of such fabled honesty that he would scrape the barrel at each delivery, lest his customer be cheated of a single drop. By his death, in 1733,

[56] *Roankyō*, 3:123; *Zenshū*, p. 274; *Selected Writings*, p. 188.
[57] *Roankyō*, 3:65; *Zenshū*, p. 257; *Selected Writings*, pp. 171–172.

Jikigyō achieved an apotheosis which could well have boggled the mind of Saikaku himself. Shōsan, certainly, when he addressed his moral instructions to the artisans and the merchants, could hardly have imagined what wonders peace might eventually produce.

Surviving documents make it possible to determine Jikigyō's career with accuracy. Letters and notes by him have been preserved. They are difficult to understand and are written in poorly spelled Japanese. Jikigyō, as he admitted, had no learning whatsoever. Certain writings of his are nonetheless revered in the Fuji cult, though the only one published is entitled *Sanjūichinichi no maki*.[58] This document contains Jikigyō's last teaching. Perhaps because it was transcribed from Jikigyō's oral instruction by a disciple, it is not as badly written as Jikigyō's letters, but the Fuji cult was assuredly not a literary movement.

Jikigyō Miroku's unusual name deserves comment. No doubt because of Kakugyō's example, names consisting of a single character followed by the element *-gyō* (practice of) were common in the Fuji *kō*.[59] In the present case, the element *jiki* (eating) reveals a concern with food. The name Miroku looks like the Japanese version of the name of the Buddha Maitreya, curiously spelled. Indeed, the thought of Maitreya does figure in the name, but this Miroku is not the canonical one. Instead, it is the Miroku of Japanese folk religion, a deity of future plenty who was evoked with particular urgency in times of famine and whose connection with Buddhism is remote.[60] Moreover, there was a prior link between Mt. Fuji and Miroku. Despite Matsudai Shōnin's clear acknowledgment of Dainichi, and the lingering presence of Dainichi in Kakugyō's name for the deity (Sengen Dainichi), the summit was also the "Inner Sanctum of the Tosotsu (Tushita) Heaven of Miroku" (*Tosotsu no naiin*).[61]

[58] In NST, 69:424–451.

[59] The Japanese term for the Tokugawa and modern cult of Fuji is Fuji kō, as distinguished from Fuji shugen, the principally medieval shugendō cult of Fuji. A *kō* is a confraternity, or sodality, of lay devotees. Fuji kō is thus a collective term.

[60] Miyata Noboru, "Fuji shinkō to Miroku," in *Sangaku shūkyō to minkan shinkō no kenkyū*, ed. Sakurai Tokutarō, Sangaku Shūkyō Shi Kenkyū Sōsho, vol. 6 (Meicho Shuppan, 1976), pp. 292–299. See also Miyata Noboru, *Miroku shinkō no kenkyū* (Miraisha, 1975), chap. 4, especially pp. 155–164.

[61] One song sung by the Fuji kō, and attributed to Kakugyō, celebrates Fuji as the "Pure Land of Amida" (Miyata, "Fuji shinkō to Miroku," p. 290). One mountain could easily support more than one paradise. At the close of the Nō play *Fujisan*, the *tsure* (Kaguya-hime) ascends to the Naiin (the Inner Sanctum of the Tosotsu Heaven) of Miroku, for Fuji, like many other mountains, was associated with Miroku. Even so small a mountain as Kasuga-yama near Nara could support at once the paradises of Amida, Kannon, and Miroku.

Jikigyō's spelling of the name Miroku (which he received, spelling and all, from Sengen) is highly significant. *Mi* means oneself, or myself, but it also means *mibun*, one's station in life. *Roku*, the word for a samurai's stipend, is the material largess which one receives from above; from a lord, from heaven, or, as in this case, from Sengen. It is also a pun on *roku*, flat, or straight. Thus the name Miroku evokes a plenty to be enjoyed in average life by the average, but true and honest, man.[62] In his last days Jikigyō said: "This teaching of miroku has nothing to do with honoring my own name. You are miroku when you have removed all evil and are perfectly straight, and when [all things] are reflected [without distortion] in the mirror of the heart."[63] This statement also implies that what the clear mirror of the heart reflects is then miroku, the true teaching of Sengen. In other words, this true teaching was Miroku, the (transpersonal) speaker himself.

The Fuji cult had been based in Edo since the latter years of Kakugyō's successor, Nichigyō Nichigan. Nichigyō was apparently a paper merchant. The trade followed by Getsugan (d. 1689), the fourth-generation sucessor, is not recorded, but it is worth noting that in 1682, he, like Kakugyō before him, was interrogated on the suspicion that he was a Christian. The fifth-generation successor, Getsugyō Sōjū, was a tobacco dealer. He was also Jikigyō Miroku's master.[64]

Jikigyō Miroku became a Fuji devotee when he was seventeen. No doubt by virtue of the same hard work and frugality which he later was to preach, he achieved considerable success in business. He also married and had a family, as was normal for a Fuji devotee. Jikigyō was assiduous in the cult and never missed the regular annual ascent of Fuji. Indeed, it is recorded that when he and his kō lodged at the Yoshida-guchi (on the north side of the mountain), he performed his devotions so loudly and so late into the night that his fellow kō members were unable to sleep. At last they complained to the *oshi* (guide) in charge of their quarters. When Jikigyō refused to desist, he was expelled from the building. Unfortunately, his reputation was such that no other oshi would have him. Only one Tanabe Jūrōemon was at last willing to take him in. This Tanabe became an important disciple and attended Jikigyō during his last days.[65]

[62] The meaning of *Miroku* is discussed by Iwashina Kosaburō, "Sōsei ki no Fuji kō: Kakugyō to Miroku," in *Fuji, Ontake to Chūbu reizan*, p. 72; and by Miyata, "Fuji shinkō to Miroku," pp. 301–302.

[63] *Sanjūichinichi no maki*, in NST, 69:444.

[64] The lineage from Kakugyō to Jikigyō is given by Inobe, "Fuji no shinkō," pp. 144–146.

[65] Inobe, "Fuji no shinkō," pp. 150–151.

By the time of this incident, Jikigyō had probably already done the inevitable: he had given away all of his personal wealth to the clerks and the manager of his business. He then continued to support himself and his family from his rounds as an individual peddler, and he devoted every effort to spreading the Fuji faith.[66] Starting about 1730, he received a series of overwhelming visions from Sengen. It was then that he took the name Miroku and began to announce the coming of the Age of Miroku.[67] In 1732 his house burned down, and having lost everything, he and his family moved to the home of a disciple. Shortly thereafter he went traveling and saw everywhere evidence of misrule and injustice. An account which he left contains sharp criticism of the bakufu and states that what he had written was "in the spirit of the book by Minamoto no Muneharu."[68] The work Jikigyō referred to is *Onchi seiyō* by Tokugawa Muneharu, who just the year before (1731) had become daimyo of Owari (Nagoya).[69]

Perhaps it was after this tour that Jikigyō had another vision from Sengen, in which Sengen instructed him to advance by five years (from 1738 to 1733) his plan for the accomplishment of the crowning gesture of his life. Jikigyō meant to achieve perfect union with Sengen by fasting to death on the summit of Mt. Fuji.

In the fourth moon of 1733, Jikigyō announced his plan in a long letter to Tanabe Jūrōemon. He said that he would start from Edo on the tenth day of the sixth moon, arrive at the Yoshida-guchi on the twelfth, and start up the mountain on the thirteenth. Indeed, this is exactly what he did. The complete list of what he had carried up the mountain with him, and of what he wore, may still be perused.[70] The key item in the list was a portable shrine (*zushi*), some three feet high, which had been carried on horseback, wrapped in matting, all the way from Edo. Jikigyō sat in this shrine during the thirty-one days of his fast, thus going far beyond the "autolatry" of Matsudaira Sadanobu and Yamazaki Ansai as described by Herman Ooms.[71] Unfortunately, he was *not* able to sit in it on the summit of Fuji. It is both comic and tragic that the Sengen (or Asama) Shrine in Fujino-

---

[66] There is a story that thanks to these rounds, he was personally acquainted with Tokugawa Mitsukuni, and that he frequented the Mito mansion in Edo. See Inobe, "Fuji no shinkō," pp. 161–162.

[67] Miyata, "Fuji shinkō to Miroku," p. 298.

[68] A long passage from this *O-soegaki no maki* is quoted by Iwashina, "Sōsei ki no Fuji kō," p. 73.

[69] According to Iwashina ("Sōsei ki no Fuji kō," p. 73), Muneharu had distributed a copy of this work to each of the *han* retainers when he became daimyo.

[70] It is given in its entirety by Inobe, "Fuji no shinkō," pp. 152–153.

[71] Herman Ooms, *Charismatic Bureaucrat: A Political Biography of Matsudaira Sadanobu* (Chicago: University of Chicago Press, 1975), pp. 43–46.

miya, which by then had jurisdiction over the top, should at the last minute have forbidden him to do so. Jikigyō had to settle for the Eboshi-iwa, a spot just above the seventh station on the mountain's north side.

Jikigyō thus fulfilled his vow to "stand in the Inner Sanctum of the Tosotsu Heaven, and to save all sentient beings."[72] While so enshrined, he was possessed almost continuously by Sengen. He took only one cup of snow water per day, and each day addressed to Tanabe Jūrōemon the teachings which Tanabe recorded in *Sunjūichinichi no maki*. Jikigyō had predicted that he would survive thirty-one days. On the tenth day of the seventh moon, the twenty-ninth day, he noted the fine weather which had prevailed ever since he had begun his fast, and ascribed this to the blessings of Sengen.[73] On the thirteenth day, the last, he started his teaching by saying, "I have temporarily appeared in the human realm."[74] When his instruction was over, he urged his disciple to pass on the teaching and said, "Well now I am going home." Then he rinsed his mouth, recited the prayers and litanies of Fuji, and at last closed his eyes. "It is beyond doubt," Tanabe wrote, "that Sengen had entered into him. I wept, closed the doors [of the shrine], heaped stones over it, and made my way down the mountain."[75]

Jikigyō's death had a tremendous impact on the cult. People were awestruck, and the cult grew rapidly from then on.[76] Indeed, some

[72] *Sanjūichinichi no maki*, in NST, 69:426.

[73] Ibid., p. 447.

[74] Ibid., p. 449.

[75] Ibid., p. 450. However, it appears from a detailed account written by Jikigyō's disciple and patron in Edo that Jikigyō did *not* actually die on the thirteenth day of the seventh moon, the predicted day. According to this account, Tanabe returned to the shrine on the sixteenth, to say farewell. He thereupon heard a voice from within the shrine (now completely covered with stones), bidding him return the next day for a last injunction. Early the next morning, therefore, Tanabe came back. The voice then urged him to grasp Jikigyō's four cardinal principles: uprightness, compassion, kindness, and frugality. After a silence, Tanabe asked if there would be no further need of him, and if he might go now. There was no answer. After asking again, and again receiving no answer, Tanabe went back down the mountain (Inobe, "Fuji no Shinkō," pp. 153–154).

[76] Regarding the awe in which people held Jikigyō, Iwashina ("Sōsei ki no Fuji kō," p. 72) quoted a passage from the diary of Itō Sangyō (d. 1809), an important successor. In somewhat free translation this passage says: "Everyone nowadays oohs and aahs about the Eboshi-iwa, but in Miroku's own time no one had any idea what he had in mind. They say he was a very difficult man. . . . Now everyone who has heard the least word about him is full of Miroku this, Miroku that. But if Miroku came back to life right now, they would find him a difficult man indeed, and quite unpleasant to be with; and they would have even less to do with him than before."

of the Fuji kō came to consider Jikigyō rather than Kakugyō as their ultimate founder.

Jikigyō's thought as expressed in *Sanjūichinichi no maki* can be summarized as follows. To begin with, Jikigyō asserted the superiority of Japan over all the other countries, calling Japan the origin of the sun and moon, of the four directions, and of the four seasons.[77] Of course, it was Fuji which was the center of Japan. Thus Jikigyō called Fuji the "pivot-stone of the Three Lands," and the "unitary Buddha (*ichibutsu ittai*) where appear the sun and moon."[78] Again, Fuji being the origin of all things, he said: "In the Inner Sanctum of the Tosotsu Heaven of the countless worlds, there is a single jewel (*tama*). This true jewel (*magatama*) becomes form. Lord Miroku teaches that it is the origin of light in the east."[79]

Thus it is natural that Jikigyō should have said, "The Mountain (Fuji) is called the Bosatsu (bodhisattva)."[80] There is a tradition that another name for Fuji is Kokushūzan, or mountain of heaped-up grain.[81] Jikigyō gave this thought great weight. He taught that it is above all rice (the essential food), which is both the product and the nature of Mt. Fuji. He therefore called rice "the true Bosatsu" (*makoto no bosatsu*), writing "Bosatsu" with the character for "rice."[82] Thus he held that the essential body of Sengen/Miroku, and, at the same time, the essential blessing bestowed by Sengen/Miroku, is that of food. If so, then by fasting into complete union with Sengen, Jikigyō Miroku died to feed the world.[83]

Since man thus eats "the true Bosatsu" every day, he comes to participate fully in the Bosatsu nature. Indeed, Jikigyō taught with respect to human birth that the life force of the Bosatsu which the mother eats becomes (in her womb) a shining light, which is then born as a child.[84] The human realm into which this child is born is the Tokugawa world. There is no thought of open disorder in it, for the time of Kakugyō and of Shōsan was already distant; nor is there any idea that it might not last forever. On the other hand, there is no talk either of the shogun. The ordering principle for Jikigyō's

---

[77] *Sanjūichinichi no maki*, in NST, 69:427.

[78] Ibid.

[79] Ibid., p. 443.

[80] Ibid., p. 427.

[81] I do not know the origin of this tradition, but I have seen its traces in more than one account of Fuji.

[82] See, for example, *Sanjūichinichi no maki*, in NST, 69:428.

[83] Miyata develops this theme in "Fuji shinkō to Miroku."

[84] *Sanjūichinichi no maki*, in NST, 69:428.

world was not an active, conquering leader but a mightily still mountain—Kakugyō without Ieyasu, as it were.[85]

What particularly concerned Jikigyō, therefore, was maintenance of stability and harmony. Thus he advocated ideals of right conduct which were quite noncontroversial in Tokugawa times, though he did give to these certain touches of the Fuji cult itself.

Jikigyō urged the faithful to practice perfect filial piety, "in complete accord with the Way of Heaven."[86] Elsewhere he said, "To be fully filial toward one's father and mother is to give full reverence to Sun-and-Moon Sengen Daibosatsu."[87] Jikigyō stressed particularly that the estate which one has received from one's parents is a "borrowed thing" (azukarimono) temporarily entrusted to one by heaven; and that equally in the case of the wealth which one has amassed, it is the "function of man" (ningen no yaku) to pass this estate on intact to his descendants.[88] Moreover, he listed the true essentials of right action as follows: compassion (jihi), kindness (nasake), helpfulness (tasukari), and frugality (fusoku). Virtuous conduct guided by these principles will be rewarded by rebirth in a position of greater wealth and power (umaremasu).

The key to such success is thus diligent attention to one's proper work in the world. Jikigyō often spoke of the four classes, confirming both the hierarchical distinctions between them and their ultimate unity.

That which is in accord with the honoring of heaven and earth is the [system of the] four classes: warriors, farmers, artisans, and merchants. In their work they interpenetrate and mutually assist one another, so that they are the foundation for the ordering of all things. . . . All [from top to bottom] are fundamentally one.[89]

Moreover, he insisted that since all four classes depend for their livelihood upon rice, "the true Bosatsu," the fundamental character of Sengen in the world is in fact visible to all.[90]

Thus Jikigyō did not actually encourage specialized religious pursuits. In this he manifested a similar contradiction between personal life and teaching, and for much the same reason, to Suzuki Shōsan.

---

[85] This is not to say that Fuji was not still volcanically active. Indeed, an important eruption took place in 1707, and the skies over Edo were darkened with ash.

[86] Sanjūichinichi no maki, in NST, 69:430.

[87] Ibid., p. 435.

[88] Ibid., p. 431.

[89] Ibid., p. 435.

[90] Ibid.

Of course, his Fuji cult was entirely a lay movement without special priesthood. Yet a devotee like Jikigyō could give an enormous amount of time to religious work and act, in fact, very much like a priest or monk. On this score, Jikigyō urged the four classes to adhere diligently to their work. He did not exclude pilgrimages to holy sites (such as Fuji), but he taught that people should not go to excess in this direction. "The path of today's household work," he said, is far more important."[91] However, he did acknowledge a genuine role for the deities which people might judiciously visit. He said: "The clan deities (*ujigami*) enshrined in the villages, and the [deities of the] lofty mountains to which people go on pilgrimage clear away the demons and disasters which afflict the people; and Sun-and-Moon (Sengen) has made them officers (yakunin) to guard mankind."[92] Shōsan had already defined Buddhist priests as yakunin, and the members of the four classes as well. Jikigyō took the thought one step further and pressed even the deities into a kind of government service, as appointees of the "pivot-stone of the Three Lands."

The Fuji cult affirmed the full equality of women as participants in the cult. Jikigyō taught that menstruation does not render a woman impure.[93] While Shōsan, who included women in his teaching, did not address this issue, he did give voice to the traditional Buddhist view that women are utterly governed by desire and thus deep in bad karma, and it was only after expressing this view (in language taken largely from *Tsurezuregusa*) that he reminded his reader, "Women are the mothers of Buddhas, and are absolutely not to be slandered."[94] Jikigyō, on the other hand, cited the traditional view only to state immediately that it was wrong. "There is nothing evil about women," he said, "and there is no reason to call them evil."[95] Furthermore, both for men and women Jikigyō asserted that no arduous purification was necessary before climbing the mountain, and that except for the night before the climb, devotees were also free to eat fish and meat.[96] Such statements probably represented no great in-

---

[91] Ibid., p. 431.

[92] Ibid.

[93] Ibid., pp. 428–429. This is not a completely new thought in Japanese religion. There is a legend, associated no doubt with the Jishū, that when the Heian poetess Izumi Shikibu, on pilgrimage to Kumano, came within sight of the main shrine, she discovered that she was menstruating. She therefore assumed that she could go no further, lest she pollute the shrine. The deity, however, sent her a message to proceed, and assured her that her condition involved no pollution.

[94] *Mōanjō, Zenshū*, p. 57; *Selected Writings*, p. 47. See *Tsurezuregusa*, no. 107.

[95] *Sanjūichinichi no maki*, p. 436. He did not, however, question their conventionally defined place in society.

[96] Ibid., p. 445.

novation with respect to the cult in Jikigyō's time, but the rules for the medieval shugendō of Fuji had undoubtedly been quite otherwise. Jikigyō's views reveal the trend toward secularization of religion so evident in Tokugawa times.

Yonaoshi

Herman Ooms, in his study of Matsudaira Sadanobu, describes the varied disasters which afflicted Japan in the 1770s and 1780s and the rash of peasant uprisings which accompanied them.[97] These uprisings were due not only to natural calamities, but also to excessive taxation and mismanagement encouraged by the economic difficulties of the samurai class and of the bakufu and *han* themselves. Under these circumstances, Matsudaira Sadanobu, whose reputation is that of an exceedingly orthodox Confucian statesman, came to appear to the people of his han as a savior and was greeted by them with these words: "Gratitude for having redressed the world" (*yo no naka o naoshi kudasaru katajikenasa yo*).[98] In a time of poverty and distress, Sadanobu had restored security and thus seemed to have accomplished locally what in those years was the object of faith or hope for many: yonaoshi, or "renewal of the world."

Yonaoshi was obviously not far from the spirit of the Fuji cult as exemplified by Jikigyō Miroku, and in the late eighteenth century this tendency of the cult surfaced for all to see. Jikigyō himself may have announced privately the coming of the age of Miroku, but he never mentioned the idea in *Sanjūichinichi no maki*. Those who followed him, however, developed the cult into a millenarian movement which proclaimed the Age of Miroku more and more insistently. At last in 1789, one Soyo, the wife of a cult leader, addressed to the bakufu a petition which contained this passage:

> It has not yet reached the ears of those in authority that Miroku is initiating his age, and renewing all things, for as long as this world shall last, and for as long as heaven and earth shall endure. We therefore beg that the Age of Miroku be proclaimed. The documents pertaining to Miroku are on the north side of Mt. Fuji (the Yoshida-guchi). If these are requisitioned, and the teachings of Miroku examined, their correctness will stand forth, and there will be no more calamitous rains or droughts. The initiating of the Age of Miroku is our most earnest prayer. We

[97] Ooms, *Charismatic Bureaucrat*, pp. 7–8.
[98] Ibid., p. 63.

therefore beg that [the bakufu] undertake to proclaim the Age of Miroku.[99]

Contemplating these words, one seems to hear Suzuki Shōsan, some 140 years before, speaking of how he burned to convince the shogun to proclaim the True Dharma. Shōsan, too, was anxious, for he feared that the great promise of the Tokugawa achievement might not be fully realized. Like Shōsan, Soyo appealed to the bakufu to proclaim the great and, to her mind, obvious truth which would restore peace to the world forever. Perhaps this was the same truth which the bakufu, with all its responsibilities, had indeed been trying to grasp through the study of Confucian thought ever since the days of Ieyasu. If this is the idea which dawned on Shōsan in his own last days, one can understand his distress. According to a disciple who spoke just after Shōsan's death, "When people asked him lately about his illness, he wouldn't answer the question. He'd just ask, 'Why isn't there anything different about Buddhism? Why isn't there anything different about Buddhism?' Really, that's all he said up to the very day he passed away."[100]

Confucianism proper is far from the discourse, let alone the actions, of the three men discussed in this essay. Yet these three, and others more or less like them, shared with avowed Confucian thinkers a close interest in public peace. In this, I maintain, they were not under any particular Confucian influence. Instead, they were addressing in other ways the same concerns which moved so many to study Confucian philosophy. It is obvious that Confucianism was the dominant mode of thought in Tokugawa times. However, it is also obvious that the issues of social order and ethical living can be approached from other points of view than the distinctively or parochially Confucian. The three subjects of this paper did so, and it is not impossible to imagine that in another time, or in another land, their ideas might themselves have become, or have represented, an orthodoxy. But if they might have disagreed with the Confucians intellectually (or the Confucians with them), they and the Confucians surely were in substantial emotional accord. The good they wanted for their world was quite similar. Like the Confucians, they took the structure of their society as a given, and addressed much of their teaching to the general problem of keeping this society running smoothly. For Suzuki Shōsan and Kakugyō Tōbutsu in the early seventeenth century, Ieyasu was an impressive leader indeed, and both (in fact or in legend)

[99] Quoted by Miyata, "Fuji shinkō to Miroku," p. 286.
[100] Roankyō, 3:133; Zenshū, p. 278; Selected Writings, p. 191.

proposed to him and to his successors principles to foster the long life of his shogunal dynasty. Jikigyō, in the early eighteenth century, appealed to quite standard social virtues; even Soyo, in 1789 (the year the Bastille fell in Paris), believed that the bakufu could somehow, by proclamation, make Miroku's renewal of the world a sensible fact. It is true, however, that the Fuji kō were banned many times by the bakufu in the late-eighteenth and early-nineteenth centuries.[101] No doubt the bakufu saw in this trumpeting of a new and more perfect age subversive possibilities of which the Fuji cult members themselves may not have been aware. Meanwhile, one wonders what Shōsan, tough-minded as he was, would have been doing and saying in Bakumatsu times. It would have been like him to champion the bakufu's own ideals against the entrenched interests of the bakufu itself, without quite seeing the conflict between the two.

[101] Miyata, "Fuji shinkō to Miroku," pp. 285–286.

FIVE

CHARACTERISTIC REPONSES TO CONFUCIANISM IN TOKUGAWA LITERATURE

BY DONALD KEENE

The literature of the Tokugawa period might be said to have begun with Confucianism. The special character of this literature was prefigured by an event of 1599. In that year, Fujiwara Seika (1561–1619), a twelfth-generation descendant of the great Fujiwara Teika, at the request of the warlord Akamatsu Hidemichi, punctuated some of the Chinese classics for reading in Japanese. This was not the first introduction of Confucianism to Japan—Confucian studies had of course been pursued in Japan since the sixth and seventh centuries A.D. at the latest—but never before had the correct way of reading the classics been made available to persons who were not in a select circle of disciples. Knowledge of the Confucian texts was transmitted as esoteric learning and was a rare privilege, open only to the chosen few, at times only to members of the Kiyohara and Nakahara families. This manner of transmission was typical of Japan, where the secrets of each branch of art and learning tended to be passed down from father to oldest son or from master to senior disciple, rather than made available for all to study. The insistence on lineage was as much true of Confucian scholars as of Shingon monks or *Waka* poets. Often the secrets that were so jealously guarded proved, when they were finally revealed, to be no more than trivia. Nevertheless, without a knowledge of the secrets, no man could count himself a full-fledged master, whether of Confucianism, the Way of Poetry, or the Way of Nō. When Fujiwara Seika broke the tradition of secrecy, even to the limited extent of punctuating texts, he was in effect ending medieval traditions and opening the way to the popular that would typify the Tokugawa period.

Other men, inspired by Seika's example, followed him in the work of enlightenment. In 1603 Hayashi Razan, who had been studying the Ch'eng-Chu texts of Neo-Confucianism at the Kenninji, a Zen monastery in Kyoto, decided to offer public lectures for the benefit of young Confucian scholars and physicians. Razan, though he was later to be known as among the most conservative of Neo-Confucian philosophers, was enthusiastic about nonesoteric transmission of learning, possibly as the result of influence from his teacher, Fujiwara Seika. He persuaded Matsunaga Teitoku (1571–1643), a scholar of Japanese literature, to join him in the public lectures. Teitoku was reluctant to take the unprecedented step of lecturing publicly on teachings which he had privately received, and only after Razan's father and uncle had joined in the persuasion, urging Teitoku to make Razan's experiment respectable by participating, did he at last consent. The texts that Teitoku lectured on, *Tsurezuregusa* (Essays in Idleness) and *Hyakunin isshu* (One Hundred Poems by One Hundred Poets), would be of enormous importance in the education carried out in the Tokugawa period, but until this time they had been relatively little known, largely because of the secrecy with which the commentaries had been transmitted.

Of course, the new approach to learning represented by the public lectures did not put an end to the secret traditions, but the characteristic literary arts of the Tokugawa period were remarkably free of the old secrecy. Matsuo Bashō (1644–1694), for example, left no secrets to his chosen disciples, though some were later forged; furthermore, in contrast to Nō, with its many closely guarded secrets, the plays of Chikamatsu Monzaemon (1653–1725) were transmitted without an aura of mystery. Although much of Tokugawa literature, especially during the first half of the period, was written by members of the samurai class, it was prevailingly popular, and the social status of writers was not of great importance when it came to receiving and transmitting knowledge of how to write or perform the texts.

It may seem strange that Confucianism should have driven the first wedge into the medieval tradition of secrecy. The Tokugawa regime, with its mania for orderliness, had looked to Confucianism to maintain the existing state of things; but Hayashi Razan, though he soon afterward became a lecturer to Tokugawa Ieyasu, was (initially at least) so enthusiastic about Neo-Confucian texts that he wished to encourage all capable men to study them and to "investigate things" in the manner advocated by the founders of Neo-Confucianism.

Confucianism assumed many forms in Tokugawa literature. First of all, it was an integral part of the Chinese culture which enjoyed such enormous prestige at the time. Works written by a Japanese which incorporated Chinese themes generally contained an admixture of Confucianism. The extreme respect for Chinese letters was most pronounced in the poetry and prose which Japanese wrote in classical Chinese. The composition of *Kanshi* (Chinese verse), which continued well into the Meiji era, was of as great importance to Tokugawa scholars as writing Waka had been to the Heian courtiers. A good Kanshi, even if it contained no doctrinal message, had to reveal familiarity with Chinese literature by means of allusions that evoked a kind of resonance and gave depth to the poet's words. The Japanese tried imagining themselves as Chinese gentlemen-scholars of the past. However little inclined a man might be to writing poetry, he felt obliged to live up to his role of gentleman-scholar and to demonstrate his proficiency at handling Chinese metrics and rhyme. Insofar as his compositions were not merely exercises, the sentiments expressed, appropriate to a Confucianist who knew no taint of worldly gain, were serene.

A Japanese who wrote classical Chinese, when not seeking to create an impression of dignity, would sometimes parody his subjects by treating familiar Japanese materials in the imposing language of the Chinese classics. The Japanese were, of course, well aware that Chinese literature included not only the works of philosophy and history which the Confucians rated at the summit of literature, but poetry that expressed emotions of a kind not generally associated with Confucian philosophy. Indeed, some Japanese also knew works of popular Chinese literature, even pornography, but this knowledge rarely intruded into the patterns of thought of Japanese intellectuals. Rather in the manner of some contemporary Japanese who, even if they know Western literature, suppose that the Europeans and Americans, unlike themselves, are dispassionately rational in affairs of the heart, the Japanese of the Tokugawa period tended to think of the Chinese as learned and eminently dignified but lacking in Japanese spontaneity. Confucian philosophy, insofar as it openly appears in Tokugawa literature, tends to be cold rather than warm, appealing to the intellect rather than the heart.

Confucian sentiments, in diluted or distinctively Japanese adaptations, are found in many varieties of Tokugawa literature. Perhaps the most striking examples are in the plays of Chikamatsu, which have often been described in terms of the principles of *giri* (duty) and *ninjō* (human feelings) which they are said to embody. These terms, though borrowed from Chinese and considered to be essential elements of Confucian teachings, acquired strongly Japanese meanings. Minamoto Ryōen has distinguished two varieties of giri, the first being the natural human response to another person's kindness, the second a "cold" giri which often is based on the fear of what people may think or is dictated by an awareness of obligations that have to be carried out, much though they go against natural feelings.[1] The

---

[1] Minamoto Ryōen, *Giri to ninjō* (Chūō Kōronsha, 1969), p. 49.

conflict between social obligations and personal desires is indeed a conspicuous feature of Chikamatsu's plays, but however strong the claims of giri may be, human feelings always triumph over other considerations. That is why so many of Chikamatsu's plays end with the death of the protagonists; the only lasting victories of ninjō are in the "other world."

The victories of ninjō are chronicled in Chikamatsu's *sewamono* (domestic tragedies), in which the unhappy lovers, despairing of any solution to their problems in this world, choose what seems to be an infinitely desirable escape from their difficulties—dying together, confident of rebirth on the same lotus in Amida's paradise. Chikamatsu's preoccupation with the conflicting claims of giri and ninjō inevitably deprived his sewamono of some of the variety we expect of a great dramatist. Ever since the 1880s, he had been called the Japanese Shakespeare—by some people, anyway—but he clearly belongs to a much later stage of world history than the first Shakespeare. His heroes are not royal personages like Hamlet or King Lear, men who are free to live according to or opposed to society as they please, but little men who have no choice but to exist within a social framework. In this sense they are more Confucian than Shakespeare's heroes, but each of them, in the end, can no longer accommodate himself to what society expects of him, and therefore has no choice but to die.

In some of the plays the motivation is inadequate and the audience may be left wondering if the love suicides were really necessary. If, say, someone in *Sonezaki shinjū* (Love Suicides at Sonezaki) could have induced the wicked Kuheiji to confess the truth about the money he borrowed from Tokubei, neither Tokubei nor Ohatsu would have had to die. Indeed, in a revised version of the play, Kuheiji was made to reveal what actually happened, but, typically for the Japanese theater, his confession came too late to save the star-crossed lovers. The audience at the Japanese theater would have felt cheated without the one resolution to worldly problems that seemed absolute. *Love Suicides at Sonezaki*, despite this failing, is a beautiful and successful work because Chikamatsu was able, thanks to his magnificent poetry and the many deft touches he gave to the drama, to impart to the unfortunate lovers—a clerk in a soy shop and a prostitute—something of the grandeur of tragic figures, but this is still, of course, a far cry from the Shakespearean counterparts.

In Chikamatsu's best works, such as *Love Suicides at Amijima*, the factors of giri and ninjō create an impression of inevitability. Jihei's love for the prostitute Koharu is complicated by his feelings of giri toward his wife, Osan. This giri stems from real affection and is not the "cold" giri imposed by a marriage contract. Similarly, Osan's love for Jihei is complicated by a sense of giri toward Koharu who, at Osan's request, has refused to join Jihei in a lovers' suicide. When Osan realizes that Koharu may kill herself, now that she has been deprived of the joy of dying with the man she loves, she is far from feeling satisfied that a rival for Jihei's affection is out of the way; Osan insists that Jihei buy up Koharu's contract and free her from the licensed quarter, even though she knows in advance that if Jihei brings Koharu home it can only result in misery for herself. Koharu is also bound by giri: she is aware that she has stolen Osan's husband and that Jihei's costly visits to the licensed quarter have ruined his business and caused great suffering to his wife and children.

Jihei tries to control his overpowering love for Koharu. In fact, a part of him desires nothing more than to live up to what society expects of him as a husband and father; but in the end his love for Koharu makes a double suicide seem like the only course open to him. However, even when Jihei and Koharu reach the place where they are to die, they talk mainly about their giri to Osan. Koharu fears that Osan will suppose that she lured Jihei into a lovers' suicide and broke her promise to give him up. Jihei, hoping to calm such anxiety, cuts off his hair at the base of the top knot and declares:

> As long as I had this hair I was Kamiya Jihei, Osan's husband, but cutting it has made me a monk. I have fled the burning house of the three worlds of delusion; I am a priest, unencumbered by wife, children or worldly possessions. Now that I no longer have a wife named Osan, you owe her no obligations either.[2] (P. 422)

Of course, we are unlikely to feel satisfied with Jihei's gesture. The symbolic act of slashing off his hair was intended to suggest his renunciation of worldly ties, but the ties exist all the same. Chikamatsu does not reveal what happened to Jihei's family after his death (though nineteenth-century adapters of Chikamatsu's play did), but surely we are not meant to understand that Osan was really satisifed by Jihei's gesture or that she and her children lived happily ever after. After Koharu also cuts her hair and, at least in intention, becomes a nun, Jihei says:

> We have escaped the inconstant world, a nun and a priest. Our duties as husband and wife belong to our profane past. It would be best to choose quite separate places for our deaths, a moun-

[2] Page numbers in parentheses in this chapter refer to Donald Keene, trans., *Major Plays of Chikamatsu* (New York: Columbia University Press, 1961).

tain for one, the river for the other. We will pretend that the ground above the sluice gate is a mountain. You will die there. I shall hang myself by this stream. The time of our deaths will be the same, but the method and place will differ. In this way we can honor to the end our duty to Osan. (P. 422)

But these acts of giri pale before the ninjō that governs their love suicides. Chikamatsu condoned their suicides, as we know from the last words of the play:

The tale is spread from mouth to mouth. People say that they who were caught in the net of Buddha's vow immediately gained salvation and deliverance, and all who hear the tale of the love suicides at Amijima are moved to tears. (P. 425)

This was not the usual judgment on a love suicide. Other writers of Chikamatsu's day who treated love suicides were severer; one account of the same love suicide at Sonezaki that Chikamatsu had dramatized concluded sternly, "they polluted the woods of Sonezaki."[3]

For Chikamatsu the deaths of the unhappy lovers were clearly not a pollution. The lovers die because they cannot bear to live any longer in a world which causes them such unhappiness. They are also determined to display their true feelings in an incontrovertible manner. This determination was shared not only by the characters in Chikamatsu's play but by many people who actually lived at the time. The word *shinjū*, which is generally translated as "love suicide" or "double suicide," means only "within the heart," and was used to designate actions that demonstrated what was actually inside a person's heart. How can one prove that one's love is genuine and not merely a pretense? The prostitutes of the seventeenth century first put into practice various acts intended to prove the sincerity of their feelings, though often such acts were no more than the artifices of women who were anxious to hold valuable customers. The pledges of sincerity called shinjū began with oaths of fidelity, then moved on to dramatically more painful acts such as tearing out a fingernail, cutting off a lock of hair or tattooing the name of the beloved on one's person, and finally to cutting off a part of a finger. The ultimate pledge, of course, was demonstrating one's willingness to die for the beloved; this was the origin of the love suicides known as shinjū.

The necessity of behaving in a way that will satisfy society, even if it violates one's inmost feelings, creates an atmosphere of insincer-

---

[3] Quoted in Hara Michio, "Sonezaki no shinjū no igi," in *Chikamatsu ronshū*, 1:68–69.

ity that must be broken if true feelings are to be recognized. Jihei, supposing that he has been betrayed by Koharu when he overhears her say that she no longer wishes to die with him, returns to his family and pretends to be concerned once more with his business, though, in fact, he can think of nothing but Koharu. He even signs an oath stating that he will break his ties with Koharu under penalty of being afflicted otherwise by the Buddhist deities. He imprints the oath with a seal of blood. His wife, Osan, seems satisfied with this shinjū, but once Jihei's brother and aunt have left, he slumps down again, obviously incapable of forgetting Koharu. This is too much even for the long-suffering Osan, who turns on him with these words, "You still haven't forgotten Sonezaki, have you?" (p. 407). (Sonezaki was the name of the licensed quarter where Jihei visited Koharu.) But Jihei denies that his tears have been caused by love for Koharu. He declares:

> If tears of grief flowed from the eyes and tears of anger from the ears, I could show my heart without saying a word. But my tears all pour in the same way from my eyes, and there's no difference in their color. It's not surprising that you can't tell what's in my heart. I have not a shred of attachment left for that vampire in human skin. (P. 408)

The problem is how to tell what is in the human heart. Does Jihei himself know what is in his own heart? He insists that he has not a "shred of attachment" left for Koharu, and his tears are caused by mortification, because his rival Tahei is to have his own way with Koharu. But we may doubt this even as he speaks, and we certainly will doubt it when, the same night, Jihei makes his way to Sonezaki and sees Koharu again.

The conflicts experienced by Jihei between love for Koharu and duty to his family, between the unruly passion he feels for Koharu and the quiet affection he feels for Osan, or even between what he thinks he feels and what he actually feels, are found in many forms in the plays of Chikamatsu. In some plays, such as *Nebiki no kadomatsu* (The Uprooted Pine), the Confucian background of giri is made more specific. In this play Jōkan, the father of the hero Yojibei, refuses to part with his money in order to buy off a man who has falsely accused Yojibei of having attacked him. Various people try to persuade Jōkan to be more lenient with his son, but he obdurately refuses. In the course of a game of chess with Yojibei's father-in-law, Jibuemon, Jōkan declares, "Even if my king is run through, even if his head is exposed on a prison gate, I won't give up my gold and silver" (p. 331). Here, not only king but "gold" and "silver" have double meanings, referring to the names of the chess pieces but also to Yojibei and Jōkan's money. Jibuemon, angered by such miserliness, throws the chess pieces in Jōkan's face, but still Jōkan does not move a muscle. But, in response to Jibuemon, who expresses regret that he, a former samurai, permitted his daughter to marry a merchant's son, Jōkan replies:

> A samurai's child is reared by samurai parents and becomes a samurai himself because they teach him the warrior's code. A merchant's child is reared by merchant parents and becomes a merchant because they teach him the ways of commerce. A samurai seeks a fair name in disregard of profit, but a merchant, with no thought to his reputation, gathers profits and amasses a fortune. This is the way of life proper for each. (P. 332)

The opinion which Jōkan expresses runs counter to the assumption of the Neo-Confucians that the only worthwhile life for a man was as a scholar (or, in the Japanese context, a samurai-scholar). But, in fact, the merchants in Chikamatsu's plays are not admirable because of their merchantly virtues but because, to the degree that it is possible for them, they behave like samurai. Jōkan himself, a little later in the play, appears with a mousetrap and demonstrates to Yojibei's wife how it is possible for a mouse to escape from the trap. Obviously, he is referring to Yojibei, who is now in Jōkan's custody, but Jōkan cannot openly pronounce the words. Bound as he is by samurai morality, he reveals what is in his heart by an elaborate allegory. When Yojibei realizes for the first time that his father is not actually miserly, he is moved to express samurailike sentiments. He refuses to escape, although that is his father's dearest wish, because he, too, follows a code of morality:

> No, that's impossible. They say that a man's highest duty as a father is to show compassion for his child, and as a child to serve his father. I am in my father's custody now. If I escape and Hikosuke dies, they will immediately arrest my father in my place and behead him. Even if Hikosuke recovers, my father will be guilty of having allowed his charge to escape, and they will punish him accordingly. My father has fulfilled his duty as a parent by showing a compassion indifferent to danger. But I have disobeyed my father's wishes in everything, to this very day. If I were to crown my sins by running away and saving my life at the expense of his, I could never mingle in human society again, not if I lived a hundred or a thousand years. Life in this world would be intolerable. I don't wish to disobey him

again—causing him grief gives me no pleasure—but I ask you to let me die as I am. I would like, by giving up my life, to discharge the filial duties of a lifetime. (P. 339)

The opening of this passage is paraphrased from the Confucian classic *The Great Learning*, and the emphasis given to duty and to filial piety bespeaks strong Confucian influence.[4] But Jōkan is not to be outdone in Confucian virtue by his son. This time he openly urges Yojibei to escape and threatens to kill himself otherwise. Yojibei at last accedes: one kind of filial piety has taken precedence over another, the urgent need to save his father's life being more urgent than the obligation to satisfy the formal requirements of filial piety.

Yojibei escapes, but not alone. He is accompanied by Azuma, the courtesan he loves. Yojibei's wife is naturally distressed that a rival is going off with her husband, but she is obliged to look after Jōkan as a good daughter-in-law, and obviously Yojibei, who has already shown signs of cracking, is in no condition to take care of himself. The wife says:

I should be the one going off with my husband—that's the proper way. Why has such a thing happened to me? Here I am sending him off in a chair for two with that woman I've envied and hated so. (P. 341)

The wife's feelings are not revealed to anyone; she maintains a dutiful, obedient attitude toward her husband and stifles her jealousy. But Yojibei, though free at last to be alone with the woman he loves, derives no joy from it. The third act opens with a *michiyuki*, usually the journey of the lovers to the place of their suicide, but here the strange journey of the demented Yojibei, who is hardly aware of what he is doing, and the courtesan Azuma, who unsuccessfully attempts to bring him back to his senses.

Yojibei's madness had been caused by the enormity of the decision he has made: to abandon his father, who surely will be punished for having allowed Yojibei to escape. He tells Azuma: "After spending the night with you, I weep for the father I have lost, I long for my wife. My heart is one but torn in two, like the notes of the cuckoo which passes us now, telling its name" (p. 343). Yojibei's words and actions verge on the comic because they are so disordered, but he is not in any sense a figure of fun. We realize that he has been under extreme pressure of giri—not the cold, but the warmest giri—and he is motivated by sincerity. This quality, in all the plays of Chika-

---

[4] *The Great Learning* (Commentary), 3:3, itself an allusion to the *Shih ching* (Book of Odes).

matsu, is redeeming: Chūbei (in *The Courier for Hell*) embezzles a samurai's money, Yosaku (in *Yosaku of Tamba*) persuades a child to commit a crime, and Gonza (in *Gonza the Lancer*) deceives his fiancée and takes up with a married woman, but they are all forgiven because at the critical moment they demonstrate their purity of soul. Sincerity, more than righteousness or wisdom, was exalted by Chikamatsu, just as it was by Yamazaki Ansai.

In some of Chikamatsu's plays giri seems cold, if not in motivation, in the acts performed according to its dictates. For example, in *Meido no hikyaku* (The Courier for Hell), Chūbei, having broken the seal on money belonging to a daimyo, has no choice but to flee Osaka. He and his beloved Umegawa go to the one place which seems likely to afford refuge, the village in Yamato from which he originally came. But Chūbei was given in adoption by his real father to the widow Myōkan; therefore, Chūbei and his father are no longer related legally. Moreover, the father believes it would be a breach of giri if he were even to look at the son whom he has given away. The father, Magoemon, asks Umegawa, "What do you think? Would there be any harm in my seeing him?" She answers, "Who will ever know? Please go to him." But he replies, "No, I won't neglect my duty to his family in Osaka" (p. 193). The legal formality of separation between father and son clearly has not killed their love, but neither Chūbei nor Magoemon wishes to transgress the letter of the agreement of adoption. They therefore forfeit their last opportunity to see each other before Chūbei is apprehended and carried off by the police.

Again, in *Hakata kojorō nami makura* (The Girl from Hakata), Sōshichi's father, acting according to his concept of giri, refuses to see his son who has become a smuggler, but when Sōshichi desperately needs his help the father breaks a hole in the wall to pass Sōshichi the document he must give the other smugglers. This extreme expedient was adopted so as not to violate the letter of giri even when yielding to the claims of ninjō.

Giri sometimes seems inhuman in the demands it makes on people to suppress their natural emotions, but ninjō, if given free rein, is destructive. Giri denies the individual's right to be happy at the expense of society and in so doing preserves society, as ninjō unchecked by giri must eventually destroy society.

It goes without saying that Chikamatsu was not guided solely by his concern for giri and ninjō. His chief objective was to write a successful play for the puppet theater. Frequent changes of mood and bold actions were special requirements of this theater, as opposed to a theater of actors; after all, an immobile puppet is no more than a lifeless creature of wood and cloth. This, no doubt, accounts for some of the exaggeration in the plays and such implausible actions as Sōshichi's father breaking a hole in the wall, rather than pass the needed document to his son in a less spectacular way. But no matter how implausible a scene may read in print, it must have been convincing to Chikamatsu's audiences. Love suicides did not occur every day, and the conflicting claims of giri and ninjō did not torment most people in the audience, but Chikamatsu's plays had verisimilitude. They certainly were not intended as models for Japanese to imitate, but were affecting representations of real elements in Tokugawa society, exaggerated or simplified for dramatic effectiveness.

In Chikamatsu's *jidaimono* (historical plays), the conflict between giri and ninjō is drawn with heroic strokes. Very little in a play like *Kokusen'ya kassen* (The Battles of Coxinga) happens on a merely human level. Ri Tōten, when he wishes to signal the Tartars (Manchus) that he will join their plot against the Ming dynasty, does not send a note or even a messenger: he gouges an eye and reverently offers it to the Ming emperor on a ceremonial baton. The emperor, we are told, is highly pleased with this extraordinary show of loyalty and does not suspect that the gesture has a sinister meaning. This kind of extravagant gesture is frequent in the plays written by dramatists after Chikamatsu, and we are sometimes given several different explanations of what they mean. Ri Tōten gouges his eye ostensibly by way of apology to the Tartars for the seeming ingratitude of the Chinese:

> I acted as a loyal minister should when I accepted your country's help a few years ago and saved my country, without taking a grain of rice for myself. But now men would break promises, incite armed disturbance, trouble the emperor, and afflict the people, and worst of all, cause it to be said that China is a beastland which knows no gratitude. This would be a disgrace to the dynasty and a disgrace to the country. It is now the task of a loyal minister to sacrifice himself, to reassure the emperor and to wipe out our country's shame. Behold what I do! (Pp. 199–200)

Later on, the loyal minister Go Sankei interprets the gesture quite differently. He says—and we discover he is correct—that Ri Tōten gouged his left eye as a signal to his Tartar confederates. "Ri Tōten gouged out his left eye, which belongs to yang and corresponds to the sun, as a warrant to his allies that he would deliver this great bright land of the sun into the hands of the Tartars" (p. 204). Ri Tōten is a villain, and Chikamatsu is not attempting to suggest that his actions are typical of the Chinese. Indeed, he sometimes denies that Chinese and Japanese are basically different: "Though the ways of Japan and China differ in many respects, in essence they are one" (p. 229). But elsewhere in the play the Chinese and Japanese ways are often contrasted.

Chikamatsu probably had little factual information about the China of his day, and it would be foolish to read *The Battles of Coxinga* for historical information; however, as an indication of what the Japanese thought about the Chinese it is most instructive. Coxinga's childhood name is Watōnai, meaning "between Japan and China," a reference to his Chinese father and Japanese mother. At the command of his father, who formerly was an official of the Ming, Watōnai has studied the Chinese classics of military strategy, but he has also examined the records of battles fought by Japanese generals of ancient and modern times, and both are equally valuable. When Watōnai crosses to China, determined single-handedly to drive out the Manchus and restore the Ming, he encounters in the Bamboo Forest of a Thousand Leagues a fierce tiger which he subdues, with some effort, with a charm from the Great Shrine of Ise. Watōnai and the tiger then join forces to subdue a party of Chinese soldiers. Then, we are told:

> NARRATOR: They join their hands in supplication and weep bitterly, their faces pressed to the ground. Watōnai strokes the tiger's head.
> WATŌNAI: Vile creatures! You who despise the Japanese for coming from a small country—have you learned now the meaning of Japanese prowess, before which even tigers tremble? (P. 227)

Watōnai accepts the surrender of the Chinese but insists that they shave their foreheads in the Japanese fashion.

So far this may suggest the kind of patriotic effusions that have been written at one time or another in many countries asserting their superiority to still other countries, but Watōnai is half Chinese, and it is essential that his Chinese half not be contemptible. We are told about him, "Here is a warrior endowed with wisdom and love, a marvel of the ages" (p. 245). "Wisdom" in *The Battles of Coxinga* is generally associated with the Chinese, rather than the Japanese, as bravery is associated with the Japanese—again, an echo of Yamazaki Ansai. Watōnai's opposite number is not his Japanese wife, a simple though courageous young woman, but his Chinese half sister, Kinshōjo. When she meets her half brother for the first time, human feelings impel her to admit him at once to the Castle of the Lions, but her duty to her absent husband forbids her to allow foreigners, even close relatives, within the stronghold. The Chinese soldiers on the wall menace the small party of visitors from Japan, but even they are at last moved, and consent to admitting Watōnai's mother, provided she is trussed head and foot. As she goes into the castle, the bolt of the gate drops with an ominous thud. "Kinshōjo's eyes grow dim: weakness is the way of the Chinese woman. Neither Watōnai nor Ikkan weeps: this is the way of the Japanese warrior" (p. 235).

Inside the castle, Kinshōjo demonstrates her solicitude toward her stepmother. She tells her maids, "Filial affection and duty both make me feel greater obligation to this mother who did not bear me than to my real mother" (p. 236). Then, for comic relief, we are told about the dinner which is prepared for Coxinga's mother: "If it please you, my lady, we prepared a meal most carefully—rice cooked with longans, soup made with duck and fried beancurd, pork in sweet sauce, steamed lamb, and beef-paste cakes. We offered these dishes to her ladyship, but she only said, 'How disagreeable! I don't like such food at all' " (p. 237). To a Japanese of Chikamatsu's time, such dishes would have sounded not only exotic but weird, rather like the dish of monkey brains which even today is mentioned by someone whenever the subject of Cantonese cuisine comes up.

Presently Kinshōjo's husband, Kanki, returns. Watōnai's mother urges him to join her son in overthrowing the Tartars and restoring the Ming. He eventually agrees, but the next instant he draws his sword and is about to kill Kinshōjo, to the consternation of the stepmother. He explains:

> If . . . I should become your son's ally without having crossed swords or shot a single arrow, I am sure that the Tartars would say—knowing Kanki is not a man to be frightened by tales of Japanese martial prowess—that I lost my courage and forgot my duties as a soldier because I was tied to my wife's apron strings and influenced by her relatives. If such is their gossip, my sons, grandsons, and even my remote descendants will be unable to escape disgrace. I would kill my dearly beloved wife in order to be able to join Watōnai cleanly—not influenced by his relation to my wife, and revering still the principles of justice and fidelity. (P. 240)

Kinshōjo agrees and expresses her willingness to die, showing that Chinese women are also courageous: "I am capable of such loyalty. I do not regret sacrificing for the sake of filial piety this body I have received from my parents" (p. 241). But Watōnai's mother will not accept this arrangement:

If I allow you to die now, people will say that your Japanese stepmother hated her Chinese stepdaughter so much—though they were separated by three thousand leagues—that she had her put to death before her eyes. Such a report would disgrace not only me but Japan, for people would say, judging the country by my acts, that the Japanese were cruelhearted. The sun that shines on China and the sun that shines on Japan are not two different lights, but the Land of the Rising Sun is its origin, and there you will find humanity, justice, and the other constant virtues. Could I, having been born in the Land of the Gods, where mercy is honored above all virtues, look on as my daughter is killed and then still go on living? I pray that these ropes that bind me will reveal themselves as the sacred ropes of the Japanese gods and strangle me on the spot. (P. 241)

This mélange of Confucian ideals and Japanese patriotism once again suggests Yamazaki Ansai. Chikamatsu, and no doubt his audiences, accepted the fact that China was a bigger country than Japan, and that it had produced the sage, but Japanese claims to respect were not to be lightly put aside. Many other examples of the same sentiments occur in the course of the play. Common to the utterances of both Kanki and Watōnai's mother, as quoted previously, is the fear of what people will say. One can hardly imagine a Shakespearean hero being disturbed by such a consideration!

At the end of the third act, Kinshōjo further demonstrates her courage with one of the extravagant "signals" with which this play abounds: she informs Watōnai that his request for Kanki's collaboration has been refused by stabbing herself and sending her blood flowing through a pipe to the place outside the castle walls where Watōnai is waiting. Her death and that of Watōnai's mother enable Kanki, who is now free of all possible entanglements, to declare himself Watōnai's ally. He bestows on him the name of Coxinga, Lord of the Imperial Surname, and together they leave the castle to do battle with the Tartars.

In the last act, the victorious forces of Coxinga and Kanki reach Nanking, where the king of Tartary and Ri Tōten are entrenched. Coxinga's Chinese colleagues propose various stratagems for capturing the city, but Coxinga, remembering his mother's dying injunction that he must consider the king of Tartary as the enemy of his mother and sister, is uninterested. He declares: "I shall attack boldly, challenge both the King of Tartary and Ri Tōten at close quarters, then cut them to shreds. If I fail to kill them in this fashion, I shall be guilty of unfilial conduct towards my mother, though I perform a million other martial feats, though I prove myself loyal to my sovereign and just to my fellow men" (pp. 263–264). Above all, he intends to fight in the Japanese rather than the Chinese manner, and this involves bold confrontation of the enemy rather than martial cunning. The only help he needs is from the Japanese gods. "I humbly beg the great goddess Amaterasu to vouchsafe her protection. The divine strength of Japan has enabled me to rise from the common people, capture many cities, and to become now a prince of the Chinese empire, honored by all" (p. 264).

Coxinga's father, Tei Shiryū, has other plans. He intends to capture Nanking all by himself, or to die in the attempt. He leaves Coxinga a note saying: "I returned to China, foolishly imagining that I might repay my debt to the emperor of the Ming, but I have achieved nothing, have won no glory. . . . Tonight I shall go to the walls of Nanking and, dying in battle, shall leave a fair name in Japan and China" (p. 264). Unfortunately for Tei Shiryū, however, he is captured and the Tartar king and Ri Tōten use him as a shield against Coxinga. Ri Tōten cries out:

> Coxinga, you crawled forth from your insignificant country, Japan, and ravaged all China. . . . Your outrageous insolence has compelled us to bind your father in this fashion. Shall we cut his belly in the Japanese manner? Or will you and your father agree to return to Japan immediately? (P. 267)

Coxinga briefly wavers, but at the end he and his men take the castle in one irresistible display of main force. They let the Tartar king escape, but Coxinga himself beheads Ri Tōten, "the cause of all our griefs, a monster guilty of the Eight Grave Crimes, the Five Inhuman Acts and the Ten Villainies" (pp. 268–269).[5]

I have discussed *The Battles of Coxinga* in detail because it was the most popular work of Chikamatsu and because it displays, more than his other plays, the influence of Confucianism in his expression. Chikamatsu's knowledge of Confucianism was probably derived mainly from the standard classics that formed the core of the education of Japanese boys of the samurai class. He was also familiar with anthologies of Chinese literature and with Japanese adaptations of Chinese literary works. Probably he was not concerned with a distinction

[5] The Eight Great Crimes were those of treason and atrocity as defined by the Taihō penal code of A.D. 701. The Ten Villainies were the killing of living beings, theft, adultery, lying, the use of obscene language, cursing, being double-tongued, covetousness, anger, and foolishness. The Five Inhuman Acts were patricide, matricide, wounding Buddha's person, killing his immediate disciple, and murdering a Buddhist priest.

between Confucianism and Neo-Confucianism. Confucianism itself may have been interchangeable with morality and ethics, both lacking in Shinto and the variety of Buddhism one finds in the plays.

Chikamatsu is always respectful concerning Shinto, in the manner of some of the Neo-Confucian philosophers, but he is openly critical of the Buddhist clergy in various works. For example, at the end of *The Courier for Hell*, just after Chūbei's father has credited the escape of Chūbei and Umegawa to the saving grace of Amida, a voice cries out that the unhappy lovers have been caught, throwing doubt on the efficacy of the old man's prayers. An anti-Buddhist bias was of course common to Neo-Confucians, and Chikamatsu seems to have shared their feelings. Anti-Buddhist sentiments are not systematically presented and do not occur in all the plays; indeed, the emphasis in the love suicide plays on the happiness of being reborn in Amida's Western Paradise demonstrates that Chikamatsu could not renounce the comfort promised by Buddhism for the life after death. But in this life, he seems to say, Confucianism is the code that men must obey.

Obedience to Confucian principles does not necessarily bring happiness. The conflicts between giri and ninjō are sometimes pushed to painful extremes. In *Yosaku from Tamba* the lady-in-waiting Shigenoi must reject her long-lost son, though it pains her exceedingly, because of her giri to the princess she serves; she fears that if people discover that her son is a horse driver it will reflect adversely on the princess's reputation. In *Horikawa nami no tsuzumi* (The Drum of the Waves of Horikawa), the samurai Hikokurō, learning that his wife has been unfaithful to him during his absence, feels it is incumbent on him to kill both his wife and her lover. The wife, anticipating this action, plunges a dagger into her breast; hence "a moving display of resolve" (p. 80). Hikokurō impassively unsheathes his sword and deals his wife the coup de grâce. Hardly is the wife dead than her sister, her adopted son, and her sister-in-law all express rage at the man who led the wife astray and insist on accompanying Hikokurō when he wreaks his vengeance. At this point Hikokurō, giving way to his human emotions, cries out: "If you think so much of your mother, sister or sister-in-law, why didn't you beg me to spare her life? Why didn't you suggest that she put on Buddhist robes and become a nun?" (p. 81). The narrator adds: "Lifting the lifeless body in his arms, he shouts his grief, and the others are carried away by tears of sympathy. The misery of it! This the heartbreaking conduct demanded of those born to be samurai" (p. 81).

There is perhaps nothing specifically Confucian about these sentiments, but the ideals of the samurai had already been expressed by

Yamaga Sokō in terms that closely accord with those voiced by Chi-kamatsu in his plays about the samurai class. The conflict between giri and ninjō tends to become less conspicuous in the plays written after Chikamatsu, if only because the sewamono, the domestic tra-gedies, were reduced to the status of scenes within long historical dramas and did not exist independently. This meant that giri, gen-erally of the "coldest" kind, tended to be the motivating force behind the actions of the characters, and ninjō was either resolutely brushed aside or given only momentary consideration. In Takeda Izumo's play Ōtōnomiya asahi no yoroi (Prince of the Great Pagoda, Armor in Morning Sunlight), Saitō Tarozaemon causes the deaths of his son-in-law and his daughter, beheads his grandchild, and finally cuts off his own head, all out of giri to the Prince of the Great Pagoda.

In Chūshingura, the most impressive of the post-Chikamatsu pup-pet plays, the ideals tend to be reduced to one, loyalty, as the title itself, The Treasury of Loyal Retainers, indicates. Every action of Yu-ranosuke, the central character, is impelled by his sense of loyalty as a samurai. Such loyalty was not earned, but is absolute, a point that is generally overlooked by producers of film and television versions of the play who, no doubt to make the vendetta more palatable to modern audiences, insist on the nobility, generosity, and so on, of Lord En'ya Hangan (the historical Asano Takuminokami). But such efforts miss the point of the play, which is that even if En'ya Hangan were a cruel or stupid master, his retainers would have been just as loyal, just as determined to avenge his death. The code of samurai behavoir, which Yamaga Sokō had instilled into the historical Asano and his men, made no exceptions to the requirement of loyalty.

Loyalty, of course, is not a uniquely Japanese virtue, but the em-phasis given to this one virtue in Chūshingura is noteworthy. Loyalty was traditionally associated with filial piety, but little attention is given to fillial piety in this play. Rikiya develops from a shy, gentle young man into a heroic personification of loyalty, but this is not the result of filial devotion to his father, Yuranosuke. Rather, he has become aware of his grave responsibilities as a retainer, however jun-ior, of Lord En'ya Hangan; his loyalty, therefore, stems from giri. Filial piety would assume major importance in Japanese drama during the early-Meiji period, when many of Kawatake Mokuami's plays contained the word kō (filial piety) in the title and filial piety was recognized as the equivalent within the family of loyalty within the state.

In late-Tokugawa drama, notably the Kabuki plays written by Tsuruya Nanboku, the traditional values, including giri and loyalty, are parodied, a reflection of the general decline of morals and ideals.

In Nanboku's plays there is not even the surface attempt to promote *kanzen chōaku* (encouragement of virtues and chastisement of vice) that is found in the novels of Bakin and other contemporary writers. His plays suggest instead a moral collapse that reveals itself in the perverse pleasure Nanboku takes in drawing moustaches on the poster art of Confucian ideals. Nanboku's most famous play, *Tōkaidō Yotsuya kaidan* (Ghost Story of Yotsuya on the Tōkaidō), was intended to be performed in conjunction with *Chūshingura*. The performances were spread out over two days; on the first day, the actors performed half of *Chūshingura* plus the first three acts of *Ghost Story*, and on the second day, the remainder of both plays. The effect of such a performance must have been to cast doubts on the ideals of *Chūshingura* by presenting, in a much closer and more realistic manner than the older work, the lives of retainers when they were not busy avenging their lord.

If one had to judge by the Kabuki dramas written during the late Tokugawa period, the Confucian ideals were dead; but even when they were most conspicuously ridiculed in the theater, they continued to affect the lives of most Japanese. The theater is a mirror of society, but it may magnify, diminish, or hopelessly distort. The one thing one can say with certainty is that as long as something appears in the mirror, no matter how crooked or warped, it still exists in society and has compelled the attention of the makers of mirrors.

SIX

NATURE AND ARTIFICE IN THE WRITINGS OF OGYŪ SORAI (1666-1728)

BY SAMUEL HIDEO YAMASHITA

No other Tokugawa Confucian scholar has received the attention that has been given to Ogyū Sorai (1666–1728), and certainly none has been made to represent so much. Despite all this attention, however, Sorai's ideas have not always been understood. Most of his interpreters have seen him formulating his ideas in opposition to those of the Ch'eng brothers—Ch'eng Hao (1032–1085) and Ch'eng I (1033–1107)—and Chu Hsi (1130–1200), which appears not to have been the case;[1] they have assumed that Sorai was preoccupied with the Ch'engs and Chu Hsi, when he was apparently not; they also have identified the Ch'eng-Chu orthodoxy popular in Japan in the seventeenth and early-eighteenth centuries with the views of the Ch'engs and Chu Hsi, an identity that never existed.

Fortunately, the recent work of Japanese and American scholars—most notably, Abe Yoshio, Okada Takehiko, and Wm. Theodore de Bary—has shown that Sorai and the other principal thinkers of the Ancient Learning school (J., *kogakuha*), Yamaga Sokō (1622–1685) and Itō Jinsai (1627–1705), were preoccupied not with the original writings of the Ch'engs and Chu Hsi, as has been alleged, but rather with later versions of their views.[2] This is not surprising, since, as Abe, Okada, and de Bary have demonstrated, the Ch'eng-Chu or-

---

[1] See Inoue Tetsujirō, *Nihon Shushigakuha no tetsugaku* (Fuzambō, 1936), p. 598; Maruyama Masao, *Nihon seiji shisōshi kenkyū* (Tōkyō Daigaku Shuppankai, 1952), pp. 25–38, 44–50, 52–61, 64–67, 78–138, 200–201, 204–205; Iwahashi Junsei, *Sorai kenkyū* (Meichō Kankōkai, 1969), pp. 72, 309; Imanaka Kanshi, *Sorai-gaku no kisoteki kenkyū* (Yoshikawa Kōbunkan, 1966), pp. 14–15; Kanaya Osamu, "Soraigaku no tokushitsu," in *Ogyū Soraishū*, Nihon no Shisō, no. 12, ed. Kanaya Osamu (Chikuma Shobō, 1970), 12:3.

[2] Abe Yoshio, *Nihon Shushigaku to Chōsen* (Tōkyō Daigaku Shuppankai, 1971), pp. 493–496, 528–531; Wm. Theodore de Bary, "Sagehood as a Secular and Spiritual Ideal in Tokugawa Neo-Confucianism," in *Principle and Practicality: Essays in Neo-Confucianism and Practical Learning*, ed. Wm. Theodore de Bary and Irene Bloom (New York: Columbia University Press, 1979), pp. 139-180.

thodoxy widely known in Japan in the late-seventeenth century actually originated in Yi- and Ming-Dynasty interpretations of the Ch'engs and Chu Hsi. Noting the obvious affinities between the Ancient Learning school thinkers and certain Ming Confucians, de Bary has argued that the views of Sokō, Jinsai, and Sorai grew out of one of several varieties of the Ch'eng-Chu orthodoxy introduced to Japan in the seventeenth century—that which gave greater weight to the external and physical reality, affirmed the emotions and desires, promoted empirical study, advanced a pragmatic statecraft, and was identified with Lo Ch'in-shun (1465–1547), Wu T'ing-han, Wang T'ing-hsiang (1474–1544), and others[3]—and thus were more than just a response to the Ch'engs and Chu Hsi.[4]

This argument applies more accurately to Jinsai and Sokō than to Sorai, however. Unlike Sokō and Jinsai, Sorai did not fully endorse the new monistic ontologies, naturalistic ethics, and pragmatic statecraft inspired by the new strains of Neo-Confucianism introduced from the continent. Although, like them, he denied the existence of transcendental ideas and argued for the primacy of an active material force, he also recognized and valued more highly another ontological dimension represented by the static and concrete artifacts of classical Chinese civilization. Similarly, he agreed with his predecessors' affirmation of the physical nature, emotions, and desires, but insisted on the importance of cultivating the nature and regulating the emotions and desires by writing literary compositions in classical styles and rehearsing ancient ritual etiquette. Finally, although his statecraft was informed by the pragmatism inspired in part by a new historicism, Sorai balanced continuing historical change with the timeless institutions created by the sages and early kings and called for a revival of these institutions as a solution to the social and economic problems of the 1720s. What this suggests is that Sorai did not completely agree with Sokō and Jinsai, or indeed with the partisans of the externally oriented varieties of Ming Neo-Confucianism with whom he shared a great deal. The subtlety of their disagreements leaves little doubt that although Sorai's views were congenial to theirs, his own attitude toward their views was ambivalent. I shall argue in this essay that this ambivalence reveals a new and important development in Tokugawa Confucianism.

[3] de Bary, "Sagehood as a Secular and Spiritual Ideal," pp. 143, 153–154, 167, 174. See also Abe, *Nihon Shushigaku to Chōsen*, pp. 496–497, 503–512, 514–517, 520–522, 530–531; Bloom, "On the Abstraction of Ming Thought: Some Concrete Evidence from the Philosophy of Lo Ch'in-shun," in de Bary and Bloom, *Principle*, pp. 69–113; and Okada Takehiko, *Sō-Min tetsugaku josetsu* (Bungensha, 1977), pp. 327–355.

[4] de Bary, "Sagehood as a Secular and Spiritual Ideal," pp. 143, 153–154, 167, 174.

Sorai's new conception owed much to his study of classical and modern Chinese literature which taught him, among other things, the importance of literary form. He had long believed that in order to approach the sages and early kings as well as the civilization they created, one had to study the classical Chinese texts. His rationale was simple: "Whereas in ancient times there were sages, in modern times there are none. Thus must learning look to the past."[5] When Sorai spoke of the "past," he was referring not just to the Three Dynasties period but also to the classical Chinese texts that were the repository of classical Chinese civilization. "Look back," he wrote to a fellow Confucian, "the bones of the ancients are rotted and gone, and only their writings survive."[6] The texts he had in mind were the *Lun-yü* (Analects of Confucius), *Tso chuan* (Tso Commentary), *Kuo yü* (Conversations from the States), *Shih chi* (Records of the Historian), *Han shu* (History of the Former Han), and the Six Classics.[7] Of these the most important for Sorai were the Six Classics, in particular the *Shih ching* (Book of Odes), *Shu ching* (Book of History), *Li chi* (Book of Rites), and *Yüeh ching* (Book of Music).[8]

Sorai singled out the Six Classics because they evinced what he considered proper reverence for heaven. "What is recorded in the Six Classics," he noted, "is essentially to revere heaven, and this is the first principle for those intent on learning the Way of the Sages."[9] Sorai accepted only those texts that exhibited the proper reverence for heaven and, by extension, for the sages and early kings. Furthermore, he was, as we shall see shortly, fiercely critical of those texts that failed to manifest this reverence.

In Sorai's eyes, the Six Classics were also the record of the myriad deeds and achievements carried out by the sages and early kings on heaven's order, and as such these texts were the principal repository of the civilization they had established,[10] the other sources being the *Analects* and the extant Chou and Han histories.[11] And so it follows that "those wishing to search for the Way of the Sages have to search within the Six Classics" and, because the Six Classics were "incom-

[5] Ogyū Sorai, *Gakusoku*, in Yoshikawa Kōjirō et al., eds., *Ogyū Sorai*, NST, 36, 257.

[6] "Kutsu Keizan ni kotau," in NST, 36:533.

[7] Ibid., p. 529.

[8] *Benmei*, NST, 36:211, and "Tō Kenjutsu ni kotau," in NST, 36:517. The other two of the Six Classics were the *I ching* and *Ch'un ch'iu*.

[9] *Benmei*, NST, 36:235.

[10] Ibid., pp. 210, 249–250; *Bendō*, NST, 36:200; *Sorai sensei tōmonsho*, NRI, 3:188.

[11] See "Kutsu Keizan ni kotau," in NST, 36:528, and *Sorai sensei tōmonsho*, NRI, 3:177, 199.

plete,"[12] within other pre-Six Dynasties texts as well.[13] Indeed, Sorai's literary archaism, as well as the new ethics and statecraft it inspired, rested entirely on this record.

Another reason for Sorai's regard for the Six Classics was that they transmitted the various forms of classical Chinese civilization: the *Odes* taught poetry, the *History* prose, the *Rites* ritual etiquette, and the *Music* ritual music. Their importance to Sorai was simple: they comprised the teachings of the sages and early kings, and every educated man was expected to have mastered them.[14]

Yet another reason for Sorai's prizing the Six Classics was their authoritative style. His high regard for the form of the Six Classics is apparent in this letter to the Confucian scholar Yabu Shin'an (1689–1744):

> Confucius said, "I have transmitted what was taught to me without adding anything of my own. I have been faithful to and loved the ancients," and "I am simply one who loves the past and who is diligent in investigating it." Even Confucius, who was endowed with a sage's intelligence, was satisfied merely to cherish the Way of the Early Kings. Thus do we know that nothing needs to be added to the Way of the Early Kings.
>
> Following Confucius's death, Hsün-tzu and Mencius expanded the most important of his teachings, and from their time up to the age of the Ch'eng brothers, Chu Hsi, Lu Hsiang-shan, Wang Yang-ming, and their followers, the Way has waxed and waned with the passage of time; and after the Ch'engs, Chu Hsi, Lu Hsiang-shan, and Wang Yang-ming, there have been no sages.
>
> How is one to know whether the Way of the Ch'engs, Chu Hsi, Lu Hsiang-shan, and Wang Yang-ming diverges from [the Way of the] Early Kings? Those who declare that they are the same assume the position of a sage when they say this, and this is something I could never do. [Similarly], those who declare that they are different also assume the position of a sage when they say this, and this too I could never do.
>
> All we can know for sure is literary form (C., *tz'u*; J., *ji*), although even this waxes and wanes with the passage of time. I started out by studying the theories of the Ch'engs and Chu Hsi and by imitating the diction of Ou-yang Hsiu and Su Shih, be-

[12] "An Tanpaku ni kaesu," in NST, 36:537.

[13] "Sō Shin'an ni atau," in NST, 36:505.

[14] *Benmei*, NST, 36:249–250; "Sō Shin'an ni atau," in NST, 36:508; "Tōmon tsuki," in NST, 36:511; "Tō Kenjutsu ni kotau," in *Soraishū* (1740 ed., University of Tokyo Library), 25:15a–17a.

lieving all the while that their writings were one with the Way of the Early Kings and Confucius. Obviously, I believed this only because I was accustomed to Sung prose styles (C., *wen*; J., *bun*). Later, the theories of the Ming writers [Li P'an-lung and Wang Shih-chen] changed my thinking. They taught me that words had ancient as well as modern meanings, and armed with this knowledge, I reread the writings of the Ch'engs and Chu Hsi and gradually realized that their style was not at all like that of the early kings and Confucius. I then searched for what was called the ancient language (*kogen*) in pre-Six Dynasties texts, including the Six Classics, and before long, I understood the Six Classics perfectly. Such were the benefits of my learning the classical style (*kobun*).[15]

Besides presenting another reason for Sorai's high regard for the Six Classics, this is as clear a statement of the aims and methods of Sorai's neoclassical philology—his "study of ancient literary styles" (C., *ku-wen-tz'u-hsüeh*; J., *kobunjigaku*)—as can be found in any of his writings, and it reveals both the underlying assumptions and the preferred method of his philology.

Sorai's philology both rested on and supported his intense belief in heaven and his reverence for the sages and early kings. The passage just quoted also indicates that Sorai may have thought of himself as a sage. By describing first Confucius' most famous and sage act—his refusal to do anything more than transmit the Way of the Sages—and then by announcing his own reluctance to do anything more than invoke the authority of the classical texts, Sorai does encourage this comparison. Nonetheless, Sorai's message is clear: those making a personal judgment set their own standards and, worse yet, "assume the position of a sage." To do so was the height of irreverence, and such irreverence was anathema to the religious Sorai. The truly reverent should, like Confucius, honor the classical texts, which were both a record of heaven's will and the repository of that civilization created by the sages and early kings on heaven's order. And Sorai condemned those of his contemporaries whose faith in themselves and in the Ch'engs and Chu Hsi "exceeded their faith in the early kings and Confucius."[16] Thus it was chiefly to do honor to heaven, its agents, and their creations that Sorai ascribed primary textual au-

[15] "Sō Shin'an ni atau," in NST, 36:505. I have used Arthur Waley's translations of Confucius' famous pronouncements on his attitude toward the past. Arthur Waley, *The Analects of Confucius* (New York: Vintage Books, 1938), pp. 123, 127.

[16] "An Tanpaku ni kaesu," in NST, 36:541; see also *Sorai sensei tōmonsho* NRI, 3:190, 195, 198.

thority to an assortment of classical texts—mostly histories written before the end of the Former Han, anthologies of mid-T'ang poetry, and, of course, the Six Classics—finding in them the standards by which to evaluate and judge other texts.

It was the Ming critics Li P'an-lung (1514–1570) and Wang Shih-chen (1526–1590) who taught Sorai to distinguish ancient and modern literary styles (C., *wen-tz'u*; J., *bunji*). Following them, he argued that the ancient literary styles had been displaced by modern ones during the Sung period and that this displacement was the culmination of a trend that had begun in the Six Dynasties period. Up until the Sung period, Sorai noted, the prevailing prose styles had been unquestionably classical. This was because those writing before the Sung, including Han Yü (768–824) and Liu Tsung-yüan (773–819), had faithfully imitated the style of the classical texts, whereas those writing during and after the Sung, beginning with Ou-yang Hsiu (1007–1072) and Su Shih (1036–1101), disdained the ancient literary styles in favor of novel and unorthodox styles. What also separated the ancient and modern styles, according to Sorai, was the emphasis that each gave to form and content. Whereas those who preferred the ancient styles freely used the diction, figures, devices, and rhetorical patterns found in the classical texts, those who preferred the modern styles were absorbed with exposition and argument and consciously eschewed the entire store of classical literary forms. Thus, concluded Sorai, the "ancients" valued form over content, and the "moderns" content over form.[17]

In his later writings, even as he acknowledged his debt to Li and Wang, Sorai claimed to have accomplished what they never had. "Li and Wang," he wrote, "were most interested in superior narrative pieces [such as the *History of the Former Han, Records of the Historian, Conversations from the States,* and the *Tso Commentary*] and never had the time to consider the Six Classics. I applied their method to the Six Classics, and this is what distinguishes me from them."[18] And so with some justification, Sorai considered the application of the new stylistic criteria to the Six Classics his own achievement.

What Sorai found so intriguing about this difference between the classical and modern literary styles that he had learned from Li and Wang was that it could be verified empirically. Here Sorai shared his contemporaries' interest in empiricism, and their attraction to the "reality of the actual physical nature of man and things" encouraged

[17] *Sorai sensei tōmonsho*, NRI, 3:188; "Sō Shin'an ni atau," in NST, 36:507; "Tō Kenjutsu ni kotau," in NST, 36:517; "Kutsu Keizan ni kotau," in NST, 36:528–529; and "An Tanpaku ni kaesu," in NST, 36:538.

[18] "An Tanpaku ni kaesu," in NST, 36:537.

by at least one of the new Ming varieties of Neo-Confucianism, that associated with Lo Ch'in-shun. Given the impact Lo Ch'in-shun's writings had on Hayashi Razan (1583–1657), the founder of the school where Sorai studied for a time, his inclination toward empiricism is not at all surprising.[19] He claimed that to reconstruct the lost language, one had only to follow his own example: to read and reread the classical texts until one could discern just how much modern writers had diverged from these texts. Near the end of his life Sorai wrote: "What I call the ancient language is a reconstruction from ancient texts. If one collates each word [that occurs in these texts], the divergence of ancient and modern literary styles will become abundantly clear."[20] It was this process of reconstruction that comprised Sorai's method and promised to reveal what he called ancient literary forms (ji).[21]

It was on these grounds, then, that Sorai condemned all those who wrote in modern, particularly Sung, literary styles. To him, no one deserved this condemnation more than the partisans of the Ch'eng-Chu orthodoxy whose divergence from the ancient literary forms was obvious. Their divergence from the "ancient language," he observed, was the result of their not realizing that the ancient and the modern languages differed and their relying on Chu Hsi's commentaries on the classics.[22] It was manifested in their preference for modern over ancient prose, their penchant for replacing the old meanings of words with new ones, and their attraction to a Taoist and Buddhist philosophical terminology.[23]

The Ch'eng-Chu scholars' preference for modern prose styles was reflected in their own writings which were stylistically quite modern. Those who doubted that their prose was modern, wrote Sorai, had only to compare their styles with classical styles or to try to read the

[19] Abe, *Nihon Shushigaku to Chōsen*, pp. 514–517, 520–521, 530.

[20] "Koku Taiga ni kaesu," in NST, 36:518.

[21] Sorai had not always used the term "literary form." In *Distinguishing Names*, he used the word "language" (*gen*) where he might have used "literary form," as when he wrote, "Culture refers to the *Odes, History, Rites,* and *Music*. Thus, that which one is to study and know is found in knowing language and knowing propriety" (*Benmei*, NST, 36:250). Later, he scrupulously distinguished "literary form" and "language," noting that "literary form is the refinement (*bun*) of language, and language seeks refinement" ("Hei Shihin ni atau," in NST, 36:503).

[22] *Bendō*, NST, 36:207; *Benmei*, NST, 36:231, 241; *Sorai sensei tōmonsho*, NRI, 3:188, 200; *Chūyōkai*, in *Nihon Meika Shisho Chūshaku Zensho*, vol. 1: *gakuyō-bu ichi*, ed. Seki Giichirō (Ōtori Shuppan, 1973), p. 3 (hereafter cited as NMSCZ); "Fushun Sanjin ni atau," quoted in Iwahashi, *Sorai kenkyū*, pp. 251–252; "Sō Shin'an ni atau," in NST, 36:507; "Sui Shindō," in NST, 36:510; and "Koku Taiga ni kaesu," in NST, 36:518.

[23] "Sō Shin'an ni atau," in NST, 36:505, and "Kutsu Keizan ni kotau," in NST, 36:529.

classics without their commentaries. Or one could even do as Sorai himself had done and first master the classics before reexamining the modern commentaries.[24] Though more demanding and arduous, Sorai promised that the latter approach would reveal how different modern prose was from that of the classical texts.[25] He remembered both his own discovery some years earlier that there indeed was a classical language and his attendant realization that the Ch'eng-Chu scholars were neither conveying what the sages, early kings, and Confucius had said nor using their literary style.[26]

More subtle but no less important was what Sorai regarded as the Ch'eng-Chu scholar's misreading of the classical texts. He cataloged dozens of examples of what he considered skewed interpretations of important words and phrases in these texts, interpretations familiar to his readers, most of whom subscribed to one or another variety of the Ch'eng-Chu orthodoxy. One of his frequently cited examples was the phrase "heavenly principle and human desire" (C., t'ien-li jen-yü; J., tenri jin'yoku). Sorai asserted that it did not mean what the Ch'eng-Chu scholars said that it did. "Heavenly principle" did not refer to the sages, nor did "human desire" mean the total annihilation of desire, as they argued. How could it? To be completely without desires was physically impossible, and to identify the sages with heavenly principle was sacrilegious.[27] Classical writers never would have been able to advance such ideas. Sorai found equally irreverent the Ch'eng-Chu interpretation of the phrase "exhausting principle" (C., ch'iung-li; J., kyūri). In classical texts, he noted, it was meant as a paean to the sages' creation of the "changes" (C., i; J., eki), but the Ch'eng-Chu scholars insisted on interpreting the phrase to mean knowing the principle inherent in all things.[28] All of this was evidence that they "read the ancient language in terms in the modern."[29]

Even more troubling to Sorai than the Ch'eng-Chu scholars' misinterpretations were the numerous Buddhist and Taoist words they

---

[24] Ibid.

[25] "Koku Taiga ni kaesu," in NST, 36:518.

[26] Sorai never forgot his discovery of the "ancient language." It occurred sometime after 1704 or 1705 when he came across the writings of Li P'an-lung and Wang Shih-chen in a massive collection he had just bought from an insolvent bookdealer. To his great surprise, he found that he could not read them, the reason being that Li and Wang wrote in a classical style and amply peppered their compositions with words and phrases drawn from the Chinese classics. See "An Tanpaku ni kaesu," in NST, 36:537.

[27] "Sō Shin'an ni kaesu," in NST, 36:508.

[28] Benmei, NST, 36:216, 250; "Sō Shin'an ni atau," in NST, 36:506; and "An Tanpaku ni kaesu," in NST, 36:538.

[29] Bendō, NST, 36:207.

introduced into the Confucian lexicon. The most obvious examples were the words *li* (J., *ri*) and *ch'i* (J., *ki*). When these two words occurred in the classics, he observed, they meant something quite different from what the Ch'eng-Chu scholars presumed they meant. In fact, it was the Taoists who first used *li* and *ch'i* to mean "principle" and "material force."[30] Further, what was true of principle and material force was also true of countless other Ch'eng-Chu concepts, and Sorai assiduously cataloged them, pointing out always their divergence from the classics. Thus, whether a word or phrase occurred in the Six Classics and whether later scholars correctly interpreted it in its original sense were of great importance to Sorai; for these reasons, he concluded that the Ch'eng-Chu commentaries on the classics were of more harm than use.

Sorai also accused Ch'eng-Chu scholars of willingly obscuring not only a more ancient stratum of meaning in the classics but also the ancient culture preserved in those texts, thus guaranteeing their ignorance of what he called "ceremonial forms" (C., *shih*; J., *koto*).[31] These ceremonial forms were the established patterns of conduct and ritual performance that gentlemen (C., *chün-tzu*; J., *kunshi*) learned

---

[30] *Sorai sensei tōmonsho*, NRI, 3:197; "Hei Shihin ni atau," in NST, 36:503; "Sō Shin'an ni atau," in NST, 36:506; an "An Tanpaku ni kaesu," in NST, 36:538.

[31] I have translated *shih* (J. *koto*) as "ceremonial form" because this appears to be what Sorai meant when he used the word. He spoke repeatedly, for example, of "practicing the ceremonial forms" (*koto o narau*). See *Benmei*, NST, 36:249–250; and *Chūyōkai*, NMSCZ, 1:3. He also identified *shih* with ritual as he did in the following from a letter to Mizutari Hakusen: "When I search for the classical past, I always do so by means of literary and ceremonial forms. When it comes to ceremonial forms, nothing is more detailed than the three Rites—the *I li* (Rites of I), *Chou li* (Rites of Chou), and the *Book of Rites*." In both cases, neither "thing" nor "affair" would make much sense. See "Sui Shindō," in NST, 36:512.

Both James Legge and Berhard Karlgren define *shih* in this way. In a gloss on the passage from the *Great Learning* that reads, "Things (C., *wu*, J., *mono*) have their roots and branches. Affairs (*shih, koto*) have their beginnings and ends," Legge writes:

The adherents of the old commentators say, on the contrary, that this paragraph is introductory to the succeeding one. They contend that the illustration of virtue and renovation of the people are doings (*shih*), and not things (*wu*). According to them, the *things* are the person, heart, thoughts, etc., mentioned below, which are the "root," and the family, kingdom, and empire, which are "the branches." The *affairs* or *doings* are the various processes put forth on those things. This it seems to me is the correct interpretation.

Legge, trans., *The Four Books* (Shanghai, 1923; reprint ed., New York: Paragon Book Reprint Corp., 1966), p. 310.

Bernhard Karlgren's catalog of the classical meanings of the word *shih* includes the sense in which Sorai seems to have used it. Bernhard Karlgren, *Grammata Serica Recensa* (Stockholm: Museum of Far Eastern Antiquities, 1964), pp. 255–256.

when they studied the decorum appropriate to certain social and ritual occasions and when they practiced the rudiments of the six classical arts—ritual, music, archery, horsemanship, calligraphy, and mathematics. Because gentlemen were expected to conform to these ceremonial forms when conducting or participating in social and ritual events and performing any of the six arts, they were considered the repository of propriety, the fount of good form. Moreover, the ceremonial forms were "external" and complex, existing outside the self and requiring years of disciplined study and cultivation.[32] Sorai was careful to point out that the ceremonial forms did not originate within the individual or within the mind, as the Ch'eng-Chu scholars suggested, but rather had been created by the sages and early kings at heaven's request and were preserved in the classical texts, particularly the *Book of Rites, I li* (Rites of I), and *Chou li* (Rites of Chou).[33]

These ancient ceremonial forms resembled the ancient literary forms and had the same relevance to ancient etiquette that the ancient literary forms had to ancient prose. That Sorai intended these ceremonial and literary forms to be parallel is suggested by his identification of the ceremonial forms with the *Book of Rites* and *Book of Music*, and the literary forms with the *Book of Odes* and *Book of History*. "In my view," he wrote, "the *Book of Odes* and *Book of History* are literary form, and the *Book of Rites* and *Book of Music* are ceremonial form. Meaning (C., *i*; J., *gi*) is to be found in literary form, propriety (C., *li*; J., *rei*) in ceremonial form."[34] He put it even more succinctly when he wrote, "The Six Classics are ceremonial and literary form."[35]

Sorai's identification of the ceremonial forms with the *Rites* and *Music* also meant that the ceremonial forms, like the literary forms, could be verified empirically and with patience and care could be reconstructed. To Sorai, when one had achieved as accurate and complete a reconstruction of the ancient literary and ceremonial forms as possible, one not only had retrieved the ancient artifacts but also had demonstrated the proper reverence toward those responsible for their creation—the sages, early kings, and, of course, heaven. As his allusions to the *Analects* imply, Sorai believed that this was the kind of reverence that Confucius had exhibited when he described himself as a lover of the past and a transmitter rather than a creator; it was also the kind of reverence that Sorai himself felt and fostered in his time.

[32] *Benmei*, NST, 36:250, 253, and "Sui Shindō ni kaesu," in NST, 36:512–513.
[33] "Tōmon tsuki," in NST, 36:513.
[34] Ibid., p. 512.
[35] "Kutsu Keizan ni kotau," in NST, 36:529.

Sorai's literary and ceremonial forms were not, however, an end in themselves and were to serve an important epistemological and political purpose.

It is the [extant classical] texts that allow one to know the ceremonial and literary forms. Today many have abandoned these ancient ceremonial and literary forms and speak on the authority of principle and their own minds. How are they to know whether or not they agree with the ancients? These days, those who invoke the authority of the classics are not expressing the true meaning of the classics but rather are speaking in accordance with their own minds. Since none is expressing the true meaning of the classics, all are fated to have different views of the Way. How, then, is one to decide [which is correct]?[36]

Sorai considered those who trusted "their own minds" to be not only disrespectful because they "assumed the position of a sage," something that he could not tolerate, but also uninformed because they ignored the classics. By doing this, they encouraged serious misinterpretations of the classical civilization of China, offended heaven and its agents, and denied themselves what Sorai believed was the proper foundation for both order and knowledge.[37] He therefore denounced them as "being of the same ilk as the Sung thinkers," and ironically those he condemned included Itō Jinsai.[38]

It is ironic because Jinsai was as much Sorai's intellectual mentor as were Li P'an-lung and Wang Shih-chen. Apparently, Sorai never realized this, or if he did, he could not bring himself to admit it, citing only his obligation to Li and Wang. Although he owed much to the Ming varieties of the Ch'eng-Chu orthodoxy, particularly that identified with Lo Ch'in-shun, this influence was mediated by Ha-

---

[36] Ibid., pp. 533–534.
[37] "An Tanpaku ni kaesu," in NST, 36:538.
[38] "Kutsu Keizan ni kotau," in NST, 36:530.

Sorai had little love for Jinsai, owing to an unfortunate incident that occurred in the early 1700s. In 1703 Sorai wrote Jinsai a remarkably warm and admiring letter, which for unknown reasons Jinsai never answered. The letter might have been forgotten had matters ended there, but they did not. The unanswered letter was appended to Jinsai's posthumous biography without Sorai's permission, and he was understandably furious.

Sorai wrote dozens of angry little notes about Jinsai, in which he belittled his ideas, questioned his integrity, berated his intelligence, and even cataloged the grammatical, orthographic, and stylistic infelicities of his classical Chinese prose. Most of these criticisms were included in Ken'en zuihitsu (Jottings from a Miscanthus Garden). Although Sorai later regretted these attacks on Jinsai and although he was a great admirer of Jinsai's cosmology, he still seemed to harbor a grudge and was not very generous in his assessments of Jinsai.

yashi Gahō (1618–1680), Razan's successor, and in this sense was indirect.[39] Sorai's debt to Jinsai, in contrast, was more direct and is especially evident in his view of reality.

As is well known, Jinsai's ontology was diametrically opposed to that of the Ch'engs and Chu Hsi, but it differed in ways that have not been fully recognized. Most modern commentators have noted that whereas the Ch'engs and Chu Hsi distinguished a transcendental dimension represented by principle and a vitalistic dimension represented by material force, Jinsai rejected the transcendental dimension and retained the vitalistic dimension. This, the prevailing view of Jinsai's ontology, suggests that he denied Chu Hsi's dualistic conception and advanced a monistic conception in its place. In fact, however, Jinsai's was also a dualistic conception: besides the vitalistic dimension identified with material force, he also recognized a characteristically static dimension that he identified with what he called "concrete things" (ki); both ontological dimensions were physical, but one was active, the other static. Jinsai's use of the term "concrete thing" reveals that the inspiration and justification for his new conception was that famous passage in the I ching that reads: "Hence that which is antecedent to the physical form exists, we say, as the Way, and that which is subsequent to the physical form exists, we say, as concrete things."[40]

That Jinsai and Chu Hsi disagreed in this way is indicated further by their glosses on the passage from the Changes just quoted. As might be expected, Chu Hsi explicitly separated transcendental and vitalistic dimensions when he observed, "that which enables yin and yang is the Way [read principle]" and "yin and yang are material force."[41] Jinsai, in contrast, refused to recognize the existence of transcendentals—in this case, a transcendental Way. The Way, he countered, is not, as Chu Hsi argued, the "course" or source of yin and yang but merely the "circling of yin and yang," and with this assertion he collapsed Chu Hsi's dualism.[42] Jinsai also strenuously objected to Chu Hsi's characterization of material force as "the concrete things that are subsequent to physical form."[43] Whereas Chu Hsi fused material force and concrete things, Jinsai separated them, and by doing so established his own dualistic conception. Both of his criticisms of Chu Hsi's views are summarized in the following passage: "Let us

[39] Abe, Nihon Shushigaku to Chōsen, pp. 514–517, 520–521, 530.

[40] James Legge, trans., I ching (New York: Causeway, 1973), p. 377.

[41] Chu Hsi, Chu Tzu yü-lei, chap. 74.

[42] Itō Jinsai, Gomō jigi, NST, 33:115.

[43] Chu Hsi, Chu Tzu wen-chi, chap. 40, quoted in Kusumoto Masatsugu, Sō-Min jidai Jugaku shisō no kenkyū (Chiba: Hiroike Gakuen Jigyōbu, 1972), p. 223.

compare this [matter of principle and material force] to a folding fan. A fan's creating wind is the Way, the paper and bamboo it is made of are concrete things. . . . Chu Hsi is wrong when he describes a fan's creating wind as a concrete thing and the principle behind its producing wind as the Way. How can one make material force out to be a concrete thing?"[44] In Jinsai's conception, there existed only action (the "fan's creating wind") and stasis ("the paper and bamboo [the fan] is made of") but no prior cause or explanatory principle. Likewise, the Way, yin and yang, and material force existed in one ontological dimension and concrete things in another. This was the dualistic conception that Sorai accepted.

At first glance, however, Sorai seems to have rejected Jinsai's new ontology. He contended, in several places, that Jinsai and Chu Hsi were saying the same things. For example, in a comment on Jinsai's reading of the passage from the *I ching* that was the *locus classicus* for his ontology, Sorai conveniently overlooked the metaphysical significance of Jinsai's view of yin and yang when he wrote: The reason that Jinsai interprets the alternation of yin and yang as the Way is not the same as Chu Hsi's. It is just that Jinsai abhors the word 'principle.' "[45] Equally uncharitable were Sorai's comments on Jinsai's use of the words "material force" and "concrete things." Referring to Jinsai's characterization of a "fan's creating wind" as the "Way" and the paper and bamboo it is made of "as concrete things," he accused Jinsai of being "blind to the [meaning] of the passage on that which is antecedent to and that which is subsequent to physical form."[46] Despite these denunciations, Sorai's ontological views did closely resemble Jinsai's.[47] Like Jinsai, he refused to recognize the transcendental dimension so favored by Chu Hsi and acknowledged only the vitalistic and concrete dimensions that Jinsai described in his later writings.[48] Although Sorai did not use the words "material force" and "concrete things" in tandem, as Jinsai did, he did divide reality into active and static dimensions, with the result that despite his apparent differences with Jinsai, most of which were personal rather than philosophical, their ontologies had the same dualistic structure.

Jinsai and Sorai did, however, emphasize different ontological dimensions. Whereas Jinsai was most concerned with the vitalistic dimension, Sorai was concerned chiefly with the static dimension, because he believed that the vitalistic dimension of reality was

---

[44] Itō Jinsai, *Gomō jigi*, NST, 33:123.

[45] "Sō Shin'an ni atau," in NST, 36:506–507.

[46] *Benmei*, NST, 36:246.

[47] Ibid., pp. 245–246, and "Sō Shin'an ni atau," in NST, 36:506.

[48] *Benmei*, NST, 36:246.

unknowable, at least by those not endowed with a sage's intelligence, precisely because it was active. "A fool, when he has made one or two successful predictions, will think that he achieved this through his own intellectual power, but this is not at all the case: it was due to the assistance of heaven and earth and ghosts and spirits."[49] Given the limitations of human intelligence, what then was one to do? Sorai suggested that one use the devices and concepts that the sages had created to compensate for human ignorance. There was, for example, divination (*bokuzei*) which permitted one to communicate with spirits and to fathom heaven's intentions.[50] There were also concepts like "change" and yin and yang which the sages devised to allow ordinary people to see what would otherwise have been imperceptible,[51] namely, "the processes of the Way of Heaven" (*tendō no ryūkō*) and "the natural [transformations] of the ten thousand things" (*banbutsu no shizen*).[52] But even these concepts, indeed all such concepts, warned Sorai, were still "conjectural" (*suiryō no sata*) and ultimately a matter of belief.[53] Far more certain than divination or these compensatory concepts was the civilization of ancient China as recorded in the classical texts. In the language of Sorai's neoclassical philology, if heaven, the sages, early kings, spirits, and the active processes of the cosmos could not be known, what could be known were the creations of the sages and early kings, including the literary and ceremonial forms, preserved in the Six Classics. The latter, being static and concrete, were accessible to anyone who could read the ancient language. And knowledge of the ancient literary and ceremonial forms would make it unnecessary "to seek the principle of the ten thousand things of heaven and earth, the mystery of human nature, destiny, Way, and virtue, or the source of rites and music."[54] Moreover, those who studied and mastered the ancient literary and ceremonial forms not only achieved certainty, they also demonstrated their reverence for heaven.

Sorai's acceptance of Jinsai's dualistic ontology helps to explain the special place of ancient literary and ceremonial forms in his new Confucian discourse. Although anyone acquainted with the language of the classical texts could master the literary and ceremonial forms created by the sages and early kings in accordance with heaven's will and preserved in these texts, Sorai also believed that this mastery

---

[49] *Sorai sensei tōmonsho*, NRI, 3:181–182.
[50] *Benmei*, NST, 36:239.
[51] Ibid., p. 247.
[52] Ibid.
[53] *Sorai sensei tōmonsho*, NRI, 3:158–159, 172.
[54] *Benmei*, NST, 36:250.

could be used to counter certain views popular in his time. Ancient ceremonial forms, for example, could be used to check the new naturalistic ethics advocated by Jinsai and others, and ancient literary forms could temper what Sorai regarded as the excessive intellectualism and subjectivity of contemporary Ch'eng-Chu scholars. In short, Sorai envisioned the ancient literary and ceremonial forms serving both a political and an epistemological purpose.

Although one can understand Sorai's misgivings about those who, like the disciples of Yamazaki Ansai (1618–1682), subscribed to an internally oriented and spiritual variety of the Ch'eng-Chu orthodoxy, one cannot understand his fear that Jinsai's new ethics would create chaos. After all, Sorai shared Jinsai's obvious interest in the "reality of the actual physical nature of man and things" and the new empiricism that he encouraged. He was also partial to any scholar who shared these views, including even Kaibara Ekken (1630–1714), a supporter of the Ch'eng-Chu orthodoxy. In fact, Sorai so admired Ekken's work that he once admitted that Ekken's views "anticipated my own" and regretted that he had never met him.[55] His recognition of the achievements of a Ch'eng-Chu scholar, albeit one of an empirical bent, suggests that Sorai could be as tolerant of a monistic ontology as he was of Jinsai's new dualistic ontology, and for the same reasons. His admiration for Ekken is also important as a tacit recognition of the affinities between his views and certain varieties of Ming Neo-Confucianism, since Ekken was as ardent an advocate of the externally oriented variety of the Ch'eng-Chu orthodoxy as existed in the late-seventeenth and early-eighteenth centuries, with the possible exception of Andō Seian (1622–1701).[56]

Despite his support of the movement away from transcendental to physical reality, Sorai was troubled by its ethical and political implications, implications that were most apparent in Jinsai's writings. Sorai agreed, for example, with Jinsai's denial of the Ch'eng-Chu notion of an "original nature" (C., *pen-jan chih hsing*; J., *honzen no sei*) and his description of human nature as both active and material.[57] Like Jinsai, he referred to human nature as the "physical nature" (C., *ch'i-chih chih hsing*; J., *kishitsu no sei*),[58] as he did in a letter to Yabu Shin'an in which he explained that if the sages differed from one another, it was because each had a distinctive "physical nature."[59] But Sorai also observed that if human nature exhibited these two

[55] "Chiku Shun'an ni atau," in *Soraishū*, 27:18a–b.
[56] Abe, *Nihon Shushigaku to Chōsen*, p. 521.
[57] *Benmei*, NST, 36:240.
[58] Ibid.
[59] "Sō Shin'an ni atau," in NST, 36:508.

traits of the material force—liveliness and physicality—it also must manifest a third trait, diversity, or what he once called the "infinite plenitude of everything within heaven and earth."[60] It was this diversity that inspired his doubts and misgivings. After all, it was not just each of the sages that was uniquely endowed but also each person in the world,[61] and it was not just people's natures that were different, but also their minds; as Sorai put it, people's minds were as different as their faces.[62] This being the case, "people's perceptions [of the world] varied according to their natures,"[63] and this infinite diversity, if unchecked, could lead to an anarchy of perception and, in turn, even to political and social disorder.

In fairness to Jinsai, we should remember that as concerned as he was with the positive features of human nature which he called, following Mencius, the "four beginnings" (C., *ssu-tuan*; J., *shitan*), he did not stop with human nature but went on to prescribe a rigorous praxis that promised "to extend and develop" (C., *k'uo-ch'ung*; J., *kakujū*) the innate moral endowment into virtue. On his part, Sorai refused to believe that human nature contained the beginnings of virtue and that one could attain virtue by extending and developing this innate moral potential. His refusal to recognize the importance of both the innate moral endowment and practice in Jinsai's ethics explains why he consistently misinterpreted Jinsai's arguments[64] and often misrepresented them, as he did when he suggested that Jinsai's notion of extending and developing the four beginnings to achieve virtue put him close to Chu Hsi.[65]

The more fundamental problem, however, was that Jinsai and Sorai had different views of the sources of virtue. Sorai insisted that Jinsai's contention that one could achieve virtue by extending and developing one's nature reversed the natural order of cultivation. The starting point should not be human nature or its presumed innate moral proclivities, but rather classical Chinese literature and culture. "What Jinsai calls virtue," he observed, "refers merely to what exists before virtue is achieved" and is the "concept" (*na*) of virtue, not its "substance" (*jitsu*).[66] This was because human nature was morally neutral and had no authority of any kind. Virtue had to originate in the civilization of ancient China which was imbued with the author-

---

[60] *Benmei*, NST, 36:247.
[61] *Gakusoku*, NST, 36:258, and *Benmei*, 36:212, 240.
[62] "Kutsu Keizan ni kotau," in NST, 36:534.
[63] *Benmei*, NST, 36:244.
[64] Ibid., pp. 212, 241–243.
[65] Ibid., p. 212.
[66] Ibid. See also *Bendō*, NST, 36:206.

ity of the sages, early kings, and heaven.[67] Jinsai had not realized this, observed Sorai, because he lacked the proper reverence for heaven and its agents.[68]

Moreover, Sorai insisted that human nature could not be accepted as it was but had to be refined; he proposed that this be done through the literary and ceremonial forms preserved in the *Odes, History, Rites*, and *Music*. Sorai considered these forms the best means of refining human nature because the sages had created them with the diversity of human nature in mind and as a foil to this diversity. In *Benmei* (Distinguishing Names), Sorai compared this process of refining human nature by means of ceremonial forms to the sages' transformation of what he called the "original substance" (*moto*) into a "refined form" (*bun*):[69]

> Consider the case of archery. Archery came about because of the efficacy of the bow and arrow in dominating the realm, and this is what is meant by the original substance (*moto*). Later, the sages embellished archery with rites and music, and this is what is meant by refined form (*bun*). The phrase [in the *Rites of I*] "archers are little concerned with hitting the target" reveals that the sages were interested in having those who practiced the art become familiar with rites and music and, in the process, establish their virtue. It tells us too that they were not very interested in the original function of archery; [that is], in whether or not the original function of archery had been lost. . . . The sages were concerned not with original substance but refined form.[70]

A similar dichotomy is implicit in Sorai's advice on refining one's nature by mastering the literary forms. "In expressing one's views," he cautioned his contemporaries, "one should never blurt them out impulsively or choose one's words capriciously. Instead, one should memorize [and use] to express one's thoughts the ancient words that

[67] *Benmei*, NST, 36:212, 214, 219.

[68] Ibid., pp. 212, 214, 227.

[69] Ibid., p. 252. Here Sorai was using the word *wen* (J. *bun*) as Confucius did in the *Analects*, and I follow Wing-tsit Chan and D. C. Lau in rendering *wen* as "refinement." See Chan, *A Source Book in Chinese Philosophy* (Princeton: Princeton University Press, 1964), p. 29, and Lau, *Confucius: The Analects* (New York: Penguin Books, 1979), p. 83.

For a discussion of the various meanings of the word, see James J. Y. Liu, *Chinese Theories of Literature* (Chicago: University of Chicago Press, 1975), pp. 7–9, and David McMullen, "Historical and Literary Theory in Mid-Eighth Century," in *Perspectives on the T'ang*, ed. Denis Twitchett and Arthur Wright (New Haven: Yale University Press, 1973), pp. 321–322.

[70] *Benmei*, NST, 36:252.

have been transmitted and that exist in the cosmos."[71] When one had done this, one would have embodied the "particulars of [the sages'] teachings" (oshie no jōken), or what he called "concrete form" (mono).[72] And here he stressed the importance of practice (okonai), observing that it was only by actually rehearsing classical etiquette and ritual and actually writing in classical styles that one truly embodied the ancient literary and ceremonial forms, refined one's nature, and achieved virtue.[73]

We should not think, however, that Sorai's distinction between human nature and the literary and ceremonial forms was absolute. He denied that once a measure of culture and literary sensibility had been achieved, one could then completely disregard one's nature. Appreciating as he did the diversity of humanity, Sorai could never have sanctioned this without contradicting himself. Instead, he argued that indeed both human nature and the literary and ceremonial forms were necessary, citing as his locus classicus Confucius' discussion of the respective merits of "natural substance" (C., chih; J., shitsu) and "refined form" (C., wen; J., bun).[74] As Sorai explained, it was not simply that both the unrefined and the refined were important but that the refined form should respect the unrefined nature. He regularly reminded his readers that when cultivating themselves they should not overlook the distinctive features of their own natures.[75] In his analogy, they had to study their own natures as carefully as carpenters and swordsmiths had to study the materials of their trades; and just as carpenters took into account the grains and textures of the woods they fashioned into structures, and just as swordsmiths considered the special strengths and weaknesses of the metals they hammered into knives and swords, they, too, had to consider their own natural tendencies as they went about refining their natures.[76] Why this was necessary should now be apparent: one's natural endowment was a gift from both one's parents and heaven, and to deny it or to seek to convert it into something else was both unfilial and sacrilegious. This, in any case, was Sorai's rejoinder to both Jinsai and those who subscribed to the new naturalistic ethics inspired by Ming Neo-Confucianism.

It was on these grounds that Sorai criticized those of his contemporaries who adhered to the internal and spiritual forms of the Ch'eng-

[71] Ibid., p. 254.
[72] Ibid.
[73] Ibid., and "Tōmon tsuki," in NST, 36:511–512.
[74] Analects, 6:16.
[75] "Sō Shin'an ni atau," in NST, 36:507–508, and Chūyōkai, NMSCZ, 1:9.
[76] Chūyōkai, NMSCZ, 1:44.

Chu orthodoxy popularized by Fujiwara Seika (1561–1619) and Nakae Tōju (1608–1648), and represented in his time by the disciples of Yamazaki Ansai. He centered his attack on their notions of mind (C., *hsin*; J., *kokoro*) and principle.[77] In his attack on their view of mind, Sorai began by denying the existence of transcendentals. Whereas they spoke of a universal "moral mind" (*dōshin*) and described the mind as possessing "innate goodness" (*ryōshin*), Sorai insisted that there were only individual minds, which "like human faces were never the same"[78] and were devoid of any moral endowment.[79] Believing this, it was not difficult for him to criticize his contemporaries' preoccupation with mind, that is, their own minds, and to mock their claim that everyone possessed a mind like a sage's and that this shared endowment enabled anyone, with the proper effort, to become a sage.[80] In Sorai's view, this could not be proved and indeed was like "painting thunder and ghosts." Although it may not seem so at first, the issue of whether there was a universal mind or only particular minds was a seminal one: if one believed that there was a universal mind, then one might make it the foundation for self-cultivation and even political and social order. According to Sorai, this is what those who still subscribed to the Ch'eng-Chu orthodoxy did. On the other hand, if one believed that there were only particular minds, then one would have to find a new foundation for personal cultivation and order, which also would check the dangers posed by the infinite diversity of human minds. The latter is what Sorai attempted to do, and, as we have seen, he found such a foundation in classical Chinese culture, particularly in classical Chinese ceremonial forms. Consider his having written, with the *Book of History* as his *locus classicus*, that ritual propriety, a ceremonial form, should be used to order one's mind.[81]

To Sorai, however, the best illustration of his contemporaries' preoccupation with metaphysics and the danger of that interest was their notion of principle. Chu Hsi had described principle as transcendental and universal, which Sorai could not accept, convinced as he was that anything originating in human consciousness was sure to

[77] "Kutsu Keizan ni kotau," in NST, 36:533.

[78] For Chu Hsi's views on the moral and human minds, see Wing-tsit Chan, *A Source Book in Chinese Philosophy*, pp. 615–616, 628. See also Ogyū Sorai, *Sorai sensei tōmonsho*, NRI, 3:162, and "An Tanpaku ni kaesu," in NST, 36:541.

[79] *Chūyōkai*, NMSCZ, 1:3; "Tōmon tsuki," in NST, 36:516; "Ryūsen Naisansei ni kaesu," in NST, 36:516; and "Kutsu Keizan ni kotau," in NST, 36:533–534.

[80] *Bendō*, NST, 36:207.

[81] *Benmei*, NST, 36:220, 242.

be subjective, arbitrary, and lacking in "fixed standards."[82] One should not think, however, that Sorai was opposed to principle as such, for clearly he was not. He recognized, for example, that "all affairs and things naturally possess principles" and, more fundamentally, that all humans were endowed with the capacity to think and that principle was a product of that faculty.[83] At the same time, he carefully separated contemporary conceptions of principle and his own. To Sorai, what his contemporaries called "principle" was just an idea, a "theory" (rikutsu), as he put it, and thus as diverse as those who imagined them.[84] What Sorai called principle was more than just an idea or theory imagined and spun in the mind's eye; it was grounded in and corroborated by the classical texts and assumed the particular and knowable forms of ritual and music, or what he called ceremonial form. "The Way of the Sages never speaks of principle," he wrote."Deeds (waza) are made to hold principle. Discard [these] deeds and employ only principle, and principle will lack standards."[85] Here Sorai uses "deeds" instead of "ceremonial form." Similarly, the very language of the classical texts—the literary forms—provided something more specific and concrete and, as Sorai would have it, more objective than principle. As the sages and early kings spoke of literary norms but never of principle, one had to use these norms to determine principle, and when one did this, Sorai declared, "then perception would have definite standards and principle a foundation."[86] Once again, what made this possible was the omniscience of the sages and early kings, which enabled them "to [study] principle exhaustively and to establish norms," that is, the literary and ceremonial forms.[87]

Yet Sorai's criticisms of contemporary Ch'eng-Chu scholars are not what they seem. Although there is no denying that he opposed those who stressed the introspective and spiritual side of Chu Hsi's philosophy, and indeed Chu Hsi himself and the Ch'engs as well, this is not all. A close reading of Sorai's objections suggests that they were formulated against those interpreters of the Ch'engs and Chu Hsi who, following the lead of the Ming Confucians Lo Ch'in-shun, Wu T'ing-han, Wang T'ing-hsiang, and others, advanced new monistic ontologies, espoused naturalistic ethical doctrines, and promoted evidential research. Consider, for example, Sorai's view of

[82] Ibid., p. 244; "Sō Shin'an ni atau," in NST, 36:506; and "Kutsu Keizan ni kotau," in NST, 36:530.

[83] Benmei, NST, 36:244.

[84] Taiheisaku, NST, 36:455.

[85] Ibid., p. 461.

[86] Benmei, NST, 36:244.

[87] Ibid., p. 244, 248.

mind and human nature. When he attacked those who, in loyalty to Chu Hsi, assumed the existence of both a "moral mind" and a "human mind," an "original nature" and a "physical nature," he appears to have assumed, in contrast, that there were only individual minds and physical natures, an assumption he shared with Jinsai and those of his contemporaries who embraced the new naturalism. Sorai, however, did not stop there. Worried about the dangers posed by individual minds and merely physical natures, he urged his contemporaries to regulate their minds and to refine their natures by rehearsing ancient ritual etiquette and writing in classical styles. Yet even though Sorai called for the regulation of eccentric human minds and the refinement of diverse human natures, he also insisted that the process of regulation and refinement respect the particular minds and natures being cultivated. And it is Sorai's unmistakable ambivalence toward the new naturalism that explains his criticisms of the Ch'engs and Chu Hsi and their loyal Japanese followers.

Sorai's ambivalence is even more apparent in his discussion of principle. When he challenged contemporary conceptions of principle, he was questioning both the dualistic and monistic conceptions of principle. If transcendental notions of principle were unacceptable, so, too, were purely empirical conceptions, for in Sorai's view both equally reflected their authors' minds.[88] Principle, he argued, had to be grounded in the ancient literary and ceremonial forms. "If one [first] grasps the meaning [of the language] of the early kings, [and then] uses that to arrive at principle, then perception will have standards and principle will be achieved."[89] Sorai's insistence that anything produced by the mind and uncorroborated by the Six Classics was bound to be subjective reveals why he objected to contemporary metaphysics. He had gone beyond his predecessors and contemporaries who promoted evidential research. Empirical study was acceptable, Sorai seemed to be saying, but it had to be directed at the classical texts and had to assist in the excavation of those ancient literary and ceremonial forms that would supply the "standards" for principle. Clearly, Sorai's view of the new monistic ontologies and the empiricism they encouraged was duplicated in his criticisms of the Ch'engs and Chu Hsi and their adherents.

Thus Sorai was responding primarily to Jinsai, those who subscribed to the externally oriented variety of Ming Neo-Confucianism, and to what he perceived as the particular hazards of the new naturalistic ethics and monistic ontologies. What this reveals, then, is

[88] Ibid., p. 244.
[89] Ibid.

the subtle tension within Sorai's writings. He began by affirming physical nature and reality, as Jinsai and the advocates of the externally oriented strain of the Ch'eng-Chu orthodoxy had, but then went on to recognize what he considered to be the dangers of the new naturalistic ethics and monistic ontologies. As a defense against these dangers, Sorai offered the ancient literary and ceremonial forms and, indeed, the entire edifice of classical Chinese civilization. Although he seemed to deny physical nature and empirical reality, he was actually affirming them and asking only that physical nature be refined by the literary forms and checked by the ceremonial forms. The proof of this is his insistence that these literary and ceremonial forms respect human nature and reality. Indeed, Sorai was trying to establish a delicate balance between the newly affirmed "reality of the actual physical nature of man and things" and the great civilization created by the sages and early kings. It was these two dimensions—the one natural, the other artificial—and their balance that comprised the structure of Sorai's thinking on ethical matters.

This same balance between nature and artifice appears in Sorai's views on statecraft, but in a different guise. In *Taiheisaku* (A Proposal for a Great Peace) and *Seidan* (A Discourse on Government), the memorials that Sorai presented to the shogun Tokugawa Yoshimune (1684–1751), there is a conspicuous tension between the ever-changing historical reality and the institutions created by the sages and early kings. In order to understand this, one first has to understand Sorai's view of history.

Like many of his contemporaries, especially those influenced by the new Ming varieties of Neo-Confucianism, Sorai subscribed to a new historicism that recognized both the ubiquity of historical change and the uniqueness of each historical moment. As was true with his contemporaries, Sorai's historicism seems to have been spawned by the vitalistic cosmologies advocated by Jinsai and others of his time. We are sure that Sorai accepted the new cosmologies, for we have not only his own declarations to this effect but also the more certain evidence provided by his own writings. Consider the following from his *Ken'en zuihitsu* (Jottings from a Miscanthus Garden): "Heaven and earth are active beings as are people. Thus does the Way of Heaven and Earth luxuriate without end and the transformations of affairs and things multiply—ten, a hundred, a thousand, ten thousand times over—without cease."[90] The repetition of the phrases "heaven and earth are

[90] *Ken'en zuihitsu*, in *Ogyū Sorai zenshū*, ed. Imanaka Kanshi and Naramoto Tatsuya (Kawade Shobō, 1973), 1:483. See also *Sorai sensei tōmonsho*, NRI, 3:158, and "Tōmon tsuki," in NST, 36:514.

active beings" (*tenchi katsubutsu nari*) and "people are active beings" (*hito katsubutsu nari*) in Sorai's later writings leaves little doubt that he accepted the most basic premise of the new cosmologies, namely, that change, not stasis, is the normal condition of the cosmos, including humanity.[91] The idea that change—in this case linguistic and literary change—is both omnipresent and the result of perpetual human activity is reminiscent of Jinsai's famous assertion that "liveliness" is the chief trait of the cosmos and everything in it.[92] And this, together with the fact that he indicates in a number of places his admiration for Jinsai's vitalistic cosmology, makes it likely that Sorai's cosmological conceptions owed much to Jinsai.[93]

Sorai's later writings confirm de Bary's observation that the Ming Neo-Confucians' vitalistic cosmologies, particularly the emphasis on renewal and growth, "helped to produce a new attitude toward history, seeing it as more than the endless repetition of dynastic cycles or degeneration from an ideal past."[94] The strengthening of Sorai's historicist assumptions over time may also have been because his own research demonstrated that language and literary style actually did change from age to age. The following passage, from *Jottings from a Miscanthus Garden*, suggests that Sorai had long believed this: "All people have a language. At times it is plain; at other times ornate. How can one speak of consistency? Some words will be pronounced similarly but have different meanings, other words will have the same meanings but will be pronounced differently. How can one speak of consistency? Why is this so? It is because people themselves are active beings."[95] As we saw earlier, the discoveries that language and literary style changed from age to age and that ancient and modern languages and styles differed inspired Sorai's call for a close and empirical reading of the classical texts.

Although Sorai continued to believe that "as ages change, they carry their languages with them," one does find in his later writings two subtle changes in his historicism. Earlier, under the inspiration of the Ming writers Li and Wang, Sorai had been preoccupied with linguistic and literary changes and with the reasons for these changes, but he now was equally concerned with the historicity of language and literary style; that is, he was concerned not just with the fact that

---

[91] The phrases appear several times in *Sorai sensei tōmonsho*, NRI, 3:153, 166, 177.

[92] Itō Jinsai, *Gomō jigi*, NST, 33:116.

[93] *Benmei*, NST, 36:240.

[94] Wm. Theodore de Bary, "Neo-Confucian Cultivation and the Seventeenth Century Enlightenment," in *The Unfolding of Neo-Confucianism*, ed. Wm. Theodore de Bary (New York: Columbia University Press, 1975), p.113.

[95] *Ken'en zuihitsu*, in *Ogyū Sorai zenshū*, 1:474.

language and literary style did change, but also with the features themselves of the language and literary style of specific periods. Moreover, Sorai's interests were no longer limited to language and literary style but now included ideas, ceremonies, customs, and institutions. His explications of Chinese philosophy, for example, were almost always historical. An example of this is his account of how human nature (C., *hsing*; J., *sei*) came to be an issue in Confucianism:

> It was because Tzu-ssu and Mencius were surpassed by Lao-tzu and Chuang-tzu [who described virtue as artificial] that they advanced the theory that human nature was good. And Hsün-tzu, in turn, recognizing that the theory of an innately good nature would lead to the abolition of ritual and music, asserted that human nature was evil. All of their arguments were meant to rescue their ages. Is this not understandable?[96]

According to Sorai, what was true of ideas was also true of customs and ceremonies: they, too, changed from age to age and were distinctive in each period. Ritual and music, the quintessential ceremonial forms of ancient China, were a good example: created by the sages Yao and Shun to bring order to the realm, they reflected the period of their creation,[97] and as historical artifacts, they, too, went out of vogue and were replaced in the Ch'in dynasty by laws and codes.[98] Their replacement was evidence that institutions, too, changed and reflected the periods of their creation. Here is Sorai's account of this important change:

> Because the Three Dynasties period was an age of feudalism and the Ch'in, Han, T'ang, Sung, and Ming ages of commanderies and prefectures, the institutions in the two periods differed dramatically. In the [earlier] feudal age, the realm was divided among the various lords, and the emperor directly governed only a small area. The vassals of feudal lords received hereditary stipends and held fiefs in perpetuity. Although talented individuals were employed, a person's status was fixed so that a knight was always a knight and a lord always a lord. Thus was it a world in which people felt secure and were at peace. It was less the laws and regulations, which were vague and imprecise, than the munificence of the various lords and the dutifulness of their subjects

---

[96] *Bendō*, NST, 36:204.
[97] Ibid., p. 201.
[98] *Gakusoku*, NST, 36:258.

that made possible order in the realm. The inculcation of honor [also] was given great importance.[99]

Institutions in the two periods differed, Sorai continued, because the periods themselves were different:

> In the age of commanderies and prefectures, there were no feudal lords, and knights were knights only for the duration of their lives and received modest salaries instead of fiefs. They had numerous subordinates, and this attested to their power and standing. . . . Because they were appointed by the emperor for three-year terms, officials usually sought, above all else, to demonstrate the efficiency of their administrations. As it was possible for one to rise from the rank of commoner to a ministerial post, many aspired to high positions. This, then, is how [the institutions of the] Three Dynasties and [those of] later ages differed.[100]

The uniqueness of the ideas, customs, ceremonies, and institutions of distinct ages, and indeed of the ages themselves, was, to Sorai, axiomatic.[101]

Yet Sorai's acceptance of the new historicism was only conditional. Although he recognized that change was the essence of history and that each age or period was different, he also argued that classical Chinese civilization was changeless and timeless. "In the teachings [of the sages]," he wrote, "there is neither past nor present. [Their] Way has neither past nor present. . . . What fails to hold true for both past and present cannot be considered the Way or teachings of the ancient sages."[102] This is so, he added on another occasion, since "the teachings of the ancient sages span past and present, and the value of their teachings is the same for distant as for recent ages."[103] What Sorai was implying was that although ideas, customs, ceremonies, and institutions did change over time, those created by the sages and early kings were timeless, a perfect foil to perpetual change, and thus could be revived in any age. This was possible, he explained, first because the sages and early kings were able "to see the future" and to anticipate the ills and problems in the times ahead;[104] and second, because they created institutions that "accorded with hu-

---

[99] *Sorai sensei tōmonsho*, NRI, 3:154–155.

[100] Ibid., p. 155.

[101] *Benmei*, NST, 3:211, and *Sorai sensei tōmonsho*, NRI, 3:202–203.

[102] *Sorai sensei tōmonsho*, NRI, 3:190; *Benmei*, NST, 36:256; and "An Tanpaku ni Kaesu," in NST, 36:538.

[103] *Sorai sensei tōmonsho*, NRI, 3:193. See also *Benmei*, NST, 36:250–251, and *Taiheisaku*, NST, 36:448.

[104] *Taiheisaku*, NST, 36:409.

man nature," presumably an infinitely diverse human nature, and with the emotions.[105] Given Sorai's faith in the omniscience of the sages and early kings, his claim that the civilization they created was timeless and universal is not at all surprising.

Nor is it surprising that his personal faith was the foundation of his proposals for political and economic reform. In *A Proposal for a Great Peace* and *A Discourse on Government*, Sorai attributed the obvious inadequacies of existing institutions to the fact that they had simply evolved over time or had been established without proper regard for either history or human emotions.[106] They were not what he called "true institutions" (*makoto no seido*) by which he meant classical Chinese institutions. Predictably, Sorai's solution to current problems was the establishment of these true institutions. He proposed specifically that the bakufu adopt the well-field system and resettle the majority of the urban population on the land,[107] replace the existing tax system with the tribute system that dated from the Three Dynasties period,[108] and remodel the inefficient bureaucracy according to the ancient Chinese Six-Office, Six-Department, and rank-in-merit systems.[109] Finally, Sorai urged his fellow samurai "to immerse themselves in the Six Classics" and in so doing master the ancient literary and ceremonial forms.[110]

Yet Sorai was not blind to the particular needs of his time and country, as his recognition of the samurai and his pragmatic proposals for administrative, economic, and social reform show. Consider, for example, his realization that the most dramatic institutional change of the day, the commercialization of the economy, was irreversible. Unlike other political thinkers of the time, notably Kumazawa Banzan (1619–1691), who called for a return to a natural economy, Sorai believed that this was impossible and called only for the self-sufficiency of the samurai. As he saw it, this would remedy samurai indebtedness to merchants and "make the samurai the 'masters' and the merchants the 'guests.'"[111] Sorai's realism is apparent, too, in his insistence that the sale of land be allowed. Questioning long-standing bakufu laws that prohibited the sale of land, Sorai argued that because the peasants had been free for some time to buy land as they

---

[105] *Seidan*, NST, 36:366; and *Benmei*, NST, 36:222, 231–232.

[106] *Seidan*, NST, 36:306–307, 312, 318–319.

[107] *Sorai sensei tōmonsho*, NRI, 3:185; *Taiheisaku*, NST, 36:478–479; and *Seidan*, NST, 36:263–267.

[108] *Seidan*, NST, 36:319–320.

[109] Ibid., pp. 346–350.

[110] *Taiheisaku*, NST, 36:449.

[111] *Seidan*, NST, 36:345.

pleased and because many, in fact, had bought their land, they also ought to be able to sell it if they wished. Why? Because the impulse to buy and sell was well established, and it was a natural inclination.[112] All this suggests that despite his belief in heaven, the sages, and early kings and despite his ardent neoclassicism, Sorai was also a realist.

Sorai's advancing both pragmatic proposals and neoclassical reforms points up the dichotomy between his realization of the particular circumstances of his age and the neoclassical solutions to them that he had gleaned from the Chinese classics. This dichotomy is also apparent in his claim that the classical Chinese institutions were based on a realistic assessment of human nature and emotions. These dichotomies remind us of those found in his discussions of ethical and literary matters, and this coincidence may explain why Sorai was so critical of existing institutions and so sure that when and if his proposed reforms were carried out, the severe social and economic crises of his day would be resolved.

Sorai's thought was distinguished, then, by its affirmation of both nature and artifice, an affirmation that assumed several different forms in his later writings. Its metaphysical form was the affirmation of both material force and concrete things as well as the ontological dimensions they represented—one active, the other static. Although Sorai accepted both dimensions, he believed that the former, with which he identified heaven, spirits, and natural phenomena, was ultimately unknowable and that only the latter could be known. And it was to concrete things, particularly the institutions and artifacts of ancient Chinese civilization and the classical texts in which they were preserved, that Sorai devoted most of his attention.

The ethical expression of Sorai's affirmation of nature and artifice was his recognition of both the physical nature, emotions, and desires, and the formal means of refining and regulating them, namely, the literary and ceremonial forms. Sorai believed that the mere affirmation of the physical nature, emotions, and desires would court disaster. This was because in each case human nature was unique, human emotion and desires unpredictable, and each person's mind hopelessly subjective, and this could only lead to institutional disorder. To counter this threat, Sorai advanced the ancient Chinese literary and ceremonial forms: not only did they refine human nature, regulate the emotions and desires, and keep particular minds in check, but they also provided objective standards and a certain authority.

[112] Ibid., p. 436.

Finally, the coexistence in *A Proposal for a Great Peace* and *A Discourse on Government* of historicist and neoclassical elements is the third manifestation of Sorai's affirmation of nature and artifice. Even as he accepted the ubiquity of both cosmic and historical change and recognized the irreversibility of many of the changes under way in his time, he also recommended the adoption of what he believed were the constant and timeless institutions that had been devised by the sages and early kings. He was convinced that this would solve the social and economic problems of his day.

Yet Sorai was not simply affirming nature and artifice, he was counterbalancing them. This is significant, as it leaves little doubt that he formulated his new ontology, ethics, and statecraft to oppose not the Ch'engs and Chu Hsi and their most devoted Japanese followers, as has long been alleged, but rather the views of those who subscribed to or were influenced by that variety of the Ch'eng-Chu orthodoxy advanced by Lo Ch'in-shun, Wu T'ing-han, Wang T'ing-hsiang, and others—Kaibara Ekken, Andō Seian, and the Hayashi. What this suggests is, first, that it was precisely because the latter group espoused a new monistic ontology centering on material force that Sorai distinguished material force and concrete things, giving greater weight to the latter; second, that it was because these same thinkers advocated ethics that affirmed the physical nature, emotions, and desires that Sorai stressed classical Chinese literary and ceremonial forms as the means of refining and regulating human nature, emotions, and desires; and third, that it was because many of these thinkers proposed pragmatic institutional reforms inspired by a new historicism that Sorai called for the revival of classical Chinese institutions. Thus those who have argued that Sorai was opposing the original Ch'eng-Chu orthodoxy have obscured his intent and achievement.

SEVEN

MASUHO ZANKŌ (1655–1742): A SHINTO POPULARIZER BETWEEN NATIVISM AND NATIONAL LEARNING

BY PETER NOSCO

One of the most interesting questions faced by Tokugawa intellectual historians is how to account for the rise of National Learning (*kokugaku*) as an ideological alternative to Confucian studies. In view of the complexity of the issue, it is not surprising that there are available several convincing alternative explanations of this phenomenon.

Perhaps the best known is what might be styled the "Maruyama thesis" which, somewhat ironically, was never intended to serve as a theory of National Learning.[1] By identifying numerous structural resemblances between the thought of Ogyū Sorai (1666–1728) and Motoori Norinaga (1730–1801), respectively the greatest of eighteenth-century Confucian and nativist thinkers, Maruyama appeared to many to be putting into place the final pieces of a puzzle that located prototypes for numerous features of National Learning within the century and a half of preceding Japanese Confucian thought. Maruyama's followers and interpreters observed that at least two central concerns of the major National Learning figures (*kokugakusha*) could be linked to one or more of the Confucian schools of the first half of the Tokugawa era: like all Confucians, the kokugakusha were concerned with the past and turned to the most ancient written sources in order to formulate a more coherent picture of archaic values and practices; and just as Ancient Learning (*kogaku*) Confucians had done with ancient Chinese texts, they attempted philologically to reinterpret and glean from those sources a Way, or, more specifically, an ancient Japanese Way (*kodō*) which, they believed, had informed and directed life during the so-called Divine Age (*Kamiyo* or *Jindai*) of Japan's primordially distant past. Indeed, one must not underestimate the importance of the Confucian thought that contributed signifi-

---

[1] Masao Maruyama, *Studies in the Intellectual History of Tokugawa Japan*, trans. Mikiso Hane (Princeton: Princeton University Press, 1974).

cantly to early-Tokugawa discourse and, in turn, helped to shape the early character of National Learning, though to suggest that National Learning represents little more than the nativist application of Confucian assumptions, as some scholars have done, does disservice to the Maruyama thesis and is inadequate as a theory of National Learning.[2]

A second widely used approach has been the "emotionalism (*shujōshugi*) thesis." According to its proponents, the exuberance and vitality of late-seventeenth-century Japan were responsible for a social and intellectual climate that proved inimicable to the puritanical stance of orthodox Neo-Confucianism vis-à-vis human emotions and desires. The "emotionalism" of the Japanese, this theory contends, required modes of thought that affirmed the affective spheres of human experience, and it was through such affirmation that, on the one hand, Confucianism in Japan became progressively more "Japanese," and, on the other, that prominent thinkers rejected Confucianism and turned to the native tradition for the sources of such affirmation. Since all major kokugakusha insisted upon the validity of emotions and desires and criticized Confucianism for its alleged weakness on this score, considerable evidence is available to support this thesis.[3]

Yet a third interpretation of the rise of National Learning relates to what has been referred to elsewhere in this volume as the "rationalism" of Tokugawa thought. The legacy of Neo-Confucianism is prominent here. To all Tokugawa Confucians save those of the late Tokugawa, the world was comprehensible, and while the nature of that comprehension might vary from one Confucian to another, the very assumption of this comprehensibility encouraged a broad range of rational and quasi-scientific inquiry in Tokugawa thought. According to this interpretation, National Learning arose in reaction against this rationalism and instead celebrated the wondrous, the nonrational, and that which lay beyond the limits of human understanding. As Motoori Norinaga pointed to this in his first important essay written at age twenty-seven: "It is those straight-laced stinking Confucians who insist that anything wondrous must be false and cannot exist. . . . There are things in the world that are beyond the ability of the ordinary mind to comprehend."[4] In fact, Norinaga ar-

---

[2] See Peter Nosco, "Nature, Invention and National Learning: The *Kokka hachiron* Controversy, 1742–46," *Harvard Journal of Asiatic Studies* 41, no. 1 (June 1981): 77–81.

[3] An example of this approach can be found in Matsumoto Sannosuke's masterful discussion of the political thought of National Learning, *Kokugaku seiji shisō no kenkyū* (Miraisha, 1972).

[4] From his *Ashiwake obune*, in Ōno Susumu and Ōkubo Tadashi, eds., *Motoori Norinaga zenshū* (Chikuma Shobō, 1968–1975), 2:45.

rived at this conclusion after five years of study under Hori Keizan (1689–1757), a Kyoto Neo-Confucian with close ties to the Sorai school.[5]

A fourth way of regarding the rise of National Learning, and the most relevant for the purpose of this essay, is to regard National Learning as the more ideological version of nativist pursuits with long roots in the Japanese tradition and more immediate prototypes in the seventeenth century. Hisamatsu Sen'ichi (1894–1976) pioneered this view in modern scholarship on National Learning when in 1927 he maintained that it was necessary to think in terms of two meanings of the word *kokugaku*. The first was kokugaku in the broad sense of the term, that is, all scholarship that took Japan as its focus instead of China (*Kangaku*); the second was kokugaku in the narrow sense, or the attempt to glean, through philological method, a Way from Japan's most ancient written sources, and the attendant attempt to elevate that ancient Way to the status of a contemporary religion.[6] In this sense, then, the broadly based nativist pursuits of the seventeenth century were the precursors of the ideological nativism of the eighteenth century.

To cite a literary example in support of this thesis, one might observe that during the seventeenth century there was a revival of interest in ancient literature and verse. Traditional genres and literary techniques were rediscovered and used to create thematically fresh prose, while literary criticism was rescued from a stagnant didacticism that had dominated perspectives on classical literature for centuries.[7] Scholars interested in verse, like Kinoshita Chōshōshi (1569–1649) and Shimokōbe Chōryū (1624–1686), resurrected the thirty-one syllable *Waka*, and in their search for Waka composed in an age prior to what they regarded as the didactic lapses of preceding generations, they turned to ever-more ancient collections of poetry until they arrived at the most ancient of all, the long neglected *Man'yōshū*. One formidable hurdle faced by these scholars was that over the centuries, the great majority of the anthology's four and a half thousand verses had become all but unreadable to contemporary Japanese, and to resolve this dilemma they turned to the new science of philology.[8]

[5] Some implications of this point of agreement between Norinaga and the Sorai school are discussed in this volume on pp. 17–18.

[6] Hisamatsu Sen'ichi, *Keichū-den* (Osaka: Asahi Shinbunsha, 1927), p. 227.

[7] To cite just one example, Ihara Saikaku (1642–1693) launched his career as an author with his *Kōshoku ichidai otoko* (1682), an irreverent tale of a satyric hero, which, like Murasaki Shikibu's classic *Genji monogatari*, contained exactly fifty-four chapters.

[8] For a discussion of seventeenth-century literary criticism and poetics, see Donald Keene, *World Within Walls* (New York: Holt, Rinehart and Winston, 1976), pp. 300–310.

Keichū's (1640–1701) commentary on the *Man'yōshū* represents the high-water mark of this seventeenth-century nativist philology and set the stage for the more ideological analyses of the same work by the eighteenth-century kokugakusha, Kamo Mabuchi (1697–1769).[9]

A similar process can be observed in the field of Shinto studies. Leading Shinto theologians of the seventeenth century sought to recast their creed using the basic assumptions and terminology of Neo-Confucianism, while major scholars of Neo-Confucianism sought to construct new Shinto theologies incorporating various elements from their comprehensive metaphysics. In general, those efforts that arose from within the traditional Shinto denominations were more successful than those that were fashioned by leading Neo-Confucians, despite obvious similarities and overlapping areas between the two. This success notwithstanding, later Shintoists of the early-eighteenth century indicated their dissatisfaction with Confucian-Shinto by inaugurating a series of attempts on the one hand to popularize Shinto doctrine, and on the other to purge Confucian and Buddhist elements from their doctrine in order to arrive at an allegedly "purer" version of Shinto as it might have been practiced in the primordially distant past. Ideologically, these Shinto purists were virtually indistinguishable from the major kokugakusha, but they have traditionally been disqualified from inclusion in the ranks of National Learning's "great men" by their relative disregard for philological method.[10]

One such Shinto purist and popularizer was Masuho Zankō (1665–1742). Also known as Masuho Nokoguchi, Zankō was a Shinto popularist once described by Ienaga Saburō as if not exactly a "forgotten" scholar in the vein of Tominaga Nakamoto (1715–1746) or Andō Shōeki (dates uncertain), then certainly as a thinker who appears, somehow, to be continually in the process of being forgotten.[11] The remainder of this essay focuses on three areas: first, the major examples of Confucian-Shinto prior to Masuho Zankō; second, a survey of Zankō's life and summary of the major features of his thought; and third, the attempt to locate Zankō ideologically, regarding him as a transitional figure midway between the syncretic Shinto discourse of the seventeenth century, that is, nativism in the broad sense,

[9] See Peter Nosco, "Keichū (1640–1701): Forerunner of National Learning," *Asian Thought and Society* 5, no. 15 (December 1980): 237–252.

[10] For discussions of National Learning in terms of its "great men," see Ryusaku Tsunoda et al., eds., *Sources of Japanese Tradition* (New York: Columbia University Press, 1964), 2:1–46; Hisamatsu, *Keichū-den*; and Nosco, "Nature, Invention and National Learning," p. 75.

[11] "Masuho Zankō no shisō," *Nihon Rekishi* 41, no. 10 (October 1951): 2.

and the fundamentalist Shinto discourse of eighteenth-century National Learning.

Syncretism is nothing new in the history of Shinto, for Shinto has always found means to respond to and accommodate itself with the major intellectual and cultural trends of Japanese history. Centuries prior to the Tokugawa when Buddhism dominated scholarly discourse, Tendai and Shingon, the most "orthodox" of Japanese Buddhism's classical denominations, took the lead in fashioning syncretic Buddhist-Shinto formulas for the coexistence of Buddhism with Shinto, and the degree of Buddhist-Shinto syncretism was at times so great as to make it impossible to demarcate the two. Still later in the fifteenth century, Shinto apologetics were written by figures like Ichijō Kanera (1402–1481) and Yoshida Kanetomo (1435–1511) who sought to reverse earlier syncretic formulas by giving Shinto priority over Buddhism.

In the early-Tokugawa period, with Neo-Confucianism at the center of the new Tokugawa discourse, leading Shinto theologians sought to transform their creed so as to displace Buddhist elements with Confucian ones, while Neo-Confucian theorists for their part recognized a potential ally in Shinto against their Buddhist rivals. Just as the more popular Pure Land denominations of Buddhism had disdained such attempts at syncretism, later Tokugawa Confucians outside the fold of orthodox Neo-Confucianism likewise found little need to devote themselves to Confucian explications of Shinto.[12] A comparison of the Chu Hsi-based Shinto of Hayashi Razan (1583–1657) with the Confucianized Shinto of Yoshikawa Koretaru (1616–1694) is illustrative of these syncretic ventures.

It may seem surprising that Hayashi Razan, that pillar of orthodoxy in Japanese Neo-Confucianism, should have taken the lead in writing the earliest Confucian commentaries on Shinto in the Tokugawa period.[13] A lesser Neo-Confucian, one with fewer institutional commitments to the philosophy, might have been more appropriate, but a lesser Confucian might likewise have lacked the erudition and confidence in his own orthodoxy to do the task properly. In his commentaries on Shinto, Razan epitomized the inclina-

---

[12] Exceptions, of course, can be found in both instances. Nichiren (1222–1282) and certain Pure Land figures retained an interest in Hachiman, just as Kumazawa Banzan (d. 1691), identified with the Wang Yang-ming school (Yōmeigaku), developed a Shinto-oriented religious system. In general, however, the "rule" holds.

[13] Razan's interest in Shinto is believed to date from his early twenties when he was still a student at the Kenninji and heard lectures on the subject from teachers of the Kiyohara school, identified with Yoshida Shinto.

tion toward comprehensiveness inherent in Neo-Confucianism, for to an orthodox proponent of the philosophy, it was inconceivable that "truths" could exist outside the Chu Hsi metaphysic.[14] Conversely, as Herman Ooms demonstrates in his chapter, Shinto (particularly in its Yoshida denomination) was never far from the center of early-Tokugawa discourse or from the thinking of the first shogun Ieyasu, and Razan may have felt it advantageous to his ambiguous status in the bakufu to devote attention to it.

Razan's first major work on a Shinto topic was his *On Japanese Shrines* (*Honchō jinja-kō*, ca. 1638–1640), and while it presents an excellent historical survey of major shrines and figures in the development of Shinto, theologically the work is dominated by clichés of a distinctly medieval vintage.[15] A more mature work and Razan's most concise statement of his theories concerning Shinto was his *Traditions of Shinto* (*Shintō denju*, 1644–1648), in which he formulated his "Shinto where Principle Corresponds to the Mind" (*ritō shinchi Shintō*).[16]

Razan sought to incorporate the Shinto Way of the Gods within the Confucian Way of the Chu Hsi school by equating principle (*ri*) with the numinous power of the native gods, thereby making the spiritual and temporal orders inseparable. He declared that "Shinto is another word for principle,"[17] identified the Shinto god Kunitoko-

---

[14] On Neo-Confucianism's inclination toward comprehensiveness, see de Bary, "Some Common Tendencies in Neo-Confucianism," in David Nivison and Arthur Wright, eds., *Confucianism in Action* (Stanford: Stanford University Press, 1959), pp. 25–49.

[15] For example, Razan virtually paraphrased the opening words of Kitabatake Chikafusa's (1293–1354) *Records of the Legitimate Succession of the Divine Sovereigns* (*Jinnō shōtōki*). The *Records* begins: "Japan is the land of the gods. Our heavenly ancestor, the god Kunitokotachi, first laid the foundations for our country, and the sun goddess Amaterasu bequeathed the rule of our land to her descendants in perpetuity." See the *Jinnō shōtōki*, in Maruyama Masao, ed., *Rekishi shisō-shū* (Chikuma Shobō, 1972), p. 155. Razan's work began: "Our country is the land of the gods. Emperor Jinmu continued the Heavenly sun-succession and established guide lines for rule, and ever since then our imperial line has continued inviolate and the Kingly Way has spread." From his *Honchō jinja-kō*, quoted in Taira Shigemichi, "Kinsei no Shintō shisō," in Taira Shigemichi and Abe Akio, eds., *Kinsei Shintō-ron, zenki Kokugaku* (Iwanami Shoten, 1972), NST, 39:511.

[16] The phrase is explained by Razan's contention that "the gods are the soul of heaven and earth. The mind is the dwelling of the deity. A dwelling is a house. For example our bodies are like a house. The mind is the master of that house and the gods are like the soul of the master. . . . When you do a good deed, it conforms to the Heavenly Way because you followed the gods of your mind. When you do evil, you are punished because you acted against the gods of your mind. This is due to the common principle underlying the connection between the gods in general and the gods of a man's mind." From Razan's *Shintō denju*, NST 39:12. The word translated here and elsewhere as "mind" (*kokoro*), to a Shintoist, also signified the heart.

[17] *Shintō denju*, NST, 39:45.

tachi with the supreme ultimate (*taikyoku*),[18] and maintained that "there are neither gods nor principle outside the mind. . . . The virtue of the gods is what administers the affairs of men; the power of the gods is what governs the country."[19] In political terms, Razan regarded the governing of man as the basis for worshiping the gods, for, in his words, "when you understand the principle of mankind, you will also automatically understand the Way of the Gods."[20]

A tension existed in all Confucian-Shinto formulations between the humanistic demands of the Chu Hsi philosophy and the religious requirements of Shinto, and in Razan's case the scales quite naturally tipped in favor of the humanistic. He maintained that "men are the masters of their gods," and insisted that "it is precisely because man exists that the gods are revered, for without man who would there be?"[21] While there is a hint of a most modern form of skepticism in his words, Razan's intent was not to question the gods' existence, but rather to demonstrate first the essential unity, the interconnectedness, of the human, divine, and natural planes of existence, and second the ability of the Chu Hsi metaphysic to express that unity in comprehensive terms.

Hayashi Razan's "Shinto where Principle Corresponds to the Mind" was the first, and perhaps the best, of Tokugawa-era Neo-Confucian attempts to recast Shinto in Neo-Confucian terms. However, Razan's Shinto was soon displaced and largely forgotten because of attempts by leading Shinto theorists a decade or two later to bring the Chu Hsi metaphysic under the umbrella of Shinto, thereby shifting the subtle religious-humanistic balance to the side of the religious. A leading figure in these attempts, and one who completes this comparison with the endeavors of Hayashi Razan, was Yoshikawa Koretaru, the Tokugawa heir to the medieval Shinto speculations of Yoshida Kanetomo.

For over a century prior to Yoshikawa Koretaru's birth, Yoshida Shinto (also known as *Yuiitsu*, or Primal Shinto) had maintained a distinct set of assumptions concerning Japan's native faith. The denomination held that Shinto was the "primal fountainhead" (*yuiitsu shūgen*) of all religions, that it was (using Confucian vocabulary) the one pure Way of man, and that it was the natural principle of heaven and earth. It further asserted that the god Kunitokotachi was responsible for all creation and was the ultimate source of this natural principle. Yoshida Shinto upheld an esoteric tradition involving four ranks,

[18] Ibid., p. 13.
[19] Ibid., p. 19.
[20] Ibid., p. 14.
[21] Ibid.

the highest of which was conferred to only one man and was meant to form a blood lineage within the Yoshida family. As was customary, in the absense of a suitable male heir to the school's secrets, adoption was used instead. Since the Yoshida was the most powerful of all Shinto denominations in seventeenth-century Japan, it was a remarkable testimony to Yoshikawa Koretaru's talents and gifts that he was selected in 1656 to inherit the highest esoteric tradition, first as an "outsider" to the blood lineage, second as a relatively young man at the age of forty, and third after having spent only three years of study within the Yoshida school in Kyoto.[22]

When Yoshikawa Koretaru reinterpreted the doctrines of Yoshida Shinto, he formulated a theology most similar to that of Hayashi Razan. For example, both creeds identified Kunitokotachi as the primary figure in the Shinto pantheon and identified him with the supreme ultimate; both shared the belief that human nature, the mind or heart, and the godhead within man were differing aspects of essentially the same metaphysical phenomenon; and both theorized that the inner godhead became obscured by desires and wants, and that in order for man to return to the pristine goodness he enjoyed at birth, he must align himself with this godhead within and the gods of heaven without.

Of course, there were also differences between the two doctrines. For example, while both Razan and Koretaru agreed that the actions of the gods were by definition correct, Koretaru expressed that cor-

[22] Koretaru was born in Omi. His ancestors had been warriors, one of whom died fighting for the forces of Tokugawa Ieyasu in the Odawara campaign of 1590. But by the time of his birth, Koretaru's family had fallen on straitened circumstances. Consequently, Koretaru was adopted by a merchant family in the Nihonbashi district of Edo. He soon tired of business life, however, and withdrew in 1651 to Kamakura, where he lived in seclusion for two years devoting his time largely to the study of works in the Shinto tradtion. In 1653 he moved to Kyoto and entered the Yoshida school, and in 1656 he became the school's director. In 1657 Tokugawa Yorinori, lord of Kishū, invited him to lecture, and in 1661 Koretaru was presented to Hoshina Masayuki whose confidence he obtained and to whom he eventually passed the secret tradition. Koretaru's evangelical strategy, like that of the Jesuits nearly a century earlier, was to seek conversions among the elite. The fact that Koretaru won an (albeit small) annual stipend from the bakufu attests to a measure of success in this respect. In his theology, he emphasized the lord-vassal relationship as the premier human relationship.

Our knowledge of Koretaru's Shinto theories derives from the writings of his adopted son, Yoshikawa Yorinaga. The following discussion of Koretaru's Shinto is based on the analysis of Taira Shigemichi in his "Kinsei no Shintō shisō," in NST, 39:522–526.

The fourth and highest of the esoteric doctrines associated with Yoshida Shinto, the *Himorogi iwasaka-den*, can be found together with Yorinaga's 1713 commentary in NST, 39:77–83. It is believed to be a faithful transmission of the esoteric oral transmission dating back to the time of Yoshida Kanetomo.

rectness in terms of one of the most basic of all Japanese virtues, *makoto*, written with the Chinese character for *ch'eng*, or sincerity.[23] Koretaru maintained that the practice of reverence (J., *tsutsushimi*; C., *ching*) was a prerequisite for the attainment of makoto, and he linked the practice of reverence to *harai*, or Shinto exorcism. Koretaru explained that outwardly this harai took the form of *misogi*, or ritual cleansing, but inwardly it consisted of the maintenance of a spiritual purity which enabled man to dispel wicked thoughts and evil notions. Koretaru also emphasized the importance of Shinto prayer (*kitō*) in helping man to ascertain the wishes of the gods, and assisting his return to a state of harmony with them.

Whatever significance these differences held for Koretaru and other members of the Yoshida school, the structural similarities between Koretaru's Yoshida Shinto and the Chu Hsi mode of thought are striking. Koretaru's makoto resembled the Neo-Confucian concept of the original nature (J., *honzen no sei*; C., *pen-jan chih hsing*) recast in the vocabulary of traditional Japanese virtue. Makoto was to be regained, according to Koretaru, either by being reverent—a practice emphasized by Chu Hsi—or by ascertaining the will of the gods, which may be regarded as the theological analogue of the Chu Hsi school's "investigation of things." For Koretaru, this divine will lay at the heart of any understanding of the world and thus resembled what Neo-Confucians called principle.

There were others in the seventeenth century who sought to reconcile the truths of Neo-Confucianism and Shinto, and of these, the two most significant were the Ise Shinto of Watarai Nobuyoshi (1615–1690) and the Suika Shinto of Yamazaki Ansai. If the Yoshida school was the most important branch of Shinto in seventeenth-century Japan, then the school which formed at the Ise Shrine was a near second, and Ise Shinto's most important Tokugawa-era spokesman was Watarai Nobuyoshi.[24] Nobuyoshi felt that Ise Shinto had become a

---

[23] While *makoto* is usually translated along these lines, its meaning was more complex implying a sincere purity of intent characterized by truthfulness and honesty.

[24] While it is customary to speak of an Ise Shrine and hence an Ise Shinto, it is important to remember that there were actually two main shrines which together formed the Ise complex, the first being the better-known "inner" shrine harboring the goddess Amaterasu, and the second the "outer" shrine dedicated to the god Toyouke, god of the five grains. There were also two sets of clergy, for the Arakida family were the hereditary wardens of the Inner Shrine, while the Outer Shrine was maintained by the Watarai family. The imperial court had been careful not to show partiality, but the Inner Shrine did enjoy a certain unspoken favoritism as the abode of the imperial ancestor Amaterasu, which, in turn, prompted a touch of resentment among members of the Watarai family. Nonetheless, when people spoke of Ise Shinto, they meant the

creed of illiterates, something he regarded as an offense to the gods.[25] To remedy this state of affairs, he dedicated his life to lecturing and writing commentaries on the Five Shinto Classics (*Gobusho*)[26] with the intention of stimulating an intellectual revitalization of the faith.

Nobuyoshi's most important expostulation of this "new" Ise Shinto was his *Chronicle of a Return to Yang (Yōfukki)*, written in 1650 at the age of thirty-five. The work was a reorganization of the creed along the lines of the Chu Hsi cosmology with particular emphasis on the *Book of Changes*, but like Yoshikawa Koretaru's Yoshida Shinto, the key elements of Nobuyoshi's Ise Shinto were drawn from the battery of traditional and native Japanese virtues. He found "profound significance in the natural correspondence between the natural Way of Heaven and Earth in our country and theirs," and stated that "this is what should be the real Shinto."[27] Nobuyoshi regarded this "real Shinto," or natural Way of Heaven and Earth, as something beyond the realm of human artifice or metaphysical speculation, and thus his use of Neo-Confucian analogy to express his doctrines was primarily an expedient. Again, like Koretaru, Watarai Nobuyoshi found an original goodness in man, but instead of makoto, Nobuyoshi described that innate virtue of man in terms of another traditional Japanese virtue, *shōjiki*, or straightforwardly correct behavior when dealing with others.[28] Nobuyoshi even formulated a rudimentary eschatology, a subject that Shinto theorists of all schools had traditionally ignored, and claimed that upon death the good man sat between the sun goddess Amaterasu and the god Amenominakanushi.[29]

Watarai Nobuyoshi was in many ways ahead of his contemporaries. His notion that "systems and cultures change with the times even in other lands; how much more so they change when their laws are applied in our own country"[30] presaged the same basic theory of

Shinto of the Watarai who compensated for their somewhat secondary position by becoming leading Shinto theorists.

[25] Nobuyoshi wrote that Shinto "has become the Way of our clergy, and outside of them no one practices or even knows of it." From his *Taijingū Shintō wakumon* (1663), quoted in Taira Shigemichi, "Kinsei no Shintō shisō," in NST, 39:532.

[26] The Five Shinto Classics were a thirteenth-century invention of the Watarai despite their claim to predate the Taika reforms of 645. The texts had been the primary scriptural authority for the Watarai family and had also been used by such other figures as Yoshida Kanetomo.

[27] *Yōfukki*, NST, 39:87. Nobuyoshi's concept of "natural" Shinto may have influenced Motoori Norinaga's early thinking on this subject. See Norinaga's *Ashiwake obune*, in *Motoori Norinaga zenshū*, 2:45, and also Shigeru Matsumoto, *Motoori Norinaga* (Cambridge: Harvard University Press, 1970), p. 63.

[28] *Yōfukki*, NST, 39:91.

[29] Ibid., p. 93.

[30] Ibid., pp. 100–101.

Ogyū Sorai by more than half a century, a fact made all the more remarkable by Nobuyoshi's utterly different ideological background.[31] Similarly, Nobuyoshi produced the first Tokugawa-era commentary on the *Nihongi* (Chronicles of Japan), an eighth-century compilation of myth and history, which he often cited as scriptural authority on Shinto cosmogony.[32]

There was also something appealing in Nobuyoshi's Ise Shinto which, like Yoshikawa Koretaru's Yoshida Shinto, was an intellectually satisfying attempt to reinvigorate Shinto theology by restructuring it along lines suggested by the Chu Hsi mode of thought. While both Yoshikawa Koretaru and Watarai Nobuyoshi denied that their intention was to fashion a Confucian version of Shinto, both nonetheless recognized the utility of Neo-Confucian vocabulary and concepts for more up-to-date versions of Shinto doctrine. Others, however, were less successful than Nobuyoshi or Koretaru in fashioning a Confucianized Shinto. Yamazaki Ansai's (1618–1682) Suika Shinto was one of those less successful experiments and marks the final major venture in the seventeenth-century Confucian-Shinto dialogue.[33]

Suika Shinto was by far the most original and inventive of all Tokugawa Shinto schools, but it did not endear its founder to either the Shinto or the Neo-Confucian intellectual establishments. Satō Naokata and Asami Keisai, students of Ansai's interpretation of Neo-Confucianism, left his school because they found his Shinto doctrines unacceptable.[34] Other critics facetiously suggested that since Ansai had begun as a student of Zen, then switched to the Chu Hsi mode of thought, and finally ended by studying Shinto, his only step left was to convert to Christianity.[35]

[31] Another interesting comparison can be found in Kumazawa Banzan's *Shūgi gaisho* where Banzan argued that, though laws (*hō*) are conditioned by time (*ji*), place (*sho*), and circumstances (*i*), the Way is comprehensive and unconditional.

[32] Miki Shōtarō, *Hirata Atsutane no kenkyū* (Kyoto: Shintō-shi Gakkai, 1969), p. 153. Commentaries on the *Nihongi* written during the medieval period include the following: Kenshō (1130–1210), *Nihongi kachū*; Jakue, *Nihongi kashō*; Urabe Kanekata (mid-Kamakura Shinto priest), *Shaku Nihongi*; Inbe Masamichi, *Jindai no maki kōketsu*; Ken'a, *Nihongi shishō*; Dōsa, *Nihon shoki shikenbun*; Ryōyo Shōkyō, *Nihon shoki shisho*; Ichijō Kanera, *Nihon shoki sanso*; Yoshida Kanetomo, *Nihon shoki jindai-shō*; and Kiyohara Nobukata (1475–1550, Yoshida Kanetomo's son), *Nihon shoki kansui-shō*.

[33] Yamazaki Ansai's interest in Shinto deepened while in the service of Hoshina Masayuki. Ansai was instructed both by Watarai Nobuyoshi and Yoshikawa Koretaru whose more highly Confucianized Shinto was well known by Masayuki (see n. 22 of this essay). In the end, of course, Ansai built on both their theories and founded his own branch of Shinto studies which dominated the last ten years of his life.

[34] Taira Shigemichi, "Kinsei no Shintō shisō," in NST, 39:503.

[35] Ibid., p. 543.

Ansai's Suika Shinto stretched the believer's faith to the limit and often involved tortuous rationalizations. His Shinto theories can perhaps be explained best by grouping them into three categories.[36] First, Ansai analyzed the traditional cosmogonic myth as a religious metaphor for the transition from the formless to the material through the transformation of yin and yang. He described the seven generations of gods responsible for the creation of Japan, the world, and Shinto, and explained the first generation, the single god Kunitokotachi, in terms of a formless god of spiritual transformation; generations two through six, in turn, corresponded to the Five Elements and represented an ineffable transition to the seventh generation, Izanagi and Izanami. According to Ansai, these two gods combined physical and spiritual transformations, and they were responsible for all creation through the power of their divine coupling. Izanagi and Izanami corresponded to the forces of yin and yang, and since man was created by their divine spirit, this spirit survived in man and united him with his gods.

Second, Ansai claimed that man, as a product of divine creation, had both a religious and filial obligation to receive the teachings of the gods and to obey their instructions. Prayer brought man closer to his gods and informed him of their instructions, but once man had received those instructions, he then had to be shōjiki, by which Ansai meant practicing reverence (tsutsushimi). Here Ansai appropriated one of the key terms of Watarai Nobuyoshi's Ise Shinto and glossed it with the Yoshida teachings of Yoshikawa Koretaru.

Third, Ansai declared that Shinto was superior to all other Ways, and as proof he offered the fact that Shinto was the native faith of the land farthest to the east, the land where the sun rises. Ansai stated that the Confucian Five Relationships and Five Virtues were the building blocks of the Way of man and that they were universal; furthermore, like Koretaru, he regarded the lord-vassal relationship as the most noble and significant of all human relationships.[37]

The major influence Suika Shinto exerted on later Shinto theorists was largely a negative one. Despite the fact that it continued to attract a following, it also came to represent the logical extreme to which the Confucianization of Shinto was susceptible, and in much the same

[36] Based on ibid., pp. 545–546.

[37] The Five Relationships were lord-vassal, husband-wife, parent-child, elder brother-younger brother, and that between friends. The Five Virtues were benevolence, righteousness, propriety, wisdom, and good faith. Koretaru had maintained that for the ordinary person, the relationship with one's spouse was sufficient for the demonstration of Shinto faith, but for the noble gentleman only the lord-vassal relationship adequately expressed the dignity of the gentleman's faith. See also n. 22 of this essay.

way that early eighteenth-century Neo-Confucians objected to the pietistic excesses of Ansai's interpretation of the Chu Hsi philosophy, two tendencies emerged in eighteenth-century Shinto thought largely as a reaction against Ansai's Shinto. The first of these tendencies, and the more conservative of the two, was the attempt to popularize Shinto by simplifying the metaphysical overlays which a century of Confucian-Shinto speculation had amassed. The other and more radical tendency was the attempt to escape the Confucian synthesis altogether. One sought to refashion a discourse, while the other heralded the advent of the new discourse of National Learning. Significantly, both tendencies are evident in the Shinto thought of Masuho Zankō.

Little is known with certainty about the life of Masuho Zankō. He was probably born in Bungo (present-day Ōita Prefecture) on Kyushu, though nothing is known of his parents.[38] In later years Zankō claimed the eighth day of the fourth month as his birthday, the same date celebrated for the historical Buddha, and though 1655 is what he claimed as his year of birth, ambiguity persists concerning the year of his death, 1742 being more likely than the still occasionally cited 1717.[39]

After early training in Pure Land Buddhism, Zankō became a priest in the Nichiren denomination, and after repressions of that denomination by the bakufu in 1691 and again in 1698, he may have switched to Tendai, eventually leaving the Buddhist priesthood at the age of forty-three.[40] He may have served the Konoe household in Kyoto and was well known in Edo and Osaka as well as the capital. In his day, he was no less known for his Shinto theories than for his reputation as an authority on sensual matters in general and red-light districts throughout Japan in particular, a reputation based on his popular work the *Endō tsugan* (1715, A Comprehensive Mirror on the Way of Love).[41]

He was what we might today call a "soapbox orator." Miwa Shis-

[38] Following Ienaga Saburō, "Masuho Zankō no shisō." Like most details on Zankō's life, there is disagreement on his birthplace. Nakano Mitsutoshi favors Matsuoka in Echigo (present-day Niigata). See his "Masuho Zankō no hito to shisō," in Noma Kōshin, ed., *Kinsei shikidōron* (Iwanami, 1976), NST, 60:401.

[39] The explanation for this curious ambiguity, despite the existence of post-1717 dated colophons by Zankō, is that the second year of Kyōhō (1717) was mistaken for the second year of Kanpō (1742), written with similar characters (see Glossary).

[40] Nakano, "Masuho Zankō no hito to shisō," in NST, 60:402.

[41] See Nagao Motoe on Zankō's reputation as an authority on nativist literature in general and the *Tsurezuregusa* in particular, in "Masuho Saichū ni tsuite," *Kokugakuin Zasshi* 21, no. 12 (December 1915): 65–66.

sai (1669–1744), a slightly younger Confucian contemporary, described him as follows: "He proceeds to the precincts of various shrines and temples where he erects a marquee and lectures on the *Endō tsugan*, interspersing his narrative with amusing anecdotes, and by being so common and familiar, he lectures on Shinto. Though both his writings and his manner may lapse into terrible vulgarity, their message actually appears, somehow, to be directed toward an invigoration of Shinto."[42] Shissai's implication is clear—that Zankō used his reputation as an authority on amorous misadventures in order to attract audiences to whom he preached Shinto.

Though Zankō was deeply influenced by the syncretic tendencies of his contemporaries in both the Shinto and Neo-Confucian camps, he made repeated vituperative attacks on Buddhism and Confucianism for their allegedly deleterious impact on Shinto practice and belief. Furthermore, in his own day he had no shortage of rivals as the numerous rebuttals to his work indicate.[43] His most important works were written during the years 1715–1719 and were known as his "eight-fold writings" (Zankō *hachibu-sho*). He spent his final years as the warden (*shinshoku*) of the Asahi Shinmei Shrine in the suburbs of Kyoto.[44]

The influence of Ise Shinto, Yoshida Shinto, and Suika Shinto are all apparent in Zankō's Shinto teachings, with the Yoshida influence perhaps the predominant.[45] Consistent with almost all Shinto thought on the subject, Zankō took an affirmative stance vis-à-vis the question of human nature, and like other nativist thinkers of his age, he was skeptical concerning the usefulness of reason in plumbing ultimate truths.[46] He asserted that from the time of Ninigi no Mikoto's passage to earth as the descendant of the sun goddess Amaterasu and as the ancestor of the inviolate lineage of divine emperors, the Japanese were naturally endowed with all virtues requisite for the harmonious functioning of their society. Chief among their virtues, he asserted, was their quality of straightforwardness (shōjiki), since this

[42] From the *Shintō okusetsu*, quoted in Ienaga, "Masuho Zankō no shisō," p. 2.

[43] Ienaga, "Masuho Zankō no shisō," p. 12.

[44] Besides *Endō tsugan*, the "eight-fold writings" include *Uzō muzō hokora sagashi* (1716), *Shinkoku kamabarai* (1718), *Suguji tokoyogusa* (1717), *Shinro no tebikigusa* (1719), *Shide tawagoto* (1719), *Tsurezure shinonome* (1718), and *Iri Wari awase kagami* (1716).

[45] See Takeoka Katsuya, "Kokugakusha to shite no Masuho Zankō no chii," *Shien* 3 (December 1931): 120, and Nakano, "Masuho Zankō," p. 405. Nakano sees echoes of Nichiren Fuju Fuse zealotry in Zankō's theology (p. 402), and also considers similarities with the Yōmeigaku and Shingaku emphasis on sincerity and the unity of thought and action (p. 412).

[46] *Shinro no tebikigusa*, NST, 39:194.

complemented their inclination toward goodness.[47] No one, in his schema, was totally wicked, since even a thief has this quality of straightforwardness just as even a gambler will betray a trace of sincerity.[48] According to Zankō, the goddess Amaterasu is the paradigm of this quality of straightforwardness, while the god Hachiman personifies purity, and the god Kasuga Myōjin exemplifies compassion.[49]

Like other thinkers of his age, Zankō was more interested in the practical application of virtue than in its comtemplation in the abstract. He explained that one of the fundamental lessons of Shinto is that each person has his status and is obliged to behave in a manner consistent with that status. In his words, "What the gods of Japan teach us today is . . . to be straightforward and to conceal nothing, neither to embellish nor to lie, to be poor if one is poor, to be rich if one is rich, and to take pleasure in the appropriate distinction between the two."[50] In a similar vein, Zankō counseled, "Do not forget your four obligations," by which he meant one's obligation to heaven and earth, one's obligation to king and country, the obligation toward one's parents, and the obligation one has toward other human beings of (presumably) relatively equal status to one's own.[51] Platitudes of this sort were common among Confucian and non-Confucian thinkers of the time and reflect what Japanese scholars often refer to as a "feudal," that is, status-oriented, morality. Such affirmations of the status quo were, of course, both ideologically "safe" and of potential use in gaining favorable official attention.

One novel feature of Zankō's social thought is his adoption of a stance curiously similar to what we might call feminism. He wrote that "in celebrating our harmonious union of yin and yang and the divine transformation, men and women are on the same level with no distinction of high and low, superior and inferior. To think of women as men's slaves or to expect them to follow men in all matters is a delusion based on Chinese manners and is a deviation from our country's Way."[52] With the exception of remarks by Andō Shōeki, active in the 1750s and early 1760s, one would be hard put to find as feminist a statement prior to the Meiji era.[53]

When discussing the Japanese Way, Zankō used several terms to

[47] Takeoka, "Kokugakusha," p. 111.
[48] *Shinro no tebikigusa*, NST 39:199.
[49] Nagao, "Masuho Saichū," p. 151.
[50] *Shinro no tebikigusa*, NST 39:197.
[51] Ibid., pp. 201–202.
[52] Ibid., p. 214.
[53] Ienaga, "Masuho Zankō no shisō," p. 7.

distinguish it from other, that is, foreign, Ways. Often he referred to it as the Way of the Gods (*Shintō*), the Way of our Country (*waga kuni no michi*), the Way of Japan (*Nihon no michi*), the Way of Harmony (*wa no michi*), or simply as the Way, but his most distinctive appellation was the term *kōdō*, which might be translated as the Way of the Lord or (still less satisfactorily) the Public Way.[54] Zankō also resorted to punning on the term *Shintō* by coining homophonous terms written with different characters. The Way of the Body (*shintō*) is what one exemplifies when one's behavior is outwardly correct, he asserted, in the same manner that the Way of the Heart (*shintō*) is what one demonstrates when one's rectification of the heart is complete. Only when both the internal and the external are present in tandem does one find the True Way (*makoto no michi*), he concluded.[55]

Though hardly inspiring as an exercise in Shinto theology, Masuho Zankō's simple, functional attitude toward morality and virtue must have appealed to those who flocked to his outdoor lectures. His doctrines were concise and easy to understand, and his ability to communicate his message with such mnemonic devices as enumeration or puns probably made it more palatable to a broad audience of townsmen. This aspect of Zankō's Shinto teachings also places him in sharp contrast to earlier Tokugawa Shinto thinkers whose arguments failed utterly to capture a mass audience.

One can picture Zankō erecting his marquee near some well-traveled intersection in one of the three major metropolises. He might begin his lecture by describing how the Way begins with male and female, husband and wife, as its fountainhead. The relationship, he might continue, is based on harmony (*wa*) just as it was in most ancient times before the Japanese became absorbed in the Ways of other countries and allowed this native fundamental Way to go awry. With his audience having by this juncture increased, he might now subtly shift his argument by claiming that this native ancient Way is none other than Shinto, and that by returning to this Way, one might resurrect both the virtues and the pleasures that devolve from it.[56] While his theology might indicate the influence of his seventeenth-century precursors, Zankō's speculations are distinguished by their simplicity, comprehensibility, and attractiveness to a broad audience of potential believers.

Another prominent and popularist feature of Zankō's thought, and

---

[54] Zankō regarded kōdō as equivalent to Shinto, both being formed out of the combination of straightforwardness and knowledge. See Takeoka, "Kokugakusha," p. 120.

[55] *Shinro no tebikigusa*, NST, 39:202.

[56] See Nakano, "Masuho Zankō," pp. 409–410.

one in which he anticipates similar formulations by the major eighteenth-century kokugakusha, was the patriotic appeal of his assertions of the superiority of the Japanese and their native Way. An important question to ask when considering any Japanese thinker's assertion of national superiority is what is the nature of that thinker's world view. Despite the ambiguous impact of nearly a century's exposure to Christian thought, most writers of the late-seventeenth and eighteenth centuries in Japan found China the most appropriate land for comparison. A few, like Zankō and Kamo Mabuchi, included India. None, to my knowledge, referred in this context to Korea, which may indicate that Japanese superiority to Korea was taken for granted, and it would not be until the early-nineteenth century that assertions of Japanese superiority by figures like Hirata Atsutane (1776–1843) were commonly expanded to incorporate arguments directed toward European as well as Asian countries.

Zankō argued that though the Way was originally a singular Way of Heaven and Earth, through circumstances of geography and national temperament it evolved into the three Ways of Buddhism in India, Confucianism in China, and Shinto in Japan. He maintained that "teachings accord with national customs, and so the teachings of Buddha are just right for India; and the hard-to-follow teachings of Confucius are prefectly appropriate for China."[57] Since, as he put it, "understandings differ according to country and locale," then, "if the Buddha and Confucius had been born in Japan, they would have taught nothing other than the Japanese-style Way."[58]

An obvious corollary to this argument was Zankō's assertion that it was inappropriate for the Japanese to observe anything other than their own native Way. Not only would this be, as he put it, "taking a circuitous path," but it would also constitute an offense to the gods of Japan.[59] It should be noted, if only in passing, that thus far Zankō's claims are not altogether original, since similar assertions had been made by Fujiwara Seika, Yamaga Sokō, Kumazawa Banzan, and Kaibara Ekken from the Confucian camp, and by Tominaga Nakamoto, the mid-Tokugawa rationalist.[60]

What distinguishes Zankō, in this regard, is his more vigorous assertion of Japanese superiority. "What those born in Japan should

---

[57] *Shinro no tebikigusa*, NST, 39:214. The continuation of this passage contains an early use of the word *kokugaku*, used to refer to nativist studies.

[58] Ibid., p. 200.

[59] Ibid.; see also Takeoka, "Kokugakusha," p. 112.

[60] On Fujiwara Seika and Yamaga Sokō, see Takeoka, "Kokugakusha," p. 113; on Kaibara Ekken and Tominaga Nakamoto, see Ienaga, "Masuho Zankō no shisō," p. 4; on Kumazawa Banzan, see Nakano, "Masuho Zankō," pp. 410–411.

be aware of," he wrote, "is, first and above all, that there is no country . . . as worthy of esteem as Japan. They should know that among human beings, there are no people as splendid as the Japanese; there are no people as wise as the Japanese; and there is no country as prosperous as Japan."[61] India, for Zankō, represented a proud country with confidence and strength in its tradition, but it was weakened by its addiction to vice, alcohol, and licentiousness. The Chinese, likewise, enjoyed a fine reputation, but there, claimed Zankō, the poor are forced to turn to crime, sons incline toward unfilial behavior, and ministers habitually slay their lords. In India and China, their Ways evolved in such a fashion so as to accord with the specific social and moral maladies of the people. Thus Buddhism in India takes a dim view of drunkenness, and Confucianism advocates filial piety needed in China as one of several forms of discipline in hierarchical relationships.[62] Tying this argument to his view of Shinto morality, Zankō was able to conclude that since in Japan people are naturally endowed with a propensity for correct behavior, the Japanese have traditionally taught that people need only be straightforward with each other. These assertions of Japanese superiority vis-à-vis China and India are striking not only for the their intensity and vigor, but also for the extent to which they anticipate similar arguments by major figures within the National Learning tradition during the second half of the eighteenth century. The popular appeal of such arguments is obvious, and while we might take exception to Zankō's reference to Confucians as "stinking half-wits," one cannot help but suspect that an audience of townsmen might take pleasure over seeing some of the wind taken out of the Confucians' sails.[63]

A second respect in which Zankō's thought resembles that of National Learning in its more mature phase lies in his attitude toward ancient texts. Figures like Kamo Mabuchi and Motoori Narinaga shared a reverential attitude toward works like the *Man'yōshū* and the *Kojiki*, since they believed it possible to glean, through philological method, an ancient Way from those texts which they then sought to elevate to the status of a contemporary religion. Zankō's attitude was, again, remarkably similar, though as we shall see, his writings contain contradictions on this point.

For example, Zankō claimed that "if you know the message of the *Kujiki, Kojiki* and *Nihon shoki*, then what you know is nothing other than the Way of Japan."[64] He asserted that if you immerse yourself

[61] From his *Uzō muzō hokora sagashi*, quoted in Takeoka, "Kokugakusha," p. 111.

[62] Ibid., pp. 111–112.

[63] *Shinro no tebikigusa*, NST, 39:222.

[64] From *Uzō muzō hokora sagashi*, quoted in Takeoka, "Kokugakusha," p. 117.

in the study of these three scriptures, "you will know the profundities of divine virtue and Shinto will ever prosper," and despite the fact that intellectual circles in his age were approaching consensus on the issue that the *Kujiki* was a later forgery and not of its reputed antiquity, this by itself should not discredit Zankō's analysis.[65] Even Kada Azumamaro (1669–1736), the founder of National Learning according to some scholars, accepted the authenticity of the *Kujiki*.[66] The absence of reference to philological method here is conspicuous, though an intense and ideologically motivated concern with the linguistic analysis of ancient mythicohistorical sources did not emerge in the National Learning tradition until after Zankō's death.

That Zankō regarded this kind of study as central to any understanding of Shinto can also be demonstrated. He insisted that "there is no Shinto not in the tradition, just as there is no Shinto which has not been transmitted."[67] Of course, this assertion in part refutes the tradition of esoteric transmission within the Yoshida and Ise denominations of Shinto. In a sense, then, Zankō seems to be saying that the roots of a truer Shinto can be gleaned from Japan's most ancient mythicohistorical sources, and that the responsibility for studying these texts is incumbent on anyone who would profess authority as a propagator of Shinto doctrine.

Zankō's stance, however, is more complicated. While on the one hand he raised the *Kujiki, Kojiki* and *Nihongi* to the status of scripture, he also called into question their doctrinal purity. "In general," wrote Zankō, "Japan's ancient writings were destroyed in the Iruga rebellion, and those few that were preserved were ruined over the years by fire and war so that the writings that remain from middle antiquity are worthless revisions and reconstructions. They are seven-parts Indian Shinto and three-parts Chinese Shinto. Since Japanese Shinto priests are constrained by the three-parts Chinese Shinto and are laden down by the seven-parts Indian Shinto, Japan's Shinto has slowly disappeared."[68] That this contradicts his earlier assertion that Shinto has survived wholly intact goes without saying. Further complicating the situation is Zankō's assertion that "to attempt to glean a single truth from the divergent theories of the branches is to mistake and lose the true, original Way."[69] Here Zankō seems to be

---

[65] Ibid.

[66] Kada Azumamaro eventually came to regard the *Kujiki* as a later forgery. See his *Nihon shoki shindai no maki sho,* in *Kada zenshū* (Yoshikawa Kōbunkan, 1928–1938), 6:151.

[67] *Shinro no tebikigusa,* NST, 39:193.

[68] From *Shinkoku kamabarai,* quoted in Takeoka, "Kokugakusha," p. 118.

[69] *Shinro no tebikigusa,* NST, 39:194.

repudiating the very methodology he himself advocated, namely, the immersion in the study of ancient sources.

How can one resolve such contradictions? It is doubtful whether one can, and even whether one should. Zankō was, after all, a popularizer. His success was measured not by the intellectual quality or consistency of his thought but rather by the size of his following. It is unlikely that Zankō's audience was much perturbed by the presence of contradictions in his arguments, and it is questionable whether attention to these inconsistencies now serves to enhance either an appreciation or an understanding of Zankō's place in the intellectual map of Tokugawa Japan. The final assessment of Zankō's place on that map must take into account his role as a popularizer and a transitional figure, and it is to such an assessment that I now turn by way of conclusion.

In view of the similarities between Masuho Zankō's thought and that of National Learning in its more mature phase, one must rightly ask why Zankō has not traditionally been ranked among National Learning's so-called great men. The answer is twofold. First, try as he might, Zankō was unable to escape much of the vocabulary and most basic assumptions of a century's legacy of Shinto-Confucian syncretic speculation. For example, when describing the sacred precincts of a Shinto shrine and contrasting the precincts with the secular world outside, Zankō likened this to the difference between yin and yang.[70] Or again, when discussing the *torii* gateway to a shrine, Zankō explained that the kami and men were originally of one principle and one essence but in concrete terms there was a distinction. This was the reason for building torii. The original gods were colorless and formless and existed whether they were reverenced or not. Nevertheless, the gods of human transformation were an expression of reverence, and so the torii were constructed in order to express that reverence.[71] Similarly, in his explanation of the ambiguous Takamagahara (Plain of High Heaven) in the ancient mythology, Zankō identified heaven with Takamagahara, earth with the Yomi underworld, and man as the link between the two. He described Takamagahara as "the place where yin and yang are not yet divided, the term for the unity prior to order and chaos, cleanliness and filth."[72] In the midst of this high plain, he continued, man is born endowed with both the clean yang heart of high heaven and the defiled yin

[70] Ibid., p. 193.
[71] Ibid., pp. 192–193.
[72] Ibid., p. 196.

heart of the underworld, thus accounting for the complex jumble of instincts man carries as his emotional baggage.[73] While this kind of analysis was surely acceptable to those who flocked to Zankō's outdoor lectures, such use of terminology from the yin-yang and Neo-Confucian traditions was anathema to later kokugakusha like Kamo Mabuchi and Motoori Norinaga who sought to divest their teachings of any resemblance to originally nonnative ideologies.

Second, despite Zankō's avowed commitment to grounding his theology in the ancient written sources of Shinto, he did not share the passionate commitment to philological method as the means for gleaning those ancient "truths"—a commitment evident in the studies of Mabuchi and Norinaga. What bound these "great men" of National Learning together and distinguished them from their Shintoist contemporaries was this insistence upon methodology. Eighteenth-century Shintoists like Matsuoka Yūen (1701–1783) and Fujitsuka Tomonao (1714–1778) likewise sought to delve into what they regarded as the deepest roots of the faith in order to rescue the ancient creed from "polluting" foreign accretions, and their aims were scarcely distinguishable from those of National Learning, save that they had already relinquished the lead to their more linguistically oriented colleagues.

If one were to search among the major kokugakusha for an interesting figure to compare with Masuho Zankō, one would have to turn to Hirata Atsutane (1776–1843), the last of the "great men." By Atsutane's time, the major philological hurdles of deciphering the Man'yōshū and the Kojiki had already been surmounted so that Atsutane was not bound by the same methodological constraints; no less significantly for such a comparison, Atsutane like Zankō was a popularizer, and as such they were both bound to communicate their teachings in the idiom of their own ages.

In Zankō's time, notions derived from the yin-yang or Neo-Confucian cosmologies—however "foreign" they may have appeared to Zankō's more linguistically radical successors in the National Learning tradition—were no more foreign than Greco-Roman concepts would have been to a Renaissance *philosophe*. That Zankō succeeded in communicating to an audience of nonspecialists the complex, perhaps even overly complex, doctrines arrived at through intensive and innovative experimentation by Shinto and Neo-Confucian scholars was thus, if anything, a mark in his favor.

After Yamazaki Ansai's Suika Shinto, other Shinto theologies could have grown ever-more abstruse, ever-more rarified, but they did not.

[73] Ibid., p. 197.

Instead, in keeping with the spirit of the times, they became in the hands of figures like Masuho Zankō more popular and more accessible. Within a few short decades of the period of Zankō's greatest literary activity, Shinto doctrines would again be revised, this time in keeping with the new spirit of fundamentalism apparent in Confucian and even Buddhist circles. Zankō stood somewhere between these two—the broadly nativist Confucian-Shinto speculations of Koretaru, Nobuyoshi, Razan, and Ansai, and the more ideological nativism of Mabuchi and Norinaga—not wholly partaking of either but in his own way participating in the fulfillment of both.

EIGHT

JIUN SONJA (1718–1804): A RESPONSE TO CONFUCIANISM WITHIN THE CONTEXT OF BUDDHIST REFORM

BY PAUL B. WATT

No student of Japanese religion can fail to be impressed by the consensus that exists regarding the character of Tokugawa Buddhism. In studies by both Japanese and Western scholars, one finds Buddhism in these centuries commonly depicted as existing in a state of deep spiritual, moral, and intellectual decline. Although this view first emerged in the Tokugawa period itself, in modern Japanese scholarship its most persuasive spokesman has been Tsuji Zennosuke (1877–1955). In his *Nihon Bukkyō shi* (A History of Japanese Buddhism), he concludes that although limited activity can be seen in such areas as sectarian scholarship, clerical discipline, and apologetics, Tokugawa Buddhism generally was a formalized, lifeless religion led by a degenerate clergy.[1] Essentially the same view has been expressed by many of Tsuji's Japanese colleagues.[2]

Scholars writing in the West have also accepted this view for decades. Its most extreme version first appeared in 1931 when, in his widely read *Japan, A Short Cultural History*, George Sansom stated that from the time of the first shogun, Tokugawa Ieyasu (1541–1616), onward, "we hear of no distinguished prelate and no great religious reformer."[3] At about the same time, other scholars were expressing similar, if more cautiously worded, opinions on the subject. In 1930 Anesaki Masaharu (1873–1949) published his judgment that on the whole Tokugawa Buddhism "tended naturally toward over-refine-

---

[1] (Iwanami, 1952–1955). See especially vol. 9, pp. 1–284 and the concluding chapter of vol. 10, pp. 404–498, entitled "Bukkyō no suibi to sōryō no daraku" (The Decline of Buddhism and the Corruption of the Clergy).

[2] See, for example, Ōno Tatsunosuke, *Nihon no Bukkyō*, rev. ed. (Shibundō, 1973), p. 248, and Tamamuro Taijō, *Nihon Bukkyō shi gaisetsu*, 1940; reprinted in Nakamura Hajime et al., eds., *Gendai Bukkyō meicho zenshū* (Tōyōsha, 1974), 8:186–188.

[3] London: Cresset Press, 1931, p. 469.

ment and degeneracy,"[4] and in 1935 George Eliot called attention to "the phlegmatic apathy of the [Tokugawa] Buddhist clergy."[5] This position has been restated in more recent years by Joseph Kitagawa, who has written of "the moral and spiritual bankruptcy" of Tokugawa Buddhism,[6] and H. Byron Earhart, who has characterized it as "fossilized."[7]

Although this paper questions the adequacy of this characterization of Tokugawa Buddhism, it must first be admitted that the established view has considerable basis in fact. Buddhism in this period was indeed in difficult straits. As has often been pointed out, it was in the Tokugawa period that Buddhism first lost the dominant position it had maintained in Japanese intellectual history for nearly a thousand years. Confucianism now attracted many of the best minds of the age, but both the nativism of the National Learning scholars and a trend usually referred to as rationalism were also influential developments in the Tokugawa world of thought, and representatives of all three viewpoints were often directly and sharply critical of Buddhism. Never in Japanese history had the religion been placed so broadly on the intellectual defensive.[8]

In addition, Buddhism faced internal problems that eroded its religious integrity. Perhaps the most serious was what has been described as a conspicuous decline in discipline within the clergy. No doubt discipline had been a problem in earlier periods as well, but circumstances unique to the Tokugawa period seem to have aggravated it. The effect of the so-called *terauke*, or temple registration system, instituted by the government to help stamp out Christianity in Japan, has been noted in this regard. The system, which required every Japanese subject to register at a Buddhist temple, had the effect, first, of increasing the number of Buddhist parishioners and, in the end, of bringing an era of financial stability and even wealth to many Buddhist temples. In these circumstances, a significant number of clergymen seem to have lost sight of their religious calling, the worst

---

[4] *History of Japanese Religion* (1930; reprinted ed., Charles E. Tuttle, 1963), p. 306.

[5] *Japanese Buddhism* (London: Routledge and Kegan Paul, 1935), p. 315.

[6] *Religion in Japanese History* (New York: Columbia University Press, 1966), p. 166.

[7] *Japanese Religion: Unity and Diversity* (Belmont, Calif.: Dickenson, 1969), p. 70.

[8] The Confucian position vis-à-vis Buddhism will be considered later in this essay. For a brief summary of criticisms advanced by National Learning scholars, see Tamamuro Taijō, ed., *Nihon Bukkyō shi*, vol. 3 (Kyoto: Hōzōkan, 1967), pp. 104–105 and 109–110. On rationalist criticisms, see ibid., pp. 107–108, as well as Katō Shūichi, "Tominaga Nakamoto, 1715–1746: A Tokugawa Iconoclast," and "*Okina no fumi*: The Writings of an Old Man," *Monumenta Nipponica* 22, nos. 1–2 (1967): 178–193 and 194–210.

giving themselves over openly to the satisfaction of their material and sensual desires.[9]

The sectarian character of Japanese Buddhism was also exacerbated by contemporary conditions. Although it, too, had earlier roots in the tradition, dating back at least to the Kamakura period (1185–1333), sectarianism became even more pronounced in the Tokugawa centuries, and polemical exchanges between Buddhist sects were not uncommon. Here as well government policy was a major contributing factor. Stimulating this development, for example, was the government's attempt to control the Buddhist establishment by organizing the temples of each sect along strict hierarchical lines, over which officials kept a close watch from above.[10] Further reinforcing the sectarian character of Tokugawa Buddhism was the government policy of encouraging the scholarly pursuits of the clergy, while forbidding it from advocating heretical doctrines or from criticizing the doctrines of other sects. These guidelines, set down in the *Jiin hatto*, or Ordinances for Temples, had the effect of focusing Buddhist scholarship primarily on sectarian concerns.[11] There is, then, ample evidence to support the view that Buddhism in the Tokugawa period had reached a low ebb.

The universal and unquestioned acceptance which this view has enjoyed, however, has had unfortunate consequences for the study of Tokugawa Buddhism. Buddhist scholars have tended to concentrate on earlier periods in which Buddhism exhibited greater religious

[9] One contemporary observer who saw the connection between the *terauke* system and the moral laxity of the clergy was the Neo-Confucian Kumazawa Banzan (1619–1691). "In recent years," he wrote in his *Usa mondō*, "from the time of the ordinance banning Christianity on, a faithless Buddhism has flourished. Since throughout the land everyone has his parish temple (*dannadera*), unlike in the past, monks can freely indulge in worldly affairs without concern for either discipline or scholarship. . . . The freedom with which they eat meat and engage in romantic affairs surpasses that of even secular men." Cited in Tamamuro Fumio, *Edo bakufu no shūkyō tōsei* (Hyōronsha, 1971), p. 140. For a similar picture of monks in popular literature, see Ihara Saikaku (1642–1693), "A Bonze's Wife in a Worldly Temple," in Ivan Morris, trans., *The Life of an Amorous Woman* (New York: New Directions, 1966), pp. 148–153.

[10] For discussions of this system of temple organization, known in Japanese as the *honmatsu*, or main temple-branch temple system, see Fujii Manabu, "Edo bakufu no shūkyō tōsei," in *Nihon rekishi* (Iwanami, 1963), 11:142–146, and Tamamuro Taijō, ed., *Nihon Bukkyō shi*, 3:47–51.

[11] A collection of the most important *Jiin hatto* can be found in Monbushō shūkyō kyoku, ed., *Shūkyō seido chōsa shiryō*, vol. 6, in the *Meiji hyakunen shi sōsho* (Hara Shobō, 1977). Examples of the government's desire to promote scholarship among the clergy can be found throughout the *Jiin hatto*; on the prohibition of heretical doctrines and the criticism of other sects, see the "Shoshū jiin hatto" of 1665, pp. 100–101.

and intellectual vitality, while intellectual historians have focused upon Confucianism, National Learning, and rationalism as the important developments in the Tokugawa world of thought.[12] All of this has led to the neglect of significant figures in the history of Tokugawa Buddhism, figures who were aware of the crisis that Buddhism was facing and who worked for thoroughgoing reforms within Buddhism, while defending it against its critics from without. One such individual who has already been brought to light is Hakuin (1686–1769), the reviver of Rinzai Zen in Japan.[13] Jiun Sonja (1718–1804), the subject of this paper, is perhaps an even better illustration. Concerned with the revival of Buddhism as a whole rather than any one sect, and exhibiting a greater breadth of erudition than Hakuin, Jiun ultimately distinguished himself as one of the great reformers, scholars, and apologists of the Tokugawa period. It is through the study of such individuals as these that a more balanced view of Tokugawa Buddhism can be achieved.[14]

JIUN'S LIFE AND ACCOMPLISHMENTS: AN OVERVIEW

Jiun was born in 1718, thirty-two years after Hakuin, in the thriving commercial city of Osaka.[15] His father, Kōzuki Yasunori (1665–1730), was a *rōnin*, or masterless samurai, who had found work at one of the many domainal granaries located there.[16] Although there are indications that he maintained a respect for Buddhism and had a scholarly interest in Shinto, Yasunori seems to have been most attracted

---

[12] For examples of the latter, see Maruyama Masao, *Studies in the Intellectual History of Tokugawa Japan* (Princeton: Princeton University Press, 1974); Minamoto Ryōen, *Tokugawa shisō shōshi* (Chūō Kōronsha, 1973); and Ryusaku Tsunoda, Wm. Theodore de Bary, and Donald Keene, comps., *Sources of Japanese Tradition* (New York: Columbia University Press, 1958), part 4.

[13] See Philip Yampolsky, trans., *The Zen Master Hakuin: Selected Writings* (New York: Columbia University Press, 1971). It is noteworthy that although Hakuin is generally recognized as the primary molder of present-day Rinzai Zen in Japan, until the time of Yampolsky's study, he had been taken up "neither by Buddhist specialists nor by students of the language and literature of the period" (ibid., p. xi).

[14] Mention of other significant Buddhist figures in the Tokugawa period will be made in footnotes 114 through 116.

[15] *Jiun Sonja Daiwajō gojihitsu ryaku rireki* (hereafter cited as *Ryaku rireki*), in *Jiun Sonja zenshū* (hereafter cited as JSZ), ed. Hase Hōshū, 2nd ed. (Kyoto: Shibunkaku, 1974), 17:24.

[16] Jiun mentions his father's *rōnin* status in *Kaizan Daiwajō shōen hikki*, JSZ, 17:18. His father's employment at the granary of the Takamatsu domain is taken note of in Myōdō Taiju, *Shōbōritsu Kōfuku Daiwajō Kō Sonja den* (hereafter cited as *Sonja den*), JSZ, *shukan* (introductory vol.):36.

to Confucianism.[17] Jiun's mother, in contrast, was a devout Buddhist.[18] Jiun was the last son and the seventh of eight children born to this couple.[19]

In spite of his mother's attraction to Buddhism, as a child Jiun developed a passionate hatred of the religion and its clergy. In large part this was the result of the Neo-Confucian education he received as a boy, an education that led him to view all Buddhist monks as "unfilial and unrighteous" and Sakyamuni as the most deceitful teacher that ever lived.[20]

Ironically, when Jiun's father died during Jiun's thirteenth year, his last request was that his son enter the Buddhist clergy.[21] Although Yasunori's motive is unclear, it may simply have been to relieve his wife of the burden of caring for this last of the male children. Almost immediately, the responsibility for Jiun's upbringing was handed over to the Shingon priest Ninkō Teiki (1671–1750), and Jiun moved into Teiki's temple, Hōrakuji, located just to the southeast of the city.[22] At the time, Jiun vowed that he would soon return to lay life to "crush the Buddhist Dharma and establish the way of the teacher Chu Hsi," but in less than two years, he became a firm believer in Buddhism.[23]

There is no doubt that Teiki played a major role in Jiun's conversion, and he continued to shape Jiun's thinking over the next several

[17] On Yasunori and Confucianism, see the discussion in this essay of the education he provided his sons. His special interest in Shinto is indicated by his completion in 1718 of a commentary on the Shinto prayer of purification known as the *Ōharae*. This commentary is also significant since in the postscript he confesses to believing in the existence not only of the *kami* or Shinto deities, but of Buddhas as well. Although the work exists only in manuscript form, a partial quotation from the postscript can be found in Kinami Takuichi, *Jiun Sonja: shōgai to sono kotoba*, rev. ed. (Kyoto: Sanmitsudō, 1972), p. 13.

[18] In the *Kaizan Daiwajō shōen hikki* (JSZ, 17:18), Jiun notes that his mother received guidance in religious matters from the Shingon monk Kōzen Fushō (d. 1724). Jiun further tells us in his *Fuchūtōkai ki* (JSZ, 11:480) that Ninkō Teiki, Kōzen's disciple and Jiun's future teacher, continued this relationship, calling upon the Kōzuki family from time to time at their Osaka home. Also see the moving letter written by Jiun's mother to her son several years after he had entered the clergy. Prior to her composition of the letter, Jiun had been asked to give a lecture on the *Awakening of Faith*. In the letter she pleads with him not to become a "lecturer" (*kōshaku bōzu*), but to continue to devote himself to his Buddhist training (JSZ, 15:613–614).

[19] *Kaizan Daiwajō shōen hikki*, JSZ, 17:19.

[20] *Fuchūtōkai ki*, JSZ, 11:479–480.

[21] Ibid. Throughout this essay, Jiun's age is given as calculated in the traditional Japanese fashion, according to which an infant was considered one year old at birth, and two at the following New Year.

[22] Ibid.

[23] Ibid., p. 481.

years. Indeed, many of the concerns that came to dominate Jiun's adult life were first developed during the years he spent under Teiki's direct care. Teiki was a member of the Shingon Vinaya sect, a small but influential group that attached special importance to the observance of the monastic discipline, or *vinaya*, and he instilled in Jiun a clear appreciation of the centrality of the vinaya in Buddhist practice.[24] Teiki also gave Jiun his first exposure to Sanskrit.[25] Although this was only a rudimentary introduction to the reading and writing of the Sanskrit syllabary in the style known as Siddham, and was theoretically required of all Shingon priests, it marks the beginning of Jiun's lifelong interest in the language. Furthermore, Teiki was aware of the seriousness of the Confucian challenge to Buddhism and saw to it that Jiun was thoroughly acquainted with its views.[26]

Jiun's training under Teiki's direction reached its culmination in 1739 when Jiun was ordained a Shingon priest.[27] However, his understanding of Buddhism soon began to develop along suprasectarian lines. One of the earliest indications we have of this tendency in Jiun's thought is his resignation of the position of abbot of Hōrakuji in 1741, just two years after he had assumed the post.[28] Apparently not entirely satisfied with the Shingon style of meditation at this point in his life, he set out to practice meditation full-time under the direction of the Sōtō Zen master, Hōsen Daibai (1682–1757).[29] The latter resided at Shōanji in Shinshū, which required several days' travel to the northeast. With Daibai's help, Jiun seems to have made great progress, for he later wrote that it was in his twenty-fifth year while in Shinshū that, in his words, "he first felt right" (*hajimete ontō ni natta*).[30]

Problems arose here as well, however. An unexplained difference of opinion developed between Jiun and Daibai,[31] and by the time of

---

[24] The Shingon Vinaya sect was founded in the Kamakura period by Eizon (1201–1290), but soon suffered breaks in its line of transmission. It was revived in the late-sixteenth century by Shunshō Myōnin (1576–1610) and became a leading force in the movement to revive the vinaya in the Tokugawa period. In Jiun's day, there were three Shingon Vinaya centers in existence: the Shinbessho at Mt. Kōya, Jinhōji in Izumi, and Yachūji in Kawachi. Jiun trained for several years at Yachūji.

[25] Jiun received this instruction in the summer of 1731, the year after his arrival at Hōrakuji. *Fuchūtōkai ki*, JSZ, 11:481. The *Shittanshō sōjō kusetsu* (JSZ, 9: 1–100) is a later-edited record of the notes he took at that time.

[26] See p. 198 of this essay.

[27] *Injinshū*, JSZ, 16:305.

[28] *Ryaku rireki*, JSZ, 17:25.

[29] Ibid. On Daibai, see *Hōju Daibai Rō oshō nenpu*, in the *Sōtōshū zensho*, ed. and pub. the *Sōtōshū Zensho Kankō Kai* (1938), 17:497–523.

[30] See his 1776 sermon, JSZ, 14:750.

[31] Ibid.

his return to Hōrakuji in 1743, it is clear that Jiun was no more satisfied with a purely Zen understanding of Buddhism than with a purely Shingon one. Up to his death in 1804, he continued in his capacity as a Shingon priest and was also an avid practitioner of Zen. But by his late twenties he had become convinced that, rather than any contemporary sect's version of Buddhism, only a return to what he sometimes called *Butsu zaise no Bukkyō*, or Buddhism as it was when the Buddha was alive, or more frequently simply the *shōbō*, or True Dharma, would enable Buddhism to meet successfully the crisis it was confronting.

Although the concept of the True Dharma came to have special significance for Jiun, he defined it only in general terms. In his most succinct definition, he states that it entails "simply acting as the Buddha acted and thinking as the Buddha thought."[32] Elsewhere his frequent reference to the *sangaku*, or Three Branches of Buddhist Learning, indicates that in his mind it, too, served as a reliable guide to the True Dharma. This traditional formula, found in the earliest Buddhist scriptures and accepted by all but the devotional schools of Buddhism, identifies morality, meditation, and wisdom—the last including the study of Buddhist scriptures and philosophy—as the essential elements of the Buddhist path to enlightenment. As these definitions suggest, for Jiun the concept of the True Dharma ultimately encompasses the proper Buddhist way of life in its entirety. Jiun's interest in the True Dharma, however, did not lead him to revive original Buddhism in a literal sense. Jiun remained unmistakably a Mahayana Buddhist, but he sought consistently to highlight the fundamentals of Buddhist practice and thought, to stress the continuities within the Buddhist tradition, and to minimize the significance of sectarian differences.

It was Jiun's sincere desire to reinvigorate Tokugawa Buddhism with the spirit and discipline of the True Dharma that gave direction to his life throughout his adult years and that led him to the achievements for which he has earned a place in the history of Japanese Buddhism. Most notable among his accomplishments are the following.

First, Jiun was the founder of a suprasectarian movement dedicated to the revival of the True Dharma. Reflecting the emphasis he placed upon the observance of monastic discipline, the movement was known as the *Shōbōritsu*, or Vinaya of the True Dharma. Although it was not officially recognized by the government until 1786, the actual

---

[32] "Shōken," JSZ, 14:331.

founding of the movement can be dated as far back as 1745, when Jiun and a small band of disciples moved into Chōeiji, a then dilapidated temple located east of Osaka in Takaida.[33] According to Taiju, one of Jiun's closest disciples and his first biographer, by the time of Jiun's death, the movement had attracted several hundred monks and nuns into its leadership and had over ten thousand followers.[34] An 1830 list of Shōbōritsu temples, now held at Kōkiji, the main temple of the movement after 1786, indicates that there were at least twenty-eight such temples in existence at that time.[35]

Second, compelled by his desire to draw as close as possible to the original meaning of the Buddhist scriptures, Jiun achieved a degree of mastery of Sanskrit unprecedented in Japan, and this in spite of the fact that he lived in an age when there were neither Indian masters to consult nor a tradition of true Sanskrit studies to rely on.[36] He and his disciples compiled the results of their research into a one-thousand-fascicle work entitled the *Bongaku shinryō*, or Guide to Sanskrit Studies, which includes not only a catalog of available texts and fragments, Sanskrit-Chinese dictionaries and Sanskrit grammars, but also information on Indian geography, history, and customs.[37]

Third, Jiun also distinguished himself as a popular advocate of the True Dharma. In numerous sermons, faithfully recorded by his followers, he set forth its essentials in a relatively simple language for the laity. His best known work in this regard is his *Jūzen hōgo*, or Sermons on the Ten Good Precepts, a collection of sermons that Jiun presented at Amidadera in Kyoto between January and May 1774 at the request of certain members in the court of Emperor Gomomo-

---

[33] See, for example, the *Konpon sōsei*, the set of regulations that Jiun established in 1749 as a guide for those monks who joined him at Chōeiji. The term *Shōbōritsu* appears numerous times in the text. JSZ, 6:70–75.

[34] *Sonja den*, JSZ, *shukan*:46. There is no way to confirm the latter figure, but the former appears to be accurate. In the introductory volume of the JSZ, Hase includes a list of 363 individuals associated with the Shōbōritsu movement in Jiun's lifetime, 342 of whom were either monks or nuns (ibid., pp. 329–558).

[35] This list was shown to the author by the Reverend Maeda Kōhan, abbot of Kōkiji, on 16 November 1977.

[36] On the undeveloped state of Sanskrit studies in Japan at this time, see R. H. van Gulik, *Siddham: An Essay on the History of Sanskrit Studies in China and Japan*, Sarasvati-Vihara series, 36 (1956), and Nagao Gajin, "Siddham and Its Study in Japan," *Acta Asiatica*, no. 21 (October 1971), pp. 1–12.

[37] The best brief descriptions of this work can be found in Ono Genmyō, comp., *Bussho kaisetsu daijiten* (Daitō Shuppansha, 1933–1936), and Ishiyama Juntarō, "Jiun Sonja: Selected Works, Introductory Remarks," Society for the One Hundred Fiftieth Commemoration of the Death of Jiun Sonja (1953). Only tables of contents are included in JSZ (see 9:383–490).

zono (1758–1779; r. 1770–1779).[38] Jiun himself reportedly regarded it as his most important work,[39] and it continued to be an influential book in Buddhist circles well into the late-nineteenth and early-twentieth centuries.[40]

Fourth, Jiun served as an apologist for Buddhism. In the *Jūzen hōgo* and other sermons, Jiun defended Buddhism against its Confucian and rationalist critics,[41] and he responded to the revival of interest in Shinto that took place in his lifetime by advancing his own interpretation of the religion, known to later generations as *Unden Shintō*, or the Shinto transmitted by Jiun.[42] While based upon such standard sources as the *Kojiki* and *Nihon shoki*, Jiun's view of Shinto was heavily informed by the understanding of ultimate reality he had gained first through his Buddhist studies and practice.

Viewed as a whole, these activities represent Jiun's attempt to make a total response to the challenge facing Buddhism in his day. The remainder of this essay focuses upon only one aspect of this response, that made to Confucianism. Although in recent years the subject of Buddhism's response to Confucianism, or rather Neo-Confucianism, has attracted the attention of scholars of Ming (1368–1644) Buddhism in China, it has yet to be considered in the otherwise often-compared context of Tokugawa Japan.[43]

JIUN'S CONTACTS WITH CONFUCIANISM

All evidence suggests that Jiun was well acquainted with Confucianism. His earliest formal education, in fact, was at the hands of a Neo-

[38] JSZ, 11:1–453. The circumstances leading to the presentation of these sermons are related in Hōsen Erin, *Jūzen hōgo no engi*, JSZ, 12:473–486.

[39] *Sonja den*, JSZ, shukan:46.

[40] On Jiun's impact on Meiji-period (1868–1912) Buddhism, see Ikeda Eishun, *Meiji no shin Bukkyō undō* (Yoshikawa Kōbunkan, 1976), pp. 1–122, passim. Such important Buddhist leaders of the period as Fukuda Gyōkai (1806–1888) of the Pure Land sect, Shaku Unshō (1827–1909) of the Shingon sect, and the onetime Sōtō Zen monk Ōuchi Seiran (1845–1918) were all deeply influenced by Jiun's writings in general and the *Jūzen hōgo* in particular.

[41] For a discussion of Jiun's response to rationalism as represented by Tominaga Nakamoto, see Okamura Keishin, "Tominaga Nakamoto to Jiun Onkō: kinsei mikkyō no ichidōkō," *Mikkyōgaku mikkyōshi ronbunshū* (1965), pp. 141–160.

[42] Jiun's Shinto studies have been collected in JSZ, vol. 10. Among his most important works are the *Shinju gūdan*, pp. 1–190; *Nihongi shindai origamiki*, pp. 441–580; and *Mudaishō*, pp. 581–640.

[43] See Araki Kengo, "Confucianism and Buddhism in the Late Ming," in Wm. Theodore de Bary, ed., *The Unfolding of Neo-Confucianism* (New York: Columbia University Press, 1975), pp. 39–66, and Chün-fang Yü, *The Renewal of Buddhism in*

Confucian teacher. In an undated work written in later life, Jiun talks about the education he received as a child:

> My father educated all seven of his sons in Confucian texts and the martial arts. In the house, there were always several rōnin whom my father supported. . . . Among them, Takechi Shinzō was a follower of the school of Chu Hsi and gave lectures to my older brothers, Yoshinobu and Ikō, and others, on such topics as the *Analects*, the *Mencius*, the *Great Learning*, the *Mean*,[44] the *Anthology of Poetry in Three Forms*,[45] ancient documents, poetry and calligraphy. I was a child and waited upon him, always listening to what he said. When I heard the metaphor of the moon's reflection in a dish of water,[46] and that even if one's spirit should enter an evil path after death, since it has no body, the tortures of King Enma's hell are all meaningless contrivances, I took it all in. I was an ignorant child; I knew nothing else. I simply regarded his views as the most reasonable. I hated monks and the Buddhist Dharma and thought to myself, "Sakyamuni was a false and deceitful leader."[47]

It is fair to assume that Jiun became generally familiar with the basic ideas of the Chu Hsi school through Takechi's lectures. It is also clear that in the course of his education Jiun was introduced to standard Neo-Confucian criticisms of Buddhism. In the above passage, Takechi criticizes Buddhism for the irrationality of its doctrine of transmigration. Elsewhere in this same source, we learn that Jiun encountered another, more fundamental Neo-Confucian criticism of Buddhism—that it was an antisocial religion.[48] This charge had earlier been made against Buddhism in China, and although not all Confucians, particularly in the late-Ming and Tokugawa periods, embraced it with the same vigor, it was repeatedly advanced in these later periods as well. The criticism stemmed from Confucianism's commitment to the establishment and maintenance of a stable and harmonious society, one built upon the cardinal Confucian virtues of

---

China: Chu-hung and the Late Ming Synthesis (New York: Columbia University Press, 1981), especially pp. 64–100 and 223–231.

[44] That is, the Four Books.

[45] *San-t'i-shih*; a six-volume work by Chou Pi of the Sung dynasty (960–1279) on T'ang-dynasty (618–906) poetry.

[46] A metaphor used to refute the Buddhist doctrine of transmigration. Just as when the water in a dish is gone, the reflection of the moon vanishes, so, too, when the human body decays, nothing remains to transmigrate. Jiun explains the metaphor in *Jūzen hōgo*, JSZ, 11:353–354.

[47] *Fuchūtōkai ki*, JSZ, 11:479–480.

[48] Ibid., p. 480.

filial piety and loyalty and seen as an integral part of the natural order. Buddhism's characterization of the world of ordinary human experience as illusory, as well as its requirement that the Buddhist follower ultimately leave both family and society in order to attain enlightenment, made Buddhism subversive in the eyes of many Confucian thinkers. References to Neo-Confucianism in works dating from Jiun's middle years indicate that this school continued to occupy a permanent place in his thinking, although nowhere does he discuss its philosophy in detail.[49]

Jiun was also familiar with another major school of Tokugawa Confucianism, the *kogaku*, or Ancient Learning school, that arose as a reaction against the highly speculative philosophy of Sung and Ming Neo-Confucianism. The kogaku school called for a return to the study of the original texts of Confucianism—the *Analects* and the *Mencius*, and beyond them, the Five Classics[50]—and to the activist moral philosophy contained therein. Jiun first encountered Itō Jinsai's (1627–1705) branch of this school, the *kogigaku-ha*, or School for the Study of Ancient Meanings, located in Kyoto. At the age of sixteen, shortly after his conversion to Buddhism, Jiun was sent there by Teiki to study Confucian texts and Chinese prose and poetry.[51] Teiki was of the conviction, Taiju writes, that Jiun would not be able to defend Buddhism against its Confucian critics unless he had a thorough understanding of Confucian thought.[52] Jiun studied for three years at Jinsai's school, which at the time was thriving under the leadership of Jinsai's son, Tōgai (1670–1736). Jiun also became acquainted with the works of Ogyū Sorai (1666–1728), the founder of the other Ancient Learning school, the *kobunjigaku-ha*, or Ancient Textual Studies school, located in Edo. Precisely when and how Jiun became familiar with Sorai's writings is unclear, but occasional references to Sorai in Jiun's collected works show that Jiun was cognizant of his views.[53]

In considering Jiun's response to Confucianism, it is important that his role as an apologist for Buddhism not be overemphasized. He

---

[49] See, for example, *Jūzen hōgo*, JSZ, 11:352 and 422, and the sermon entitled "Gojō gokai," in JSZ, 14:627ff.

[50] The *Book of History*, the *Book of Odes*, the *Book of Changes*, the *Rites*, and the *Spring and Autumn Annals*.

[51] *Ryaku rireki*, JSZ, 17:24, and *Fuchūtōkai ki*, JSZ, 11:481.

[52] *Sonja den*, JSZ, *shukan*:27. Note, however, that Taiju errs in placing this event in Jiun's eighteenth year.

[53] In the *Fugen gyōgansan kikigaki* (JSZ, 9:3–4), Jiun takes note of the emphasis Sorai places upon Chinese language studies, and in the *Jūzen hōgo* (JSZ, 11:372–373), he describes him as one who held the belief that "there is no fixed Way in the universe," since the Way was formed gradually at the hands of the sages.

did, of course, play that role, but his response was not simply a defensive one. There was much in Confucianism that Jiun appreciated, and contact with it shaped his thinking in significant ways. Jiun's acquaintance with the Ancient Learning school, for example, can be seen as having influenced him in at least two respects. First, the Ancient Learning school's belief that what they considered to be distortions of the Confucian tradition could be rectified only by a return to the founders and the fundamentals of Confucianism seems to have stimulated similar fundamentalist tendencies in Jiun's approach to Buddhist reform. In fact, Jiun states in a later recollection of his years in Kyoto that it was while at Jinsai's school that he first felt the desire to go to India to study Buddhism.[54]

Second, it is clear that contact with the Ancient Learning school further contributed to Jiun's interest in Sanskrit. One of the chief characteristics of the kogaku school was the importance it attached to the study of the ancient Chinese language of the Confucian classics. It was felt that if the original message of the classics were to be grasped, the language of these texts had to be understood as strictly as possible within its original context. This was an especially prominent feature of the Sorai branch of the school. The striking parallel to Jiun's own attitude toward Sanskrit cannot be missed, for just as Jinsai and Sorai emphasized the study of the earliest Confucian texts in their original language, so Jiun came to emphasize the need for the study of Buddhist texts in Sanskrit. On the one hand, we may assume that Jiun's exposure to Sanskrit as a boy contributed to his appreciation of the significance of the language; moreover, it appears that Jiun was also spurred on by the activities of other Buddhists in his age who were attempting to move beyond the elementary knowledge of Sanskrit that was then the norm.[55] On the other hand, there is clear evidence that Jiun was inspired by Sorai's example. In lectures given in 1767 on the Sanskrit text of the *Bhadra-caripranidāna* (J., *Fugen gyōgansan*), Jiun singles out Sorai for praise, applauding him for requiring his students to learn Chinese. He then recommends that students of Buddhism likewise learn Sanskrit if they are to prevent the distortion of the message of the Buddhist scriptures.[56]

There is another, more general sense in which Jiun can be said to have appreciated Confucianism. As we will see, Jiun was a great admirer of the emphasis in all schools of Confucianism on the im-

---

[54] *Myōdō Taijushi kessho Fugen gyōgansan batsu*, JSZ, 15:12.

[55] Jiun mentions in passing the Sanskrit studies of, among others, the Shingon monk Jōgon (1639–1702). On Jōgon, see van Gulik, *Siddham*, pp. 133ff.

[56] *Fugen gyōgansan kikigaki*, JSZ, 9:3–4.

portance of morality. Nevertheless, since Confucian thinkers were often not similarly appreciative of Buddhism in this regard, that is, since many considered Buddhism to be undermining those values upon which, in their view, a stable social and political order should be based, Jiun was compelled to come to Buddhism's defense. Above all, he had to demonstrate that Buddhism possessed a moral philosophy that served not only its own religious ends, but larger social and political ends as well. This he did in the *Jūzen hōgo*, which stands as both his most comprehensive statement of the True Dharma and his most complete reply to the Confucians. It is to an examination of the central ideas of this work that we now turn.

SERMONS ON THE TEN GOOD PRECEPTS

As the title indicates, the focus of the *Jūzen hōgo* is the "ten good precepts," a standard Buddhist guide to proper conduct and thought that prohibits killing, stealing, adultery, lying, frivolous language, slander, equivocation, greed, anger, and wrong views.[57] Although Jiun almost nowhere mentions the *jūzen* before his presentation of these sermons in 1774, his *Jūzen no keitō*, or Lineage of the Ten Good Precepts, completed in the same year, suggests that Jiun had been aware of their special significance for some time, having first learned of them from his teacher, Ninkō Teiki.[58] By the time of the *Jūzen hōgo*, however, they had come to occupy the center of his attention, and they continued to hold an important place in his thought for the rest of his life. In these sermons, Jiun presents the ten good precepts as a unique summation of the heart of the Buddhist teachings, as well as, and indeed more importantly, an all-encompassing guide for mankind, beneficial in both the secular and sacred realms of life, practicable by all types of human beings, and eternally valid.

In chapter one, Jiun begins by pointing out the unique position the jūzen hold within the Buddhist tradition. He notes first that they are a formulation taught in all periods of Buddhist history and accepted by Buddhists of all persuasions, from the earliest Hinayanists to the latest Mahayanists.[59] By way of illustration, Jiun presents a list of

---

[57] The Japanese for each of the precepts, in order of their appearance here, is: *fusesshō, fuchūtō, fujain, fumōgo, fuakku, furyōzetsu, fukigo, futon'yoku, fushin'i*, and *fujaken*.

[58] Okamura Keishin points out that the earliest mention of the jūzen occurs in the 1748 *Jukai hōsoku*; "Jiun Sonja no shōgai to shisō," *Bokubi*, no. 127 (May 1963), p. 8. See JSZ, 6:99. Mention is also made of the jūzen in a 1761 sermon entitled "Gojō gokai," in JSZ, 14:627. On his reception of the jūzen from Teiki, see JSZ, 6:212.

[59] JSZ, 11:3.

representative scriptures (Skt., *sūtra*; J., *kyō*) and commentaries (Skt., *śastra*; J., *ron*) in which the ten good precepts appear. Included in the list are such varied texts as the *Āgama-sūtras* (J., *Agongyō*),[60] the *Fan-wang ching* (J., *Bonmōkyō*),[61] the *Satyasiddhi-śastra* (J., *Jōjitsuron*),[62] and the *Prajñāpāramito-padesa* (J., *Chidoron*).[63] To this list we may add the *Avataṁsaka-sūtra* (J., *Kegonkyō*),[64] which Jiun quotes numerous times in this regard, as well as the *Mahāvairocana-sūtra* (J., *Dainichikyō*).[65] Although these citations do not in themselves constitute a thorough-going documentation of the antiquity and wide acceptance of the jūzen, modern scholarship has, on the whole, substantiated Jiun's contention.[66]

Second, Jiun maintains for reasons that will be made clear in this essay, that all other formulations of the Buddhist precepts are encompassed within the jūzen. He speaks of them, therefore, as "the foundation" of the precepts for laymen as well as the vinaya for monks and nuns.[67] This was not the customary understanding of the jūzen within the Buddhist community, as Jiun was well aware. He notes himself that traditionally they were regarded merely as "precepts for the laity" (J., *sekenkai*) and consequently were seen as preliminary to and surpassed in value by the more detailed "precepts for the clergy" (J., *shussekenkai*).[68] In his view, however, the vinaya for the clergy is nothing more than an amplification of the jūzen. Even the practice of meditation, he states, is based upon the observance of this simple

[60] The earliest scriptures of Buddhism, reportedly recited at the first gathering of the Sangha after the Buddha's death in 480 B.C.

[61] A Mahayana text that discusses the bodhisattva precepts. Its date of composition is unknown, but it was first translated into Chinese by Kumārajīva in 406.

[62] By the Indian, Harivarman (ca. A.D. 250–350). Sometimes regarded as representing a transitional point between Hinayana and Mahayana Buddhism, the text argues the Mahayana view of the emptiness of all things in an analytic, Hinayanist fashion.

[63] Also known as the *Mahāprajñāpāramitopadesa* (J., *Daichidoron*); a commentary by Nagarjuna (ca. A.D. 150–250) on the *Mahāprajñāpāramita-sūtra*, a long scripture on the Mahayana doctrine of emptiness.

[64] The Mahayana text upon which the Hua-yen (J., *Kegon*) sect was founded in China. The earliest translation of the text into Chinese was done in the fifth century.

[65] A sutra associated with the rise of Tantric Buddhism in India in the sixth and seventh centuries. It was translated into Chinese in the eighth century and is one of the basic texts of the Shingon sect.

[66] On the formation of the jūzen in early Buddhism, see Nakamura Hajime, *Genshi Bukkyō no seikatsu rinri, Nakamura Hajime senshū* (Shunjūsha, 1972), 15:264–273. For a discussion of the place of the jūzen in the history of Buddhist ethical thought in general, see Miyamoto Shōson, ed., *Daijō Bukkyō no seiritsushiteki kenkyū* (Sanseidō, 1954), pp. 57–134.

[67] JSZ, 11:3–4.

[68] Ibid.

code.[69] Buddhist scholars may think of the jūzen as "shallow," but in fact they are "profound and vast."[70]

Jiun also begins at the outset to articulate the second and more important theme of these sermons, that of the ten good precepts as an all-encompassing guide for mankind. In the first lines of the preface, he introduces the motif of the beneficiality of the jūzen and calls attention to their importance to both the Buddhist community and the nation as a whole. "The ten good precepts are the true norms for the protection of the nation," he writes, echoing a time-honored theme in the Japanese Buddhist tradition, "and the great mooring of the all-embracing discipline of the clergy."[71] So central to the *Jūzen hōgo* is the idea of the jūzen's relevance to all aspects of life that Jiun both opens and closes the work with a reference to it. In language in part suggestive of the Confucian classic the *Great Learning*, he concludes: "If you perfect the ten good precepts, you will be more than able to cultivate yourself, set your house in order and rule your country in peace. Every one of you will be able to attain the status of even a *bhadra* or *ārya*,[72] and by gradually fulfilling the precepts, the time will come when you become one with the Buddha Body."[73] In the intervening pages, Jiun returns repeatedly to this topic, often spelling out in detail the benefits that people of all walks of life may enjoy by observing the ten good precepts.[74]

Related to this motif are those of the jūzen's universal practicability and timeless validity. In a line that becomes a refrain in the text, he touches upon both of these motifs at once. "Only the ten good precepts," he points out, "encompass all countries, the past as well as the present, the wise as well as the foolish, the clever as well as the slow, the noble as well as the humble and men as well as women; only they are the Way that can be regarded as the true Way."[75] As this passage suggests, in many respects the ten good precepts resem-

---

[69] Ibid., p. 71.

[70] Ibid., pp. 3–4. Kūkai (774–835), the founder of the Shingon sect, held a similar view of the jūzen. See Yoshito Hakeda, *Kūkai: Major Works* (New York: Columbia University Press, 1972), p. 94. Oddly, although comments made by Jiun during the last years of his life show that he had a profound respect for Kūkai, Jiun neither cites his view of the jūzen nor includes him in his *Jūzen no keitō*.

[71] Ibid., p. 2.

[72] *Kenjō*. A *bhadra* is an individual who, although he has abandoned evil ways and taken up Buddhist practice, has not yet gained insight into the truth. An *ārya* is one who has attained that insight.

[73] JSZ, 11:451.

[74] See, for example, ibid., pp. 6–7, 49–50, 51, 69, 96, 203, and 226.

[75] Ibid., p. 56. For further examples of this statement with slight variations, see pp. 51, 258, and 445.

ble a natural law in Jiun's thinking, existing wherever human beings exist, both in the past and in the present, bringing benefits to those who conform to them and hardships to those who do not. They exist, he states, "whether or not a Buddha appears in the world" to identify and expound upon them.[76] Although he believes that Buddhism alone transmits a full understanding of the jūzen, he also seeks to demonstrate their universality by quoting extensively throughout the work from non-Buddhist as well as Buddhist sources. Prominent among the non-Buddhist works are the *Book of Changes*, the *Book of History*, the *Rites*, the *Tso Commentary*, the *Analects*, the *Mencius*, the *Lao-tzu* and the *Chuang-tzu*, and the *Records of the Historian*.

Of the several claims that Jiun makes for the ten good precepts, all but one are founded upon a single all-important conception. Except for his assertion concerning the ubiquitous nature of the jūzen in Buddhist scripture, which can be demonstrated simply by pointing to textual evidence, Jiun bases his claims for the jūzen upon his understanding of the relationship between them and the Mahayana Buddhist view of ultimate reality. In Jiun's thought, the two are inextricably linked, as they are in Mahayana thought generally. In order to appreciate the claims that Jiun sets forth in the *Jūzen hōgo*, therefore, it is necessary to note briefly the view of ultimate reality that Mahayana Buddhists hold.

In no other Mahayana concept is their view of ultimate reality more fully captured than in the concept of emptiness (Skt. *śūnyatā*; J., *kū*).[77] For Mahayana Buddhists, this term represents the culmination of a line of thought that had its origins in the fundamental Buddhist doctrine of no-self (Skt., *anātman*; J., *muga*) taught first by the historical Buddha. His reflections upon the ultimate origins of human suffering led him to conclude that it was our failure to realize that all things are without a permanent self or abiding essence that causes us to suffer. Unaware of this fact, and, by implication, unaware of the utter transiency of all things, we generate desires that in the nature of things cannot be fully satisfied. The no-self doctrine was further developed in the centuries immediately after the Buddha's death in the Abhidharma literature. There, systematizers of the Buddha's teachings attempted to demonstrate the selfless nature of things by analyzing the world of everyday experience into its constituent elements or *dharmas* (J., *hō*), beyond which no self or abiding essence could be found.

[76] See, ibid., pp. 25, 46, and 55.

[77] For studies of this important concept, see T.R.V. Murti, *The Central Philosophy of Buddhism*, 2nd ed. (London: George Allen and Unwin, 1960), and Frederick J. Streng, *Emptiness: A Study in Religious Meaning* (Nashville: Abingdon Press, 1967).

The Mahayana concept of emptiness, which began to emerge around the first century B.C., had its roots in these earlier expressions of the doctrine of no-self, but differed significantly from them. On the one hand, emptiness continued to indicate the absence of an abiding essence in all things; indeed, applying the idea in an even more consistent fashion, the Mahayanists maintained that even the dharmas that the Abhidharma scholars had identified had no abiding essence. On the other hand, however, emptiness took on a positive meaning as well. It came to stand for the one unconditioned and unchanging aspect of a world that in all other respects is conditioned and transient. It became, in short, the positive ground upon which all things exist, and in time synonyms for emptiness appeared that reflect its more positive character. Mahayanists thus came to speak of it as the true nature of the dharmas or phenomenal order (Skt., *dharmatā*; J., *hosshō*), thusness or suchness (Skt., *tathatā*; J., *shinnyo*), the Buddha nature (Skt., *Buddhatā*; J., *Busshō*) within all things, and in China and Japan, principle or the absolute (C., *li*; J., *ri*) as opposed to phenomena or the relative (C., *shih*; J., *ji*). Furthermore, the Mahayanists pointed out that as the true nature of all things, emptiness is the one respect in which all of the disparate objects of ordinary experience can be said to be identical or equal (Skt., *samatā*; J., *byōdō*).

There is a corollary to this position that is also essential for the comprehension of Jiun's views regarding the jūzen. According to the Mahayanists, if all things are empty or without an abiding essence, then no thing exists autonomously, but only as it stands in relation to all other things. All particulars within the phenomenal realm, in other words, are absolutely interdependent, each serving simultaneously as both the cause and effect of all other things. This is a theme most closely associated with the important Mahayana scripture the *Avataṁsaka-sūtra*, a text whose spirit pervades the *Jūzen hōgo*.[78] However, Jiun first draws our attention to the connection between the emptiness of things and their interdependency in a lengthy meditation on a line from the *Lotus Sutra* (Skt., *Saddharmapundarīka-sūtra*; J., *Myōhō rengekyō*). In the line in question the Buddha states, "Now these three worlds[79] are all my possessions, and the sentient beings within them are all my children."[80] Jiun's comment on it is that only

---

[78] See Francis H. Cook's study of the philosophy of this sutra as elaborated by Fatsang (643–712), *Hua-yen Buddhism: The Jewel Net of Indra* (University Park: Pennsylvania State University Press, 1977).

[79] The world of desire (J., *yokukai*), the world of form (J., *shikikai*), and the formless world (J., *mushikikai*). Together they constitute the three divisions of the world of sentient beings.

[80] JSZ, 11:5. For the original context, see Leon Hurvitz, trans., *Scripture of the Lotus Blossom of the Fine Dharma* (New York: Columbia University Press, 1976), p. 72.

"if we are aware of the original emptiness of the self, possessions associated with the self, and the dharmas" can we appreciate the meaning of the Buddha's remark.[81]

Since the focus of the *Jūzen hōgo* is on the ten good precepts themselves, Jiun seldom engages in extended discussion of the concepts of emptiness and the interdependency of things. Nevertheless, it is apparent that the work rests upon the view of reality signified by such concepts. According to Jiun, all that exists is "a manifestation of the dharmatā" (*hosshō no arawareshi sugata*), and all things are "identical in their fundamental nature" (*honshō byōdō*). Of more immediate concern to Jiun, however, is that the way of life outlined in the jūzen results directly from the attainment of insight into this view of ultimate reality. The jūzen, in short, embody the implications that this view of reality has for human conduct. For Jiun, to live in accord with the ten good precepts is nothing less than to live in accord with the dharamatā, the true nature of the phenomenal order, which is emptiness.

Jiun states this point, so crucial to the central argument of the *Jūzen hōgo*, in several passages in the text. In chapter one he writes: "Although I preach the ten good precepts, there is just the one Buddha nature, the one dharmatā. Keeping your mind in harmony with the dharmatā is called good; going against it is called evil."[82] In a longer passage in the same chapter, quoted below, Jiun again discusses the relationship that exists between the jūzen and the dharmatā, although there the term "principle" rather than dharmatā is used. The activities of the body, speech, and mind that he mentions at the beginning of the passage are those governed by the ten good precepts. "The three activities of the body" refer to killing, stealing and adultery, or their opposites; "the four activities of speech" refer to lying, frivolous language, slander and equivocation, or their opposites; and "the three activities of the mind" refer to greed, anger and wrong views, or their opposites. Together they encompass all aspects of human behavior. Note, too, that here Jiun introduces the idea that principle is identical to "the original nature" of man.

When the three activities of the body, the four activities of speech and the three activities of the mind are in harmony with principle, they are called the ten good acts (*jūzengō*); when they go against principle, they are referred to as the ten evil acts (*jūfuzengō*). Being in harmony with principle means nothing other than being just as you are in your original nature, without the

[81] JSZ, 11:6.
[82] Ibid., pp. 15–16.

slightest alteration. If your body, speech and mind are one with your original nature, the ten good precepts will naturally be perfected.[83]

Proper behavior in thought, word, and deed, therefore, finally depends upon our being cognizant of and living in harmony with the dharmatā or principle, the ground of emptiness upon which all things exist. Having attained insight into the dharmatā, like the Buddha of the *Lotus Sutra*, we, too, can see our own existence as inextricably linked to that of all other beings and things and understand the folly of such acts as killing, stealing, and lying.[84] Furthermore, since we, too, manifest the dharmatā, we need only be true to our original nature in order to encounter the dharmatā and perfect the jūzen. As Jiun continually reminds us, "The jūzen are replete within you."[85]

By relating the jūzen to the Mahayana view of ultimate reality, Jiun establishes the foundation upon which he may argue the claims of the *Jūzen hōgo* mentioned previously. First, regarding the importance of the jūzen vis-à-vis other, more detailed formulations of the precepts: since, like the jūzen, all Buddhist precepts "flow out of the dharmatā" (*hosshō yori tōru suru*), true mastery of even the relatively elementary jūzen implies mastery of all other precepts as well. Jiun goes on to draw the more radical conclusion that since genuine mastery of any one of the ten good precepts presupposes the attainment of insight into the dharmatā, the practitioner who succeeds in even that deceptively simple endeavor will be able to fulfill all Buddhist precepts.[86] Indeed, since as Jiun notes elsewhere, "even the 250 precepts [for monks] are an abridgement of an abridgement,"[87] by truly mastering even one precept, the practitioner has gained a guide upon which he may rely in all aspects of his life.

Second, from the same premise, Jiun is able to assert the timeless validity and universal practicability of the jūzen. Because the dharmatā is the same in all ages, likewise are its implications for human conduct. Moreover, since it is present in all human beings as their original nature, all people, regardless of education, social status, or

---

[83] Ibid., p. 4.

[84] On the link between insight into the dharmatā or emptiness and conduct, Cook writes: "Compassion, which I am considering to be an ethical matter here, is inextricably bound up with perception. . . . It is really only the dynamic form of *prajnā*-insight, which is itself the insight into emptiness. . . . Simply stated, to act compassionately means to act in accordance with reality" (*Hua-yen Buddhism*, p. 121).

[85] JSZ, 11:16.

[86] Ibid., p. 237.

[87] JSZ, 14:563.

sexual identity, may in theory perfect the jūzen by realizing their original nature.

Third, Jiun can further maintain, also upon the basis of the relationship that exists between the jūzen and the dharmatā, that the jūzen benefit all who attempt to embrace them. Not only Buddhist monks and nuns, whose lives, it could be said, are totally dedicated to the fulfillment of the jūzen—although in their expanded form in the vinaya—but also farmers, shopkeepers, family heads, and heads of state can expect to benefit in concrete ways from their more limited efforts to observe the precepts. In Jiun's view, to the degree that any individual lives in accord with the ten good precepts, he also lives in accord with the dharmatā, and, to that same degree, he will inevitably benefit. "Although the bright light of the sun and moon makes no distinctions," Jiun writes, "high mountains and deep valleys receive their light just as it falls, according to their lots. Similarly, although the ten good precepts are equally manifest throughout the dharmatā, people receive their merits to the extent that they abide by them."[88]

Thus all may benefit by observing the jūzen, but Jiun is particularly concerned that the laity be made aware of their importance. Writing more generally about the relevance of Buddhism as a whole to lay life, he points out, "Occasionally, even a person who believes in the exalted nature of the dharma (J., hō) sees the like of Karukaya Dōshin[89] and the priest Saigyō[90] and thinks that unless he cuts himself off from [the relationships of] lord and subject, parent and child, and husband and wife, and enters mountain forests and dark valleys, he is not a follower of the dharma. This is a mistake. . . . These teachings are vast and nothing is left out. For the laity, there is the Way of the laity; for the clergy, there is the Way of the clergy."[91]

The benefits that a lay person can reap through observance of the ten good precepts have immediate value within lay life. A well-ordered family, success in business, and a well-governed state are some of the most significant benefits that Jiun mentions.[92] Jiun makes it clear, however, that the supreme benefit that an individual can gain by following the jūzen is of a different order than these; moreover, it is attainable only by the individual who devotes himself full-time to living in accord with the jūzen, that is, the Buddhist monk or nun

---

[88] JSZ, 11:6.

[89] A legendary Shingon recluse made popular through tales and drama.

[90] (1118–1190). The famous poet-priest who spent his life wandering the Japanese countryside.

[91] JSZ, 11:100–101.

[92] See, for example, ibid., pp. 50, 71, and 93.

who lives according to the vinaya. That supreme benefit is Buddha-hood.[93] A Buddha in Jiun's definition, therefore, is an individual whose every thought, word, and deed conforms to the jūzen;[94] or considering that the jūzen "flow out of the dharmatā," a Buddha may also be defined as an individual who has gained complete insight into and lives in total harmony with the dharmatā. It is at this final stage of spiritual growth that we experience fully the unity of all things of which the Buddha spoke in the *Lotus Sutra*. Not only do we regard all sentient beings as "our children," but beyond that, "All the various objects of our senses—forms, sounds, fragrances and tastes—all are one with the wondrous principle (*myōri*) and we, both in body and mind, are one with them. The mountains, rivers and earth, the grasses, trees and forests—all of these we see as our very own body."[95] The joys of this attainment, Jiun notes, are so profound as to be beyond the comprehension of ordinary men and women.[96]

Finally in this regard it is important to note that, in Jiun's view, the celibate and monastic life required of the Buddhist clergy—the life prescribed in detail in the vinaya, but captured in essence in the jūzen—is far more than a means to an end. Properly understood, it is a way of life that both leads to and proceeds from insight into the dharmatā. Consequently, the life of the Buddhist monk or nun, regardless of whether he or she has attained that insight or is still striving toward it, is a living testimony to the dharmatā, the ultimate ground of emptiness shared equally by all things. "That a monk leaves the family," Jiun writes in an earlier sermon, "is a concrete expression of the fact that he regards all things as equal (*byōdō*) and has transcended all distinctions."[97] In yet another sermon, he explains that the historical Buddha did not become a monk because he found the position of ruler—for which he was destined by birth—and the officials, subjects, palaces, and concubines that came with it to be a nuisance; rather he became a monk because he "saw all sentient beings as equal (byōdō)."[98]

Thus the monk transcends "human relations" (*jinrin*), but at the

[93] In his frequent summaries of the benefits that observance of the jūzen brings, Jiun always mentions this benefit last. See, for example, the concluding passage of the *Jūzen hōgo* translated on page 202 of this essay. Similar passages can be found in JSZ, 11:1 and 71.

[94] On one occasion, when asked, "What kind of person is a Buddha?" Jiun replied, "Simply a good person." See *Sosai mondō*, JSZ, *hoi* (Supplement):80.

[95] JSZ, 11:9.

[96] Ibid., p. 150.

[97] JSZ, 14:8.

[98] Ibid., pp. 615–616.

same time he is "a teacher of human relations,"[99] since he bears constant witness to the ultimate source of all moral values, the dharmatā. Concretely speaking, he does this by meeting the requirements of the jūzen in all respects. Therefore, although others not as far along in their spiritual development may continue to violate the precept prohibiting killing, by taking, for example, the lives of animals, the Buddhist monk, aware of the fundamental unity of all things, kills nothing.[100] Similarly, although laymen may regard fidelity in marriage as an ideal, the monk remains unmarried and chaste.[101] In sum, the Buddhist monk's function in society is to serve as a standard. He marks the final end of a path that all sentient beings are, at various stages and through innumerable lifetimes, in the process of treading.

It is apparent that in his formulation of the essentials of the Buddhist religion in the *Jūzen hōgo*, Jiun worked with the Confucian point of view in mind. Both his presentation of the ten good precepts as a summation of the Buddhist way of life and his emphasis upon the relevance of Buddhism particularly to the laity reflect his deep desire to lay to rest, once and for all, the Confucian perception of Buddhism as an antisocial religion with little guidance to offer those in the secular world. Moreover, his articulation of the rationale for the existence of the Buddhist clergy in these sermons, although certainly intended for the ears of the clergy, may also be regarded as apologia for Confucian critics. It can thus be said that Jiun's most comprehensive response to Confucianism is the understanding of Buddhism that he sets forth in the *Jūzen hōgo*.

Lest the point be missed, however, Jiun also responds directly in the text to the Confucian criticism that Buddhism is, socially and politically, a deleterious religion. In chapter two, he considers a number of charges made against Buddhism that reflect this common Confucian view. Some assert, he points out, that "the Buddhist dharma is only [a means of] cultivating the mind with the mind and is of no help to the world and no use to the people"; that in the Buddhist scriptures, "no Way exists for governing the state and the world"; that although it has various purification rituals for the Buddhist practitioner, "it is not a Way that ordinary people should follow"; or finally, that because it emphasizes the equality (*byōdōshō*) of all things, it encourages people "to show compassion equally to insects and parents alike."[102] Jiun addresses each of these charges, but his response is essentially the same in each case. Such criticisms, he states, could

[99] JSZ, 11:103.
[100] Ibid., p. 30.
[101] Ibid., p. 102.
[102] JSZ, 11:49–54.

be made only by individuals who had never seriously studied Buddhism. An examination of the religion would show that Buddhism offers guidance to all human beings, in all times and circumstances, for "within the Buddhist dharma," he reminds his audience, "there are the ten good precepts."[103]

Jiun is thus committed to defending Buddhism against Confucian criticisms in the *Jūzen hōgo*, but this stance by no means prevents him from the positive evaluation of Confucianism noted earlier. In particular, Jiun is appreciative of much that he encounters in Confucian morality. We have seen that in his thought the ten good precepts are understood as flowing directly from the dharmatā and represent the ideal for human conduct. From this perspective, Jiun is able to find value not only in the Confucian moral code, but in any moral code to the extent that it approximates the jūzen. They, too, reflect the dharmatā, although with varying degrees of clarity. Within this framework, Jiun evaluates Confucianism highly, taking special note of its assertion of the basic goodness of human nature. After stating again the Buddhist view that the jūzen are replete within us, Jiun points out, "In Confucian texts as well, it is said that the man of virtue simply does not lose the childlike mind."[104]

Consequently, Jiun embraces the Confucian virtues, since they also can contribute to the progress of the individual toward the ultimate goal of Buddhahood. Both within and without the *Jūzen hōgo*, Jiun discourses upon the value of filial piety,[105] and in regard to other Confucian virtues, he observes, "The worldly Way of benevolence, righteousness, decorum, wisdom and good faith [the so-called Five Constants of Confucianism] is included within the absolute truth (*shōgitai*) of the Buddhist dharma."[106]

At the same time, however, Jiun also takes the offensive against Confucianism and directs much of his criticism at the identical Confucian morality he elsewhere affirms. To Jiun, while valuable, Confucian morality is flawed in two important respects. First, from the Buddhist point of view, it is not based upon an accurate understanding of the nature of ultimate reality—since Confucianism fails to recognize the emptiness of all things—and thus it is incapable of leading human beings to their fullest development. Confucian morality is useful in the awakening of a moral sense in the individual and in the organization of societies and governments, but in the end it remains only a teaching for the secular world (*seken no hō*). By contrast,

[103] Ibid., p. 49.
[104] Ibid., p. 16. A reference to *Mencius*, 4:B12.
[105] See, for example, JSZ, 11:54 and 14:412–425.
[106] JSZ, 14:489.

Buddhism is able not only to countenance Confucian moral values, as illustrated previously, but also to reveal their ultimate religious significance.

Second, Jiun criticizes the abstract character of Confucian morality. He makes this point in the course of his refutation of the idea, widely accepted in both China and Japan, that Confucianism's Five Constants are identical to the Five Precepts of Buddhism, which prohibit killing, stealing, adultery, lying, and the consumption of intoxicants.[107] The first four of the Five Precepts are included in the jūzen, and in the view that equates the two, parallels are drawn between benevolence and nonkilling, righteousness and nonstealing, decorum and nonadultery, wisdom and the nonconsumption of intoxicants, and good faith and nonlying.

Jiun rejects this view, drawing attention to the contrast that exists between the abstract virtues of Confucianism and the concrete precepts of Buddhism. Benevolence, Jiun points out, is "a teaching that dates from ancient times in China, but even a thousand years later, the very meaning of the word is difficult to understand. Some give the complicated explanation that it is the principle of love (ai no ri) or the virtue of the heart (kokoro no toku); others explain it simply by love. Still others say that it is [the virtue] by which a king rules his people."[108] The meaning of the Buddhist precept prohibiting killing, by contrast, is clear. It tells an individual that "human beings are important, that they are to be respected, that killing them is a great sin, that he should not heedlessly hit or strike or wound them. Put this way," he continues, "from kings, princes and officials above to warriors, farmers, artisans, merchants, laborers and servants below, all may be taught to practice it and to take it to heart."[109] For the same reason, Jiun argues that decorum and the precept prohibiting adultery cannot be properly equated. Calling attention to the complexity of Confucian rites, he observes, "If one is not a scholar, one cannot master decorum."[110] However, both the illiterate person and the scholar can understand and practice the straightforward Buddhist precept regarding adultery.[111]

In a manner strikingly similar to that of his National Learning contemporary, Motoori Norinaga (1730–1801), Jiun also finds the

---

[107] For a discussion of the relationship between these two codes in China, see Michihata Ryōshū, Bukkyō to Jukyō rinri: Chūgoku Bukkyō ni okeru kō no mondai (Kyoto: Heirakuji Shoten, 1968), pp. 133–162.

[108] JSZ, 11:57.

[109] Ibid., pp. 57–58.

[110] Ibid., p. 61.

[111] Ibid.

important role assigned to the human intellect or reason in Confucianism a major stumbling block to the spiritual growth of its adherents. Norinaga had been critical of the rationalistic element within Confucianism primarily because of the damage that, in his view, it does to the more essential, affective aspect of human nature. Jiun disapproves for a different reason. From the Buddhist viewpoint, such reliance upon the intellect prevents the individual from passing beyond the transient realm of subject and object, within which the intellect properly operates, to an experience of ultimate reality which transcends all dualisms. It prevents the individual, in other words, from the attainment of insight into the dharmatā, an insight gained finally not through the exercise of reason but through the practice of meditation.

To Jiun, therefore, the Confucians, and particularly the Neo-Confucians of Sung times and after, appear trapped in endless rounds of overly subtle debate. They "artificially set forth such terms as 'original nature' (*honzen no sei*) and 'physical nature' (*kishitsu no sei*) and are fond merely of argumentation. Since argumentation has no end, once one has become fond of it, one is continually plagued by it."[112] In the end, Jiun includes the Confucians in a class of individuals described as "the worldly wise and clever" (*sechi bensō*), one of eight conditions recognized in Buddhism as inhibiting acceptance of the Buddhist dharma. In what is certainly his strongest statement of this point, he remarks: "Heaven despises worldly wisdom and cleverness. To be shrewd and quick is something of which one should be ashamed. The reason—being worldly wise and clever is contrary to the dharmatā."[113]

The aim of this essay has been to present briefly the life and thought of Jiun Sonja, with specific reference to his response to Confucianism, in the hope of initiating a reexamination of our current understanding of Tokugawa Buddhism. In Jiun, one can glimpse an aspect of the religion in this period that stands in sharp contrast to the negative characterization of Tokugawa Buddhism that has been commonly accepted. Admittedly, little can be claimed for Tokugawa Buddhism as a whole on the basis of a single extraordinary individual. It is important to note, therefore, that although Jiun is exceptional in many respects, he is also representative of trends character-

[112] Ibid., p. 422. The Neo-Confucians distinguished two natures in man: his "original nature," which was his pure, moral nature, and his "physical nature," which was the *ch'i* or ether within which his "original nature" was embodied.

[113] JSZ, 11:367–368.

istic of Tokugawa Buddhism generally. His Shōbōritsu was only one of several movements founded in the period that stressed the importance of monastic discipline.[114] Similarly, while Jiun had no peer in the field of Sanskrit studies, the names of other students of the language are known.[115] As for popular advocates of Buddhism and defenders of the religion against its non-Buddhist critics, their numbers are too great to list here.[116] Thus, although it is undeniable that Buddhism faced serious challenges in the Tokugawa period, it is possible to argue that significant segments of the Buddhist community had both the will and the capacity to respond to those challenges. Some may question the originality of the contributions made by Jiun and other Buddhist leaders of this period—apart, that is, from Jiun's achievements in the study of Sanskrit. In a sense, however, this criticism is beside the point. As an original philosopher, Jiun may not equal such figures as Kūkai (774–835) or the Zen master Dōgen (1200–1253). But in attempting to preserve the Buddhist dharma and to present it in terms comprehensible to his contemporaries, he shared their goal, and all indications suggest that he met with remarkable success.

The study of Jiun Sonja has implications for our understanding of fields beyond Tokugawa Buddhism, however, and in closing at least two merit brief mention. First, a knowledge of Jiun contributes to our general understanding of Tokugawa intellectual history. The restorationist or fundamentalist character of his thought, his great concern with ethical issues, his philological interests—all place him squarely within the intellectual context of eighteenth-century Japan. It could even be argued, although it has not been a concern of this essay to do so, that the rationalism of this period, of which Jiun was in part critical, is also evident in his thought. To date, however, none of

[114] Reference has already been made to the *Shingonritsu* movement. Others include Tendai's *Anrakuritsu*, founded by Myōryū (1637–1690); Nichiren's *Hokkeritsu*, represented by Gensei (1623–1668); and Pure Land's *Jōdoritsu*, represented by Kyōju (1683–1748).

[115] In addition to Jōgon, noted previously, the most often-cited Sanskrit scholars are Donjaku (1674–1742), his disciple Jakugon (1702–1771), Shōzen (1676–1763), and Tōku (1745–1816). All are members of the Shingon sect.

[116] For a brief discussion of some of the most important figures in each category, see Tamamuro Taijō, ed., *Nihon Bukkyō shi*, 3:85–91 and 111–113, respectively. Popular advocates of Buddhism mentioned there include Keikō (1740–1795) of the Tendai sect, Daiga (1709–1782) of Pure Land, Gensei of the Nichiren sect, Bunan (1603–1676) and Bankei (1622–1693) of the Rinzai sect, and Tetsugen (1630–1682) and Chōon (1628–1695) of the Ōbaku sect. Included among Buddhist apologists are Shingon's Jakuhon (1631–1701), Daiga and Bun'yū (d. 1764) of Pure Land, Nitchi (1819–1854) of the Nichiren sect, Rinzai's Chidatsu (1704–1769), and Ōbaku's Chōon.

these themes have been discussed with reference to Tokugawa Buddhism. Second, the study of Jiun Sonja bears important implications for the comparative study of Buddhism in Tokugawa Japan and in late-Ming and Ch'ing China. The parallels that exist between Jiun and the Ming Buddhist leader Chu-hung (1535–1615), for example, are instructive in this regard.[117] Although the circumstances in which they worked are by no means identical, both men lived at a time when Buddhism was troubled internally by a lack of discipline within its clergy and challenged intellectually by Neo-Confucian thinkers. Furthermore, both responded to their situations in a similar fashion, emphasizing the importance of the precepts and monastic discipline, exhibiting a special concern for the laity, de-emphasizing sectarian differences, and replying to Neo-Confucian criticisms of Buddhism while affirming the value of the Confucian moral code. Such parallels suggest that this, too, is a rich field of inquiry.

[117] On Chu-hung, see Yü, *The Renewal of Buddhism in China.*

NINE

NEO-CONFUCIAN THINKERS IN NINETEENTH-CENTURY JAPAN

BY TAKEHIKO OKADA

In their researches on nineteenth-century thought, Japanese intellectual historians have tended to concentrate on those Confucians active in the political or social arenas; as a result the work of Neo-Confucians active in other areas has not been examined, creating an incomplete portrait of the era. The work of these neglected Neo-Confucians is important both in terms of the history of Confucian thought in East Asia and in terms of the development of the Neo-Confucian study of the mind and human nature.

Several factors stand in the way of those who might wish to explicate the thought of these nineteenth-century Neo-Confucians: their writings have, for the most part, not been published or made widely accessible; what little has been written on them is replete with misunderstandings and misinterpretations; but perhaps most significantly, in order to understand fully the context of their thought, one must first examine not just the writings of Chu Hsi (1130–1200) and Wang Yang-ming (1472–1529) in China, but also the history of their Neo-Confucian followers and interpreters in China, Korea, and Japan. These thinkers of the nineteenth century regarded themselves as members of lineages which they traced back to the two masters, and their thought represents a significant development of certain aspects of the teachings of both Chu and Wang.

This essay, then, has three major aims. The first is to identify these largely neglected nineteenth-century Japanese Neo-Confucians, and to observe the relationships they formed internally as a distinct intellectual community. My second aim is to map the relationship of these Japanese Neo-Confucians *as they themselves perceived it* to Neo-Confucian lineages which they traced back to the late-Ming and Ch'ing dynasties in China, and the Yi dynasty in Korea. Third, I shall compare the views of these nineteenth-century Neo-Confucians on such topics as the mind, human nature, the appropriate role of the Neo-Confucian in politically troubled times, and so on. It is, of course, hoped that in this way meaningful comparisons may be observed between the thought and behavior of late-Tokugawa and early-Meiji

Neo-Confucians in Japan, and their counterparts some centuries earlier on the continent.

NINETEENTH-CENTURY NEO-CONFUCIAN SCHOLARS
AND TOKUGAWA CONFUCIANISM

The Neo-Confucian scholars whom I take up in this essay—Satō Issai (1772–1859) in Edo, the students of Ōshio Heihachirō (also known as Ōshio Chūsai, 1798–1837) in Osaka, and also those who had direct and indirect links to these two—emphasized both the importance of understanding based on personal experience, and the study of the mind and human nature. Among those who identified with the orthodox teachings of Chu Hsi were Ōhashi Totsuan (1816–1862) from Ueno, and the brothers Kusumoto Tanzan (1828–1883) and Sekisui (1832–1916) from Hirado. Sekisui's friend and Totsuan's student, Namiki Rissui (1829–1914) from Shimōsa, might also be said to belong to this group. Those who identified with Wang Yang-ming learning (*Yōmeigaku*) included Hayashi Ryōsai (1807–1849) from Sanuki, Yoshimura Shūyō (1797–1866) from Aki, Yamada Hōkoku (1805–1877) from Bitchū, Kasuga Sen'an (1811–1878) from Kyoto, Ikeda Sōan (1813–1878) from Tajima, and Higashi Takusha (1832–1891) from Iwakuni. From this group Totsuan, Tanzan, Sekisui, Shūyō, and Hōkoku were students of Satō Issai, and Ryōsai was a student of Ōshio Heihachirō. Ōhashi Totsuan was an acquaintance of Yamada Hōkoku and a passionate follower of Ōshio Heihachirō's Wang Yang-ming studies. Ikeda Sōan called on Issai in Edo where he had first met Totsuan, continuing their association for some time thereafter, and also had connections with Ryōsai, Shūyō, and Hōkoku. Kusumoto Tanzan and Sekisui both had direct and indirect links to these Wang Yang-ming scholars with whom they shared common goals. Higashi Takusha was a student of Shūyō and also had friendly associations with Sōan and the brothers Tanzan and Sekisui.

This interrelated group of orthodox and heterodox Neo-Confucian thinkers received and made use of Neo-Confucian learning from the late Ming and early Ch'ing, were active in intellectual circles of the nineteenth century, and were responsible for bringing fresh ideas into Japanese Chu Hsi and Wang Yang-ming studies. They were trained primarily in Edo or Osaka, but they were active in the provinces where they lectured on the study of mind and human nature, basing their theories on what they could apprehend from direct experience and observation. By propagating these teachings to their many devoted students, they made an important contribution to intellectual circles of that time.

In the study of Tokugawa Confucianism, it is important that one examine the educational system of each domain because even though the bakufu used orthodox Neo-Confucianism as its official teaching, it did not compel each domain to do the same. Since the bakufu took a tolerant attitude in these matters, each domain independently promoted its own education. This differed from the situation in early-modern China where in order to establish an educational orthodoxy, the government had to be exceedingly strict with any school that promoted teachings other than those of the Chu Hsi school. By way of contrast, Tokugawa Neo-Confucians in their respective schools might profess Chu Hsi studies or Wang Yang-ming studies, and generally did not often enage in attacks on other contending schools. There may be a connection here with the fact that Tokugawa Neo-Confucians encountered Sung, Yüan, Ming, and early-Ch'ing Neo-Confucianism at virtually the same time, and this may also be reflective of possible differences between the Chinese and Japanese temperaments.

After a rich and variegated early history, Tokugawa Confucianism peaked during the mid-eighteenth century with the Ken'en school of Ogyū Sorai at the vanguard. At that time, other schools arose including the "eclectic" (setchū), the "independent" (dokuritsu), the "ancient commentaries" (kochū), the "investigative" (kōshō), and so on, and from them emerged scholars who espoused original thought. However, because of the Ken'en school's popularity as well as the popularity of culture and learning in general, others likewise set up their own schools and vied for originality. They promoted their independent theories, rejected the restrictions imposed by their teachers, and became self-appointed authorities on Confucianism. As a result the traditional decorum of Confucian studies was lost, and the intellectual atmosphere came to resemble that which had prevailed in China during the late Ming.

One result of the rise of these various schools was that intellectual circles rid themselves of the negative effects of conventionality and came to exhibit a distinctive kind of liveliness and vigor; at the same time, however, official discipline in the age grew lax and morality decayed, with corresponding lapses within intellectual circles. The bakufu, anxious over these matters, issued in 1790 the Prohibition of Heterodox Studies, assuming that this would revitalize Neo-Confucian studies and renovate educational affairs with quasi-scientific thought. However, by this time simply promoting Chu Hsi learning in official education was not sufficient to rescue the situation. In due course the bakufu appointed Hayashi Jussai to head the Bakufu College, and he and his colleague Satō Issai strove to reinvigorate the official educational system. They championed Chu Hsi learning but refused to adopt the singular view of a "school" and maintained a tolerant attitude toward other teachings, calculating that this approach would be most effective in terms of revitalizing orthodox Neo-Confucian learning. Satō Issai in particular never accepted the notion of a single lineage or school, and after Jussai's death he espoused the theory of a common origin for the teachings of Chu Hsi and Chu's rival, Lu Hsiang-shan (1139–1193), so that some referred to Issai as "Chu [Hsi] on the outside, Lu [Hsiang-shan] on the inside." Many talented men emerged from Issai's gates and went on to active service in their respective domains, and so Issai was widely admired and recognized as a leading authority of his age.

Both the proliferation of schools and the generally tolerant intellectual climate resulted in a diminution of the distinction between orthodox and heterodox Neo-Confucian teachings. Let us now turn to an examination of a comparable intellectual climate in China some centuries earlier.

NEO-CONFUCIAN LEARNING OF THE LATE MING AND EARLY CH'ING

As mentioned previously, in order to understand Neo-Confucian learning of the nineteenth century, it is essential that one understand Chinese Neo-Confucianism of the late Ming and the early Ch'ing. Let us look first at developments in the heterodox Neo-Confucian circles of Wang Yang-ming learning. According to Wang Chi (1498–1583), Wang Yang-ming's disciple, there were six interpretations of Wang Yang-ming's doctrine of the extension of the innate knowledge of the good (chih liang-chih) after Yang-ming's death,[1] but for our purposes, it will suffice to regard these various divisions in terms of three main schools: the Existential Realization school, the Quietist school, and the Cultivation school. The Existential Realization school was the school of Wang Chi and Wang Ken (1483–1540). They emphasized the actuality and utility of innate knowledge, and they sought a kind of enlightenment experience grounded in and based on reality whereby being equates with nonbeing. They explained the immediacy of the here-and-now and emphasized direct or sudden enlight-

---

[1] Huang Tsung-hsi (1610–1695) analyzed the Wang school in terms of seven branches in his Ming-ju hsüeh-an, chaps. 10–36. See also my Ōyōmei to Minmatsu no Jugaku (Meitoku Shuppansha, 1970).

enment. While some of their followers were drawn into unproductive abstraction, Wang Chi himself was a master of actual enlightenment, and Wang Ken stressed practice and practical matters. Their techniques were simple and direct, offering an attractive Confucian alternative to the Ch'an (Zen) emphasis on enlightenment through sitting in meditation, and they conformed well to the preferences of the times. Thus the school came to predominate in its age. Among later followers of the Existential Realization school was a group that might be called a school of "independents" who claimed the strength to vanquish dragons with their bare hands, prized chivalry and valor, and rejected the rules and regulations of others.

The Quietist school began with the Wang Yang-ming follower Nieh Pao (1487–1563) and extended through to Lo Hung-hsien (1504–1564) and Liu Wen-min, as far as Wan T'ing-yen and Wang Shih-huai. Nieh Pao took "innate knowledge" and divided it into the fundamentals of emptiness and quietism on the one hand, and the practical value of inspiration on the other. By establishing fundamentals and guiding one to their utility—the so-called theory of establishing fundamentals and promoting utility—he explained quietism as the essence of Wang Yang-ming's doctrine of the extension of the innate knowledge of the good. Lo Hung-hsien, in turn, felt that this quietism had to resurrect a kind of original tranquillity. Both Nieh Pao and Lo Hung-hsien felt that the primary points of the doctrine of the extension of innate knowledge of the good were expressed better in Wang Yang-ming's middle years than in the explanations of his later years. They also tended to emphasize Wang's doctrine of forming one body with all things.

The Cultivation school was represented by Ch'ien Te-hung (1496–1574), Tsou Shou-i (1491–1562), and also Ou-yang Te (1496–1554). Ch'ien Te-hung emphasized the use of effort to achieve fundamentals, and insisted that what Wang Yang-ming had called innate knowledge could be acquired only by cultivating the quality of sincerity. Tsou Shou-i emphasized the practice of what he called loyalty and faithfulness, following goodness and correcting faults, and being careful and cautious. He expounded on the Sung Confucian concept of reverence, and he maintained that innate knowledge was the same as the principle of heaven (t'ien-li), suggesting that the thought of Sung and Ming Chu Hsi scholars was often in alignment with that of Wang Yang-ming. Ou-yang Te, much like Tsou Shou-i, emphasized the doctrine of cultivation and promoted the practice of caution, honesty, and so on. The Cultivation school in general was faithful to the principal points of Wang Yang-ming concerning the unity of theoretical fundamentals and practical effort, for they learned their lessons from the abuses of their age and asserted the need for pragmatic reforms based on ancient models.

Of the three schools, the Existential Realization school was the most popular, probably because it addressed the issues and conformed to the preferences of its age, but its followers were too ready to follow their own impulses, giving rise to occasional abuses. As a result, Hsü Fu-yüan, a student of Wang Yang-ming's friend and colleague Chan Jo-shui (1466–1560), and Hsü's student Feng Ts'ung-wu (1556–1627) tried to correct what they regarded as some of the excesses of the Existential Realization school. Hsü Fu-yüan advocated the need for extreme self-control and criticized the Existential Realization school for their theory of the individual which postulated the existence of an autonomous self and denied that this self should be inhibited or restrained.

With the previously mentioned figures as representative of major currents among the followers of Wang Yang-ming, we may now turn to their counterparts among the followers of Chu Hsi learning, starting with the Tunglin Academy, the single most important center of Neo-Confucian scholarship in the late Ming. The Tunglin Academy at this time was headed by Ku Hsien-ch'eng (1550–1612) and Kao P'an-lung (1562–1626) who, like Feng Ts'ung-wu, intended to rescue their age through their scholarship. They insisted on the actual existence of the principle of heaven, identifying human nature with principle, and by reaffirming the notion of human nature as good, they promoted the practice of self-cultivation. The Tunglin criticized Wang Yang-ming's identification of the mind with principle as well as the Existential Realization school's primary emphasis on the here-and-now. They followed Chu Hsi's notion of the investigation of things and the exhaustion of principle, but they also came to emphasize the importance of the tranquillity of principle and human nature. Accordingly, they explored the more mystical aspects of the mind and principle, thought and action, fundamentals and effort. Furthermore, by emphasizing the attainment of tranquillity and understanding based on personal experience, they sought to achieve a deepened self-awareness. Other features of Tunglin Neo-Confucianism included the practice of so-called pure conversation, and an emphasis on individual courage and integrity.

Liu Tsung-chou (1578–1645) was another of Hsü Fu-yüan's students. He regarded Chu Hsi's investigation of things from the *Great Learning* as the central point of Neo-Confucianism and like Wang Yang-ming emphasized the importance of sincere intentions. Liu Tsung-chou regarded intention as the substance of the mind and distinguished it from conscious thought. He followed Hsü Fu-yüan and advocated strict self-denial and being circumspect in solitude. According to Liu, the substance of the mind was a singular indivisible entity, and he maintained that while Confucius alone understood this, from Tzu-ssu and Mencius (371–289 B.C.) on down, scholars through Chu Hsi and Wang Yang-ming all mistakenly separated intention from mind. Like Confucians of the Tunglin, Liu Tsung-chou stressed courage and integrity and ended his life by committing suicide for his principles.

Among the next generation of early-Ch'ing scholars, Chang Lü-hsiang (1611–1674), a student of Liu Tsung-chou, also esteemed the orthodox teachings and criticized Wang Yang-ming. He stressed everyday practice and held that one had to see the principle of human nature and destiny in the practical reality of plain words and actions. Bitō Nishū (1745–1813), a Japanese Chu Hsi scholar, called this the learning of the gate of the sages and recommended it highly,[2] and Kusumoto Sekisui regarded Chang Lü-hsiang as a great Confucian who deserved to be ranked alongside the so-called three greats of the early-Ch'ing, namely, Sun Ch'i-feng (1584–1675), Li Yung (1627–1705), and Huang Tsung-hsi (1610–1695). Sekisui praised the purity and clarity of this learning, and recommended it as a Way appropriate for a time of revolutionary change.

Other features of early-Ch'ing intellectual life had an impact on nineteenth-century Japanese Neo-Confucians. These included an emphasis on statescraft and utility, the rejection of "empty" discussions of human nature and principle, an emphasis on actual meritorious deeds, a retrospective reexamination of the classics, and a revival of fidelity to the orthodox teachings of Chu Hsi. Figures representative of these themes included Sun Ch'eng-tse (1593–1675), Chang Lieh, Lü Liu-liang (1629–1683), and Lu Lung-ch'i (1630–1692). These figures were strongly biased in favor of the Ch'eng-Chu orthodoxy and endeavored to distinguish it from, and thereby reject, the teachings of Lu Hsiang-shan and Wang Yang-ming.

As we shall see, Japanese Neo-Confucians drew fruitfully from the teachings of their late-Ming and early-Ch'ing counterparts. Their response to the Existential Realization school's self-confident zeal, and their receptivity to the tranquillity of the Quietist school, the self-nurture of the Cultivation school, as well as the orthodox Neo-Confucian interest in questions on the mind, human nature, and wisdom all helped to shape the character of late-Tokugawa Neo-Confucian thought. They, of course, also found meaningful precedents in Korean thought.

---

[2] *Shisho takugen.*

Among nineteenth-century Japanese Neo-Confucian scholars versed in the learning of the early Ch'ing, probably the greatest was Kusumoto Sekisui who was also familiar with the Korean Neo-Confucianism of Yi T'oegye (1501–1570). Other Japanese Neo-Confucians like Hayashi Ryōsai, Ikeda Sōan, Higashi Takusha, and others had been exposed to Korean Confucianism, but the ones who were most familiar with T'oegye's learning were Kusumoto Tanzan and Sekisui who were introduced to him through the Kimon school founded by Yamazaki Ansai (1618–1682). Sekisui especially had great praise for him: "The various forms of Korean Confucianism before T'oegye were synthesized by T'oegye, and after T'oegye there was no one else."[3] Sekisui even recited poems in priase of T'oegye,[4] and Higashi Takusha is said to have wept upon learning that in Korea T'oegye's reputation was in decline.[5]

THE PRINCIPAL FIGURES IN NINETEENTH-CENTURY NEO-CONFUCIAN LEARNING

Turning first to the principal figures in nineteenth-century Japan who identified themselves with the teachings of Wang Yang-ming—Hayashi Ryōsai, Yoshimura Shūyō, Yamada Hōkoku, Kasuga Sen'an, Ikeda Sōan, and Higashi Takusha—what do we find? Hayashi Ryōsai, like his teacher Ōshio Heihachirō, followed Ch'ien Te-hung of the Cultivation school by referring to the substance of innate knowledge as the great emptiness, and by regarding selflessness in the context of emptiness as the original substance of the universe.[6] Selflessness for Ryōsai meant the extinguishing of all desires and selfish intentions, and he expounded the need to return to emptiness. He believed that the vital impetus underlying and unifying all things was found in nature. However, since the attainment of selflessness requires a degree of individual effort and insight, Ryōsai advocated the classic dictum from the *Great Learning* of "being watchful over oneself when alone." For Ryōsai, "being watchful over oneself when alone" brought the original state of the mind together with individual effort. Taking "being watchful over oneself when alone" as a praxis, Ryōsai advocated concentration by means of quiet sitting, retrospec-

---

[3] *Kusumoto Tanzan, Sekisui zenshū* (Fukuoka: Ashi Shobō, 1975), "Sekisui sensei yokō," kan 11, zuitokuroku 4.

[4] Ibid., kan 10, furoku 3.

[5] Letter from Higashi Takusha to Kusumoto Sekisui, in *Bakumatsu-Ishin Shushigakusha shokanshū* (Meitoku Shuppansha, 1975), Shushigaku Taikei, vol. 14.

[6] "Saiki Tokuzan Kondō sensei fukuron gakujutsu sho" (original MS).

tion, and reflection. He believed that in this way one might achieve full cultivation of the vital impetus of the empty and spiritual.[7]

Ryōsai also developed the Sung doctrine of maintaining quiescence, followed by Lo Tsung-yen (1072–1135), Li T'ung (1088–1163), Ch'en Hsien-chang, the Quietist school teachings of Nieh Pao, and Lo Hung-hsien. Of these he particularly esteemed Lo Hung-hsien's doctrine of self-criticism.[8] In this regard Ryōsai had his students make ledgers of self-criticism in which they attempted retrospection and reflection.[9]

Of the three factions of the Wang Yang-ming school, Ryōsai most respected the Quietist school. Though he found merit in the Existential Realization teachings of Wang Chi and Ken Ting-hsiang,[10] he also abhorred the excesses of the followers of Existential Realization and blamed them for distorting Wang Yang-ming's original teachings.[11] Only the Quietists Nieh Pao and Lo Hung-hsien, according to Ryōsai, were beyond reproach in this regard.[12] Ryōsai also drew on the late-Ming Neo-Confucian teachings of Ku Hsien-ch'eng (1550–1612) and Kao P'an-lung (1562–1626) of the Tunglin school, and on Hsü Fu-yüan.

Seeking a common thread in the teachings of the Ch'eng brothers and Chu Hsi on the one hand, and those of Lu Hsiang-shan and Wang Yang-ming on the other, Ryōsai declared, "In my humble opinion the special character of Ch'eng-Chu and Lu-Wang is that they all go back to the same thing, they are all teachings of sages."[13] By synthesizing the Lu-Wang and Ch'eng-Chu teachings, he was able to achieve a compromise between the two learnings of the Sung and the Ming.[14] Ryōsai's admiration for the eclectic Liu Tsung-chou was thus natural and appropriate.

Like his teacher Ōshio Heihachirō, Ryōsai emphasized filial piety, declaring, "One filial piety, ten thousand goodnesses."[15] He referred to filial piety as the classic meaning of heaven and earth, and he advocated the filial piety doctrines of Yang Chien (1141–1226) in the

---

[7] "Jikeiroku" (original MS), rōsetsu 7; "Hōsō Chūsai daikyōtaku jo" (original MS); "Saiki Tokuzan Kondō sensei fukuron gakujutsu sho"; letter from Hayashi Ryōsai to Ikeda Sōan, *Bakumatsu-Ishin Yōmeigakusha shokanshū* (Meitoku Shuppansha, 1971), Yōmeigaku Taikei, vol. 11.

[8] Letter from Hayashi Ryōsai to Ikeda Sōan.

[9] Ibid.

[10] "Kaiseki" (original MS).

[11] "Ki Kondō-ō hōfukushitsu Tokuzan sensei" (original MS).

[12] Letter from Hayashi Ryōsai to Ikeda Sōan.

[13] "Jikeiroku," rōsetsu 7.

[14] "Ruijū yōgo" (original MS), jijo, batsu.

[15] Letter from Ōshio Chūsai to Hayashi Ryōsai (original MS).

Sung, Yü Chi in the Yüan, Lo Ju-feng (1515–1558) in the Ming, and in Japan the Shingaku teachings of the Sekimon school.[16] He in particular recommended the Shingaku teachings as simple, familiar, and beneficial to the age, and he criticized the popular view of Shingaku as a vulgar teaching.[17]

A second leading figure of the group that followed Wang Yang-ming was Yoshimura Shūyō. He was a faithful proponent of the doctrines of his teacher Satō Issai and warmly praised Wang Yang-ming's doctrine of the extension of innate knowledge of the good. He was critical, however, of Liu Tsung-chou and rejected the thesis of Ōhashi Totsuan and others who held that Liu Tsung-chou had improved on certain shortcomings of Wang Yang-ming. He maintained that those who had best remedied shortcomings of the Wang school were Tsou Shou-i and Ou-yang Te, both of the Cultivation school; that others who had merit within the Wang school were Nieh Pao, Lo Hung-hsien, Wang Shih-huai, and Wan T'ing-yen of the Quietist school; and that Liu Tsung-chou was too independent and was not a true follower of Wang learning.[18]

Shūyō had particular admiration for the doctrines of the Cultivation school, and when he explained the extenion of innate knowledge, he interpreted it in terms of the practice of "extension" (ka-kujū).[19] He emphasized Wang Yang-ming's doctrine of sincere will and concluded that what was needed was effort in the direction of the practical application of virtues.[20] He criticized the Existential Realization school of Wang Chi and Chou Ju-teng (1547–1629?) and others for being too abstract and self-indulgent.[21]

In his later years Shūyō deplored excessive intellectualism, and he rejected the various lofty theories of human nature and destiny, claiming that the sin of scholarship was that it separated the mind from the body.[22] He held that man's highest duty was to discipline his thoughts and to restrict the desires,[23] and he developed a sophisticated practice of reflection that he called "self-encounter" (jihan).[24] Shūyō wrote:

[16] "Jikeiroku," rōsetsu 7; "Hōshitsu Tokuzan daikyōtaku" (original MS); "Saiki Tokuzan Kondō sensei fukuron gakujutsu sho."

[17] Letter from Hayashi Ryōsai to Ikeda Sōan.

[18] Doku ga sho rōikō (pub. 1882), kan 1, yo Ikeda Sōan.

[19] Ibid., fuson, goroku.

[20] "Doku ga sho rōbunshō" (original MS), kan jō, zuihitsu 75 jō.

[21] Doku ga sho rōikō, kan 1, "Ō Bunsei ko denbon jo"; "Doku ga sho rōbunsō" (original MS), zō Iida shi, jo.

[22] "Doku ga sho rōbunsō," Junsei shoin ki.

[23] Doku ga sho rōikō, fuson, goroku.

[24] Ibid.

A scholar need only encounter himself and should not oppose things. All maladies arise from this. If you do not oppose things, then there will be no separate things. If there are no separate things, then the self can merge with things. . . . Filial piety means being filial, and fraternal love means being fraternal. It is not a matter of wanting filial piety or wanting fraternal love. In a world with ten thousand changes every day we hold on to one place. Encountering oneself involves nothing more than this."[25]

Shūyō, in later years came to appreciate the practice of quiet sitting in the Cultivation and Quietist schools.

Yet a third figure in nineteenth-century Yōmeigaku was Yamada Hōkoku who drew his inspiration primarily from Wang Yang-ming's doctrines concerning the sincerity of one's will or intentions. As Hōkoku put it:

The primary emphasis of Wang's teaching was sincere will. The extension of innate knowledge was merely a feature of this sincere will. Nonetheless, you must use the investigation of things in order to achieve this. Without the extension of innate knowledge, you will not find the original substance of sincere will. Without the investigation of things, there will be no performing the meritorious deeds of sincere will. When both are brought along together you have sincerity of will."[26]

In this sense Hōkoku regarded sincerity as the culmination of the extension of innate knowledge, and investigating things as essential for the performance of meritorious deeds. According to Hōkoku, in this way the extension of innate knowledge might avoid abstraction and aimlessness and might become more solid. Accordingly, he devoted himself to this promotion of the extension of innate knowledge and held that without the performance of practical meritorious deeds, one would be at variance with the original teachings of Wang Yang-ming. Hōkoku in many ways resembled Ch'ien Te-hung of the Cultivation school and was known in his day as "the small Ban" because of his emphasis on meritorious deeds in the manner of Kumazawa Banzan (1619–1691).[27]

Kasuga Sen'an, Ikeda Sōan, and Higashi Takusha are our three remaining Yōmeigaku figures. Kasuga Sen'an regarded himself as a faithful follower of Wang Yang-ming's more contemplative doctrines and emphatically stressed the need for effort in terms of per-

---

[25] Ibid.
[26] *Yamada Hōkoku ikō*, kan jō, "Tōjin bōsho."
[27] Meaning, thereby, to also belittle Kumazawa Banzan.

sonal development.[28] He modeled himself on Hsü Ai (1487–1517) of the Wang school, who advocated returning to the original self as the main teaching, and he regarded Tsou Shou-i of the Cultivation school and Nieh Pao, Lo Hung-hsien, and Liu Wen-min of the Quietist school as those who understood the essential points of Wang Yang-ming. Thus he admired the teachings of Lü Tsu-ch'ien (1137–1181), who reconciled Chu Hsi's teachings with those of Lu Hsiang-shan and emphasized practical reality.[29] Sen'an in some respects personally resembled Wang Ken of the Existential Realization school, but he criticized the behavior of Wang Ken and Wang Chi for what he regarded as self-indulgence and moral laxity.[30]

Sen'an was a Yōmeigaku scholar, but he most admired the teachings of Liu Tsung-chou, that latter-day critic of the Existential Realization school. He described his impressions upon first reading Liu Tsung-chou's *Jen-p'u* (Genealogy) as follows: "I first read the *Genealogy* in the autumn and winter of 1838, and I lost myself it was so refreshing, and I understood the narrowness of my own learning."[31] He maintained that Liu Tsung-chou had for him "revealed the fruit" of Wang Yang-ming's teachings and that "Liu Tsung-chou's learning found the essence of Yang-ming."[32] Sen'an did not see the deviation from Wang's teachings that others among his colleagues claimed to have found in the writings of Liu Tsung-chou, and in Liu's doctrines of self-understanding, Sen'an claimed to have found the best of the message of Chu Hsi and Lu Hsiang-shan.[33]

Ikeda Sōan, like Sen'an, also had great respect for Liu Tsung-chou. According to Sōan, Lu-Wang learning was simple, easy, and straightforward. It also saved Ch'eng-Chu learning from intellectual incoherence and excessive constriction. He claimed that "after Ch'eng-Chu, there had to be a Wang, and after Wang there had to be a Liu. . . . Wang saved Ch'eng-Chu learning and it would not be wrong to say that Liu supplemented the essence of Wang."[34] Sōan, like Hayashi Ryōsai, respected Liu Tsung-chou's doctrines of self-criticism and being watchful when alone, and he said that these by themselves were sufficient to make Liu Tsung-chou's learning worthwhile. Like

[28] *Kasuga Sen'an ikō* (pub. 1892), kan 3, goroku, "Sen'an gūhitsu."

[29] Ibid., kan 2, yo Okamoto Keiteki sho.

[30] Ibid., kan 2, Ō Shinsai zenshū jo.

[31] Ibid., kan 1, yo Ikeda Shikei sho.

[32] Ibid.

[33] Ibid., kan 1, Kimu; letter from Kasuga Sen'an to Ikeda Sōan, in *Bakumatsu-Ishin Yōmeigakusha shokanshū*.

[34] *Seikei shoin zenshū* (1913), vol. 2, part 1, Sōan bunshū, letter to Yoshimura Shūyō.

the Ming scholar Wu Yü-pi (1392–1469), Sōan esteemed the meritorious deeds and direct experiences of the body and mind which are carried out in the context of everyday life. Sōan affirmed Lo Tsung-yen and Li T'ung's doctrine of maintaining quiescence, and Nieh Pao and Lo Hung-hsien's doctrine of quietism, and he explicated the *Mean* according to Nieh Pao and Lo Hung-hsien.[35] In this way, Sōan, who took quietism as his main point, emphasized the joyous aspects of introspection and loved Liu Tsung-chou's dying words, "Within my heart there is refreshing joy."[36] Sōan appreciated the teachings of Wang Chi and Wang Ken of the Existential Realization school and rejected later scholarship as something rife with abuses.[37] As mentioned previously, Sōan inclined sharply toward Liu Tsung-chou's doctrine of being watchful when alone, but he regarded this being watchful when alone as something based on the *Mean*, and he thought of him as someone who unified the teachings of Ch'eng-Chu and Lu-Wang.[38] Therefore, Sōan personally refused to establish an independent or separate school.[39]

Higashi Takusha, too, at first appreciated Liu Tsung-chou's teachings as something that synthesized Chu Hsi and Wang Yang-ming, but after he studied under Shūyō, he inclined more toward Yōmeigaku. Takusha was aware of the extremes of the Existential Realization school;[40] however, he took exception with Shūyō's fondness for the Cultivation school and criticism of Wang Chi and Wang Ken of the Existential Realization school, both of whom he admired.[41] He asserted that "in general, learning uses memorization to arrive at hypotheses,"[42] and he regarded memorization and self-confidence to be the essential points of learning.[43]

Thus the Yōmeigaku figures of the nineteenth century were generally in sympathy with the Cultivation and Quietist schools and

[35] Letter from Ikeda Sōan to Hayashi, in *Bakumatsu-Ishin Yōmeigakusha shokanshū*.

[36] "Ryōsai, Ryōkai dōki," Sōan bunshū, in *Seikei shoin zenshū*.

[37] "Doku Ō Shinsai zensho," Sōan dokubun, in *Seikei shoin zenshū*, vol. 2.

[38] Letter from Ikeda Sōan to Kusumoto Tanzan; letter from Ikeda Sōan to Hayashi Ryōsai; "Doku Ryūshi zensho," Sōan dokubun, in *Seikei shoin zenshū*, vol. 2.

[39] Letter from Ikeda Sōan to Hayashi Ryōsai, in *Bakumatsu-Ishin Yōmeigakusha shokanshū*.

[40] "Shōshin roku (ge)," in *Higashi Takusha zenshū* (1919), vol. 1.

[41] Ibid., "Shōshin roku (jō)," and "Fuku Kusumoto Sekisui sho," Takusha bun'yaku, *ibid.*, kan ge.

[42] Letter from Higashi Takusha to Kusumoto Sekisui, in *Bakumatsu-Ishin Shushigakusha shokanshū*.

[43] "Namiki Seishū no yo Kusumoto Sekisui," Shuō gappen 4, *Kusumoto Tanzan, Sekisui zenshū*.

critical of the Existential Realization school, though the latter found support from figures like Higashi Takusha. Satō Issai's student Okumiya Zōsai (1811–1872) liked Wang Chi, and Yoshida Shōin (1830–1859), who studied under Issai's student Sakuma Shōzan (1811–1864), read the writings of Li Chih (1527–1602) and is said to have been struck by them.[44] Zōsai and Shōin, like other nineteenth-century Wang Yang-ming supporters, tended to seek and emphasize points of agreement between the teachings of Chu Hsi and Wang Yang-ming. This was in sharp contrast, however, to those nineteenth-century Chu Hsi scholars—Ōhashi Totsuan, Kusumoto Tanzan, and Kusumoto Sekisui—who sought to separate the two lines of development and were in general more critical toward Wang Yang-ming, at times engaging in severe attacks on him.

Ōhashi Totsuan at first celebrated the concept of realization through personal experience, and like Sun Ch'i-feng, Huang Tsung-hsi, Li Yung, and others of the early-Ch'ing he found points in common between Chu Hsi and Wang Yang-ming. He attacked Feng Ts'ung-wu's criticism of Wang learning as unfair and repudiated the anti-Wang theories of Lü Liu-liang and Lu Lung-ch'i of the early Ch'ing. Later, he shifted to the teachings of Liu Tsung-chou, but in the end he regarded Chu Hsi alone as orthodox and rejected Wang, Zen, and Western Learning as dangerous heterodoxies. Ironically, Totsuan's Chu Hsi learning in the end came closest to that of Lü Liu-liang and Lu Lung-ch'i, both of whom he had once criticized.[45]

Kusumoto Tanzan and Sekisui followed the Kimon school teachings of Yamazaki Ansai which they felt, by means of its emphasis on self-cultivation, enabled one to value both innate knowledge and strenuous effort. They regarded abiding in reverence as the beginning and ending of their learning, and they sought realization through personal experience and self-understanding.[46] Tanzan interpreted this in terms of what Chu Hsi had called "making the original allotment universal." What Tanzan meant by "making the original allotment universal" was much the same as what had been known as realization through personal experience by Kao P'an-lung, and maintaining quiescence by Chou Tun-i (1017–1073), Lo Tsung-yen, Li T'ung, and the Quiestists Nieh Pao and Lo Hung-hsien. This realization or awareness derived from personal experience, and self-understanding

[44] *Yoshida Shōin zenshū*, nenpu (Iwanami Shoten, 1935).

[45] Cf. my *Kusumoto Tanzan* (Sekibunkan Shoten, 1959).

[46] *Bakumatsu-Ishin Shushigakusha shokanshū; Kusumoto Tanzan;* "Kaisetsu," in *Kusumoto Tanzan, Sekisui zenshū*; letter from Kusumoto Sekisui to Ikeda Sōan, in *Bakumatsu-Ishin Shushigakusha shokanshū*.

achieved through quiet sitting formed the principal points of Tanzan's teachings. In his later years, Tanzan was drawn to the Chu Hsi
concept of the Store of Wisdom, which is discussed later in this
essay.[47]

Sekisui also advocated awareness based on personal experience, but
he at the same time regarded everyday things to be replete with mystery, and thus emphasized the need for both physical and spiritual
effort. For Tanzan, the admonitions and commandments in Ming
Confucian writings were interesting, but he felt that the examination
of principle must be a never-ending process and that the wondrous
aspects of everyday life were only truly appreciated by the Ch'eng
brothers and Chu Hsi.[48] He had high praise for Wu Yü-pi, asserting
that, "Nowadays numbers of people study the teachings of Wu Yü-
pi."[49] Sekisui, too, again like Tanzan, favored the Kimon school's
doctrines of self-cultivation, but Tanzan's scholarly approach was more
comprehensive and subjective, whereas Sekisui's approach was more
analytical and segmented.

Sekisui's scholarship resembled that of the early-Ch'ing followers
of Chu Hsi, Lu Lung-ch'i, and Chang Lü-hsiang, and he warmly
praised both saying, "Lu Lung-ch'i was correct and great, and Chang
Lü-hsiang was spiritual and pure."[50] At the same time, he was critical
of Liu Tsung-chou's teachings which were popular at that time.[51]
Like his brother, Sekisui lectured on the doctrines of quiet sitting and
the store of wisdom, but he differed with Tanzan in his continuation
of the popular approaches of the Kimon and his conclusions concerning individual duty.

We can thus see that for nineteenth-century Japanese Neo-Confucians, including both orthodox and heterodox figures, the intellectual
controversies, affiliations, and identifications of late-Ming and early-
Ch'ing Neo-Confucians were matters of intense interest and direct
relevance. Japanese Neo-Confucians *identified* with Chinese Neo-
Confucians, whom they regarded as counterparts, for reasons that
will, it is hoped, become clearer by examining their views on several
topics that were central to their thought. By understanding how Japanese Neo-Confucians imagined their circumstances to be comparable to those of their Chinese predecessors, one can then understand

---

[47] *Kusumoto Tanzan*; and "Kaisetsu," in *Kusumoto Tanzan, Sekisui zenshū.*
[48] Letter from Kusumoto Sekisui to Ikeda Sōan.
[49] Ibid.
[50] "Sekisui sensei isho," kan 8, zuitokuroku 1, in *Kusumoto Tanzan, Sekisui zenshū.*
[51] Ibid., kan 11, zuitokuroku 4.

why their proclaimed intellectual lineage was of such importance to them.

Teachings on the Mind and Human Nature

No issue was of more personal interest to Neo-Confucians than that of the mind and human nature, and so let us begin by examining nineteenth-century Japanese views on this issue starting with the orthodox school for whom this was an issue of even greater than usual importance. Questions on the mind and human nature were linked to the exercise of retrospection and tended at this time to include a rejection of intellectualism, or what might be called "book learning." The followers of Chu Hsi had long emphasized practical efforts at renewal, as well as clear understanding based on personal experience and self-reflection. It was not that this kind of academic tradition had not already existed, but for their nineteenth-century successors these matters were altogether more profound, mysterious, and marvelous. Even Satō Issai, acclaimed as the leading authority of his age, said, "People today read books containing words with their eyes. As a result they are held back by the words and are incapable of proceeding beyond them. What they should do is to read wordless books with their hearts. Then their self-understanding will be [as deep as] a cave."[52] In the same vein, Issai wrote, "I would like to take 'reading books and quiet sitting' and to strike off the first bit," and he took realization through personal experience and self-understanding as the main points.[53]

In the minds of most nineteenth-century followers of Chu Hsi, even Issai was a step behind. In their eyes, Issai's teachings lapsed at times into academic abstruseness and were thus relatively not as advanced in terms of helping one develop self-understanding. Therefore, they did not concentrate on Issai's teachings, but rather applied themselves diligently to the refinement of each other's work. Even among his students, there were some who were critical of Issai's actions,[54] and still others who maintained that there was no real force in Issai's teachings.[55]

They imagined their teachings to be superior in terms of these themes of realization through personal experience and self-understanding because they felt they had encountered a historically un-

[52] "Saigyo jō," in Shuō gappen (furoku), *Kusumoto Tanzan, Sekisui zenshū.*
[53] Ibid., "Shigoroku."
[54] Letter from Ikeda Sōan to Kusumoto Tanzan, in *Bakumatsu-Ishin Shushigakusha shokanshū.*
[55] "Ikeda Seinosuke nikki" (original MS).

precedented set of problems for the fortunes of the country. Furthermore, in times such as these they regarded understanding based on direct personal experience as the most relevant. Factors like these were probably the cause for their turning to the Neo-Confucianism of the late Ming and early Ch'ing. They felt that the destiny of their country and welfare of the people all came back to questions of the mind and human nature, and that the connection between the vicissitudes of the teachings of the mind and human nature on the one hand and the future of the country on the other was of singular importance.[56] The following statement by Sōan conveys these concerns:

> Alas in this broad and vast universe questions of what one is to do and questions of right and wrong have never been finally resolved; and questions of safety and welfare have not even for one day been clear. Everywhere people are abandoning this land like a sinking ship. What I wish is that my colleagues might discretely address themselves to this issue, and that through diligence and perseverance a stop might be put to these abuses. Fortunately if this single seed can be planted between heaven and earth, it just might grow, as I hope, into a lucky sapling. Then might it not be helpful to the Way of the world and the mind of man?"[57]

The same Neo-Confucian scholars of the nineteenth century emphasized both the vigorous performance of practical, meritorious deeds and the importance of understanding the mind and human nature. They also argued vehemently against views gleaned from the exegeses of ancient texts, understandings based on analyses, the isolation of responsibility from moral issues, an overabundance of information and knowledge, and the parochialism of individual schools. Satō Issai had indicated the pitfalls of an overindulgence in scholarly exegesis,[58] but Neo-Confucian scholars of the nineteenth century argued this point even more forcefully. Kusumoto Tanzan, who acknowledged the importance of scholarship, nonetheless maintained: "Those who espouse the teachings of Chu Hsi in the world waste their time on exegesis while performing not a single valorous, practical, meritorious deed. I can only be amazed at how the most important teachings of Master Chu have been obscured by dark clouds

---

[56] Letter from Yoshimura Shūyō to Ikeda Sōan, in *Bakumatsu-Ishin Yōmeigakusha shokanshū.*
[57] Letter to Kasuga Sen'an in Sōan bunshū, in *Seikei shoin zenshū.*
[58] "Shibanroku."

and the four injuries."[59] These "most important teachings," according to Tanzan, were those on the mind.[60] As he put it:

If one listens to the Confucians of this immediate world of ours, those who propound Chu learning mostly deal with exegetical textual study, but there is not a single person who speaks of understanding the mind, and while there are those who quietly and cheerfully set themselves to exegesis and memorization, they merely waste their time on textual matters, and there is no one who works at the meritorious act of broad self-cultivation.[61]

According to Tanzan, the Hayashi school of orthodox Neo-Confucianism had lapsed into incoherent analysis, since it was afflicted with notions like exegesis, memorization, and broad and vast learning. Tanzan echoed Yamazaki Ansai's criticism of the Hayashi that they did not go beyond learning one or two of the empty shadows of Chu Hsi, and Ansai scolded them for this and insulted them by calling them vulgar Confucians. Because they sought the teachings of the mind and human nature through exegesis, Ansai said there was no one to step forward by performing practical and direct meritorious deeds.[62]

On this point there was broad agreement between the nineteenth-century followers of both Chu Hsi and Yōmeigaku. From the latter group, Yoshimura Shūyō likewise denounced exegesis when applied to teachings on the mind and human nature, maintaining that "exegesis and textual study are not yet sufficient to form a field of study," and "a lifetime is not long enough to make a contribution if one defends the commentaries and vies with the exegetes."[63] Of Shūyō's "Three Articles of Vigilance" (jikei sanjō), the first was the admonition "Do not become dependent on exegesis." He criticized the Kimon scholar Kaneko Sōzan (1785–1865) claiming that while he was factually well informed, he was deficient in the performance of meritorious deeds, and that ultimately he was "merely a scholar."[64]

Kasuga Sen'an and Ikeda Sōan were also among the Yōmeigaku followers who opposed what they regarded as "empty" intellectualism. Kasuga Sen'an deplored how Confucian scholarship at that time

[59] Letter from Yoshimura Shūyō to Kusumoto Tanzan, in Bakumatsu-Ishin Shushi-gakusha shokanshū.

[60] Letter from Kusumoto Tanzan to Ikeda Sōan, ibid.

[61] Ibid.

[62] "Gakushuroku" (ge), Kusumoto Tanzan sho (kan 6), Kusumoto Tanzan, Sekisui zenshū.

[63] Doku ga sho rōikō, fuson, "Goroku."

[64] Letter from Yoshimura Shūyō to Kusumoto Tanzan.

had lapsed into vapidity. "Shallow learning has spread far and wide throughout the whole country while learning of the mind and body and learning of practical value have in the long run become rare."[65] Teachings on the Way had, in his view, degenerated into sophistry, and he maintained these "so-called scholars appear to be spending their days as if discussion were the most important issue, and in due course scholarship as a whole will disappear."[66]

Among Neo-Confucian figures of that age, no one enjoyed reading more than Ikeda Sōan, but Sōan, too, criticized scholars who sought to investigate principles exhaustively and thus lapsed into shallow learning.[67] He emphasized the example of Yin T'un (1071–1142) who despite his deficiency in talents and abilities was nonetheless perfect in his practical application.[68] In this context he said that "the abuse of extensive reading is not uncommon," and it was ironic that he drew such attention to the harm that extensive reading could cause.[69]

One finds much the same view among the followers of Chu Hsi. For example, Ōhashi Totsuan was a gifted orator, but he nonetheless said:

> The learning of human nature and principle does not esteem extensive reading; rather it esteems energetic reading. Therefore one must select the important passages from the writings of the Four Masters of Lo-Min, and one must vigorously read and re-read them dozens and hundreds of times. Then when one considers and reconsiders these words and sets aside meritorious deeds of actual experience, there will come a time when, like virtue awakening from a long nap, one will escape from this and will see clearly the substance of the Way.[70]

Totusan's student Namiki Rissui also rejected extensive learning and memorization and maintained that ultimately they trivialized one's inmost feelings.[71]

Since these thinkers rejected exegesis, they also were skeptical vis-à-vis explications and commentaries on the classics. For example, Yoshimura Shūyō felt that despite the fact that reading and scholarly

[65] "Sen'an ikō," kan 2.

[66] Letter from Yoshimura Shūyō to Ikeda Sōan.

[67] "Jikei," in Sōan bunshū (jō).

[68] Letter from Ikeda Sōan to Kusumoto Sekisui.

[69] Letter from Kasuga Sen'an to Ikeda Soan, in *Bakumatsu-Ishin Yōmeigakusha shokanshū.*

[70] Letter from Ikeda Sōan to Kusumoto Tanzan. The Four Masters of Lo-Min (Lo-yang) were Chang Tsai, Chou Tun-i, and the Ch'eng brothers.

[71] Letter from Namiki Rissui to Kusumoto Sekisui, in *Bakumatsu-Ishin Shushigakusha shokanshū.*

discourse were an introduction to learning, and experience and practice were the end products of learning, scholars of his age were guilty
of mistaking the means for the ends. He stated further that while
there were many in the world who worked on explicating the classics, their knowledge was based exclusively on written characters and
was of dubious value in terms of actual and practical meritorious
deeds.[72] He maintained that as a result, rather than seeking ever to
improve their exegesis, so long as the meaning is clear in its general
outline, scholars must apply it in a sober-minded fashion and in such
a way as to obtain self-cultivation and enlightenment.[73]

According to Ikeda Sōan, on occasions when one is reading the
classics, rather than extensively reading the various analyses and
commentaries of different scholars, one should reread the classics
themselves, endeavor to achieve realization through personal experience, and discard notions based on analysis. He also held that commentaries on the classics, just like the commentators of his own age,
were inevitably seduced into citing copious references and making
boastful exaggerations.[74] Sōan spoke in this way because, like Chang
Tsai and Lu Hsiang-shan of the Sung, and Wang Yang-ming of the
Ming, he felt that the character of the sages as recorded in the classics
was basically the same as that originally possessed in one's heart.[75]
Kusumoto Sekisui was a great scholar, but he spoke for many of his
colleagues when he declared simply, "That the Ch'engs were able to
address these matters with the spirit of amateurs was fine, but this is
not an end or achievement by itself."[76]

Since they denounced the exegesis of the teachings of mind and
human nature, it is understandable that some of them were even
critical of writings in general. Yoshimura Shūyō maintained: "If your
understanding of writings is less than perfect, it is by all means fine
that you should have a look at writings and other opinions, but becoming pretentious about it is like dashing after fame and fortune.
. . . In short, how would it be if writings were few and people sought
understanding in ordinary life?"[77] Shūyō's only important work was
his *Kohon daigaku kakuchi tōgi* (Issues in Investigating Ancient Texts
of the *Great Learning*) in one volume. Sekisui said, "Writings are of

[72] "Doku ga sho rōbunshō," kan jō, zuihitsu 75 jō.
[73] *Doku ga sho rōikō,* fuson, goroku.
[74] Letter from Ikeda Sōan to Kusumoto Tanzan.
[75] Ibid.
[76] Letter from Hayashi Ryōsai to Ikeda Sōan.
[77] Letter from Yoshimura Shūyō to Ikeda Sōan.

no benefit,"[78] and praised Chu Hsi's teacher, Li T'ung, for not having any writings. And in evaluating a political tract written by Li T'ung's teacher, Lo Tsung-yen, Sekisui said (by way of flattery), "It definitely seems not to have been written [by him]!"[79]

Thus one can observe nineteenth-century Japanese Confucians turning inward, in a sense, toward these questions of human emotional understanding, while at the same time seeking to ground these understandings in the outer world of human experience. They were skeptical of the ability to acquire such understandings through scholarship or textual analysis, since they felt that the urgent issues of their own age provided an extraordinary "laboratory" of experience from which they could draw. Hence they saw meaningful antecedents for their particular dilemmas not so much in the teachings of the ancients or even those of the Sung and early Ming, but rather those eclectic formulations of the comparably troubled late Ming and early Ch'ing.

Rejection of Parochialism

It is interesting that among Neo-Confucian scholars of the nineteenth century, those who espoused the views of the Ch'eng brothers and Chu Hsi were generally critical of Yōmeigaku, whereas those who espoused the views of Wang Yang-ming tended to acknowledge the strong points of the Ch'eng-Chu orthodoxy and found use in both. Yamada Hōkoku, for example, emphasized the merits of the investigation of things within the context of the extension of innate knowledge of the good. According to Hōkoku, the merits of the investigation of things are evident, and if they are evident, then they are direct and tangible.[80] He taught Chou Tun-i's doctrine of maintaining quiescence, the Ch'eng brothers' for abiding in reverence, Lu Hsiang-shan's for honoring the moral nature, Chu Hsi's on the Way, and Wang Yang-ming's for the extension of innate knowledge, and maintained that all these paths ultimately converge.[81]

Yoshimura Shūyō said that the opinions of the Chu Hsi school were complex and their correct meaning was difficult to discern, and so he favored the teachings of Wang Yang-ming, but he said that scholars may select whichever they wish by relying on their own judgment.[82] It is said that even though Shūyō was a Wang Yang-

---

[78] "Sekisui isho," kan 9, zuitokuroku 3.
[79] Ibid., kan 11, zuitokuroku 4.
[80] *Yamada Hōkoku ikō* (kan jō), "Fuku Kasuga Sen'an."
[81] Ibid., "Tōjin bōsho."
[82] "Doku ga sho rōbunshō," zatcho.

ming scholar, on occasions when he lectured to students in his school, he used Chu Hsi's commentaries, and that barring some special request from some of his students, Wang Yang-ming's *Ch'uan-hsi lu* (Instructions for Practical Living) was not used in his lectures. Shūyō said that the doctrines of Wang Yang-ming were lofty and penetrating, while the doctrines of Chu Hsi were weighty and sober-minded, and he criticized Ōhashi Totsuan for asserting that the distinction between "orthodox" and "heterodox" was clear.[83]

Among the Wang Yang-ming scholars of this time, Ikeda Sōan was the most adamant in his rejection of parochialism. Sōan, as mentioned earlier, used Liu Tsung-chou to harmonize and improve upon the teachings of Chu and Wang: like Liu Tsung-chou, he opposed any sharp division of the two teachings as separate doctrines and any establishment of parochial views. Sōan, if one had to say which lineage, preferred Lu-Wang, but he nonetheless held that Ch'eng-Chu complemented Lu-Wang just as Lu-Wang complemented Ch'eng-Chu.[84] He maintained that both teachings focused on human ethics and morality, and while there were distinctions at the lower level of practice, ultimately both were teachings of the sages. The similarities and differences in the teachings were, he insisted, of help to one's study.[85]

Shūyō wrote the *Kohon daigaku kakuchi tōgi* in which he explained the doctrines of the investigation of things and the extension of knowledge on the basis of Wang Yang-ming's teachings. Ōhashi Totsuan, who at that time favored Liu Tsung-chou, wrote the *Tōronsho* (Work Attacking the Theory) in which he criticized Shūyō's theories, and Shūyō, in turn, wrote the *Benfukusho* (Work of Rebuttal) in which he refuted one by one the allegations of Totsuan. The two argued back and forth eventually growing hostile toward each other. Ikeda Sōan who also admired the syncretic teachings of Liu Tsung-chou disdained this parochialism and sent a letter to Shūyō in which he compared this dispute with that between Chu Hsi and Lu Hsiang-shan and urged both parties to reexamine their positions.[86] Ultimately, Sōan called attention to defects in both Chu Hsi's and Lu Hsiang-shan's teachings, concluding, that it was unnecessary to make parochial assertions so boldly.[87] In this way, Sōan arrived at a

---

[83] Letter from Ōhashi Totsuan to Kusumoto Tanzan, in *Bakumatsu-Ishin Shushigakusha shokanshū*.

[84] Letter from Ikeda Sōan to Yoshimura Shūyō.

[85] Ibid.

[86] Ibid.

[87] Ibid.

more eclectic position, but he still recognized that there were differences between the two teachings because to do otherwise, he felt, would mean being a blind follower of neither.

Kusumoto Tanzan lauded the Kimon school's version of the Chu Hsi teachings for their focus on exhaustively investigating principles. He was critical, however, of those who, like Ikeda Sōan in his opinion, emphasized being watchful when alone to the extent that it interfered with understanding the Way: "Maintaining that there is a need for being watchful when alone is a perfectly sensible position. However, when this teaching asserts, as it often has, that one need not follow the principles (dōri) of the world . . . as if there were not a shade of doubt, some people mistake the rebel for the master and adopt the rebel's notions."[88] Tanzan held that unless one establishes a comprehensive plan to investigate the principles of affairs and things tracing them back to their ultimate origins, and unless one resolves to base one's understandings on personal experience and self-reflection, one's views will grow ever shallower until one becomes a trivial person. He insisted that one exhaustively investigate principles by means of seriousness, reverence, tranquillity, and personal experience, and he gave priority to Chu Hsi learning. Accordingly, he told Sōan that "unless one serves Wang wholeheartedly and unless one serves Chu wholeheartedly, one is not serving the edification and illumination of the sages and worthies."[89]

In opposition to this, Sōan stated that even though he preferred the atmosphere of the Ch'eng-Chu, he was unable to follow Chu Hsi's commentaries on the Great Learning or the Mean, and he did not support the attitude of orthodox fidelity to the Chu Hsi teachings of Tanzan and his brother Sekisui.[90] Sōan felt that being watchful when alone had the same importance for Chu Hsi as maintaining seriousness and that this was no different from the practice of holding the mind steady or cultivating the nature. Insisting that there were no real differences between Chu and Wang and that ultimately they agreed on far more than they differed, he rejected the stance of Tanzan and Sekisui of promoting Chu Hsi learning and setting up parochial views.[91]

Kusumoto Sekisui held that while many in Japan reverenced Chu Hsi, there was no group comparable to the Kimon school of Yamazaki Ansai in terms of the number of its followers, the intensity of

[88] Letter from Kusumoto Tanzan to Ikeda Sōan.
[89] Ibid.
[90] Letter from Ikeda Sōan to Kusumoto Sekisui.
[91] Letter from Ikeda Sōan to Kusumoto Tanzan.

their conviction, or the profundity of their erudition. Tanzan and Sekisui most admired the teachings of Miyake Shōsai within the Kimon school, and according to Sekisui, since the Kimon school had become narrow-minded and obstinate after Yamazaki Ansai, the principle points of Ansai's teachings were unclear, and each of the students established his own parochial school which, in turn, subdivided into still more schools. Further, according to Sekisui, the Confucians of the Kimon school by and large held to their own theories and brought about a climate in which they could pass judgment on the faults of the former Confucians in a single sentence. Shōsai was without bias and like Tseng Tzu (505–436 B.C.) in the *Analects* understood the Master's teaching well.[92]

Ikeda Sōan, on the other hand, argued vigorously against the Kimon school. In a lengthy diatribe, he declared:

> All in all, if one is Chu Hsi, one should be Chu Hsi; why should one speak of the Kimon? Furthermore, how can one speak of Yamazaki Ansai and others as if they were interchangeable with Chu Hsi? If one is a dim-witted scholar, then so be it, but if one is a man of intelligence and excellence, then do not speak of the Kimon school. Even to my colleagues I usually express my profound reverence for the scholarship and the person of Chu Hsi, but I also say that I see no need to go so far as to read Ansai's writings.[93]

Sōan slandered the Kimon school in this way because in general the Kimon school never hesitated to attack the teachings of other schools.

Hayashi Ryōsai followed Yōmeigaku teachings and read Buddhist works in order to clarify the distinction between the Lu-Wang and Zen teachings. Accordingly, he criticized the theories of Bitō Nishū (1745–1813) who regarded Lu-Wang as Zen. Ryōsai, nonetheless, sought points of agreement between Chu Hsi and Lu Hsiang-shan concluding that both made understanding the moral nature their principal point. He also maintained that the Way of the Sages returned to filial piety in order to fill a need, and that both Chu and Lu had understood this.[94] He praised the eclectic Chu-Lu theories of Fujiwara Seika (1561–1619) and said, "My fellows immediately followed Fuji *sensei's* teachings; with their hearts they felt its correctness and with their bodies they complied with it; when I look for a single

---

[92] "So Nikokushi keisho," in *Sekisui ikō*, kan 1.
[93] Letter from Ikeda Sōan to Kusumoto Sekisui.
[94] "Ruijū yōgo."

thread among the differences, is [Seika] not what I should be wishing for?"[95]

Thus, where there was general agreement between the followers of Chu Hsi and Wang Yang-ming on the centrality of questions concerning the mind and human nature, there was also a great deal of tolerance shown by the Yōmeigaku followers toward orthodox proponents, with the possible exception of the more strident Kimon school. Further, this tolerance was not entirely reciprocated by the followers of Chu Hsi, even while they acknowledged certain areas of agreement. There were still other differences, however, between the two groups as we shall see on the next point.

Courageous Exploits and Victorious Ardor

A second issue on which the followers of Wang Yang-ming and Chu Hsi differed was political involvement. Here, too, there was an enormous range of opinion. If there are men like Yamada Hōkoku who were renowned for their knowledge of statecraft, men like Ōhashi Totsuan, Kasuga Sen'an, and Higashi Takusha who were active as imperial loyalists, and men like Kusumoto Tanzan encharged with domainal administration who participated in the epochal achievements of the Meiji restoration, there were also men like Ikeda Sōan who did not pursue a lifetime of official service but remained in the countryside, or men like Hayashi Ryōsai and Kusumoto Sekisui who at the prime of their lives declined government service and propagated their teachings. Generally, the Neo-Confucians ranked among the *sonnō-jōi* (Revere the Emperor, Expel the Barbarian) advocates and sought to protect what they regarded as the national character. Though they probably exaggerated both the magnitude of their mission and the purity of their principles, they still differed from those activists who, spurred on by their enthusiasm, dedicated themselves to affecting a radical reform of their age. This was so because they regarded the dissemination of Sung and Ming teachings on the mind and human nature to be their primary duty, in order thereby to establish ethics and morality, and to rectify public behavior for the sake of the nation. According to them, even the courageous exploits of the activists, unless they were tempered by an understanding of the mind, would inevitably lapse into opportunism, ultimately affecting adversely the welfare of the country, breaking the web of morality, and bringing hardship and misery upon the people. This kind of

[95] "Kaiseki."

attitude coursed through the writings of Neo-Confucian scholars during the late Ming.

Among the followers of Yōmeigaku, Ōhashi Totsuan was criticized by his colleagues for plotting the overthrow of the bakufu, but he insisted that the study of human nature and meritorious accomplishments formed a single entity.[96] He regarded meritorious accomplishments as a natural manifestation of the principles of human nature, and he claimed that the exhaustive investigation of principles was given priority in his teaching.[97] Thus he criticized many Confucians after the coming of the American ships to Uraga, maintaining that "those who presume to deliberate on matters like moral principles (dōgi) have not given this more than half-a-glance."[98] He felt it to be essential that courageous feats be regarded as manifestations of the principle of heaven. Insisting that courageous exploits were wrong if they were motivated by one's disposition and were boasted of, he said, "After one has achieved understanding of the principle of heaven, not only will one naturally conform to the spirit of the age, but likewise one will glean a personal sense of integrity and courage which is nothing other than the principle of heaven applied in an everyday setting."[99]

Namiki Rissui's criticism of heroics was likewise based on the same factors. Rissui, another follower of Yōmeigaku, regarded study of the mind and human nature and the establishment of morality as duties necessary to rescuing his age, and he felt that activist schemes and strategies would ironically disrupt the country. Rissui singled out Rai San'yō and Fujita Tōko in the following way:

> Scholars nowadays all regard study of the Four Books and the Six Classics as useless and stupid; they regard history and literature as useful and erudite; they do not yearn to become sages, worthies, or gentlemen, but they wish to become great heroes. As a result men's minds are demoralized, behavior has degenerated, and many blindly follow heretical doctrines. It is indeed fortunate that the world has not yet fallen apart. When you propagate the teachings of the sages and worthies, then the virtues of faithfulness, sincerity, courtesy and deference will flourish.
>
> There has never been a country wherein faithfulness, sincerity, courtesy and deference flourished that had disorder. There has

[96] Letter from Ōhashi Totsuan to Kusumoto Tanzan.
[97] Ibid.
[98] Ibid.
[99] Letter from Ikeda Sōan to Kusumoto Sekisui.

never been an instance of great men of wisdom to appear and govern the country when doctrines of heroics are popular. . . . I dare say that scholarly circles of the early-modern era have completely changed. The origins [of this change] came from Rai San'yō, and the followers of Fujita Tōko and Sakuma Shōzan encouraged it. They were so-called heroic great men. Therefore their popular abuses have overwhelmed the country. Their ill effects have been most severe.[100]

In this way, Rissui regarded the veracity and clarity of teachings to be matters of singular importance to the very life of the nation.

Among those who followed Wang Yang-ming's teachings, there were some who dreamed of his exploits and who held that they might be applied in their own age. The followers of Chu Hsi, however, had another answer. As Yamada Hōkoku warned the Yōmeigaku followers. "Your fault lies in that none of you read his writings or understand the Way.[101] Hōkoku made it clear, using the example of Wang Yang-ming's military tactics, that Yang-ming's achievements were based on the strategies of suppressing disorder, quelling upheaval, suppressing violence, and chastising traitors; these achievements, in turn, were linked to his belief in the extension of sincerity and the inherent goodness of the unity of the ten thousand things.[102]

And what of those who did commit courageous feats? They were generally regarded as having forgotten the teachings of the mind and human nature, and it was thought that unless they escaped this intoxicating ardor, they would be unable to master those teachings. As the orthodox Neo-Confucian Kusumoto Sekisui himself reflected in later years on the character of youth: "Ardor is not good. I had much ardor when I was young. . . . Even if your reasoning is fine, ardor by itself will not do."[103] Sekisui in his later years was characterized by his open-mindedness, his profound self-understanding, and the tranquil elegance of his life.

Thus, while much attention has been paid to the exploits of the most activist Neo-Confucians of the nineteenth century like Ōshio Heihachirō, Sakuma Shōzan, and Yoshida Shōin, they were anything but typical of Neo-Confucians of either main school in Japan, and in fact were roundly criticized by them. The Neo-Confucians generally believed in the suppression of disorder and the renewal of society through one or another form of self-cultivation. We shall see, none-

---

[100] Cf. Higashi Takusha, Shuō gappen 4, in *Kusumoto Tanzan, Sekisui zenshū.*
[101] "Ōbunsei kō zensho ko zō Kawaisei," in *Yamada Hōkoku ikō* (kan chū).
[102] Ibid.
[103] "Zotei yobun," in *Kusumoto Tanzan, Sekisui zenshū.*

theless, that these same Neo-Confucians sought other—and to their minds more meaningful—forms of engagement with their society.

The Rejection of Western Learning (Yōgaku) and National Learning (Kokugaku)

One is not surprised to find that Western Learning and those who engaged in it were not highly regarded by the followers of either the Ch'eng-Chu or the Lu-Wang Neo-Confucian tradition. For example, Kusumoto Sekisui claimed of Yokoi Shōnan (1809–1869) from Kumamoto, a student of Chinese Studies (*Kangaku*), that "it would appear that the man called Yokoi outwardly espouses the teachings of Ch'eng-Chu but inwardly nurtures notions of advantage and profit."[104] This was said bacause Sekisui suspected Shōnan of favoring Western Learning for reasons of personal advantage. Nineteenth-century Neo-Confucian scholars in general were critical of Western Learning which they felt was injurious to the national polity.

Ōhashi Totsuan wrote the *Hekija shōgen* (Some Words on Heresy) in which he advocated the rejection of Western Learning. Kusumoto Tanzan, in a postscript to this work, speculated that the damage done by the followers of Western Learning was worse than the ravages of floods or fierce animals. It goes without saying that the Neo-Confucian scholars of the late Tokugawa who were most critical of Western Learning—Totsuan, the Kusumoto brothers, and Ikeda Sōan—were acting out of impulses of patriotism and concern over national conditions.

Ikeda Sōan unsparingly acknowledged Western Learning's superiority to Chinese studies in the areas of astronomy, military matters, medicine, and other scientific techniques and felt at that time that their adoption was essential. However, according to Sōan, since the intention in using these techniques is primarily for their utility and the welfare of the public, if one should become a devotee of them, day by day one's habituation to advantage and profit will increase, one will forget to separate the means of duty from the ends of duty, and swept up in the sheer luxury of it, one will lose one's integrity and fidelity to principles. Maintaining that there had been a complete change in the customs of Japan and its national polity since the opening of the country to the West, Sōan alleged that Western Learning fomented an atmosphere of insubordination (*gekokujō*).[105] According

---

[104] Letter from Kusumoto Sekisui to Ikeda Sōan.

[105] Ibid.; letter from Ikeda Sōan to Yoshimura Shūyō (MS); letter from Ikeda Sōan to Yoshimura Shūyō, in *Bakumatsu-Ishin Yōmeigakusha shokanshū*.

to Sōan, since the welfare of the populace depended merely upon the establishment of morality and ethics, the dissemination of the teachings of the mind and human nature was sufficient to save the people of this time from their miserable suffering.[106] That Sōan did not exert a more positive influence on his times was due to his perception that, as a humble subject, it was impossible for him to affect the transitions of his age. He claimed that "the state of our world is troubled and is on the verge of serious difficulty. However as far as I am concerned there is nothing better than enjoying life by earnestly pursuing knowledge."[107] Accordingly, he maintained that in this age when Western Learning was flourishing and orthodox teachings were on the wane, his mission was to disseminate his teachings to one or two kindred souls in every nook and cranny of the country and to keep alive traditional morality and ethics.[108] In his later years, resigned to the ineluctable advance of Western Learning, Sōan concluded that the only appropriate response was to adopt what is useful and discard what is not from both Western and Chinese studies.[109] One can detect here a difference from the more radical posture of Ōhashi Totsuan who to the end utterly rejected Western Learning including even Western arts.

It is not surprising that in their critiques of Western Learning, nineteenth-century Neo-Confucian scholars included barbs turned toward Christianity. Ōhashi Totsuan regarded Christianity as superstition and concluded that what was needed was the Oriental reverence for heaven.[110] Ikeda Sōan maintained that Christianity was the only Western Way capable of winning over a man's mind. Sōan was critical toward religions in general, but this was because he lamented the disordered rise of sectarianism. Sōan claimed:

> It is possible that there have always been religions in our country. However with the rise of the Tokugawa family came their efforts at and espousal of these Confucian teachings, and fortunately there was not much confusion. When one comes up to the present age, Western Learning prospers. Unless our scholars and great men exert themselves in the study of [Confucian] teachings, how are they to realize that the disorder of schools

---

[106] Letters from Ikeda Sōan to Yoshimura Shyuō and Kusumoto Sekisui (MS); letter from Ikeda Sōan to Yoshimura Shūyō, in *Bakumatsu-Ishin Yōmeigakusha shokanshū.*

[107] Letter from Ikeda Sōan to Yoshimura Shūyō.

[108] Letter from Ikeda Sōan to Kusumoto Sekisui.

[109] Letter from Ikeda Sōan to Nishimura Keizō.

[110] "Hekija shōgen" (1857), kan 2.

we have had thus far in our own country is not comparable to that in the West. This is why I am so deeply concerned.[111]

He also criticized the Christian Bible by asserting: "When I had a glance recently at their New Testament and Old Testament, what they call the recorded scripture of Christianity, I saw that they are shallow, narrow, mysterious and false. I know that no one with any intelligence would promote such confusion."[112]

Sōan did not limit his criticisms to just Western Learning but also condemned the National Learning (*kokugaku*) of that time as well. National Learning scholars had rejected Western Learning in much the same fashion as scholars of Chinese studies had, but according to Sōan, their criticisms bordered on the irrational—a situation made all the more serious because of their self-proclaimed status as defenders of the national polity. As Sōan put it:

> Everywhere Western Learning has flourished, and there are also those who espouse Imperial Learning (*kōgaku*). These eccentrics have been entrusted with the national polity . . . and assert that there are no men of excellence among followers of Western Learning and other such fabrications. Scholarly circles have disintegrated, and the conditions of the present are growing dangerous. What will the morrow bring? What I wish for is that likeminded persons at this time man the towers so that even one-tenthousandth might be saved.[113]

The reference to "Imperial Learning" here probably indicates the school of Hirata Atsutane (1776–1843).

Yamazaki Ansai in his later years espoused Suika Shinto, but among his students there were both those who followed his Shinto, and those who followed his Confucianism and were critical of his Shinto. Kusumoto Tanzan followed Ansai's Confucian teachings, but with respect to Suika Shinto, Tanzan acknowledged that those whose learning was shallow or lacked ability would find it impenetrable, but since Suika Shinto was definitely not contrary to the Way of Confucius and Chu Hsi, it was no obstacle to the transmission of orthodox Confucian teachings.[114] Kusumoto Sekisui said of Suika Shinto that, since there was no shortage of theoreticians among Kimon Confucians, there were points in Suika Shinto that they, too,

[111] "Igyō yokō" (zoku).
[112] Letter from Ikeda Sōan to Yoshimura Ryūzō.
[113] Letter from Ikeda Sōan to Yoshimura Shun.
[114] "Gakushūroku" (ge), Tanzan sho (kan 6), *Kusumoto Tanzan, Sekisui zenshū*.

should look at.[115] However, Sekisui was extremely pointed in his attacks on Hirata Atsutane's version of Shinto. The members of the Hirata school were particularly numerous in Kyoto, and since they popularly rejected Confucian teachings, Kusumoto Tanzan criticized them severely, saying, "They are made up of heresies, outrages, and verbal absurdities, and they do great harm to the true orthodox teachings."[116] Sekisui also remarked, "The nonsense of Hirata Atsutane has never been worth adoption."[117]

Doctrine of the Store of Wisdom

Both Kusumoto Tanzan and Sekisui developed the doctrine of the Store of Wisdom (J., *chizō*; C., *chih-tsang*). The Store of Wisdom had originally been propounded by Chu Hsi, and Yamazaki Ansai was the first to make it clear to others in Japan. Ansai referred to it in his *Kinshiroku jo* (Preface to the Reflections on Things at Hand),[118] and wrote an epilogue on this subject for Hoshina Masayuki's (1611–1672) compilation titled *Gyokuzan kōgi*, where he took excerpts from Chu Hsi's *Chu Tzu wen-chi* and the *Chu Tzu yü-lei*. This was an area on which Neo-Confucians of the Yüan and Ming had not expounded. Accordingly, let us examine the general features of Chu Hsi's doctrine of the Store of Wisdom.

According to Chu Hsi, the three virtues of benevolence, righteousness, and propriety respectively grow out of sympathy and commiseration, shame and dislike, and respect and reverence, and are virtues whose usefulness is externally apparent. Wisdom, however, involves no more than having a sense of right and wrong, and the store of it is completely hidden inside. If one examines the four virtues of benevolence, righteousness, propriety, and wisdom from the perspective of principle, one can speak of benevolence as the creation of life, propriety as the prolonging of life, righteousness as the controlling of life, and wisdom as the store of life. Accordingly, one can speak of wisdom as the dwelling to which the life force returns. If one were to use the metaphor of the four seasons, wisdom would be symbolized by winter; if one speaks of yin and yang, movement and stillness, then wisdom would be the apex of yin and stillness; and using the metaphor of a day, wisdom would correspond to midnight.

---

[115] Letter from Kusumoto Sekisui to Namiki Rissui, *Bakumatsu-Ishin Shushigakusha Shokanshū*.

[116] Letter from Kusumoto Tanzan to Ikeda Sōan.

[117] Letter from Kusumoto Sekisui to Namiki Rissui.

[118] "Suika sō" (10), in Nihon Koten Gakkai, ed., *Yamazaki Ansai zenshū* (Matsumoto Shoten, 1936), vol. 1.

Thus the Store of Wisdom is that which gathers and stores up the ten thousand things, and conceals the images of ten thousand symbols without allaying their traces.

According to Ansai, the ones who first made it clear that there are no traces of the Store of Wisdom were the two masters Ch'eng Hao and Chang Tsai, and Chu Hsi filled in the particulars. Ansai further explicated the doctrine of the Store of Wisdom in his *Teishi shoshō* and *Chōshi shoshō*, but Ansai regarded this as the secret preserve of sages and worthies.

Among Ansai's students the one who was most concerned with the doctrine of the Store of Wisdom was Miyake Shōsai. Shōsai emphasized the element of trust that was involved.[119] Kusumoto Tanzan first became interested in the doctrine of the Store of Wisdom when he read Shōsai's words, "Wisdom is the darkness within a flame, the yin with yang. The multitudinous principles are stored within it."[120] Tanzan followed Chu Hsi's doctrine that the substance of wisdom is the quality of human nature that fathoms both the past and the future. He said: "Wisdom is inherent in winter and in righteousness. Its substance is to be alone and to store up the past, and its function is to make use of things, to generate movement, and to know what will come. It is the beginning and ending of the ten-thousand things."[121] Chu Hsi taught the Store of Wisdom, but he regarded benevolence as the highest virtue that included all others, and he did not regard wisdom as either the highest of the virtues or as the end point of the substance of the mind.

Tanzan amplified Chu Hsi's doctrine of the Store of Wisdom finding antecedents in the *Book of Changes'* "storing up the past and knowing the future" (*ts'ang-wang chih-lai*), and the concept of "centrality of the unmanifest state" in the *Mean*. He praised both Chu Hsi's use of the *Mean* to teach wisdom and the theories of Ansai, and he maintained that this was what Chu Hsi had taught first and what Ansai had pledged himself to.[122] He referred to it as one of the secrets of ten thousand ages, and alleged that there were few Yüan or Ming Confucians who understood this.[123]

According to Tanzan, wisdom was the substance of the four virtues, and accordingly it was both where the four virtues are stored

---

[119] Shōsai included Kume Teisai's "Doku chizōsetsu hikki" as an appendix to his "Chizōsetsu."

[120] "Gakushūroku" (ge), Tanzan sensei isho (kan 9), *Kusumoto Tanzan, Sekisui zenshū.*

[121] Ibid.

[122] *Chu Tzu yü-lei,* chüan 62; *Bunkai hitsuroku,* kan 3.

[123] "Gakushūroku" (ge), (kan 6), *Kusumoto Tanzan, Sekisui zenshū.*

and their ultimate source of origin.[124] Referring to wisdom as "the marvellous quality on which principle hinges," he went so far as to regard wisdom as the store of principle.[125] Tanzan felt that principle and wisdom are not separate entities, and so even if you speak of the thorough investigation of principle, it is clear that this refers to more than simply pursuing external objects.[126] The Store of Wisdom, he concluded, was even what ultimately bonded man's heavenly endowed nature to the supreme ultimate.[127]

In one of his most mystical utterances, Kusumoto Tanzan referred to the Store of Wisdom as the activating point of knowledge whereby "silence fails to see its endings and thinking fails to see its beginnings," and comparing this to the four seasons, it corresponded to midnight on the winter solstice, that is, to that moment when maximum silence has been reached and activation or movement are incipient.[128] Tanzan added, "The Store of Wisdom leaves no tracks; it is the perfect silence of winter that forms the traceless complete substance, the point of activation."[129] Dr. Kusumoto Masatsugu, Tanzan's grandson and my former teacher, explained these words in the following way:

When human knowledge is profound it leaves no traces. It is like winter when the ten-thousand things are stored away and have returned to stillness. This aspect of the human mind is imperceptible to the senses, the absolute universe, and the mind of all creation. Within its stillness it contains the potential for infinite movement. The position of the inner world of the mind reaches the position of the external world. Conversely the true meaning of the external world of activity can only be understood through the attainment of the world of constant stillness which is its opposite. Then the true community of life arises, and one can retrieve the mind of all creation. This is no different from the cultivation of profound knowledge through quiet-sitting.

Kusumoto Sekisui's doctrine of the Store of Wisdom was for the most part identical to that of Tanzan. According to Sekisui, prior to their being in an unmanifested state, benevolence, righteousness and propriety are stored in wisdom. Wisdom, therefore, "is what makes it possible to put benevolence, righteousness and propriety into prac-

124 Ibid.
125 Ibid.
126 Ibid.
127 Ibid.
128 Ibid.
129 Ibid.

tice," for within itself there is no room for practical application.[130] The distinguishing feature of Sekisui's doctrine of the Store of Wisdom was his theory of the relationships between wisdom and principle, and the mind and wisdom. According to Sekisui, wisdom and the mind together constitute something divine, but wisdom is yin and shines within, while the mind is yang and illuminates without. Accordingly, principle is the master of wisdom. This implies that principle is an active being, but it is stored within. Wisdom, on the other hand, enables one to make the distinction between right and wrong, and since it is stored within, Sekisui maintained that "wisdom is the store of righteousness."[131]

It is fascinating that orthodox Neo-Confucians in nineteenth-century Japan rediscovered this doctrine of the Store of Wisdom, just as Yamazaki Ansai had done two centuries earlier. Just as events in their own age were growing more urgent and change was growing more obviously irreversible, they turned to perhaps the most mystical of all Chu Hsi's teachings seeking a virtually physical source of inspiration in the deepest recesses of the mind.

One might then imagine that such orthodox Neo-Confucian thinkers as the Kusumoto brothers had little concept of or concern over the appropriate role of the intellectual in times such as their own. One would, however, be mistaken. Let us look at the views of Kusumoto Sekisui on just this issue, before proceeding to our final conclusions.

Among nineteenth-century Neo-Confucian scholars, no one argued more articulately than Sekisui the importance of personal duty (meibun). In his later years Sekisui reminisced in the following manner: "Now that I am over sixty, there are a few things that I have seen and that I have attained. I place my faith on the two characters of moral obligation (giri) and the two characters of loyalty and filial piety (chūkō), for these from ancient times have not changed in the slightest."[132] He insisted that "one should devote all one's energies to distinguishing between the gi (righteousness) and ri (profit) of the word giri (moral obligation). The entire difference between becoming a gentleman and remaining a small person lies in this."[133]

Sekisui was most strict in his personal behavior and vehemently detested the popular pursuit of profit or gain. His theory of personal duty was in fact patterned on that of Miyake Shōsai and Asami Keisai

[130] "Zuitokuroku" (1), Sekisui sensei isho (kan 8), Kusumoto Tanzan, Sekisui zenshū.
[131] Ibid.
[132] Furoku 1, Sekisui ikō.
[133] "Zuitokuroku" 2, Sekisui isho, kan 9.

(1652–1711) and other primarily Kimon school Confucians.[134] According to Sekisui, the rectification of names was the primary responsibility in ethical behavior and few Confucians in his age understood or practiced this truth.[135]

Among the various aspects of personal duty, Sekisui emphasized the responsibility of the lord-vassal relationship, and therefore he espoused imperial loyalism (kinnō) regarding service in domainal administration as unrighteous. According to Sekisui, daimyos understood the Way of the lord, but they did not understand the Way of the vassal, because they thought of their people as something their ancestors acquired through distinguished military service and had lost consciousness of the fact that the land and people were the private property of the throne. Therefore, he maintained: "Loyal samurai and men of benevolence do not serve the bakufu or daimyo."[136] He himself declined an official stipend at the age of thirty-nine and returned to his village insisting that "not serving the military houses is the highest form of loyalty."[137] Not surprisingly, Sekisui also lectured on imperial loyalism and taught the theory of legitimacy of the southern court based on works like the Jinnō shōtōki, and the Dai Nihonshi.[138]

The Neo-Confucians of the nineteenth century in Japan were a livelier, more sensitive, and more intellectually active group than has thus far been imagined. Deeply concerned over the question of how they were to respond to the momentous changes they were to witness during their lifetimes, they found meaningful intellectual and personal prototypes among the late-Ming and early-Ch'ing Neo-Confucians in China who had confronted a comparable set of circumstances. Though they were trained largely in the metropolitan areas of Edo or Osaka, they tended to return to their native provinces and to shun active engagement in the political transformation of their age. They saw their primary obligation in terms of their responsibility to establish morality through their teachings and personal example. They were particularly concerned with the long-standing Neo-Confucian questions of the mind and human nature, but while they (at times outspokenly) affirmed their commitment to a deepened understanding of these questions, they in the same breath tended to

---

[134] "Zuitokuroku" 4, Sekisui isho, kan 11. Sekisui criticized both Chinese and Japanese Confucian writings for their treatment of meibun.

[135] "Zuitokuroku" 2, Sekisui isho, kan 9.

[136] Ibid.

[137] "Zuitokuroku" 1, Sekisui isho, kan 8.

[138] "Zuitokuroku" (yō), Sekisui isho, kan 12.

disdain such discussions when they lapsed into what they regarded as vapid intellectualism.

The thought of these Neo-Confucians was by no means uniform, but they agreed upon far more than they disagreed. While they might differ on the extent to which the teachings of Chu Hsi and Wang Yang-ming were ultimately compatible, their attitude toward Western Learning, National Learning, and other contemporary issues inclined toward a consensus. They regarded themselves as the heirs to a rich and profound intellectual tradition that enjoyed a timeless relevance, but within that tradition they were nonetheless able to ask and find new questions, new approaches, and, in the final analysis, new answers.

TEN

NAKAE CHŌMIN AND CONFUCIANISM

BY SANNOSUKE MATSUMOTO

The questions that I propose to raise here for consideration are how Nakae Chōmin (1847–1901, also known as Nakae Tokusuke), an intellectual representative of Meiji Japan, inherited Confucianism in the formation and development of his thought, and how this Confucianism operated within his thought. It is my hope that the clarification of these issues will not only be helpful in the consideration of continuities between Tokugawa-era Confucianism and the thought of Meiji Japan, but also that it may likewise contribute new insights to the consideration and evaluation of Tokugawa thought from the perspective of the formation of modern thought in Japan. I propose to examine these questions while focusing primarily on the concept of freedom within Chōmin's thought.

Nakae Chōmin was born in 1847 in Kōchi in Tosa province on the island of Shikoku. His father was a Tosa domainal "foot soldier" (*ashigaru*). From an early age Chōmin studied Chinese, English, and Western Learning, and in 1865 he was officially dispatched by Tosa to a school in Nagasaki where he studied French. Thus began Chōmin's lifelong study of France. After the Meiji restoration of 1868, he moved to Edo and continued his study of France in the school of Mitsukuri Rinshō. He also taught French studies in the school of Fukuchi Gen'ichirō. In 1871 Chōmin, who longed for an opportunity to study in France, joined the Ministry of Justice, and in the autumn of that year he sailed from Yokohama to France accompanying the government mission headed by Iwakura Tomomi (1825–1883) as a foreign student from the Ministry of Justice. After residing for about six months in Lyon, he moved to Paris and carried on as a foreign student until his return to Japan in 1874. France had restored republicanism after its defeat in the war with Prussia, and Chōmin's visit to France directly followed the collapse of the Paris Commune before the government troops. While France was making the transition to the Third Republic, Chōmin was in contact with Saionji Kinmochi (1849–1940) and Baba Tatsui, a liberal of aristocratic descent. Chōmin was inspired by French liberalism during his stay in Europe, and it was also at this time that he acquired his lifelong interest in the social contract theory of Rousseau.

Having returned to Japan in 1874, Chōmin opened a private school for French studies (later known as the Futsugaku Juku) in his home in Tokyo, and the next year he became director of the Tokyo School of Foreign Languages (Tōkyō Gaikokugo Gakkō). However, he resigned his directorship within some three months and entered the newly established Senate (Genrōin) where he served as secretary until January 1877. Thereafter he was engaged in the translation of a number of European legal works and other projects, but he soon became involved in the popular rights movement and in 1881 joined the newspaper *Tōyō Jiyū Shinbun*. With Saionji as the president of the paper and himself as its editor, Chōmin raised numerous significant issues within its pages. However, by not joining the Liberal party (Jiyūtō) founded in October of that same year, Chōmin limited his future role in the party to that of an "outsider."

Chōmin began to concentrate on introducing American and European political theory to Japan, and in 1882 he started publication within his school of a journal titled *Seiri sōdan* (Collection of Political Principles), later known as *Ōbei seiri sōdan* (Collection of European and American Political Principles). This journal began the serial publication in October 1882 of Chōmin's annotated translation of Rousseau's *Contrat Social* under the title *Min'yaku yakkai*.

In this manner, Chōmin concentrated primarily on the construction of a theory of popular rights, but with the dissolution of the Liberal party in 1884 and the subsequent stagnation and disintegration of the popular rights movement, Chōmin grew committed to a refocusing of the influence of popular rights and came to exert a leadership role in the movement. Chōmin's introductory work on European philosophy, his *Rigaku kōgen* (pub. 1886), and perhaps his most representative works, the *Sansuijin keirin mondō* (pub. 1887) and *Heimin no mezamashi* (pub. 1887), all date from this period.

The government, fearing the possible revitalization of the popular rights movement, suddenly promulgated in the summer of 1887 the Peace Preservation Law in order to expel the leadership of the movement from Tokyo. Chōmin, along with others, felt the impact of this decree and suffered the hardship of having to leave Tokyo with his family. Having removed himself to Osaka, he became editor of the newspaper *Shinonome Shinbun*, which began publication in January 1888, and he wrote numerous essays of exceptional quality. Thereafter confronted with the establishment of the first Diet and committed to the resurrection of the Liberal party, Chōmin was elected to the Diet as representative from Osaka with the support of the much abused and discriminated against Burakumin population. He soon became disillusioned, however, by the readiness of his colleagues in the lower house of the first Diet to compromise with the government, and in February 1891 he resigned from the assembly.

For a time he tried his hand at several ventures including a railway project, but success eluded him and in 1901 he was diagnosed as having cancer and was informed that he had a year and a half to live. Chōmin immersed himself in his writing and authored in August of that same year his *Ichinen yūhan* (A Year and a Half), entrusting its publication to his protégé Kōtoku Shūsui (1871–1911). The work won immediate acclaim, and Chōmin responded by writing a sequel titled *Zoku ichinen yūhan* (A Year and a Half, Continued) which was published in October of that same year. Just two months later, however, he died in Tokyo from cancer of the esophagus. As final summations of Chōmin's philosophy, both *Ichinen yūhan* and its sequel can be said to rank among the most important works for an understanding of his thought.

CONFUCIAN LEARNING AND MORALITY IN CHŌMIN'S THOUGHT

Though in recent years attention has increasingly been paid to the relationship between Chōmin and Confucianism, this connection had already been recognized in the Meiji period by Kōtoku Shūsui, just after Chōmin's death. Shūsui maintained in the "Record of the Memorial Service for the Late Master Chōmin" (*Ko-Chōmin koji tsuitōkai no ki*) that, "What I have found most moving today has been the attention paid to the emphasis our teacher placed on the teaching of virtues and how this teaching drew its fundamental points from Confucius and Mencius. I likewise share this view completely."[1] Of course, as is well known, Confucianism lay at the heart of Chōmin's education, and the fact that Chōmin's main work, *Min'yaku yakkai*, was written in Kanbun (Chinese) may well be emblematic of the depth of Chōmin's Confucian education.

As a youth Chōmin had studied Confucian classics at the domainal school, the Bunbu-kan. After returning to Japan from study in France, he also studied at Takatani Ryūshū's academy for Chinese studies, the Saibikō, and later at Okamatsu Ōkoku's (1820–1895) school, the Shōseishoin. Recently, it has been discovered that about 1880 Chōmin studied in Mishima Chūshū's (1830–1919) school, the Nishōgakusha.[2] Chūshū was a domainal Confucian in Matsuyama of Bitchū

---

[1] From the *Heimin Shinbun*, 20 December 1903, in *Kōtoku Shūsui senshū*, 1:28.

[2] Fukushima Masao, "Mishima Chūshū to Nakae Chōmin," *Shisō*, no. 641 (November 1977), pp. 84–100.

(present Takahashi in Okayama Pref.) who studied under Satō Issai (1772–1859) at the Shōheikō and later became head of the Matsuyama domainal school.

In the early stages of the Meiji era when, in the spirit of enlightenment (*bunmei kaika*), Western scholarship, knowledge, and technology were introduced in large measure, Chōmin suggested instead that traditional Confucian morality was of great significance since it constituted a spiritual support of the people, and he frequently restated this assessment. For example, in February 1875 when Chōmin assumed the position of director of the Tokyo School of Foreign Languages, feeling acutely the need to establish regulations for the school, he expressed his intention to add "the teachings of Confucius and Mencius" to the curriculum in order to cultivate systematically the moral qualities of his students. As a result, he clashed with the educational authorities and in May found himself forced to resign.[3] Further, in recent years the work *Sakuron* (Policy), which one can assume was written by Chōmin in August or September of that same year, has been discovered and introduced. In that work, too, Chōmin made an appeal for revitalizing the "study of the classics" and emphasizing "benevolence, righteousness, loyalty and faithfulness" in order to resist the frivolous tendencies among students that in his mind had originated with the introducton of Western science and technology after the Meiji restoration.[4] Moreover, in an essay titled "Gensei" (Principle of Government, 20 December 1878) published in the collection *Keiun meisei roku* (Selection of Literary Works Competing for Progress) by Takatani Ryūshū's pupils, in the context of a criticism of the spirit of utilitarianism in enlightenment, Chōmin praised China's "Policies of the Three Dynasties" (*sandai no hō*): "There was righteousness between lord and vassal, affection between parent and child, separateness between husband and wife, sequence between senior and junior, and good faith between friends, and nothing more was needed to cultivate one's person or to govern man. Accordingly, the people inclined toward morality and suffered from neither invasion nor rebellion for the sake of profit or gain."[5]

From these examples we can begin to sense Chōmin's positive attitude toward Chinese learning. Chōmin's concern with Chinese learning amounted to more than simply seeking Sino-Japanese compounds when translating Western words, and under the govern-

---

[3] *Kōtoku Shūsui senshū*, 3 vols. (Sekai Hyōronsha, 1927), 1:118.

[4] Matsunaga Shōzō, "Nakae Tokusuke no *Sakuron* ippen ni tsuite," *Shisō*, no. 650 (August 1978), pp. 45–65.

[5] In Matsunaga Shōzō, comp., *Nakae Chōmin shū*, Kindai Nihon Shisō Taikei, vol. 3 (Chikuma Shobō, 1974), p. 179.

ment's suppression of expression, it went beyond using Confucianism as his personal "camouflaged weapon for expressing the truth."[6] One can thus state that the links between Chōmin and Confucianism lay deep within the internal structure of his thought.

Rigi

The word rigi (truth, or principle and justice) is one of the key words that underlie Chōmin's thought. As the expression "the mind of rigi which is the original substance of civilization" suggests,[7] it means the principles and norms of modern civilization. Consequently, it is frequently used to designate principles like freedom, equality, civil rights, and so on, as in "the principle (ri) of equality," "the justice (gi) of freedom," or in saying that "civil rights is the highest principle; freedom and equality are the highest justice."

There are also instances when it suggests "the goodness of principle and justice," that is, a universal morality for mankind, as opposed to "the beauty of the material," as in his "distinction between rigi and the material." For example, this is the rigi he referred to in the context of explaining the importance of maintaining moral strength rather than depending on "the beauty of the material" (that is, the economic, military, scientific or technical) when it comes to the pursuit of the nation's international independence:

No matter how much these arts and sciences may advance, no matter how much their influence may grow, no matter how much their reputation may flourish, if the son tyrannizes his father, if the husband rebukes his wife, if people deceive their friends, or if any manner of wickedness should occur, then what? No matter how strong our nation may be and no matter how weak our neighbors, if we send our soldiers against our neighbor without cause, then what? The reason that material things will ultimately fail to prevail over principle and justice is because of the distinction between what is fundamental and what is trivial (honmatsu no betsu).[8]

As Shimada Kenji has indicated,[9] the word rigi was drawn from Mencius where it meant "that of which the mind will similarly ap-

---

[6] Kawano Kenji, Nakae Chōmin, Nihon no Meicho, no. 36 (Chūō Kōronsha, 1970), p. 21.

[7] Sansuijin keirin mondō, in Matsunaga, Nakae Chōmin shū, p. 4.

[8] From Ichinen yūhan (1901), in Matsunaga, Nakae Chōmin shū, p. 140.

[9] Shimada Kenji, "Chōmin no aiyōgo ni tsuite," in Kinoshita Junji and Etō Fumio, eds., Nakae Chōmin no sekai (Chikuma Shobō, 1977), p. 230.

prove,"[10] that is to say, what all persons in common perceive to be good. Even when Chōmin held with respect to rigi that "the words principle and justice are commonplace,"[11] this can probably be regarded as his alternative, and somehow paradoxical, expression of what Mencius meant by "that of which the mind will similarly approve." Chōmin even spoke elsewhere of rigi as "the most brilliant principles (*dōri*) under heaven."[12]

Chōmin's use of Mencius' concept of rigi is indicative of a broader indebtedness of Chōmin's Confucian thought to Mencius. In this regard Shimada Kenji has stated, "What can be called Chōmin's Confucianism, in the final analysis, can be called Mencius-style Confucianism."[13] In fact, Chōmin recognized and acknowledged this intellectual debt:

> Civil rights is the highest principle; freedom and equality are the greatest justice. Ultimately anyone who opposes principle and justice (rigi) will suffer retribution. There may be a hundred imperialisms but none will ever destroy principle and justice. The imperial sovereign should be revered, but this reverence depends on his revering principle and justice. This principle even existed in China where early on Mencius and Liu Tsung-yüan [773–819] observed it, and it is not an exclusive possession of the West."[14]

At this juncture, I shall turn to a consideration of Chōmin's concept of freedom, and an examination of ideological and structural continuities between Mencius' thought and Chōmin's conception.

Being Endowed with Freedom

It is possible to discern two distinct concepts of freedom in Chōmin's thought, the one being a concept of "negative freedom," and the other a concept of "positive freedom." The former is a concept of "freedom as a natural endowment" and corresponds to what Chōmin referred to when he spoke of "the right of freedom that is bestowed on man by heaven, gives man his free will, and makes possible the

[10] *Mencius*, 6A:7.

[11] Shimada, "Chōmin no aiyōgo ni tsuite," in Kinoshita, *Nakae Chōmin no sekai*, p. 230.

[12] From *Ichinen yūhan*, in Matsunaga, *Nakae Chōmin shū*, p. 125.

[13] Shimada, "Chōmin no aiyōgo ni tsuite," in Kinoshita, *Nakae Chōmin no sekai*, p. 231.

[14] From *Ichinen yūhan*, in Matsunaga, *Nakae Chōmin shū*, p. 125.

creation of life."[15] This concept rests on the assumption that the natural desire "to create life" is to be respected as part of mankind's heavenly (endowed) nature, and the acknowledgment that the maintenance of this desire is nothing less than a right.

The fundamental meaning of this right of freedom is negative in the sense that it interprets freedom as man's being free from all manner of interference or obstruction that might threaten his natural desire for self-preservation. This natural freedom, in Chōmin's case, enjoyed priority over the artificial order dictated by the state or society. This freedom was not construed as anarchic or as a factor destructive of the social order leading mankind toward "a battle of all versus all" (bellum omnium contre omnes), but rather as a factor supportive of that order. Further, Chōmin added a connotation of original "principle" that grounded the artificial order with ontological justification. He stated: "What conforms to the Way of life we call goodness, and what departs from the Way of life we call evil. As long as man continues to exist, he will regard life thusly and will pursue good fortune in this manner. . . . No matter what, man's heavenly [endowed] nature will be like this. That which is like the heavenly [endowed] nature is the Way. Wherever the Way exists, rights necessarily follow. Accordingly, it is the single highest right a man has in life and is the fountainhead that generates all the other rights."[16]

Chōmin constructed his concept of principle and justice—that "civil rights is the highest principle; freedom and equality are the greatest justice"—as a logical and direct extension of his notion of freedom as a natural endowment. In other words, where Mencius discovered rigi, or rather "that of which the mind will similarly approve," primarily in the moral qualities of benevolence and righteousness (jingi), Chōmin located it first and foremost in the "freedom as a natural endowment" that originates in the natural desire of "creating life." In this respect, one can observe elements of both continuity and discontinuity in the respective analyses of Chōmin and Mencius.

The "Cultivation" (Baiyō) of Freedom

Chōmin's perception of mankind was intimately linked to two of his previously mentioned assumptions: first, that "freedom as a natural endowment," that is, mankind's natural right of freedom, was not a

---

[15] Min'yaku yakkai, 31:1.

[16] "Kenri no minamoto," Jiyū Shinbun 5 (July 1882), in Matsunaga, Nakae Chōmin shū, p. 225.

factor injurious to the social order but rather was supportive of that order; and second, that he situated the artificial social order of man in the context of that original "principle" from which all order directly devolves. Chōmin's was an extremely idealistic view of mankind. It held, in essence, that mankind, having received its nature from heaven, possessed something (at least latently or potentially) equivalent to an inherent capacity to establish norms for itself and to construct order by itself so as to achieve satisfaction in life. "The reason that the people are the people," maintained Chōmin, "is directly because they possess the ability to create by themselves a constitution," by which he meant that "the people are sovereign."[17]

Likewise in his *Sansuijin keirin mondō* (pub. May 1887), Chōmin had the "Western gentleman" speak the following words: "Alas, the ruler is a man, and we people too are men. Both of us are common in our humanity. Is it not shameful that we people cannot rely on ourselves alone to create life, but that we are dependent upon others for the creation of life?"[18] Here, too, Chōmin explained that the formation of social order that enables the people to create life under conditions of public peace is not a characteristic that should be regarded as the sole prerogative of the ruler, but rather as something that the people themselves can achieve by exercising their rights.

Of course, even Chōmin was not totally blind to the limits of human achievement, including the construction of social order by man. He felt that certain conditions were essential for this achievement including the "cultivation" (*baiyō*) of freedom and its attendant "development" (*chōtatsu*). He maintained, for example, that "freedom is truly a natural endowment. However, if you do not wish to cultivate it, it will certainly not be able to develop well by itself."[19]

Chōmin's concept of freedom implied the existence of a certain moral quality or spiritual power which, through "cultivation" by the exertion of personal intellectual effort, could achieve an extension of its functions or applications. Thus he held that it was only when people had fully developed their sense of the power of freedom that people might for the first time utilize their inherent capacity ("the reason that the people are the people") to construct order, that is, an

[17] "Kokkai mondō," *Tōyō Jiyū Shinbun*, 6 July 1881.

[18] Matsunaga, *Nakae Chōmin shū*, p. 21. It is of profound significance that Chōmin's phrasing is suggestive of that in *Mencius* (4B:28) where it states: "Shun was a man, and I too am a man. Shun made the laws of our world, and these were worthy of being handed down to later ages. I am no more than a villager. This is properly a matter for [my] concern. And what should concern Shun? Just that he be like Shun."

[19] "Kansho kyōiku," *Tōyō Jiyū Shinbun*, 27 March 1881, in Matsunaga, *Nakae Chōmin shū*, p. 188.

order of the sort that would enable them to reap good fortune and to achieve peace in their actual social life.

Chōmin discussed this concept of freedom, that is, the cultivation of a certain abstract power, as a kind of spiritual freedom when, for example, he used the concepts of *liberté morale* and "freedom of spirit." According to Chōmin, "Liberté morale means developing one's spirit and thought perfectly with every ounce of strength and without ever encountering external restraint."[20] In other words, liberté morale meant not merely enjoying freedom from outside impediment—"without ever encountering external restraint"—but rather seeking to have the workings of the human spirit through its freedom demonstrate its power completely—"developing one's spirit and thought perfectly with every ounce of strength."

It is in this sense that one can speak of a "positive freedom" in contrast with a "negative freedom" in Chōmin's thought. Since Chōmin regarded this freedom of the spirit as the fountainhead of social activity, he stressed the necessity for "training" (*kan'yō*) by describing freedom as "probably what I should use most when training properly to bring the mind to rest."[21] Chōmin explained this "training" or "cultivation" of freedom in *Sansuijin keirin mondō* where he described how to make the transition from a perception of freedom as a right conferred from above ("graciously bestowed civil rights") to a right acquired through the personal power of the people ("expansive civil rights"). He placed emphasis on the "*cultivation* of this [freedom] using moral vigor (*dōtoku no genki*) and academic nourishment (*gakujutsu no jieki*)" [emphasis added].

Chōmin's emphasis on the "cultivation" of freedom suggests a connection with the thought of Mencius, who stressed "nurturance" (*yō*), maintaining that "if something receives its proper nurturance, it will grow; if something loses its proper nurturance, it will decay."[22] As is well known, Mencius with one hand held an idealistic view of mankind taking the position that human nature was good, while with the other hand he taught the necessity of human effort in the area of moral cultivation as an adjunct to human nature's basic goodness. As his maxim "preserving the mind and nurturing the nature" suggests, the concepts of "preserving" and "nurturing," that is, the cultivation of man's original nature, hold a conspicuous place

<hr/>

[20] "Shasetsu," *Tōyō Jiyū Shinbun*, 18 March 1881, in Matsunaga, *Nakae Chōmin shū*, p. 182.

[21] Ibid.

[22] *Mencius*, 6A:8.

in the thought of Mencius, and may even be said to constitute the nucleus of that thought.[23]

Of course, the activity of "nurturing" (*yashinau*), as Mencius described it, presupposed on man's part a degree of moral "goodness," and specifically the virtues of "benevolence and righteousness." However, in Chōmin's case, the activity of "cultivation" was a relatively comprehensive concept that embraced numerous meanings, in much the same way that Chōmin's rigi meant a universal human morality that included "the essence of civilization" and was summed up in such notions as "freedom and equality" and "civil rights." This was only natural for a Japanese intellectual like Chōmin who had received his baptism in the thought of eighteenth- and nineteenth-century European liberalism.

Therefore, when Chōmin expounded on the "cultivation" of freedom, he certainly included within this concept the cultivation of those intellectual and rational aspects of man's free spiritual faculties that awaited such "development." For example, according to Chōmin, it was necessary for men to discover the "truth" (*shinri*) and to advance the cause of "humanity," for these would never be realized merely through individual, "complacent self-cultivation" (*dokuzen jiyō*). Rather it was only through the "intercourse" (*kōsai*) of many persons serving as the bearers "respectively of all thought" that "truth" and "humanity" might best be fulfilled. "He and I are not the same," declared Chōmin. "Present-day people are not the same as the ancients; and people from east, west, south and north are not the same as others from east, west, south and north. These differences multiply in variation and divide people from each other, and yet the course of humanity advances ever forward with great strides. This is entirely due to the power of these very differences in thought."[24] In other words, Chōmin understood this "cultivation" of freedom to be inseparable from a certain human spiritual development which, through the free interaction and struggle between the individual and those distinctive and manifold forms of thought that derive from different life experiences and value systems, can be reckoned in terms of both the activation of the individual intellect and the maturation of mental faculties.

However, what should be noted is that Chōmin's concept of freedom included not just this intellectual aspect identified with rational faculties or the intellect, but also a subtle undercurrent of volunta-

[23] Ibid., 7A:1.
[24] "Shisō wa yoroshiku intoku subekarazu," *Tōyō Jiyū Shinbun*, 2 April 1881, in Matsunaga, *Nakae Chōmin shū*, p. 193.

ristic or moralistic tendencies that were inseparable from this intellectual aspect. It is necessary, for example, to recall that even in his explanation of how to bring about the transition from "graciously bestowed civil rights" to "expansive civil rights," he regarded both "moral vigor" and "academic nourishment" as absolute essentials. His "cultivation" of freedom was thus at one and the same time a problem in terms of the quantitative expansion of "intelligence" (*chishiki*) or the "intellect" (*chiryoku*), and that quality of "mettle" (*kiryoku*) which draws on one's sense of moral justice.

Even in his explanation of liberté morale, after defining it in terms of "developing one's spirit and thought perfectly with every ounce of strength and without ever encountering external restraint," Chōmin continued by stating, "This is what the ancients referred to as the 'single strong and moving power' (*kōzen no ikki*) identified with righteousness (*gi*) and the Way."[25] Of course, this "single strong and moving power" was what Mencius called "the strong, moving power" (*kōzen no ki*), and in the same sense in which it is discussed there— "exceedingly great and exceedingly strong, if nurtured by uprightness and unimpaired, it will fill all between heaven and earth"—it referred to that vital spirit which, if cultivated with rectitude, will be of volume and power sufficient to overflow heaven and earth, but which if lacking will mean that mankind per se will likewise lose its vitality.[26]

Chōmin likened liberté morale, that is, "freedom of spirit," to this "strong, moving power" sustained by moral conduct. For him this meant not only a measure of spiritual freedom unfettered by the external power and authority of "political and religious organizations" (*seifu kyōmon*), but also that quality of freedom undisturbed by those evil, internal desires expressed as "the five desires and six evils" (*goyoku rokuaku*). This is probably what Chōmin meant by that power of moral conduct or "mettle" which transcends the limits of the "intellect."

In other words, Chōmin felt that all human beings have certain inescapable requirements by virtue of their "emotional nature" (*jōsei*). "Man," he claimed, "desires clothing for his warmth, food for his sustenance, action for his goodness, and wisdom for his illumination."[27] However, it was not until one endeavored to satisfy these wants (the "emotional nature") that for the first time human progress

---

[25] "Shasetsu," *Tōyō Jiyū Shinbun*, 18 March 1881, in Matsunaga, *Nakae Chōmin shū*, p. 182.

[26] *Mencius*, 2A:2.

[27] "Shukushi," *Tōyō Jiyū Shinbun*, 18 March 1881, in Matsunaga, *Nakae Chōmin shū*, p. 183.

became possible. Chōmin situated this "mettle" or "moral vigor," or rather this "strong, moving power"—that incipient power that sustains these endeavors internally, gives "vital spirit" to the "emotional nature," and even causes it to develop in the fundamentals and particulars of mankind—in liberté morale, that is, in the workings of the free spirit.

When Mencius was asked about the areas of his own strength and development, he identified two elements in his response: "I understand words, and I nourish my strong, moving power well."[28] Itō Jinsai (1627–1705) in his commentary on the writings of Mencius explicated this passage in the following manner:

> The main points of Mencius' teachings are preserving the mind, and nourishing the nature. "Understanding words" means preserving the mind, and the "nourishing of power" means nourishing the nature. When you understand words, you preserve the mind, and when you preserve the mind, you illuminate wisdom. When you illuminate wisdom, you have no confusion as to the right and wrong or good and bad of words. Accordingly by knowing words one is able to preserve the mind. The nature, originally, does not move and is set into motion by material force. When you nourish material force even in the slightest degree, you likewise obtain the nourishment of your nature. Accordingly by nourishing power one is able to nourish the nature.[29]

As this commentary shows, Jinsai understood that "nourishing the nature" occupied an extremely important position in scholarship on Mencius, and he regarded the "nourishing of material force" as the most important means of "nourishing the nature." According to Jinsai, when Mencius spoke of "the goodness of human nature," this "nature" did not mean the "original nature" (honzen no sei) with which all men are endowed at the moment of birth, but rather the variegated "physical" (kishitsu) nature. In Jinsai's view, this was the primary factor behind Mencius' assertion that through effort in cultivation and education human beings develop and incline their "nature" toward goodness.

Similarly, Jinsai regarded Confucius' famous dictum on the subject—"By nature men are alike but through practice they differ"[30]—

[28] Mencius, 2A:2.
[29] Mōshi kogi, in Seki Giichirō, comp., Nihon meika shisho chūshaku zensho (Ōtori Shuppan, 1973), 9:56.
[30] Analects, 17:2.

as perfectly consistent with Mencius' and his own views.[31] In the passage just quoted, Jinsai maintained that "the nature, originally, does not move and is set into motion by material force." This exemplified his conviction that human nature possessed the potential or latent ability to incline toward goodness, but in order actually to incline the nature toward goodness and to have it grow, it was essential that the nature be cultivated in a lively and vigorous fashion.

It should now be obvious that Jinsai's understanding of Mencius' view of mankind, that is, that human nature is good but requires preserving and nourishing, bears a striking resemblance both structurally and ideologically to Chōmin's thoughts on the subject of the "cultivation" of freedom. For example, while Chōmin regarded freedom as part and parcel of the natural endowment shared by all human beings, he likewise taught the necessity of its cultivation. "Human beings have freedom as a natural endowment," declared Chōmin, "and freedom truly is a natural endowment. However, unless you cultivate it, freedom will definitely not be able to develop well by itself."[32] In other words, while Chōmin believed that freedom was a natural endowment ("heavenly nature" or *tensei*), he did not regard freedom as something that would "be able to develop well by itself" if it were not "cultivated." To look at freedom from yet another perspective, one might compare it to what Jinsai maintained: "The nature, originally, does not move and is set into motion by material force."

In concrete terms, how did Chōmin interpret this "freedom of spirit" which he compared to Mencius' "single strong and moving power" when he spoke of the power that required "cultivation" through the workings of the free spirit? In this regard the essential point is that Chōmin postulated the existence of a particularly acute form of moral sensibility—what one might call moral sentiments—that was held by all mankind, a sensitivity that might even be likened to a moral sense of pain. For example, in an essay titled "Kokumin no tomo" (The Nation's Friend) he wrote, "There is nothing more beneficial to progress than the emotions of resenting and weeping."[33] Similarly, while warning the former samurai aristocracy about its customary penchant for "doom-saying and resentment" (*hika kōgai*), he advised them that it was important that they continue to preserve a "spirit of constancy" (*setsugi no kokoro*), and in the same vein he urged their "becoming both moral and intellectual figures capable of

[31] *Mōshi kogi*, in Seki, *Nihon meika shisho chūshaku zensho*, 9:233–234.

[32] "Kanshō kyōiku," in Matsunaga, *Nakae Chōmin shū*, p. 188.

[33] "Kokumin no tomo," no. 15, *Shinonome Shinbun*, 8 February 1888, in Kuwabara Takeo, ed., *Nakae Chōmin no kenkyū* (Iwanami Shoten, 1966), p. 287.

using the arts and sciences in tandem with a nobility of character."[34] In other words, for Chōmin emotions were what supported the very foundation of human society, and he likened "a man without emotions to a tree or a stone."[35]

However, the endowment and development of emotions were not identical in each individual. For example, Chōmin asserted that the so-called concerned patriots (*aikoku yūsei no shi*) had developed "a kind of emotion" that might be called "political emotion." Thus according to Chōmin, "Those who have these emotions are acutely sensitive to the gain or loss, benefit or harm of the state, the ebb and flow of rights and freedom, and the weal or woe of the people, and when they come into contact with matters from a political perspective, they are themselves incapable of repressing their emotions or inhibiting their feelings."[36]

In other words, the moral mettle that Chōmin hoped would develop and expand throughout society by virtue of the "cultivation" of freedom can thus be seen to originate in these "acutely sensitive" reactions to the ebb and flow of the state, the people, freedom and rights, and so on. Chōmin pursued the logical implications of this position by regarding the actions, thoughts, and feelings of the bearers of these emotions as "equivalent to the national welfare, social wisdom, and public opinion." It was "with them," he declared, that "the spirit of the country is formed, the energy of the country is nourished, and they become the country's bullwark of freedom and rights."[37]

This emphasis on moral feelings also reminds us of elements of continuity between the thought of Chōmin and that of Mencius. Mencius, too, in his explanation of the moral ideals of benevolence and righteousness, vigorously asserted that moral feelings which he called "the Four Beginnings" are naturally given to human beings, and he emphasized their significance. The "Four Beginnings," of course, included the mental qualities of "commiseration," "shame and dislike," "respect and reverence," and "right and wrong."[38] The example of the "mind of commiseration" is famous: if a person sees a child about to fall into a well, he will be alarmed and startled and will seek to rescue the child. This feeling is what Mencius called the

---

[34] "Shizoku shokun ni tsugu," *Shinonome Shinbun*, 18 March 1888, in Kuwabara, *Nakae Chōmin no kenkyū*, p. 293.

[35] "Sōshi ron," *Shinonome Shinbun*, 23 January 1888, in Kuwabara, *Nakae Chōmin no kenkyū*, p. 278.

[36] Ibid., pp. 278–279.

[37] Ibid.

[38] *Mencius*, 6A:6.

"mind of commiseration," and he asserted that the extention and completion of this feeling were represented by the virtue of "benevolence." When Mencius stated that "if one follows these feelings, one creates goodness," he meant that moral goodness, that is, benevolence, righteousness, propriety, and wisdom, was simply the "amplification" (*kakujū*) of those feelings he called the Four Beginnings.[39]

As mentioned previously, Itō Jinsai was the Tokugawa-era figure who more than any other called attention to this point. Jinsai regarded the *Analects* and especially the *Mencius* as the most important texts in the formation of his own personal scholarship. I have already discussed how Jinsai regarded the theme of "preserving the mind and nourishing the nature" as constituting the nucleus of Mencius' thought, and it goes without saying that Jinsai's outlook, described previously, was profoundly influenced by his understanding of what Mencius called "the nature."

The one whom Jinsai criticized most with respect to the meaning of this "nature" was Chu Hsi. According to Chu Hsi, "benevolence and righteousness" were "names for the nature," and he maintained that "the nature is equivalent to principle."[40] In opposition to Chu Hsi's view, Jinsai insisted that "benevolence and righteousness" were "universal virtues" (*tenka no toku*) and "names for morality" (*dōtoku no mei*), but were not "names for the nature." He discussed Mencius' theory that "human nature is good" in the following way:

> People simply understand their own particular nature, but they do not understand what these natures have in common. That they necessarily possess minds that are startled and touched when seeing a youngster just about to fall into a well is similar to a fire blazing upwards or water flowing downwards. It is the same today as of old, and holds true for sage and fool alike. This is the same. This is what Mencius called the goodness of human nature. This is what emerges when the goodness of the physical nature is clarified, and it cannot be discussed apart from this physical nature. Earlier Confucians did not understand this notion, and in vain they equated human nature with principle. Therefore, they could not explain the fact that one's nature is not the same as one's physical nature. Then they insisted that there are two aspects, the original [nature] and the physical [nature]. The confusion arose from having two names for the single nature.[41]

---

[39] Ibid., 2A:6.
[40] Cf. Itō Jinsai, *Gomō jigi*, NST, 33:40, 51.
[41] *Mōshi kogi*, in Seki, *Nihon meika shisho chūshaku zensho*, 9:242.

In this regard Jinsai maintained that the "nature is life." He stated that "human nature is the basis for life and implies what one is by nature."[42] The dispositions which people receive at birth are fundamentally variegated. However, the "mind of commiseration" is a feeling that is within one's nature and is held in common by all dispositions. Mencius' theory that "human nature is good," according to Jinsai's understanding of it, represented an elaborate discourse on that aspect of the human personality that inclines toward morality. For this reason, against the "doctrine of returning to beginnings" that Chu Hsi taught—the theory that took the moral course to mean extinguishing emotions and desires and returning to one's original condition in which one's "nature" is equivalent to principle—Jinsai advocated "amplifying" (kakujū) human emotions and "preserving and nourishing" (son'yō) the nature.[43] In this way, Jinsai emphasized the significance of "material force" and the "physical," as well as feelings and wants, in his discussions of morality. "Even though all people understand that they do good and avoid evil," Jinsai explained, "everyone still vacillates and shrinks from the task, and those who do not do good are deficient in their material force and have not yet become magnificent. If you nourish this [nature] in even the slightest degree, you will be unable to resist its strong and powerful magnificence."[44] One may thus conclude that there are common threads in Jinsai's views on the subject and Chōmin's explanation that what causes people to tend toward good actions is that over and above their ability to "understand" good and evil, they have feelings of partiality which Chōmin called "loving good and detesting evil."[45]

In this brief essay, by concentrating on Nakae Chōmin's concept of freedom, I have examined first whether it is possible to indicate common elements between the thought of Chōmin—or rather his particular ideological formation—and the ideological formation of Mencius, especially as it was understood by Itō Jinsai, and second how those shared concepts functioned in their respective modes of thought. This examination is intended as no more than a preliminary inquiry, as mentioned at the outset, into the more complex question of the identification of continuities between Tokugawa Confucianism and Meiji intellectual history. I would hope, one day, that an opportunity might arise to conduct a comprehensive inquiry into the subject.

[42] Ibid.
[43] Ibid.
[44] Ibid., p. 56.
[45] Rigaku kōgen (1886), in Hayashi Shigeru, comp., Nakae Chōmin shū, Meiji Bungaku Zenshū (Chikuma Shobō, 1966), 13:28.

LIST OF CONTRIBUTORS

Donald Keene, Professor of Japanese at Columbia University, is currently writing the first volume of an intended four-volume history of Japanese literature. *World Within Walls* (Holt, Rinehart and Winston), which will be the second volume when the series is completed, was published in 1976; it is devoted to the literature of the Tokugawa period and discusses many of the issues treated in his essay.

Sannosuke Matsumoto is Professor of Japanese Political Thought in the Faculty of Law of the University of Tokyo. His numerous publications include *Kokugaku seiji shisō no kenkyū* (The Political Thought of Kokugaku), *Tennōsei kokka to seiji shisō* (The Imperial System and Political Thought), *Nihon seiji shisōshi gairon* (Outline of the History of Japanese Political Thought), and *Meiji seishin no kōzō* (The Structure of the Meiji Spirit). In English he has also written "The Idea of Heaven: A Tokugawa Foundation for Natural Rights Theory," in T. Najita and I. Scheiner, eds., *Japanese Thought in the Tokugawa Period* (1978).

Kate Wildman Nakai earned her doctorate from Harvard University and teaches Japanese history and thought in the Department of Comparative Culture of Sophia University in Tokyo. A study of Arai Hakuseki analyzing his thought against the background of bakufu politics is forthcoming from Harvard University Press.

Peter Nosco earned his doctorate from Columbia University and teaches in the Institute of Asian Studies, St. John's University (N.Y.). He has translated Ihara Saikaku's *Some Final Words of Advice* (Charles Tuttle, 1980) and has articles on Tokugawa thought in *Asian Thought and Society* (5:15) and *Harvard Journal of Asiatic Studies* (41:1). He is currently working on a study of Tokugawa nativist thought.

Takehiko Okada is Professor Emeritus and former Dean of the College of General Education of the University of Kyushu. Among his numerous publications on Chinese and Japanese Confucian thought are *Ōyōmei to Minmatsu no Jugaku* (Wang Yang-ming and Confucianism of the Late-Ming), *Kusumoto Tanzan, Sō-Min tetsugaku josetsu* (An Introduction to Sung and Ming Philosophy), *Kinsei kōki Jugakushū* (Writings of Late-Tokugawa Confucians, NST, vol. 47), and *Edoki no Jugaku* (Tokugawa Confucianism). In English he has authored "Practical Learning of the Chu Hsi School: Yamazaki Ansai and Kaibara Ekken," in W. T. de Bary and I. Bloom, eds., *Principle and Practicality.*

Herman Ooms is Associate Professor of History at the University of Illinois at Chicago, where he has taught since 1972. He started his graduate training in Belgium (licentiate in philosophy), holds an M.A. degree from the University of Tokyo (anthropology) and a Ph.D. degree from the University of Chicago (history). He has published *Charismatic Bureaucrat: A Political Biography of Matsudaira Sadanobu, 1725–1829* (University of Chicago Press, 1975). His *Tokugawa Ideology: Early Constructs, 1570–1680* is forthcoming from Princeton University Press.

Royall Tyler received his doctorate from Columbia and has taught at the University of Wisconsin in Madison. He has published *Selected Writings of Suzuki Shōsan* (Ithaca: Cornell University China-Japan Program, 1977), no. 13 in the series Cornell University East Asia papers. His current research is on Japanese ideas of the sacred landscape.

Paul B. Watt is Assistant Professor of Religion at Columbia University where he received his doctorate. His fields of interest are Japanese and Chinese religious thought, with particular emphasis upon Buddhism, and he is currently at work on a book-length study of the life and thought of Jiun Sonja. He has also taught at Grinnell College in Iowa.

Samuel H. Yamashita received his doctorate from the University of Michigan in 1981, spent a year as a postdoctoral fellow in the Japanese Institute at Harvard University, and is Assistant Professor of History at Pomona College. His chief interests are the intellectual history of the Tokugawa and Meiji periods, Neo-Confucianism, and East Asian historiography. He is doing further work on the Ancient Learning school and compiling an anthology of Japanese Confucian writings.

GLOSSARY FOR CHINESE, JAPANESE, AND KOREAN NAMES AND TERMS IN THE TEXT

Abe Yoshio 阿部吉雄
Agongyō 阿含経
ai no ri 愛の理
aikoku yūsei no shi 愛国憂世の士
Akamatsu Hidemichi 赤松秀道
Aki 安芸
Amaterasu 天照
Amenominakanushi 天之御中主
Amida 阿弥陀
Amidadera 阿弥陀寺
Andō Seian 安東省庵
Andō Shōeki 安藤昌益
Anesaki Masaharu 姉崎正治
Arai Hakuseki 新井白石
Asaka Tanpaku 安積澹泊
Asama 浅間 (cf. Sengen)
Asami Keisai 浅見絅斎
Asano Takuminokami 浅野内匠頭
Asayama Soshin 朝山素心
ashigaru 足軽
Ashikaga 足利
Ashikaga gakkō 足利学校
Ashikaga Takauji 足利尊氏
Ashikaga Yoshimitsu 足利義光
Ashikaga Yoshiteru 足利義輝
Azuchi 安土
azukarimono 預リ物
Azuma 吾妻

Baba Tatsui 馬場辰猪
Bairi 梅里
baiyō 培養
bakufu 幕府
banbutsu no shizen 万物の自然
Banmin tokuyō 万民徳用
Benfukusho 弁復書

Benmei 弁名
Bitchū 備中
Bitō Masahide 尾藤正英
Bitō Nishū 尾藤二洲
bokuzei 卜筮
Bongaku shinryō 梵学津梁
Bonmōkyō 梵網経
bu 分
buke 武家
Buke jiki 武家事紀
Buke shohatto 武家諸法度
bun 文
Bunbu-kan 文武館
Bungo 豊後
bunji 文辞
bunmei kaika 文明開化
Buppō 仏法
Burakumin 部落民
bushi 武士
bushidō 武士道
bushō 武将
Busshō 仏性
Butsu zaise no Bukkyō 仏在世の仏教
byōdō 平等
byōdōshō 平等性

Ch'an 禪
Chan Jo-shui 湛若水
Chan, Wing-tsit 陳榮捷
Chang Lieh 張烈
Chang Lü-hsiang 張履祥
Chang Tsai 張載
Chao 趙
Ch'en Hsien-chang 陳獻章
ch'eng 誠
Ch'eng-Chu 程朱

269

Ch'eng Hao 程顥
Ch'eng I 程頤
Chen-kuan cheng-yao 貞觀政要
ch'i 氣
ch'i-chih chih hsing 氣質之性
Chidoron 智度論
Ch'ien Te-hung 錢德洪
Ch'ien-tzu wen 千字文
chih 質
ch'ih-ching ching-tso 持敬靜坐
chih liang-chih 致良知
Chih Po 智伯
chih-tsang 智藏
Chikamatsu Monzaemon 近松門左衛門
Chin 晋
Ch'in 秦
Ch'ing (dynasty) 清
ching (seriousness, reverence) 敬
chiryoku 智力
chishiki 智識
ch'iung-li 究理
chizō 智藏
Chōeiji 長栄寺
Chōshi shoshō 張子書抄
chōtatsu 暢達
Chou 周
Chou Ju-teng 周汝登
Chou li 周禮
Chou Tun-i 周敦頤
Chu Hsi 朱熹
Chu Tzu wen-chi 朱子文集
Chu Tzu yü-lei 朱子語類
Ch'uan-hsi lu 傳習錄
Chuang-tzu 莊子
Chūbei 忠兵衛
Chu-hung 袾宏
chūkō 忠孝
Ch'un ch'iu 春秋
Chung-yung 中庸
chün-tzu 君子
chūsei 中世
Chūshingura 忠臣蔵
Chūyō 中庸

Dai Nihonshi 大日本史
Daigaku 大学

daimyō 大名
Dainichi 大日
Dainichikyō 大日経
daishinkun 大神君
Daitokuji 大徳寺
danka 檀家
darani 陀羅尼
Dazai Shundai 太宰春台
den 伝
dōgaku 道学
Dōgen 道元
dōgi 道義
dokuritsu 独立
dokuzen jiyō 独善自養
dōri 道理
dōshin 道心
dōtoku no genki 道徳の元気
dōtoku no mei 道徳の名

Eboshi-iwa 烏帽子岩
Echū 恵中
Edo 江戸
eki 易
ekisei kakumei 易姓革命
En no Gyōja 役行者
Endō tsugan 艶道通鑑
En'ya Hangan 塩谷判官

Fan-wang ching 梵網經
Feng Ts'ung-wu 馮從吾
fudai 譜代
Fudō 不動
Fugen gyōgansan 普賢行願贊
Fuji 富士
Fuji kō 富士講
Fujinomiya 富士宮
Fujita Tōko 藤田東湖
Fujita Yūkoku 藤田幽谷
Fujitsuka Tomonao 藤塚知直
Fujiwara 藤原
Fujiwara Seika 藤原惺窩
Fujiwara Teika 藤原定家
Fujufuse Nichiren 不受不施日蓮
Fukuchi Gen'ichirō 福地源一郎
fusoku 不足
Futsugaku Juku 佛学塾

270

gakujutsu no jieki 学術の滋液
gekokujō 下剋上
Genrōin 元老院
Genroku 元禄
Gensei 原政
Getsugan 月旺
Getsugyō Sōjū 月行創忡
gi (justice, meaning, righteousness) 義
Gion monogatari 祇園物語
giri 義理
giron 議論
Go Sankei 呉三桂
gō 号
Gobusho 五部書
Godaigo 後醍醐
Goen'yū 後円融
Gokameyama 後亀山
Gokomatsu 後小松
Gomomozono 後桃園
Gokōmyō 後光明
Gomurakami 後村上
Gonza 権三
goshu 五主
Gotaigyō no maki 御大行の巻
goyoku rokuaku 五欲六悪
Goyōzei 後陽成
gyō 行
Gyokuzan kōgi 玉山講義

ha 覇
Hachiman 八幡
Haga Noboru 芳賀登
hajimete ontō ni natta 初めて穏当に
　なった
Hakata kojorō nami makura 博多小女郎
　波枕
Ha Kirishitan 破吉利支丹
Hakuin 白隠
Hamamatsu 浜松
han 藩
Han (dynasty) 漢
Han 韓
Han Hsien-ti 漢献帝
Han shu 漢書
Han Yü 韓愈
Hanazono 花園
harai 祓

hatamoto 旗本
Hattori Nankaku 服部南郭
Hayashi Gahō 林鵞峰
Hayashi Jussai 林述斎
Hayashi Kinpō 林錦峰
Hayashi Razan 林羅山
Hayashi Ryōsai 林良斎
Heian 平安
Heimin no mezamashi 平民の目ざまし
Hekija shōgen 闢邪小言
hennen 編年
Hideyoshi 秀吉
Higashi Takusha 東沢瀉
hika kōgai 悲歌慷慨
Hikokurō 彦九郎
Hirado 平戸
Hirata Atsutane 平田篤胤
Hisamatsu Sen'ichi 久松潜一
hito katsubutsu nari 人活物也
Hitoana 人穴
hō 法
Hogo shū 反故集
Hon'ami 本阿弥
Honchō hennen roku 本朝編年録
Honchō jinja-kō 本朝神社考
Honchō tsugan 本朝通鑑
hongi 本紀
honmatsu no betsu 本末の別
honshō byōdō 本性平等
Honzan-ha 本山派
honzen no sei 本然之性
honzen no sei (Jiun) 本然の性
Hōrakuji 法楽寺
Horikawa nami no tsuzumi 堀川波鼓
Hori Keizan 堀景山
hosa 輔佐
Hōsen Daibai 法撰大梅
Hoshina Masayuki 保科正之
hosshō 法性
hosshō no arawareshi sugata 法性のあ
　らわれし姿
hosshō yori tōru suru 法性より等流
　する
Hsiao-hsüeh 小學
hsing 性
Hsü Ai 徐愛
Hsü Fu-yüan 許孚遠

Hsün-tzu 荀子
Huang Tsung-hsi 黃宗羲
Hyakunin isshu 百人一首

i 義
I ching 易經
I li 儀禮
ichibutsu ittai 一仏一体
Ichijō Kanera 一條兼良
Ichinen yūhan 一年有半
Ienaga Saburō 家永三郎
Ihara Saikaku 井原西鶴
Ikeda Mitsumasa 池田光政
Ikeda Sōan 池田草菴
Ikkyū 一休
Ikō 伊蒿
Imagawa Yoshimoto 今川義元
Inga monogatari 因果物語
Iruga 入鹿
Ise 伊勢
Itō Jinsai 伊藤仁斎
Itō Tōgai 伊藤東涯
Iwakuni 岩国
Iwakura Tomomi 岩倉具視

jen 仁
Jen-p'u 人譜
ji (ceremonial form) 事
ji (literary form) 辞
Jibuemon 治部右衛門
jidaimono 時代物
jihan 自反
Jihei 治兵衛
jihi 慈悲
Jiin hatto 寺院法度
jikei sanjō 自警三条
jikei seiza 持敬静坐
Jikigyō Miroku 食行身禄
jin 仁
Jindai 神代
jingi 仁義
Jinnō shōtōki 神皇正統記
jinrin 人倫
jinsei 仁政
jitsu 実
Jiun Sonja 慈雲尊者

Jiyūtō 自由党
Jōkan 浄閑
jōsei 情性
jūfuzengō 十不善業
junii gondainagon 従二位権大納言
jusan'i gonchūnagon 従三位権中納言
Jusha 儒者
jūzen 十善
jūzengō 十善業
Jūzen hōgo 十善法語
Jūzen no keitō 十善の系統

Kabuki 歌舞伎
Kada Arimaro 荷田在満
Kada Azumamaro 荷田春満
Kaibara Ekken 貝原益軒
kakaku 家格
kakubutsu 格物
Kakugyō Tōbutsu 角行藤仏
kakujū 拡充
kakumei 革命
Kakure Kirishitan かくれキリシタン
Kamakura 鎌倉
kami 神
Kami no michi 神の道
Kamiya Jihei 紙屋治兵衛
Kamiyo 神代
Kamo Mabuchi 賀茂真淵
kanazōshi 假名草子
Kanbun 漢文
Kan'eiji 寛永寺
Kaneko Sōzan 金子霜山
kang 綱
Kangaku 漢学
kan'i 官位
Kanki 甘輝
Kanpō 寛保
Kansei igaku no kin 寛政異学之禁
Kanshi 漢詩
Kantō 関東
kan'yō 涵養
kanzen chōaku 勧善懲悪
Kao P'an-lung 高攀龍
Karukaya Dōshin 刈萱道心
Kasuga Myōjin 春日明神
Kasuga Sen'an 春日潜菴

272

Kawatake Mokuami 河竹黙阿弥

Kegonkyō 華厳経

kei 敬

Keichū 契沖

Keiun meisei roku 奎運鳴盛録

Ken'en 蘐園

Ken'en zuihitsu 蘐園随筆

Kenmu 建武

Kenmu shikimoku 建武式目

Kenninji 建仁寺

Ken Ting-hsiang 耿定向

ki ("concrete things") 器

ki (material force) 気

kiden 紀伝

Kii 紀伊

Kimon 崎門

kinnō 勤皇

Kinoshita Chōshōshi 木下長嘯子

Kinshiroku jo 近思録序

Kinshōjo 錦祥女

kiryoku 気力

kishitsu no sei 気質之性

kishitsu no sei (Jiun) 気質の性

kitan 忌憚

kitō 祈禱

Kiyohara 清原

Kiyomizu monogatari 清水物語

kō (confraternity) 講

kō (filial piety) 孝

kobun 古文

kobunjigaku 古文辞学

kobunjigaku-ha 古文辞学派

Kōchi 高知

Ko-Chōmin koji tsuitōkai no ki 故兆民居
　士追悼会の記

kochū 古注

kodō 古道

kōdō 公道

kogaku 古学

kōgaku 皇学

kogakuha 古学派

kogen 古言

kōgen 公言

Kōgen 光厳

kōgi 公儀

kogigaku-ha 古義学派

Koharu 小春

Kohon daigaku kakuchi tōgi 古本大学格
　致贐議

Koishikawa 小石川

Kojiki 古事記

Kokka gakkai zasshi 国家学会雑誌

Kokka hachiron 国歌八論

kokoro no toku 心の徳

koku 石

kokugaku 国学

kokugakusha 国学者

Kokumin no tomo 国民之友

Kokusen'ya kassen 国性爺合戦

Kokushūzan 穀聚山

kokutai 国体

Komagome 駒込

ko-ming 革命

kongen 根元

Konoe 近衛

kōsai 交際

Koshitsū 古史通

kōshō 考証

koto ("ceremonial forms") 事

Kōtoku Shūsui 幸徳秋水

kouta 小歌

ko wu 格物

kōzen no ikki 浩然の一気

kōzen no ki 浩然之気

Kōzuki Yasunori 上月安範

kū 空

Ku Hsien-ch'eng 顧憲成

Kuheiji 九平次

Kujiki 旧事記

Kūkai 空海

Kumamoto 熊本

Kumazawa Banzan 熊沢蕃山

Kunitokotachi 国常立

kunshi 君子

k'uo-ch'ung 擴充

Kuo yü 國語

Kusumoto Masatsugu 楠本正継

Kusumoto Sekisui 楠本碩水

Kusumoto Tanzan 楠本端山

ku-wen-tz'u-hsüeh 古文辭學

kyō 経

Kyōhō 享保

273

Kyōto 京都
kyūri 究理
Kyūshū 九州

Lao-tzu 老子
li (principle) 理
li (propriety) 禮
Li chi 禮記
Li Chih 李贄
Li P'an-lung 李攀龍
Li T'ung 李侗
Li Yung 李顒
lin 麟
Liu Tsung-chou 劉宗周
Liu Tsung-yüan 柳宗元
Liu Wen-min 劉文敏
Lo Ch'in-shun 羅欽順
Lo Hung-hsien 羅洪先
Lo Ju-feng 羅汝芳
Lo-Min 洛閩
Lo Tsung-yen 羅從彥
Lu 魯
Lu Hsiang-shan 陸象山
Lü Liu-liang 呂留良
Lu Lung-ch'i 陸隴其
Lü Tsu-ch'ien 呂祖謙
Lun-yü 論語

magatama 真玉
Magoemon 孫右衛門
magokoro 真心
makoto (cf. ch'eng) 誠
makoto no bosatsu 真米
makoto no michi まことの道
makoto no seido 誠の制度
Manchu 滿洲
Man'yōshū 万葉集
Maruyama Masao 丸山真男
Masuho Nokoguchi 増穂残口
Masuho Zankō 増穂残口
Matsudai Shōnin 末代上人
Matsudaira Sadanobu 松平定信
Matsumoto Sannosuke 松本三之介
Matsunaga Shōsan 松永昌三
Matsunaga Teitoku 松永貞徳
Matsuo Bashō 松尾芭蕉
Matsuoka Yūen 松岡雄淵

Matsuyama 松山
meibun 名分
Meido no hikyaku 冥途の飛脚
Meiji 明治
Meireki 明暦
Meng-tzu 孟子
mi 身
mibun 身分
michiyuki 道行
Mikawa 三河
minamoto 源
Minamoto no Muneharu 源の宗春
Minamoto Ryōen 源了圓
Ming 明
Mino 美濃
mi no hodo o mamori 身の程を護り
Min'yaku yakkai 民約訳解
Miroku 弥勒
Mishima Chūshū 三島中洲
misogi 禊
Mito 水戸
Mitsukuri Rinshō 箕作麟祥
Miwa Shissai 三輪執斎
Miyake Kanran 三宅観瀾
Miyake Shōsai 三宅尚斎
mizugori 水垢離
Mōanjō 盲安杖
mono ("concrete form") 物
Morohashi Tetsuji 諸橋轍次
moromoro no minamoto 諸々の源
Mōshi 孟子
moto 本
Moto-Murayama 元村山
moto no chichihaha 繦褓
Motoori Norinaga 本居宣長
mu 目
muga 無我
Murayama 村山
Muromachi 室町
Mutsu 陸奥
Myōhō rengekyō 妙法蓮華経
Myōkan 妙閑
myōri 妙理

na ("concept") 名
Nagasaki 長崎
Nagoya 名古屋

Nakae Chōmin 中江兆民
Nakae Tōju 中江藤樹
Nakae Tokusuke 中江篤介
Nakahara 中原
Namiki Rissui 並木栗水
Namu Amida Butsu 南無阿弥陀仏
nasake 情
Nebiki no kadomatsu 寿門松
nenbutsu 念仏
Nenbutsu sōshi 念仏草子
Nichigyō Nichigan 日行日旺
Nichiren 日蓮
Nieh Pao 聶豹
Nihon Bukkyō shi 日本仏教史
Nihon kokuō 日本国王
Nihon no michi 日本の道
Nihongi 日本紀
Nihon seiji shisōshi kenkyū 日本政治思
　想史研究
Nihon shoki 日本書紀
Nikkō 日光
ningen no yaku 人間の役
Ninigi no Mikoto 瓊々杵尊
Ninin bikuni 二人比丘尼
ninjō 人情
Ninkō Teiki 忍綱貞紀
Niō Zen 仁王禅
Nishōgakusha 二松学舎
Nitta Yoshisada 新田義貞
Nō 能
Noguchi Takehiko 野口武彦

Ōbei seiri sōdan 欧米政理叢談
Oda Nobunaga 織田信長
Ōdai ichiran 王代一覧
Ōgimachi 正親町
Ogyū Sorai 荻生徂徠
ohanashishū 御咄衆
Ōhashi Totsuan 大橋訥菴
Ohatsu お初
Ōita 大分
Ōjin 応神
Okada Takehiko 岡田武彦
Okamatsu Ōkoku 岡松甕谷
Okayama 岡山
Okegahazama 桶ケ狭間
okonai (cf. "gyō") 行

Okumiya Zōsai 奥宮慥斎
on 恩
Onchi seiyō 温知政要
Ōnin 応仁
Ōsaka 大阪
Osan おさん
oshi 御師
oshie no jōken 教の條件
Ōshio Chūsai (Heihachirō) 大塩中斎
　（平八郎）
Ōtōnomiya asahi no yoroi 大塔宮曦鎧
Ou-yang Te 歐陽德
Ou-yang Hsiu 歐陽修
Owari 尾張

pa 覇
Paekche 百済
pen-jan chih hsing 本然之性
pien-nien 編年
Po Yi 伯夷

Rai San'yō 頼山陽
rei 礼
reibutsu 霊物
retsuden 列伝
ri (principle) 理
ri (profit) 利
Ri Tōten 李踆天
Rigaku kōgen 理学鉤玄
rigi 理義
rikutsu 理掘
Rinzai Zen 臨済禅
ritō shinchi Shintō 理当心地神道
Roankyō 驢鞍橋
rōjū 老中
roku (flat) 陸
roku (stipend) 禄
ron 論
Rongo 論語
rōnin 浪人
ronsan 論賛
ryō 両
ryōshin 良心

Saibikō 済美黌
Saigyō 西行
Saionji Kinmochi 西園寺公望

Saitō Tarozaemon 斉藤太郎左衛門
sakashira さかしら
Sakuma Shōzan 佐久間象山
Sakuron 策論
sandai no hō 三代の法
sangaku 三学
Sanjūichinichi no maki 三十一日の巻
sankō 三光
Sansuijin keirin mondo 三酔人経論問答
Sanuki 讃岐
san'yō 算用
Satō Issai 佐藤一斎
Satō Naokata 佐藤直方
sechi bensō 世智弁聡
sehō 世法
sehō no kongen 世法の根元
sei 性
Seidan 政談
seifu kyōmon 政府教門
sei-i tai shōgun 征夷大将軍
Seikyō yōroku 聖教要録
Seiri sōdan 政理叢談
Seizansō 西山荘
seken no hō 世間の法
sekenkai 世間戒
Sekigahara 関ケ原
Sengen Daibosatsu 仙元大菩薩
Sengen Dainichi 仙元大日
Senjimon 千字文
sensei 先生
setchū 折衷
Setsugi no kokoro 節義の心
sewamono 世話物
shakabutsu 釈迦仏
Shang shu 尚書
Shigenoi 滋乃井
shih ("ceremonial forms") 事
shih ("substance") 實
Shih chi 史記
Shih ching 詩經
Shiji tsugan 資治通鑑
Shimabara 島原
Shimada Kenji 島田虔次
Shimokōbe Chōryū 下河部長流
Shimōsa 下総
Shingaku 心学
Shingon 真言

shinjū 心中
Shinjūten no Amijima 心中天の網島
shinkun 神君
Shinonome Shinbun 東雲新聞
shinri 真理
shinshoku 神職
Shinshū 信州
Shintō (Way of the Body) 身道
Shintō (Way of the Gods) 神道
Shintō (Way of the Heart) 心道
Shintō denju 神道伝授
shi o narau 死を習ふ
shitan 四端
shitsu 質
sho shinbutsu no moto 諸神仏の元
Shōanji 正安寺
shōbō 正法
Shōbōritsu 正法律
Shōgitai 勝義諦
Shōgoin 聖護院
shōgun 将軍
Shōheikō 昌平黌
shōjiki 正直
Shōkōkan 彰考館
shōō kōrai 彰往考来
Shōseishoin 紹成書院
Shōtoku Taishi 聖徳太子
Shu 蜀
Shu Ch'i 叔齊
Shu ching 書經
shugendō 修験道
shugyō 修行
shujōshugi 主情主義
shukun 主君
Shun 舜
shussekenkai 出世間戒
Soga no Umako 蘇我馬子
Sonezaki shinjū 曾根崎心中
sonnō-jōi 尊王攘夷
son'yō 存養
Sōshichi 惣七
soshitsu 宗室
Sōtō Zen 曹洞禅
Soyo そよ
Ssu-k'u t'i-yao 四庫提要
Ssu-ma Kuang 司馬光
ssu-tuan 四端

Suika 垂加

suiryō no sata 推量の沙汰

Sumiyoshi daimyōjin 住吉大明神

sun 寸

Sun Ch'eng-tse 孫承澤

Sun Ch'i-feng 孫奇逢

Sunpu 駿府

Su Shih 蘇軾

Sushun 崇峻

Suzuki Shōsan 鈴木正三

Ta-hsüeh 大學

taigi meibun 大義名分

taigyō (great practice) 大行

taigyō (great work) 大業

Taiheisaku 太平策

Taiju 諦濡

taikyoku 太極

Tajima 但馬

Takaida 高井田

Takamagahara 高天原

Takamatsu 高松

Takatani Ryūshū 高谷龍洲

Takechi Shinzō 武市新蔵

Takeda 武田

Takeda Izumo 竹田出雲

Takeuchi Shikibu 竹内式部

Tako 多胡

Tako Tokitaka 多胡辰敬

tama 玉

Tanabe Jūrōemon 田辺十郎衛門

T'ang 湯

T'ang (dynasty) 唐

tasukari 助り

tatami 畳

Tayasu Munetake 田安宗武

Tei Shiryū 鄭芝竜

Teishi shoshō 程子書抄

tenchi katsubutsu nari 天地活物也

Tendai 天台

tendō 天道

tendō no ryūkō 天道の流行

tenka 天下

tenka no toku 天下の徳

Tenkai 天海

tenri jin'yoku 天理人欲

tensei 天性

tenshi o hasamite 天子を挾みて

terauke 寺請

t'ien-li 天理

t'ien-li jen-yü 天理人欲

Tōgai 東涯

Tōkaidō Yotsuya kaidan 東海道四谷
怪談

Tokubei 徳兵衛

Tokugawa 徳川

Tokugawa Hidetada 徳川秀忠

Tokugawa Iemitsu 徳川家光

Tokugawa Ienobu 徳川家宣

Tokugawa Ietsuna 徳川家綱

Tokugawa Ieyasu 徳川家康

Tokugawa jikki 徳川実紀

Tokugawa Mitsukuni 徳川光圀

Tokugawa Muneharu 徳川宗春

Tokugawa Tsunaeda 徳川綱條

Tokugawa Tsunashige 徳川綱重

Tokugawa Tsunayoshi 徳川綱吉

Tokugawa Yorishige 徳川頼重

Tokugawa Yoshimune 徳川吉宗

Tokushi yoron 読史余論

Tōkyō 東京

Tōkyō Gaikokugo Gakkō
東京外国語学校

Tominaga Nakamoto 富永仲基

toppitsu 特筆

torii 鳥居

Tōronsho 討論書

Tosa 土佐

Tōshō 東照

Tōshōgū goikun 東照宮御遺訓

Tosotsu no naiin 都卒の内院

Tōyō Jiyū Shinbun 東洋自由新聞

Toyotomi 豊臣

Toyotomi Hideyoshi 豊臣秀吉

ts'ang-wang chih-lai 藏往知來

Ts'ao P'i 曹丕

Ts'ao Ts'ao 曹操

Tseng Tzu 曾子

tso-ch'an 坐禪

Tso chuan 左傳

Tsou Shou-i 鄒守益

Tsuji Zennosuke 辻善之助

tsumetachi-gyō 爪立行

Tsurezuregusa 徒然草

Tsuruya Nanboku 鶴屋南北
tsutsushimi 敬
Tu Yu 杜佑
T'ung-chien kang-mu 通鑑綱目
Tunglin 東林
tz'u 辭
Tzu-chih t'ung-chien 資治通鑑
Tzu-ssu 子思

Ueno 上野
ujigami 氏神
umaremasu 生れ増す
Umegawa 梅川
Unden Shintō 雲伝神道
Uraga 浦賀
utai 謡
Utsunomiya Ton'an 宇都宮遯菴

wa 和
wa no michi 和の道
waga kuni no michi 我国の道
Wajima Yoshio 和島芳男
Waka 和歌
Wan T'ing-yen 萬廷言
Wang Chi 王畿
Wang Ken 王艮
Wang Shih-chen 王世貞
Wang Shih-huai 王時槐
Wang T'ing-hsiang 王廷相
Wang Yang-ming 王陽明
Wani 王仁
Warongo 和論語
Watanabe Mōan 渡辺蒙庵
Watarai Nobuyoshi 度会延佳
Watōnai 和藤内
waza わざ
Wei 魏
wen 文
Wen 文
wen-tz'u 文辭
Wu 吳 (kingdom)
Wu 武 (king)
Wu T'ai Po 吳太伯
Wu T'ing-han 吳廷翰
Wu Yü-pi 吳與弼

Yabu Shin'an 藪震菴

yaku 役
yakunin 役人
yamabushi 山伏
Yamada Hōkoku 山田方谷
Yamaga Sokō 山鹿素行
Yamagata Daini 山県大弐
Yamato 大和
Yamazaki Ansai 山崎闇斎
Yang Chien 楊簡
Yao 堯
yashinau 養う
Yi 李
Yi T'oegye 李退溪
Yin T'un 尹焞
Yin-yang 陰陽
yō 養
Yōfukki 陽復記
Yōgaku 洋学
Yojibei 与次兵衛
Yokohama 横浜
Yokoi Shōnan 横井小楠
Yōmeigaku 陽明学
Yomi 黄泉
yonaoshi 世直し
Yoritomo 頼朝
Yosaku 与作
Yoshida 吉田
Yoshida-guchi 吉田口
Yoshida Kanetomo 吉田兼倶
Yoshida Shōin 吉田松陰
Yoshikawa Koretaru 吉川惟足
Yoshimura Shūyō 吉村秋陽
Yoshino 吉野
Yoshinobu 義陳
Yü 禹
Yü Chi 虞集
Yüan 元
Yüeh ching 樂經
Yuiitsu 唯一
yuiitsu shūgen 唯一宗源

Zankō hachibu-sho 残口八部書
zazen 坐禅
Zen 禅
zoku 賊
Zoku ichinen yūhan 續一年有半
zushi 厨子

INDEX